THE NORTHERN COLONIAL FRONTIER

THE
NORTHERN
COLONIAL
FRONTIER
1607-1763

△

DOUGLAS EDWARD LEACH

Vanderbilt University

HISTORIES OF THE AMERICAN FRONTIER
Ray Allen Billington, General Editor
Howard R. Lamar, Coeditor

UNIVERSITY OF NEW MEXICO PRESS
Albuquerque

To Brenda

FOREWORD

When, a generation ago, historians first attempted the formidable task of telling the unified story of the westward march of the American frontier, they normally began with the pre-Revolutionary decade, when pioneers pierced the Appalachian barrier to emerge on the fringes of the Mississippi Valley. Their assumption, apparently, was that the mere process of crossing the mountains magically transmuted Easterners into frontiersmen and endowed them with the forest skills that have made Daniel Boone and Davy Crockett the nation's folk heroes. The colonists who had pushed civilization across the coastal plain and mountain foothills were clearly men of lesser stuff, unworthy of a place in the saga of westward expansion and undeserving of designation by that pulse-tingling word, "pioneers."

This view of the settlement process was both inaccurate and harmful. It was inaccurate because the frontier was already a century and a half old when just after the French and Indian War the first venturesome souls cut logs for their cabins on the upper reaches of streams that emptied into the Mississippi. Indeed, the history of American westward expansion, chronologically speaking, was already nearly half spent. For nearly a hundred and fifty years before 1760 men and women had moved westward, more slowly than in later years, but with results no less significant. During those years they had learned, by painful trial and error, the arts of pioneering. They had discovered which crops would grow on virgin soils and how to build log cabins; they had acquired the skills needed to protect themselves from Indians and the means of utilizing the countryside to provide for their every need. The forest rangers who, clad in green-dyed buckskin, carrying their long rifles, and eager to use their hunting knives on the scalps of red-skinned foes, roamed the borderlands with Major Robert Rogers in the French and Indian War bore but faint resemblance to the Pilgrim Fathers who faced starvation amidst the plenty of Plymouth in the dawn days of the continent's conquest. The lessons learned in this earlier time made possible the more dramatic sweep westward of the nineteenth century.

The neglect of this chapter in the history of westward expansion not only distorted the truth but did lasting harm. Later frontier historians, lulled into believing that this distant period was unimportant, centered their research on the Mississippi Valley and Far West. So few paid attention to the colonial frontier that even today vast gaps in our knowledge of that foundation era persist. Modern scholars have hesitated to attempt a general history of the period, knowing that to do so would mean hours of archival research to fill the chinks with a solid mortar of knowledge. He who ventures into this neglected subject has no simple task of synthesis before him; back-breaking labor in Clio's garden is needed to produce a well-rounded account.

This background is necessary to appreciate both the usefulness and importance of this fine book. Professor Douglas E. Leach, already well known for his study of King Philip's War, has written in the pages that follow the first connected history of the northern colonial frontier to appear in print. To do so, he has not only immersed himself in the existing monographic literature but has burrowed deep into the archival sources on both sides of the Atlantic. The result is an interpretive synthesis that not only tells a connected story for the first time but makes important contributions to our knowledge of a germinal period in our nation's history.

To catalogue the new information that he has unearthed or the fresh viewpoints that he has suggested would require almost as many pages as Professor Leach has used. Not the least notable among his achievements are his reappraisal of the story of New England expansion to embrace the northern frontier, the robust re-creation of the life of the typical pioneer, the well-knit account of the fur trade as a major force in the economy and in diplomacy, the appraisal of the often-forgotten role played by land speculators in westward expansion, the clarification of the imperial rivalries that underlay the four wars of the period, and the revelation of the part played by missionaries and the religious impulse in pushing civilization westward. Only an expert in every aspect of the period will be able to recognize his many contributions.

Yet Professor Leach has not written for the specialist alone. His lively prose, spiced with apt quotations, will carry the reader forward with all the excitement of a good frontier tale. Equally enticing is his refusal to clog his narrative with well-known facts; he has chosen instead to give his readers only a skeleton framework of information and to flesh this with thoughtful interpretation to a degree seldom found in such a study. This book is not only captivating to read but also informative, and the reader will lay it aside with the realization that he has painlessly absorbed a vast amount of information.

This volume is one of eighteen in the Holt, Rinehart and Winston *Histories of the American Frontier* series. Like the others in the series, it tells a complete story; it may also be read as part of the broader history of westward expansion told in connected form in these volumes. Each is being written by a leading authority who brings to his task an intimate knowledge of the period he covers and a demonstrated skill in narration and interpretation. Each will provide the general reader with a sound but readable account of one phase of the nation's frontiering past, and the specialized student with a documented narrative that is integrated into the general story of the nation's growth. It is the hope of the authors and editor that this full history of the most American phase of the American past will help the people of the United States to understand themselves, and thus be better equipped to face the global problems of the twentieth-century world.

The Huntington Library   Ray Allen Billington
November 1965

PREFACE

For nearly three hundred years, beginning in the first decade of the seventeenth century, Americans struggled to conquer the wilderness that stretched three thousand miles, from the beaches of the Atlantic to the shores of the Pacific. Always their principal objective on a succession of expanding frontiers was to tame this wilderness to their own uses, transforming it into a seat of civilization. During the first half of the period, down to about 1763, most of this pioneering activity was confined to a relatively narrow zone bounded on the west by the great chain of the Appalachian Mountains. In fact, not until the era of the American Revolution did Anglo-American pioneers in any considerable numbers begin to burst through the mountain barrier and spread out into the vast region of the Mississippi Valley. After that, they kept going all the way to California. We call the long, harsh struggle with this wilderness continent "the frontier experience."

How wonderful it would be if someone could write a history of the westward movement from the Indian point of view. Such a book would be quite different from the histories we now have on our shelves, including this volume. To read such a book might be almost like stepping through Alice's looking-glass into a strange world whose main outlines we recognize but whose inhabitants and occurrences astonish us by their perverse unorthodoxy. They would baffle us simply because they would belong to a frame of reference with which we have had no experience. Certainly the mind of the American Indian, conditioned by a history and culture vastly different from that of Europe, apprehended the events of the westward movement in a way quite different from that of the pioneers.

Before the arrival of the first Europeans, the Indians of the northern frontier lived in a world of their own. It was a world of forest, river, lake, and seashore, large in scope and completely innocent of European influence. These aborigines, apparently, had no conception of other beings' inhabiting the earth—people different in complexion and drastically different in their way of life. Suddenly the first men from Europe appeared. They were light-skinned, sometimes blond-headed, clothed in woolen garments and metal armor, conveyed in waterborne craft of wonderful design, and equipped with weapons of strange appearance and frightful power.

The very first contact with these strangers must have come to the Indians as something of a shock. To understand the feelings of the moment we may imagine ourselves suddenly confronted by a delegation of super-intelligent beings just arrived from outer space. But the analogy breaks down even as we formulate it, for our science fiction has long been preparing us for such an event; it is not entirely new in our minds. Even an invasion of little green Martians could not surprise us quite so completely as the coming of the first Europeans must have surprised the Indians.

Astonishment was followed by suspicion and awe. Then, with more experience of the white men and their ways, and particularly as the Indians came to have dealings with the Europeans in trade and settlement of land, the early sense of awe gave way to resignation, and often resentment. Resentment, in turn, easily developed into hatred. When the Indians became aware of the true consequences of the European intrusion, their natural inclination was to employ whatever forms of resistance seemed feasible at the time. Thus conflict between Indians and whites became a notable feature of the westward movement. A wise student of the Indian problem has said:

> No one can blame the Indians for fighting to preserve their country. At the same time it is difficult to blame the settlers, caught up as they were in one of the great mass movements of mankind. That does not mean that we must condone the crimes committed by those who cheated and murdered to gain their ends. It means only that we should not be unfeeling toward either side as we look back on the clash of races, remembering that there was then no way of controlling the vast migration — much like an explosion — which Columbus' discovery of America touched off.[1]

Actually, it is highly unlikely that we shall ever be able to read the history of the early westward movement from the Indian point of view, for what historian now can possibly express the Indian mind with any degree of authenticity. The Indians themselves left no systematic record of their experiences and reactions, and the reservation Indian of today is not at all the same being as the woodland Indian of colonial times. Not a person alive at this moment can speak from the mind of a seventeenth-century Algonkin or Iroquois. Only the existence of an extensive histor-

---

[1] Paul A. W. Wallace, *Indians in Pennsylvania* (Harrisburg, Pa., 1961), p. 141.

ical literature enables any of us to speak even from the mind of the colonist, and then only imperfectly.

So we are, as it were, imprisoned within the bounds of our own heritage, and must view history from where we stand. But we can and should endeavor to understand as completely as possible the *Weltan-schauung* of other peoples, even those whose total experience is radically different from our own. It is worth remembering that no matter how different the heritage, there is a common core of humanity in all men; whether viewed in the light of religion or sociology, we are all indeed brothers. Realization of this fact is essential for the student of history. Although the modern American cannot think through the mind of the Indian, he may achieve an understanding of him, and in any case should try to appraise him and his history with a fair and balanced mind.

Our view of the early westward movement must of necessity be closer to that of the white pioneer than to that of the Indian, because the pioneer's heritage is ours also. We are much more the heirs of Western civilization than of the American wilderness, although we owe much to both. So the reader will not be surprised to discover that this book is constructed frankly within the perspective of the Anglo-American settlers who inhabited the colonies from New England to Pennsylvania, and not within that of the Indians. It is the author's sincere belief that this has been done without the sacrifice of justice or truth, which would be a price too great to pay.

Quotations from the sources have been carefully transcribed, so that they might be utilized with complete confidence. In the interests of uniformity and readability, however, certain minor changes have been made. For example, the letters *v* and *u*, *i* and *j*, are employed in accordance with modern usage, and the old *y* (or thorn) is rendered as *th*. Likewise all superior letters, as in *y^e*, have been lowered, while the various contractions, such as *w^{ch}*, have been expanded to their full spelling. Thus *y^e* becomes *the*, and *w^{ch}* becomes *which*. Dates before 1752 are given Old Style, with a double-year designation where appropriate.

The work of research and writing over a period of years has been accomplished only with the invaluable assistance of many institutions and individuals. I should like to express my thanks to each, without attempting to enumerate all. To future researchers I especially recommend the basement room in the Massachusetts Archives where those able and cheerful custodians, Mr. and Mrs. Leo Flaherty, manage to combine efficiency with hospitality. I also recall with gratitude the extraordinary kindness of the late Dr. Albert B. Corey of the New York State Library. Vanderbilt University has been generous in granting a leave of absence and other forms of encouragement, all contributing to the progress of the work. Morale as well as quality of output have been repeatedly elevated by the buoyant spirit and wise counsel of the general editor of the series, Professor Ray Allen Billington. My thanks go also to Professor Alden T. Vaughan of Columbia University for making available the manuscript of his forthcoming book *New England Frontier: Puritans and Indians, 1620–1675;* to the personnel of the Joint University Libraries at Nashville for various kinds of assistance, including a hideaway for uninterrupted work; and to my research assistants, Charles F. Cummings and Chester R. Young.

A special word of gratitude and love is reserved for my wife Brenda, and our two children Carol and Bradford, whose patience, understanding, faith, and support have been all-important.

Nashville, Tennessee Douglas Edward Leach
November 1965

CONTENTS

LIST OF MAPS

AND ILLUSTRATIONS

MAPS

ILLUSTRATIONS

Following 108

An early eighteenth-century map of the Iroquois country and the
    eastern Great Lakes
Diorama of an Iroquois hunting group
Interior of an Algonquian wigwam as reconstructed at Plimoth
    Plantation
Letter from the Eastern Indians to the Governor of Massachusetts
    concerning the fur trade
Examples of wampum
A pioneer housewife husking corn
The main street in a well-ordered frontier village
Tools and implements used by the pioneer farmer
A Palatine plow, dated 1759
New England pioneers erecting a dwelling
A thatch-roofed cottage such as was built by the Pilgrims
Mortise and tenon construction
A log being turned into planks at the saw pit
Pioneer tools

Following 162

◁ **1** ▷

The Challenge of the Unknown Wilderness

*E*arly in the sixteenth century, European adventurers began to visit the northern frontier, the region extending from present-day Maine to Pennsylvania, skirting along the irregular coast in their bluff-browed, high-pooped vessels. To them it was a land of mystery, both inviting and repelling, with an unseen hinterland whose nature and extent were as much unknown as the world beyond the grave,

> *The undiscovered country from whose bourn*
> *No traveller returns, . . .*

If these inquisitive mariners ventured ashore in this forested region, perhaps to renew their supplies of wood and water or to truck with the dark-skinned natives, they seldom lingered long but hastened back to the relative security of deck and cabin. The true pioneers and frontiersmen, people who came to put down roots and make this land their own, did not enter the scene until the opening of the seventeenth century. For the northern frontier, there was no Walter Raleigh and no Lost Colony.

Our story really has its beginning on a spring morning in 1602 when

1

the English bark *Concord,* Captain Bartholomew Gosnold commanding, made land somewhere on the coast of Maine. Reaching a rocky headland that would afford some shelter, the *Concord* dropped anchor with a splash that startled the hovering gulls. Gosnold had come with a purpose: to plant a small settlement to serve primarily as a base for economic exploitation of the country, the first such English attempt since the Roanoke disaster.

Scanning the landscape with excited curiosity, the newcomers saw stretching away toward the north and the south a variegated shoreline of rugged, rocky points separated by occasional coves with beaches of sand and open reaches of flat marshland. Just beyond loomed the somber green backdrop of the forest, the realm of the unknown, extending on into the interior as far as eye could see. This was no mere island in the sea; this was a continent of vast yet unknown potential. Gosnold's men feasted their eyes upon it with a mixture of admiration and apprehension.

Then from the nearby headland there came a small craft making its way steadily toward the anchored vessel. In it were eight American Indians, naked for the most part, except for the skins of animals. Their leader, however, was wearing garments of European origin, evidence of previous contact with the fishing vessels that had been visiting the New England coast for many years. As the boatload of Indians came close aboard the *Concord,* both parties by signs and gestures made clear their peaceful intentions, after which the dark-skinned natives clambered boldly up the ship's side and stood on the deck before Gosnold and his men.[1]

There was great significance in this moment of encounter. Without any particular awareness or insight, the Englishmen were being introduced to the two great barriers destined to challenge the pioneers in America for almost three centuries. The terrain itself—vast, often forbidding—was to be a geographical obstacle, and the Indians, desperately striving to hold their homeland against the advancing tide of European settlement, were to assume the role of a human obstacle. Since these two barriers stand like unmistakable landmarks across the length and breadth of the westward movement in American history, anyone who wishes to know the real story of the pioneers must first acquaint himself with the land over which they advanced and the Indians they encountered.

*G*EOGRAPHY, the physical characteristics of land and water on the face of the earth, has always served as a controlling factor in history.

The course of human migrations, the founding and development of civilizations, the emergence of nations with their evolving economies and policies, all have been profoundly influenced by the facts of geography. A navigable river invites travel and trade, while a mountain range hinders such intercourse. Deep, rich soil encourages agriculture, while rocky or sandy ground either turns men to other pursuits or condemns them to grinding poverty. Thus man plans and achieves under the dictates of nature.

The seacoast from the Bay of Fundy to Delaware Bay is both inviting and forbidding: inviting because of its many indentations and river mouths, which afford numerous havens for sea-battered ships; forbidding because of its rocky ledges spelling doom for the unwary seafarer. In northern New England especially, the coast is "stern and rock-bound," although even in that area quiet harbors and coves with sandy beaches may be found. Casco Bay, Boston Harbor, Narragansett Bay, New York Harbor, and Delaware Bay, which offer excellent anchorage for seagoing vessels, were quickly noted by the early explorers. All along the coast, in places where the land was low and the forest did not crowd upon the edge of the sea, extensive salt marshes of tough green grass reached as high as a man's waist or higher.

And there was the forest, sometimes majestic and stately, sometimes dark and awesome, but always fascinating to those seeing it for the first time. Some men seemed enchanted by it and never broke free of its spell. They became what we might call "compulsive pioneers." The early explorers sent back to England lists of the various kinds of trees they had seen, for wood and wood products were an important natural resource, and England's own forests were being depleted. North of the Piscataqua River in New Hampshire the evergreens—spruce, cedar, and especially the tall, straight pine—predominated. Farther south were seemingly endless stands of hardwoods—oak, walnut, chestnut, beech, and many others.

It would be a mistake to think of the American forest in the seventeenth century as a nearly impenetrable tangle of trees and underbrush. On the contrary, the newly arrived settlers found extensive areas of open land and even the remains of planting fields that had once been cleared by the Indians for their agriculture. In the thick of the woods, with great trees on every side, the ground might be almost entirely free of low brush, so that the forest reminded many an English settler of a well-kept woodland preserve in the old country. For this the pioneers could thank the Indians, who habitually in the fall of the year burned over large areas of forest land in order to facilitate hunting. The places to avoid were what the English came to know as "swamps"—extensive stretches of marshy land often covered with a dense growth of trees and brush, difficult to push through, damaging to clothing and tender hides, and often infested with poisonous reptiles.[2]

What a pioneer thought of the forest depended largely upon his immediate situation. If the struggle for survival was proving hard and dangerous, he would be likely to view his immediate environment with considerable distaste and wish himself back among the sheltering hills of the old country. Early Puritan settlers had a favorite term for their forbidding countryside; they called it a "howling wilderness," and sometimes it was literally that when a pack of wolves was on the prowl. But many men, especially in circumstances of relative prosperity and security, found the wilderness beautiful and exhilarating. William Penn was enthusiastic about American woodlands made lovely by a profusion of wild flowers.[3] Thomas Pownall, an Englishman who served as governor of Massachusetts, was equally impressed:

> The general Face of the Country, when one travels it along the Rivers through Parts not yet settled, exhibits the most picturesque Landscapes that Imagination can conceive, in a Variety of the noblest, richest Groupes of Wood, Water, and Mountains. As the Eye is lead on from Reach to Reach, at each Turning of the Courses, the Imagination is in a perpetual Alternative of curious Suspense and new Delight, not knowing at any Point, and not being able to discover where the Way is to open next, until it does open and captivates like Enchantment.[4]

Perhaps he was responding to a dash of the magic that occasionally made pioneers out of solid, substantial city dwellers.

Any heavily laden pioneer, other considerations being equal, would prefer to make his way along a navigable river by boat rather than toil overland through the forest. The rivers were channels of communication and transportation, wilderness highways, as it were. Sometimes the pioneer thought that nature, in laying out her highways, had done well by him; but often he found her perverse, especially when she blocked his way with dangerous rapids and falls.

Almost all the major rivers of the northern frontier east of the Appalachian Mountains follow a generally southward course to the sea. Unlike the St. Lawrence, they do not give access to the great interior region of the continent. One look at the course of the St. Lawrence River shows the principal reason why the French were able to move far into the heartland of America at an early date. The English had no such advantage. For the early explorers and pioneers seeking new routes, however, each river mouth was an invitation to investigate. The rivers that figure largest in our story are the Penobscot, the Kennebec (first known as the Sagadahoc), the Piscataqua, the Merrimack, the Connecticut, the Mohawk-Hudson combination, the Delaware, and the Susquehanna. West of the Appalachian Mountains is an entirely separate system dominated by the beautiful Ohio, *la belle rivière* of the French.

Of particular importance was the water route lying along the length of a trough reaching from the valley of the St. Lawrence to the western end of Long Island. Here the traveler—or an invading army—might proceed from the St. Lawrence River to New York by way of the Richelieu River, Lake Champlain, Lake George, and the Hudson River, the only difficult overland stretch being the wilderness section between Lake George and the upper Hudson. Moreover, cutting into this important north-south route from the direction of the Great Lakes was an east-west trough containing the Oswego River, Lake Oneida, Wood Creek, and the Mohawk River. Because of rapids and necessary portages this east-west route was not easy, but it did afford the English colonies their best gateway through the Appalachian Mountains to the region of the Great Lakes. The Hudson-Champlain route together with the related Mohawk route played a major role in the drama of the northern frontier.

Rivers were important not only as routes of entry but also because the bottom land on either side was usually the most favorable for agriculture. Streams and rivers enriched the terrain through which they flowed, affording good planting land and highly valued meadow land for the maintenance of cattle. Uplands, on the other hand, were likely to offer only thin, undesirable soil, and were therefore avoided by pioneering farmers so long as better land was available along the rivers. Too, a flowing stream could provide the waterpower necessary to operate sawmills and gristmills. Finally, rivers were important to the pioneers because they offered the easiest means for sending agricultural products back to the coastal markets.

From the moon, no doubt, our earth looks as smooth as an orange; even the high Himalayas rising to almost 30,000 feet above sea level would flatten out when seen at such a distance, and the northeastern part of the United States, whose highest mountain is barely 6,000 feet above sea level, would appear to be quite flat. But to a pioneer emerging from the forest to catch a western vista, the prospect could be strikingly different. A topographical map shows that much of the land area from Maine to Pennsylvania is hilly and even mountainous. Innumerable streams twist their way around and through the highlands, and lakes of all sizes and shapes nestle in the natural basins. This was of immediate concern to the frontiersman because mountains are barriers, streams may offer a way through, and lakes often mean good hunting and fishing.

The great belt of mountains known as the Appalachians is a multi-layered barrier separating the east coast from the Great Lakes region and the Mississippi Valley. Its component ranges constantly influenced the course of settlement. The backbone of New Hampshire consists of the irregular and rather formidable range of the White Mountains, and to the west, beyond the Connecticut River, lie the Green Mountains of Vermont, whose southern extension into Massachusetts is known as the Berkshires. From the top of this range one looks westward to the Champlain Valley, beyond which rises the jumble of the Adirondacks in the angle of the Hudson and the Mohawk. From New York through Pennsylvania the Appalachians, sprawling along a broad belt of territory, are formed in a multitude of parallel ridges and chains, the most prominent of which is the Alleghenies separating eastern Pennsylvania from the upper valley of the Ohio River. The whole Appalachian system, in fact, is a barrier, not so much because of its height but because of its width, and because its parallel ranges lie, for the most part, directly across the paths of westward advance.

*T*HE INDIANS, the second great barrier to the westward movement, have fascinated American observers from colonial times to the present. Opinions as to their character and the role they played have ranged between two extremes. Colonists who suffered under the cruelty of Indian warfare tended to view the native Americans as savage barbarians, treacherous and bloodthirsty. Samuel Penhallow, contemporary historian of Indian warfare, spoke the mind of many a colonist when he called the Indians "bloody pagans . . . monsters. . . . Who are as implacable in their revenge, as they are terrible in the execution of it; and will convey it down to the third and fourth generation." "No courtesy," he continued, "will ever oblige them to gratitude; for their greatest benefactors have frequently fallen as victims to their fury."[5]

In Pennsylvania, on the other hand, where for many years relations between the races were unusually good, there was a widely held opinion that the Indians were of reasonable mind and peaceful intent. The Quakers built their Indian policy on this hopeful assumption, and William Penn could remark with calm assurance, "Don't abuse them, but let them have Justice, and you win them."[6] Indeed, there existed in colonial America a school of thought, perhaps most clearly represented by the Mennonite leader Francis Daniel Pastorius, which held that before the coming of the white men the Indians had lived in a state of natural innocence, undefiled by the corruptions of civilization. Pastorius put the case in positive terms: "They strive after a sincere honesty, hold strictly to their promises, cheat and injure no one. . . . I fully believe that in the future, at the great day of judgment, they will come forth with those of Tyre and Sidon, and put to shame many thousands of false nominal and canting Christians."[7]

The two opposing viewpoints were arrived at through a complex of experience and circumstances. Both have been expressed again and again ever since in the historical literature of the white race. Neither will entirely satisfy the discerning student. Modern research, not only in the field of history, but also in anthropology and ethnology, has brought us much closer to a satisfactory understanding of why the Indians, when confronted with the intrusion of Europeans, acted as they did. We are now less interested in pointing the finger of guilt at one race or the other; instead, we try to probe ever deeper into the history of the frontier experience in order to enlarge our comprehension of human behavior under the difficult circumstances of competition between two markedly different—one must even say inherently antagonistic—ways of life.

What were the Indians of the northern frontier really like? What was their appearance, and how did they live? Actually there existed in the area under consideration two major Indian cultures, the Algonquian and the Iroquoian. All tribes can be classified with one or the other culture, the primary consideration being linguistic, but including also such matters as social organization and architecture. The Iroquoian tribes were concentrated in an area extending from Lake Champlain through the Mohawk Valley to Lake Erie. Elsewhere, from northern New England to Chesapeake Bay, were tribes speaking the Algonquian tongue. Although this cultural division increases the difficulty of presenting a brief but accurate picture of Indian life, we may still achieve the necessary understanding if we concentrate on aspects that were generally similar throughout the Algonquian area about the middle of the seventeenth century, with subsequent attention to some distinguishing features of Iroquoian culture.

A typical Algonquian village consisted of a cluster of low huts, or *wigwams*, described by one observer as

> . . . very strong and handsome, covered with close wrought mats, made by their women of flagges, rushes, and hempen threds, so defensive, that neither raine, though never so sad and long, nor yet the winde, though never so strong can enter. The top through a square hole giveth passage to the smoke, which in rainy weather, is covered with a pluver.[8]

Such wigwams were constructed by placing poles in the ground around the perimeter of a round or oval floor plan, then bending and binding them so as to form a domed framework, upon which a covering of bark or mats was fastened. A gap at one or both ends of the wigwam gave access to the interior. Although dark and smoky, this home was eminently practical for its inhabitants. It could be constructed easily and quickly, was weathertight, and could be kept moderately warm in all seasons.

Indians of the Eastern woodlands lived by agriculture and hunting. Their basic crop was maize (Indian corn), but they also grew beans and squashes, and sometimes tobacco. Tending the crops was usually the business of the women, who also kept house, dressed skins, and made clothing for the family. The planting field lay just beyond the cluster of huts. There in the springtime the squaws used primitive planting sticks or hoes to make holes in the earth at regular intervals. In each hole they buried some seed together with a fish as fertilizer. Later the soil would be carefully "hilled up" around each growing stalk of corn. It was common practice among these Indians to plant corn and beans in the same "hill" so that the bean plants would have the cornstalks to climb on.[9]

The men hunted and fished, not for sport, but to survive. With many centuries of experience behind them the Indians were wise in the ways of nature. Their ability to follow and interpret the tracks of animals is well illustrated in a story told by a colonist who had lived among them. "I was once travelling a little way behind several Indians," said John Gyles, "& heard them Laughing very merrily: when I came to them, they shew'd me the Track of a Moose, and how a *Wolverin* had climb'd a Tree, and where he had jump'd off upon the Moose; and the Moose had given several large Leaps, and happening to come under a Branch of a Tree, had broke the *Wolverin's* hold and tore him off: and by his Track in the Snow, he went off another [way], with short steps, as if he had been stun'd with the Blow."[10] Playing Dr. Watson to the Indians' Sherlock Holmes, Gyles saw it all very clearly once the signs had been shown and explained to him.

Using bows strung with moose sinews and arrows of straight young elder, the Indians stalked moose, deer, bear, and other game. They set ingenious traps and snares for birds and animals. They took fish in weirs or speared them as they swam, and in winter they fished for them through the ice. Boys were taught the necessary skills at an early age, so that they would become good providers. The diet thus derived from field, forest, and stream was further supplemented when the squaws went to the seashore to gather shellfish—lobsters, clams, and mussels. But all too frequently nature was unkind; crops withered and game was scarce. Then the Indians tightened their belts and tried to survive on nuts, roots, and water.

The people of the village generally migrated in accordance with a seasonal plan. In summer they might live near the planting fields; in winter they would set up their huts in a more protected location; and at the time of spring fishing they could be found encamped near the falls of their favorite river. Even a semipermanent village site might be abandoned after a decade or so of use, as the fertility of planting fields and the supply of wood approached exhaustion. When traveling overland the Indians carried their baggage on their backs, for they had no vehicles or draft animals. They followed age-old trails through the forest or made their way along the watercourses in hollowed-out logs or bark canoes.

Every member of the village belonged to a clan, which consisted of all persons related by blood as well as those who had married into the clan. A village included portions of several clans, these forming subdivisions among even a small population. Family matters were settled within the family itself, clan matters by a clan council, and village matters by the village leader and his council. The village was a distinct economic and political entity, but it might be closely related to several nearby villages, forming with them a sort of "band." Villages and bands were part of a larger structure called the tribe, which to a very limited degree may be considered the equivalent of a nation. The principal leader of the tribe was known as the *sachem,* a highly respected member usually chosen by vote of the entire tribe or its council of lesser leaders, called *sagamores.* Not infrequently, in practice, the honor of the sachemship remained within a particular family generation after generation, becoming almost hereditary.

Each tribe occupied territory whose bounds were clearly understood. Generally speaking, all tribal land except that in the immediate vicinity of the villages was available to all members of the tribe for hunting. Planting fields and garden plots, however, belonged to particular groups or families. Even here the land was not "owned" in the sense understood by Europeans; it was merely occupied and utilized under a temporary arrangement that might be altered whenever conditions warranted a change. In a transfer of land from one group or family to another, only the right to make use of the land was granted, and the agreement was valid only so long as it satisfied the particular Indians affected. We see immediately that the Indian concept of land tenure was in sharp contrast to the European concept of absolute and perpetual title. Within this contrast lay the germs of grievous misunderstanding and bitter conflict.[11]

The Indians believed in a supernatural world of good and evil spirits. Every spirit had a will and a personality, in fact, might be appealed to and cajoled. Wisest and most experienced in matters of the supernatural were men known as *shamans* or *powwows,* who served as priests and medicine men, resorting to magic in order to consult the spirits and heal the sick. Such special capability, of course, made the powwow an awesome figure, with influence sometimes rivaling that of the sachem himself.

Almost all contemporary observers agreed that the Indians were physically well formed, agile, and tough. Peter Kalm, the Swedish botanist who traveled extensively in the northern colonies, called them "tremendously rugged."[12] This characteristic is explained by two circumstances: hard conditioning from birth and the likelihood that infants born with physical defects seldom survived. Child-rearing was oriented toward preparation for survival in the wilderness, where life was often harsh. In Maine, it was said, the Indians would take their two-year-old children and "cast them into the Sea, like a little dogge or Cat, to learne them to swimme."[13] The rule was "sink or swim," and the Indians had no Society for the Prevention of Cruelty to Children to militate against such practices.

Among many tribes the sweat bath was popular. As one observer reported, the Indians "Use hot baths on all occasions by the water side, heat a stone & put it into the hole where they sit & in the height of their sweat leap or run into the water."[14] Or sometimes

> They dance round a hot Fire, till they are almost ready to faint, and are wet with Sweat; and then run out, and, striping themselves naked, expose their Bodies to the cold Air, and, if there be Snow upon the Ground, roll in it till they are cold, and then return to their Dancing again, and when they are hot, and tir'd, cool themselves in the same Manner, and, it may be, repeat this four or five Times in a Night.[15]

This behavior might have been comprehensible to a Finn on the Delaware, but to the Puritans of New England it was pure evidence of Indian savagery.

If the Indians exposed their bodies to the elements more than the Europeans considered modest or prudent, they at least gave themselves some form of protection, for it was common practice among the Indians to anoint their bodies with grease derived from animals such as the bear and the raccoon, or even with fish oil. This was supposed to protect them against the cold of winter and the hot sun and biting insects of summer. That this habit may have had something to do with the reluctance of the English to socialize with the Indians in confined quarters is hardly to be doubted.

Indian clothing consisted mostly of animal skins. The basic costume in summer was a simple breech clout passed between the legs and secured at front and back by a belt or girdle. Women usually wore a simple form of skirt.[16] Footwear consisted of soft-soled moccasins made from the skin of moose or deer. When the weather became cold, other garments were added—deerskin leggings and warm robes or cloaks of fur. After the coming of the white traders, Indians made more and more use of English woolens and European-style clothing, but throughout the colonial period the native garments remained much in evidence. Sometimes articles of clothing were embellished with white and colored beads arranged in patterns. The usual headgear for men consisted of a decorated band bearing feathers of the eagle or turkey. Hair styles varied from tribe to tribe, but women usually wore their hair long, and the men often plucked or shaved some portion of the head, leaving a tuft of hair on one side or along the top. On special occasions the Indians decorated their faces with pigments of various colors.

In political organization and fighting power the Five Nations of the Iroquois Confederacy far surpassed the loosely related Algonquian tribes of New England and Pennsylvania. Occupying the region south and east of Lake Ontario, these five Iroquoian "nations," or tribes—the Mohawk, Oneida, Onondaga, Cayuga, and Seneca—controlled the most important crossroads of communication and trade of the entire northern frontier. The most feasible route between the English colonies and the Great Lakes ran through the heart of their country. Moreover, so strong was the determination of these tribes and so great their combined resources that by the eighteenth century they would be able to bring under their sway other Indian groups over a much larger area. Indeed, the will of the Iroquois was to be feared and respected throughout a large part of the northern frontier. In 1722 the northward-trekking Tuscarora were admitted to the Confederacy, which thereafter became known as the Six Nations.

The characteristic feature of the Iroquoian village was the type of dwelling known as a longhouse. This was a rectangular structure with vertical, windowless side walls, a door at each end, and a semicylindrical roof. The exterior was covered with slabs of elm bark overlapping like shingles. Such a dwelling might be about eighteen or twenty feet wide and some sixty or more feet long.[17] The interior was divided into open-faced rooms or booths on either side of a central corridor extending the length of the longhouse from door to door. Each booth was occupied by a family, the two families opposite each other sharing a common cooking fire in the center of the corridor between them. A longhouse, then, was a communal dwelling in which lived some ten or a dozen related families, all under the stern supervision of the senior female resident.

Fond as they were of expressive figures of speech, the Iroquois liked to compare their Confederacy to a longhouse. They said that the Mohawk guarded the eastern door and the Seneca the western door, while in the center, within the domain of the Onondaga, burned the council fire of the Five Nations. To the Onondaga council came the chosen leaders from each of the tribes to deliberate on matters concerning them all. Here was practiced the Iroquoian art of oratory, whose effectiveness was noted and admired by numerous colonial leaders. In especially important deliberations, such as the conclusion of a treaty, major points were emphasized by the giving of strings and even belts made of *wampum*. This consisted of small cylindrical beads laboriously made from sea shells and carefully drilled through the longitudinal axis so that they could be strung together. Some were white, others dark blue or purple. When strung in combinations, they could be made to form meaningful patterns and designs, thus serving as a kind of record. The Indians used wampum also as currency in their trade.

There was a long and bloody record of hostility between the Iroquois and the Algonkins, and, to make matters worse, the various Algonquian tribes sometimes warred with one another, enjoying no fraternal peace such as the Iroquois had established among themselves. In fact, warfare seems to have been almost a natural condition of Indian life in the American wilderness. In general, the kind of warfare practiced by these Indians, Algonkins and Iroquois alike, was private rather than public, an affair begun and carried on by individuals and groups rather than by the tribe as a political unit. A common objective was personal revenge. The aggrieved party would announce his intention of taking revenge and then, usually in the frenzied ceremonial of a war dance, recruit a band of volunteer warriors to go with him. Retaliation of course bred counterretaliation, leading to what may well be described as a blood feud.

Also present as a motivating factor was the yearning for glory. Every young Indian male who aspired to full manhood in the tribe, marriage, and a place at the council fire sought to prove his valor by besting an enemy in mortal combat. The head or scalp of the victim was incontrovertible evidence of victory, and a cherished trophy.[18] Indian warfare was largely a matter of sporadic raids rather than prolonged campaigns. Each warrior went armed with a good tough bow, a quiver of arrows, and some sort of club or hatchet. Skill in stalking was put to maximum use in approaching the enemy, and the favorite tactic was the hidden trap or ambush. When the battle was joined, it was every man for himself. Yelling fiercely to terrorize the enemy, the individual warrior would dart from cover to cover, pausing now and then to shoot an arrow at a similarly elusive target. Finally at grips, there would be a club-swinging melee terminated perhaps by a swift scalping and equally swift retreat. Actually, this kind of warfare caused far fewer mortal casualties than the uproar would seem to indicate, but it was a most effective way of working off youthful energy.[19]

Scalps were not the only trophies brought back from a successful raid. Live prisoners were highly prized, especially by the Iroquois, who wanted them for two purposes. Most important was the custom of adoption into the tribe. This usually was the fate of women and children captives. In addition, many warrior prisoners were adopted by Iroquois widows to replace their dead husbands. Cadwallader Colden, the eminent colonial authority on the Iroquois, pointed out the significance of this custom when he wrote,

> It has been a constant Maxim with the Five Nations, to save the Children and Young Men of the People they Conquer, to adopt them into their own Nation, and to educate them as their own Children, without Distinction; These young People soon forget their own Country and Nation; and by this Policy the Five Nations make up the Losses which their Nation suffers by the People they loose in War.[20]

In other words, the drain of many decades of fierce warfare was to some extent counterbalanced by the infusion of fresh blood. Once fully adopted, the former prisoners were considered members of the tribe in good standing and were treated as such.

Male captives not selected for adoption customarily were put to death by prolonged torture. Anyone interested in learning the details of these horrible orgies will find them graphically described in the literature known as captivity narratives. There can be no doubt that sadism played a significant role, but it was more than that. Torture was a test of manhood, and the captive warrior who could undergo his cruel fate without whimpering, indeed, even mocking the worst efforts of his tormentors, won a degree of grudging admiration. In some instances cannibalism was practiced by the Iroquois, who were known to tear out the living heart of a victim and eat it, apparently in the belief that the sufferer's courage could be ingested.[21] Among the Iroquois, torture of captives seems to have been an important tribal rite; the Algonkins adopted the practice and used it as a form of retaliation. As for the European colonists, they too occasionally showed an appalling capacity for inflicting cruelties upon their Indian enemies, although they always looked upon Indian torture as the basest kind of savagery.

Many pioneers discovered, perhaps to their surprise, that the Indians could be both hospitable and kind. On numerous occasions settlers in distress received invaluable assistance from sympathetic natives. But unfortunately a mutual spirit of good will was not sufficiently strong to prevent deadly competition and conflict. If the Indians helped the process of settlement, they also hindered the advance of the frontier, and on balance must be reckoned a serious obstacle to the westward movement.

*A*MERICAN TERRAIN—forested, mountainous, vast, and largely unknown; and the American Indian—extremely resourceful and skillful in his own environment, and fierce when antagonized; these constituted the two major obstacles encountered by the westward-moving pioneers. These obstacles were there from the beginning; they had to be dealt with at the outset of the frontier experience. Facing these ominous barriers in 1602 Captain Gosnold's men, remembering Roanoke, quailed and quit just five weeks after their arrival. Instead of remaining to hold the little post they had constructed on Cuttyhunk Island off the southern shore of Cape Cod, they insisted on going back to England with the ship. So it was that the first English habitation north of Roanoke Island was left to rot. It would be five years before English pioneers again attempted a settlement on the northern frontier.

◁ **2** ▷

The Coastal Pioneers:
Plymouth and New Netherland,
1620–1664

G osnold's favorable report concerning the natural resources of New England induced other mariners to visit the area during the next few years, with the result that in 1607 a second colonizing expedition arrived to establish a trading settlement at the mouth of the Kennebec River, then known as Sagadahoc. These new pioneers began to construct a fortified village, and of course made contact with the local Indians, whose furs they coveted. Unlike Gosnold's irresolute crew, this group managed to last through one "extreme unseasonable and frosty" winter, but then gave up the venture, abandoned their settlement, and sailed away.[1] Once again the American wilderness had repelled a feeble invasion from the Old World.

For the next ten years English promoters such as Sir Ferdinando Gorges, who were interested in exploring the New England area, limited their endeavors to periodic fishing and fur trading voyages. But all this time English seamen were becoming more and more acquainted with the land and its inhabitants. It is not unlikely that from time to time during this period small groups of fishermen lived for months at a time

15

in crude huts on the Maine coast where they maintained stages for curing their fish. The enterprising Richard Vines, with several other men, apparently even spent the winter of 1616–1617 in a camp at the mouth of the Saco River.[2] Although this kind of pioneering was sporadic and insubstantial, it did add to the reservoir of English experience, thereby increasing the chances for successful colonization in the future.

In 1611 and again in 1614, unfortunately, certain English seafarers actually kidnaped small groups of Indians on the coast of New England, either taking them to England as curiosities or selling them into slavery. The consequence was to plant fear and hatred of the white men in the hearts of the coastal tribes, thereby undermining whatever hospitality they had hitherto been inclined to show the European intruders. Nevertheless, for many years there would be no massive resistance to any settlements made along the coast between the Penobscot River and Narragansett Bay, because of an epidemic that swept through the native villages of that area starting in 1616. Whole communities were decimated, villages and planting fields were abandoned, and the land lay open to the English.[3]

A SMALL GROUP of English refugees known as the Pilgrims, including women and children as well as men, in the frigid weeks of late 1620 was to found the first permanent settlement on the northern frontier. The Pilgrims were materially one of the weakest and spiritually one of the strongest groups of pioneers that ever ventured into the American wilderness. That they not only survived but even succeeded in their venture to establish a little haven of their own is something of a wonder to those who do not understand the power of the resources they did have.

Among the settlers who now contemplated a new life in a new land were a number of young men who had attached themselves to the expedition more for adventure and personal gain than for religious idealism. Realizing that they were now beyond the reach of English law, they let it be known that they had no intention of submitting to the authority of the Pilgrim leaders and would do as they pleased in this free land. Here indeed were the seeds of future trouble, perhaps even rebellion. So at the very outset the lawlessness of the remote frontier hurled its challenge at men who believed in the reign of law. The Pilgrims met that challenge with a decisiveness that would inspire many another group in like circumstances. They drew up a compact pledging obedience to the decisions of the group for the welfare of the group, and managed to persuade forty-one adult males to sign it. This "Mayflower

Compact" is the first example of what has become known as a "plantation covenant"—or less elegantly in the nineteenth century as a "squatters' agreement"—that is, a written compact among a group of pioneers who, finding themselves outside the protecting arm of the law, establish a basis for law among themselves. Such frontier compacts constitute a practical demonstration of group initiative in the face of extraordinary conditions, revealing how the ordinary processes of civilization can be adapted to a wilderness situation. There is nothing mystical or magical in this. The Pilgrims, and other groups after them, simply faced up to potential anarchy and, drawing upon experience and common sense fortified with a firm determination to make things work out right, devised a practical way to prevent it.[4]

At a place where a hillside sloped easily to the water's edge, with a brook nearby, the Pilgrims planted their settlement and called it Plymouth. The hill offered good possibilities for defense; the soil appeared to be reasonably fertile, and because the site had been occupied by Indians prior to the plague the land was already clear of trees. As quickly as possible the men erected a number of small crude huts.[5]

The first winter was a frightful experience, mainly because of disease caused by dietary deficiencies and other deprivations endured during the long voyage across the ocean. The Plymouth people were but the first in a long succession of pioneers condemned to undergo the hazards of life on the frontier under the added handicap of ship-bred illness. Fresh air and clear water often were not sufficient to overcome the erosive effects of long weeks spent beneath the hatches of a seventeenth-century merchantman. During the first winter at Plymouth almost exactly half of the settlers died of scurvy and other maladies.

Techniques of survival in a winter wilderness were learned by bitter experience. One afternoon, for example, two Plymouth men lost their way deep in the woods. They were without food, their clothing was thin, and soon the temperature began to drop as darkness closed in. To add to their terror some wild animals, probably wolves, set up a howling that seemed to signify a special craving for choice English flesh. With that eerie sound helping the cold to chill their blood, the two benighted ones passed the dreadful hours pacing the ground at the foot of a tree into which they might scramble if the wild beasts should come upon them. Next day, suffering greatly from exposure, they finally found their way back to Plymouth, to the great relief of their friends and their own inexpressible joy.[6] Thus these tenderfoot pioneers learned how important it is to keep track of landmarks and direction when exploring the forest.

Relations with the Indians early became a matter of concern at Plymouth. One day as the spring of 1621 was drawing near, an Indian suddenly appeared, walked in among the Pilgrims, and addressed them in broken English. This was Samoset, a sagamore from the coast of Maine, who had picked up some knowledge of English from contact with fishermen. Dignified and hospitable, he arranged for the Pilgrims to meet Squanto, one of the Indians kidnaped in 1614, who had spent some time in England. With Squanto came Massasoit, the esteemed sachem of the Wampanoag tribe, whose territory lay along the eastern shores of Narragansett Bay about thirty miles southwest of Plymouth. Massasoit and the Pilgrim leaders met together and made a solemn agreement to live in amity, a treaty that was faithfully observed so long as Massasoit lived. This peace, obviously, was of great advantage to the little colony during its feeble years. Indians, said one resident of Plymouth, "were wont to be the most cruellest and trecherousest people in all these parts, even like Lyons, but to us they have beene like Lambes, so kinde, so submissive, and trustie, as a man may truely say many Christians are not so kinde, nor sincere."[7]

Squanto attached himself to the Plymouth community and became a sort of wilderness guide to these inexperienced pioneers. William Bradford, the Pilgrim leader, called him "a special instrument sent of God," who "directed them how to set their corn, where to take fish, and to procure other commodities, and was also their pilot to bring them to unknown places for their profit . . . ."[8] With Squanto's aid the Pilgrims acquired experience that helped to bridge the tremendous gap between the environment of western Europe and that of the American wilderness, a process that was to be an essential part of frontier endeavor for decades to come.

In formulating an Indian policy the Pilgrims had little precedent to guide them. True, they had picked up all sorts of information about the natives of the New World, tales brought to Europe by explorers, reports from Jamestown and the coast of Maine, but much of this information was fragmentary and even misleading. When called upon to meet the problem head on, not as a matter of theory but as a matter of practical politics, the Pilgrim leaders tended to follow their own instincts, and the Indian policy they evolved served them remarkably well, all things considered. Stated briefly, their policy was to offer friendship, deal justly, and refuse to be intimidated. When the powerful Narragansett tribe, which resented the intrusion of the English and their liaison with the Wampanoags, sent to Plymouth a warlike challenge in the form of a bundle of arrows wrapped in a snakeskin, the doughty Pilgrims sent the snakeskin back stuffed with bullets. The Narragansetts got the point.[9] On another occasion, getting wind of an Indian plot, Captain Miles Standish and a party of Plymouth men demonstrated how ruthless the English could be, when they surprised and slew several of the conspirators.[10] By such methods—conciliation if feasible, decisive action if not—Plymouth managed to maintain itself in the face of latent Indian hostility not yet ready or able to break out into open war.

As for economic development, the Pilgrims quickly demonstrated both imagination and adaptability, qualities much to be prized on a wilderness frontier. They had come to America expecting to live by fishing, farming, and trading with the Indians. Experience soon taught them to forget about commercial fishing, and they found agriculture in New England for the most part unrewarding except as a means of subsistence. It was the Indian trade that was the key to economic solvency for Plymouth. Not having planted their settlement at the mouth of a river, the Pilgrims sought out the trade by skirting along the coast in both directions in order to establish contact with Indians who had access to the beaver grounds of the interior. At first the Pilgrims traded corn for furs, but soon they were making excellent use of wampum, which many of the tribes coveted but could not make for themselves. In time the Plymouth traders established posts on the Kennebec and Penobscot rivers in Maine, at the head of Buzzard's Bay, on Narragansett Bay, and on the Connecticut River above the site of Hartford. Business flourished, and year after year large quantities of skins and furs, especially beaver, were shipped to England to help pay the colony's debts. Until 1640 the fur trade of Plymouth was a monopoly reserved to a small group of the colony's leaders who had taken upon themselves the obligation to liquidate the public debt.

In the meantime, occasional ships from England brought newcomers to the colony, with the result that the population, so badly depleted during the winter of 1620–1621, grew considerably. This, in turn, led to a need for more land, especially pasture and meadowland to accommodate the increasing herds of cattle. Bradford and other leaders were most reluctant to have the people disperse to remote places, but the need for land was not to be denied, and, beginning about 1628, the process of expansion began. Individuals and small groups found land that pleased them elsewhere along the edge of the harbor or farther along the coast, and then secured permission and made arrangements to move. One by one new villages and farms were established, with snug frame houses, outbuildings, and fenced fields. In this way there came into being such towns as Duxbury, Scituate, Marshfield, and Barnstable.

Even before Plymouth began sending out offshoots, other small English settlements had begun to appear at various points along the coast to the north.[11] In each of these, whatever its nature and purpose, Englishmen were testing their ability to survive the challenge of the wilderness, gaining experience, developing techniques. Some of the new settlements were transitory; they made mistakes fatal to pioneers. Others groped their way through the first crucial months and years to permanence and relative security. One thing was certain—English New England was beginning to grow, and the wilderness was beginning to recede from an increasing number of select spots along the edge of the sea. At two places in particular, the mouth of the Piscataqua River and the rocky peninsula of Cape Ann, English colonists were appearing in ever-growing numbers and, as usual, their purposes were largely, if not entirely, economic—to catch fish and trade for furs. Plymouth watched the appearance of these pioneering communities to the north with a combination of relief and apprehension—relief because they meant added strength against the forces of the wilderness, apprehension because they brought with them to America the worldly corruption that the Pilgrims were trying to escape.

*T*HE ENGLISH were not the only nationality to arrive early on the northern frontier. Soon after the Hudson River was first explored in 1609, Dutch vessels began visiting its hill-crested shores to acquire the valuable peltry that the natives had to offer. By 1614 the Dutch had established a crude trading post, Fort Nassau, on a low island at the present site of Albany. Seven years later the Dutch government granted a charter, with exclusive rights of trade and colonization in North America, to a private business organization known as the Dutch West India Company. Under the sponsorship of this group the first shipload of actual settlers, most of them French-speaking Walloons, arrived at Manhattan Island in 1624. Some proceeded upriver to establish Fort Orange where Albany is now located; others went south to the Delaware River and constructed a new Fort Nassau. Both of these forts were intended primarily as centers for the Indian trade. The island of Manhattan, present site of New York City, was just a temporary stopping point until 1626, when the Dutch village of New Amsterdam was begun. Soon other small pioneering communities were started at Hoboken, Bergen, and Hackensack.

In theory, if not always in practice, Dutch policy with respect to Indian lands was prudent and just. The Company viewed its colony of New Netherland as a commercial base rather than an expanding agricultural settlement, and so could afford an enlightened attitude toward Indian rights. Any land grants made under the Company's charter were contingent upon prior or subsequent purchase from the native proprietors, without coercion or fraud. This policy was in effect during the entire period of Dutch control, until 1664.[12] Likewise, early instructions from the Company required the colonists to avoid involvement in disputes among the Indians except in the role of peacemakers.

In the meantime the fur trade, which was the foundation of the colony's economy, was growing with gratifying speed. As early as 1626 the city of Amsterdam in Holland received from New Netherland a cargo that included 7,246 beaver skins, a large number of otter, and a few mink, wildcat, and muskrat.[13] Pieter Barentz, described by a contemporary chronicler as a man familiar with several Indian dialects, stands as a good example of the early Dutch fur trader, visiting the tribes in his trading sloop and carrying away valuable bundles of skins.[14]

By law, only the Company could engage in the fur trade, but everyone who saw the profits to be made wished to participate. Even some of the directors of the Company were not satisfied with the exclusive monopoly, in which they shared as members, but sought to gain direct personal access to the trade. Accordingly, they devised a scheme by which the Company would authorize wealthy investors to establish huge manorial estates in New Netherland, ostensibly to foster agricultural settlement but actually to enable the estate owners to conduct the fur trade on their own territory. The profits from the trade would cancel out the expenses of the manor and still leave goodly amounts for personal enrichment.[15]

In 1629 the Company was persuaded to issue a document known as the "Freedoms and Exemptions Granted by the West India Company to all Patroons, Masters, or Private Persons who will plant Colonies in New Netherland."[16] It offered princely grants of territory, with feudal jurisdiction, to such members of the Company as would undertake to transport and settle within four years fifty colonists above the age of fifteen. The settlers would become agricultural tenants of the grantee, or patroon, for a fixed term of years, being subject to his jurisdiction during that time. In this way it was expected that the population of New Netherland would be increased and the colony strengthened without appreciable expense to the Company itself.

Although several patroonships were undertaken by ambitious men, only one proved to be of any great importance, that of the wealthy Amsterdam merchant Kiliaen Van Rensselaer. This vast estate extended for miles along both shores of the Hudson River above and below Fort Orange, embracing hundreds of thousands of acres of virgin land. With a pride not inconsistent with the scope of his domain, the patroon named his feudal manor "Rensselaerswyck." To it he brought pioneering farmers, building houses for them and even providing subsistence during the first difficult months. In time the Hudson shores of Rensselaerswyck became a region of scattered farms together with necessary accommodations such as smithies, brick kilns, sawmills, and gristmills.[17] Wealth and planning paved the way for these pioneers, but at the sacrifice of a large measure of personal freedom and self-determination.

Immigrants who came to New Netherland as free men rather than as tenants found it relatively easy to become independent farmers. That the Company was not averse to the establishment of small, independent farms is shown by the fact that the Freedoms and Exemptions of 1629 made provision for grants of lesser size than the patroonships. In 1640 the Company agreed to grant tracts of about two hundred acres each to free immigrants who brought with them five other settlers.[18] Under these conditions independent farming developed fairly steadily.

Dutch farmers in New Netherland, like most agricultural pioneers along the northern frontier, sought to turn the wilderness into prosperous farms by modifying the practices of European agriculture to fit the conditions of the New World. But in a colony so deeply involved in the fur trade and with nearby Indians clamoring for European products in exchange for furs, nearly every farmer was tempted to dabble in the traffic, despite the Company's monopoly. As a result, the theoretical monopoly proved impossible to maintain. The first major breach came with the concessions made to the patroons in 1629. The patroons, in turn, found their own private monopolies equally chimerical in the face of almost universal trading on the part of their tenants. As a matter of fact, neither the Company nor the patroons really objected to the fur-trading activities of individual settlers provided the settlers subsequently offered their peltry to the monopolists at reasonable rates. About 1639 the Company abandoned all pretence of a monopoly, threw open the fur trade to residents of the colony, and henceforth sought to derive its fur-trading income primarily from duties imposed on the traffic.[19]

In the early years of the colony, down to about 1639, Dutch relations with the Indians were quite good. The Dutch colonists respected the Indians little, loved them even less, but recognized the value of a practical accommodation for the sake of successful colonization and trade. There was constant contact between the races, with a minimum of friction, an achievement largely made possible by the relatively slow growth of the colony's population. The Indians rejoiced in the advantages of their commercial relations with the Dutch and, as some of the colonists put it, came "as lambs among us."[20] Nevertheless, over the years Indian resentment began to accumulate. A certain amount of friction between them and the Dutch was inevitable. Dutch cattle would wander into Indian cornfields, and half-wild Indian dogs would prey upon Dutch livestock. Perhaps more serious was the fact that the colonial authorities refused to make firearms available to certain groups of local Indians lest they become a menace. This proved to be a handicap to those Indians when their enemies somehow managed to obtain guns from other sources.

The coming of Willem Kieft in 1638 to be the colony's chief executive marked the beginning of serious trouble between the two races.[21] Kieft came to New Netherland determined to enhance his reputation by leading the rather feeble colony to a new level of strength and prosperity. For Indians, whom he regarded as primitive creatures, he had a dangerously low reserve of tolerance and understanding. Indeed, it seems apparent that Director Kieft, by his attitude toward the American Indians, placed himself squarely in the long, futile procession of European imperialists who, for several centuries and in some cases even down to recent times, have looked upon backward native people as a nuisance either to be molded into a pattern convenient for the colonizing power or else crushed. This, together with the previous accumulation of Indian resentment, spelled trouble.

Starting in 1640 the Raritan Indians and other local groups began to indulge in acts of violence against the colonists, with attendant bloodshed. The Dutch retaliated in kind, although there is reason to believe that the majority of the settlers would have preferred peaceful accommodation to all-out war. It was Kieft who welcomed the chance to strike a decisive blow that would humble the Indians for all time and clear the way for Dutch expansion. The opportunity came in February 1643 when the local Indians found themselves under attack by tribesmen from farther up the river, either Mahican or Mohawk. In terror, they hurried to the Dutch for protection and huddled in two camps not far from New Amsterdam. Then some of the leading citizens came to Kieft with a proposal that cold steel and hot blood were the answer to the Indian problem, and the sooner the better. The governor agreed. On the night of February 25, after careful preparation, a force of well-armed men proceeded to the two camps of refugee Indians, where they fell upon the unsuspecting natives, slaying men, women, and children. When the frightful work was over, at least eighty Indians were dead.[22]

The tribes were not slow to seek vengeance for this outrageous act and like aroused hornets swarmed in upon the territory occupied by the Dutch, even to the very gates of New Amsterdam. They attacked farms, burned buildings, and slew whatever they found alive. Under these conditions many utterly discouraged settlers abandoned the colony and made their way back to Europe. Two circumstances saved the colony from almost total disaster: the various bands of Indians were not firmly united under a determined leadership, and the warriors were not amply supplied with guns and ammunition. Taking advantage of these weaknesses, the colonists were able to rally and strike some decisive blows of their own, chopping up the Indians piecemeal. Kieft's War, as the conflict has come to be known, dragged on until August 1645, when a general peace was arranged.

One modern commentator has labeled Kieft's War "the one really black spot on the record of the provincial government's treatment of the Indians."[23] That is, perhaps, a slight exaggeration in favor of the Dutch, but it does emphasize that under Kieft relations between Indians and whites reached an all-time low—this when peaceful accommodation would not have been unduly difficult. The frontier was not yet crowded; the Dutch population was not yet pressing hard upon the Indians. Wrongs on both sides were isolated cases and should have been treated as such. To expect the Indians, divided as they were, to come forward with the constructive kind of leadership so greatly needed was futile. The Dutch had the potential for it, but failed to produce. Moreover, Kieft's War well demonstrates that a policy of extermination, all too often seized upon by frontiersmen as a quick answer to the Indian problem, not only lacks moral justification but falls far short of solving the problem.

In the long run it was agriculture rather than the fur trade that provided the greatest stimulus to frontier expansion in Dutch New Netherland. After the founding of the settlements at Fort Orange and Manhattan in the 1620s came the gradual process of settling the Hudson Valley between them, as well as the desirable land at the western end of Long Island. Because the population increased only haltingly, especially in the early decades, the Dutch frontier underwent a very gradual expansion, and in times of trouble even suffered severe setbacks. Step by step the pioneering farmers sought out fertile sites, acquired land by purchase from the natives, and broke the sod with the plow. Usually the farmers settled in groups, for security as well as companionship, so that typically the frontier advanced by the establishment of agricultural villages. In this way the Jersey shore became occupied, the area around present Brooklyn was settled, and a nucleus of farming families became established at the Esopus in the 1650s.[24]

As was usually the case during the course of the westward movement, persons primarily involved in the fur trade opposed the advance of the farming frontier, in New Netherland not so much for fear that the fur-bearing animals would be driven away as from apprehension that advanced settlements would intercept the trade before it could reach the established centers. This attitude was especially prevalent at Beverwyck, the village that had grown up alongside Fort Orange, a place almost totally dependent upon the fur trade. The merchants of Beverwyck were full of suspicion when a discontented group of pioneers from that community, under the leadership of an experienced frontiersman named Arent Van Curler, in 1661 migrated northwestward to a select site on the south bank of the Mohawk River, where they founded the village of Schenectady. Unable to prevent this advance of the frontier, Beverwyck had to satisfied with an official decree prohibiting any trading with the Indians at the new settlement. Since the fur merchants remained suspicious and voiced repeated complaints, the colony government in 1663 forbade the residents of Schenectady even to transport or possess any Indian trading goods.[25] The founding of Schenectady represents the northernmost advance of the Dutch frontier, and, significantly, the motive for its settlement was more agricultural than commercial.

*M*EANWHILE, the slowly expanding Dutch frontier was being sharply challenged by rival frontiers on the east and south. From the east came a creeping tide of English from New England who had founded communities of their own kind on the eastern part of Long Island and even on the mainland not many miles from New Amsterdam. The westernmost of these English villages submitted to Dutch jurisdiction but inevitably chafed under the dictatorial rule of the Dutch governors. Like many frontiersmen after them, having ventured into the wilderness and come to terms with it, they resented being kept in tight leading strings by distant officials ensconced in paneled offices. Representatives of the English villages in New Netherland plainly told the Dutch governor in 1653 that the arbitrary enactment of new laws or orders affecting the lives or property of the people without the consent of their representatives was "contrary and opposed to the granted Freedoms of the Dutch Government, and odious to every freeborn man, and principally so to those whom God has placed in a free state on newly settled lands. . . ."[26] Conflict over this principle of freedom continued through the remainder of the Dutch regime, with many Dutch colonists joining the English pioneers in protest.

To the south, along the Delaware River (called by the Dutch the South River), New Netherland was boldly challenged by a Swedish frontier. Since 1620, when Captain Cornelis Jacobsen May explored the Delaware, the Dutch had shown a continuing interest in the area, primarily because the river was another entryway to the fur country. For a brief two years in the mid-1620s they maintained a trading post at the mouth of Timber Creek, about opposite the entrance to the Schuylkill River. In 1631 they attempted a real settlement at Lewes, just inside Cape Henlopen, but the effort foundered with an Indian massacre.[27] After that the Dutch concentrated their effort almost entirely on the lucrative fur trade with the willing natives.

In 1638 the picture was suddenly complicated by the arrival of a

Swedish colonizing expedition under the command of Peter Minuit, formerly director-general of New Netherland. Minuit and his colonists built Fort Christina where Wilmington now stands, bought extensive tracts of land from the local Indians, and commenced their own trading operations. Naturally, the Dutch resented this intrusion into what they considered their own territory, but for the time being were too weak to do more than protest.

With the arrival of the corpulent but amazingly energetic Governor Johan Printz early in 1643, the colony of New Sweden entered upon its most vigorous period of development. To complicate the situation still further, a small group of English traders from New England had constructed a blockhouse near the mouth of the Schuylkill, and were preparing to reap the profits of the Indian trade. Thus the contest for domination of the Delaware River, with its valuable fur trade and rich farmland, began to shape up as a tricornered spat. Mustering what strength they could, the Dutch burned down the English post and transported the interlopers to New Amsterdam.[28]

For a while the Dutch and the Swedes maintained a fairly cordial relationship as they competed with each other for land and furs, but inevitably the competition produced friction and ill feeling. In 1645 Printz peremptorily expelled a Dutch trading sloop from the area, and the contest entered a new phase. In the fur trade, position was all-important, for the Indians brought their furs down the rivers and would be likely to stop at the first trading post they saw. The most audacious move in this Swedish-Dutch game of chess came soon after the Dutch erected a new fort on the Schuylkill. The Swedes, under orders from Printz, calmly put up a blockhouse of their own directly in front of the Dutch fort and so close that the latter was not visible from the river. By such bold action Printz was able to humiliate and weaken his rivals until by 1648 the Swedish colony was virtually master of the fur trade in the Delaware River.

A hundred years after these events, tales of the early days in New Sweden were still being told: how the pioneers sometimes had to journey many miles overland to obtain salt from New Netherland, how farmers in the fields were protected against hostile Indians by armed guards, how the Indians came to fear and respect the Swedish pioneers because of their toughness, and how the Swedes themselves gradually changed under the conditions of the New World and became more and more like Indians.[29] Whatever the validity of these reports, it is certain that the Scandinavians made good pioneers. On the whole they treated the Indians well without being condescending; they exploited the fur trade of the Schuylkill Valley with considerable success; and they developed an agriculture that demonstrated the virtues of hard work, resourcefulness, and adaptation. Their houses and barns were built of logs laid horizontally, an important prototype of the familiar log cabin of the later American frontier.[30]

The Dutch in New Netherland and the Swedish pioneers of the Delaware River, because of the small scope of their ventures and the sometimes pretentious way in which they undertook them, frequently have been cast as the buffoons in American colonial history for purposes of comic relief. But considering the small number of people involved, the inadequate backing they received from their respective home governments, and what they accomplished under heavy handicaps, such treatment really is quite unfair. Both nationalities proved themselves able and courageous pioneers; both made significant contributions to the development of the American frontier.

New Sweden's apparent vitality and strength under the dynamic leadership of Governor Printz was deceptive; the colony rested on no firm foundation of support from the mother country. This became clear when in 1655, two years after Printz had departed for home, the resolute Dutch director-general Peter Stuyvesant led a strong military expedition against the Swedish positions. New Sweden collapsed like a house of matchsticks. The settlers were allowed to remain if they would accept Dutch jurisdiction, and many did so. As the Dutch did little to colonize the area, it remained predominantly Swedish in character for years to come.

While Stuyvesant was on the Delaware conquering New Sweden, war with the Indians broke out again at New Amsterdam, the first of three such conflicts during the rule of this pugnacious governor. The causes of these outbursts of violence were various, and neither side can claim perfect innocence. Worth noting is the fact that the population of the colony increased from only about two hundred inhabitants in 1625 to some seven or eight thousand in 1664.[31] It is clear that the expansion of agricultural settlement in New Netherland irritated and alarmed the Indians, producing ever more serious friction along a thin, irregular frontier. No genuine modus vivendi for the two cultures had been found. As a consequence the Dutch paid a heavy price in lives and property, and the Indians suffered equally serious losses, which they had little prospect of recouping. In the matter of Indian relations, the fairly good Dutch beginning rocked on to its grim conclusion in 1664. After that the problem belonged to the English conquerors of New Netherland.

*D*URING THE FIRST decades of pioneering the European settlers began to learn the most fundamental lessons that the frontier, a harsh and exacting instructor, had to teach. Those lessons, put into practice by determined and resourceful men, made possible the westward expansion of the frontier during the remainder of the colonial period. For one thing, through actual experience the true nature of the country became better known. It was found to be neither the paradise that some enthusiasts had claimed nor the hell so dolefully described by the disillusioned. Brave and adventurous settlers soon discovered the truth that lay somewhere between these views, and that was important because the actual conditions, once known, could be anticipated and prepared for. Careful advance planning, including arrangements for enough supplies to sustain life during the first difficult year, was found to be the necessary foundation for a new settlement on the frontier.

Good organization and discipline were also important. Some if not most of the early pioneers came to the wilderness because they were impatient with the usual restraints imposed by civilized society. All too often such individualists, when they found their freedom, showed little concern for the rights and security of others. The difficulties and dangers of frontier living often required teamwork, and when this was lacking the consequence might be failure and even starvation. Such might well have been the fate of Plymouth had there been no Mayflower Compact and the will to make it effective. Thomas Weston's trading settlement at Wessagusset (Weymouth) in 1622–1623 showed how quickly a colonizing venture could slide toward disaster when constructive leadership and discipline were lacking.[32]

Good motivation proved to be another important key to successful colonization. Men who had strong, positive reasons for coming to the wilderness seemed to weather the early vicissitudes better than those who were careless opportunists. When the going became rough, men without adequate motivation were likely to cut cables and run; others, under the same dangers and hardships, stuck it out because they had a goal worth fighting for. The settlers at the Kennebec in 1607 did not have sufficiently solid reasons for being on that bleak hillside—they quit; the Pilgrims in 1620 understood thoroughly why they were on their bleak hillside at Plymouth—they stayed. It is interesting to observe how motivation sometimes could be strengthened by altering certain conditions, when experience indicated that a change was desirable. An example of this occurred in 1623 when the leaders at Plymouth realized that their communal form of agriculture was not offering sufficient inducement to produce maximum effort and began to allot farmland to individuals. As soon as this was done, individual initiative improved significantly, and the whole community enjoyed the benefits.[33]

Indeed, one of the most valuable lessons derived from the Plymouth experience was that somewhere between the extremes of rugged individualism and complete subordination of the individual to the group lay a middle course which, if prudently pursued, would contribute most to the successful growth of a pioneering community. Late in 1621 Deacon Robert Cushman preached at Plymouth a sermon in which he extolled the virtues of teamwork, asserting that "nothing in this world doth more resemble heavenly happinesse, then for men to live as one, being of one heart, and one soule; neither any thing more resembles hellish horror, then for every man to shift for himselfe."[34] Fortunately, when too much "togetherness" was found by experience to be harmful to the plantation's welfare, the Pilgrims were wise enough to avoid going to the opposite extreme, and sought and found the preferable middle ground—a happy blend of group control and individual freedom.

The early pioneers also discovered the great value of Indian friendship. Although the presence of the natives was viewed as something of an annoyance if not always a danger, the Indians could not simply be wished away but had to be dealt with as one of the conditions of frontier living. Pioneers who managed to establish friendly relations with the Indians usually fared best. Friendly Indians such as Squanto and Massasoit could be extremely valuable to a young pioneering settlement, for they could provide food in times of acute shortage and show the frontiersmen how best to utilize the resources of their new environment. If need be, too, neighboring Indians could serve as a buffer against more distant, hostile tribes. The Dutch record in the matter of Indian relations shows how easily good intentions could be eroded under frontier conditions. The inevitable racial friction of an expanding frontier, where the rough edges of both races rubbed against each other, bred contempt and hatred, which in turn led to violence. There were acts of bad faith on both sides, sometimes the product of deep misunderstanding but often indicative of a deteriorating philosophy of human relations on the part of civilized Europeans.

The experience of New Netherland reveals other serious mistakes —selection of inferior leaders, preoccupation with profits at the expense of long-range progress, maintenance of dictatorial techniques of control among a people who were developing a pioneer's appetite for self-determination, and retention of governmental authority by a private company either unwilling or unable to give the colony the massive support it desperately needed. Like many another frontier, that of New Netherland proved corrosive to the great distinctions of class and wealth prevalent in Europe, being truly a frontier of budding opportunity for uncommon men of common rank.[35] Apparently Dutch frontiersmen were much like those of other nationalities under similar circumstances—inclined to be impatient with constituted authority, contemptuous of Indians, greedy for material gain in an environment where those who lagged were quickly left behind, prone to settle problems by an easy resort to action rather than prolonged discussion.[36]

Always there was the danger that the rush for land and profits would obliterate less tangible forms of wealth such as culture and religion. Education, for example, was long neglected or kept half-starved in New Netherland, as indicated by the complaint of two clergymen in 1657, that "although some parents try to give their children some instruction, the success is far from satisfactory, and we can expect nothing else than young men of foolish and undisciplined minds."[37] To cherish learning on a raw frontier took extraordinary devotion and sacrifice; many pioneers, absorbed in the day-by-day struggle for survival and success, were not willing to pay the price. Yet in many ways the Dutch pioneers built well, creating solid homes, substantial villages, and prosperous farms where before there had been only a forest. That New Netherland failed to develop sufficient strength to prevent its absorption by the English is more justly attributable to planners and profiteers in old Amsterdam than to pioneers in New Amsterdam and the Hudson Valley. Much the same comment may be made about New Sweden.

The greatest secret of successful living on the frontier was to have the will and ability to modify habitual practices in the light of new conditions. People of rigid habits often failed to make a successful transition from civilization to frontier, for they were unable to alter their ways to meet the peculiar demands of a wilderness environment. This does not mean that Europeans had to become Indians to survive, but they did have to be able to draw upon the resources of common sense and the experience of others, including the Indians, to solve problems that were radically different from anything they had previously known. The adoption of maize as a basic crop where soil and climate proved less favorable for European grains is a notable example. Even Indian recipes found their way into pioneering kitchens when hunger hovered by the hearth, with the result that such dishes as succotash and johnny-cakes still come steaming hot to many an American table.

New Plymouth, New Netherland, New Sweden—all of these are interesting and significant examples of early pioneering endeavor in the American wilderness. But, as communities they were relatively weak in wealth and numbers, and consequently handicapped in their development. This became especially evident as a vastly more numerous and powerful wave of English colony builders swept in from across the Atlantic to challenge the wilderness as it had not been challenged since the great days of Spanish conquest. They were to leave upon the land a mark that is clearly apparent in American life even to the present day.

◁ **3** ▷

The Tidal Wave of the English,
1630–1675

*T*he year 1630 was to see the beginning of a momentous influx of settlers from the British Isles, but a casual observer traveling the length of the coast from the Kennebec River to the Delaware in the early spring of that year would have seen little to suggest the fact. A few scattered outposts along the coast of Maine, a small community of fishing folk at Cape Ann, the Pilgrim colony within the protecting arm of Cape Cod, a covey of Dutch pioneers at Manhattan Island, an occasional trading vessel anchored in a sheltered harbor—these were the sparse evidences of continuing European interest in the northern frontier. Almost everywhere the forest still prevailed; the Indians, as yet, remained scarcely disturbed in their own way of life. But the impression was deceptive, for in 1630 the tide of history was gathering force and a great migration was in the making.

In England a commercial organization known as the Massachusetts Bay Company was skillfully transformed by its Puritan leaders into an agency dedicated to establishing in New England a combined refuge and laboratory of Christian living for God's company of saints. To this end a sincere and dedicated country squire, John Winthrop, led to Massachusetts the first contingents of what was to become, in effect, a tidal wave of Puritan settlers. During the next ten years some two hundred more ships, bearing in all about sixteen thousand colonists, were to follow. The impact of this migration was tremendous, expanding the area of settlement many miles inland.

The fishing colony at Cape Ann, already strongly Puritan in character, readily allowed itself to be absorbed into the new and larger enterprise, becoming the nucleus of the Massachusetts town of Salem. But Winthrop and his people preferred the area near the mouth of the Charles River to the rocky peninsula of Cape Ann, and proceeded to set up their dwellings not far from where the town of Boston was to grow. As a matter of fact, so great was the influx of settlers that before long a little flock of tiny pioneering villages sprang up in the vicinity.

Unlike the Pilgrims ten years earlier, the Winthrop migration had the advantages of careful preparation, influence in high places, considerable wealth, and a leadership of wide learning and experience. Too, the season was more advantageous, and the Indians were even more docile at Boston than at Plymouth. But it must not be supposed that conditions during the early stages of the venture were easy—the harshness of the new and strange environment saw to that. Until houses could be built, the newcomers had to live in tents or Indian-style wigwams. Hunger, the all-too-frequent companion of frontiersmen, lurked in the new community. One early settler recalled:

> The then unsubdued Wilderness yielding little Food, many a Time if I could have filled my Belly, tho' with mean Victuals, it would have been sweet unto me. . . . *Bread* was so very scarce, that sometimes I tho't the very Crusts of my Father's Table would have been very sweet unto me. And when I could have *Meal & Water and Salt* boiled together, it was so good, who could wish better?[1]

As in early Virginia and Plymouth, corn acquired from the Indians helped tide the pioneers over the difficult early months until a crop could be harvested. One hungry colonist traded a puppy for a peck of grain. Occasionally provisions arrived by ship from England or Virginia, whereupon the leaders of the colony would have the precious food purchased for the populace as a whole and distributed to individuals according to need.[2] As yet, there was little of the rugged individualism so often associated with the American frontier.

Some reports sent back to England emphasized the bounty of the Massachusetts frontier, probably in the hope of attracting more settlers.[3] The truth was that although the soil in the vicinity of Boston was not impossibly sterile, it was not remarkably fertile either, and much of it was rocky and shallow. After five or six years of cultivation the soil, it was said, became "barren beyond belief." The lowland hay or marsh grass, which grew luxuriantly, was found to have a low nutritive value: "our beasts grow lousy with feeding upon it, and are much out of heart and liking." One disillusioned woman among the colonists exclaimed with disgust, "The air of the country is sharp, the rocks many, the trees innumerable, the grass little, the winter cold, the summer hot, the gnats in summer biting, the wolves at midnight howling, &c."[4] She was not the last of her sex to regret having let herself be enticed to the frontier.

One problem that was to become typical of the expanding frontier during the next two centuries cropped up early in Massachusetts—wage and price inflation caused by a shortage of man power and supplies. The colony government met the problem with a policy of strict controls and achieved some measure of success. This, too, violates the stereotype of an unregulated frontier society, but the Puritans were not interested in stereotypes—they were determined to employ whatever measures were necessary to assure the success of their undertaking, including the subordination of individuals to the general good.

*E*XPANSION of settlement in southern New England was so rapid and diverse that it may well be described as explosive. Behind this dynamic movement lay a variety of causes. Political and religious troubles in England combined with the vaunted opportunities in America to draw thousands of Puritans and like-minded Englishmen across the sea. The new arrivals swelled the population, increasing pressure on available land in the original communities, especially good meadowland for the keeping of cattle. In addition, many ambitious men were lured farther and farther inland in the competitive trade with the Indians, each man seeking to establish his base of operations closer to the Indians than the posts of his rivals. There was also a strong religious motive underlying Puritan expansionism—the compelling urge to preserve religious purity by withdrawing from a society infected with error, or conversely, to protect orthodoxy by expelling from society the advocates of erroneous opinions. One or more of these causes may be detected in nearly every instance of new settlement prior to 1675.

Ipswich, on the coast twenty-five miles north of Boston, was settled in 1633 under the apprehension that if the English did not move into the area the French would do so.[5] Two years later a group from Ipswich pushed five miles farther up the coast to begin a settlement at Newbury. At about the same time twenty-one families newly arrived from England established themselves at Weymouth, a dozen miles south of Boston,

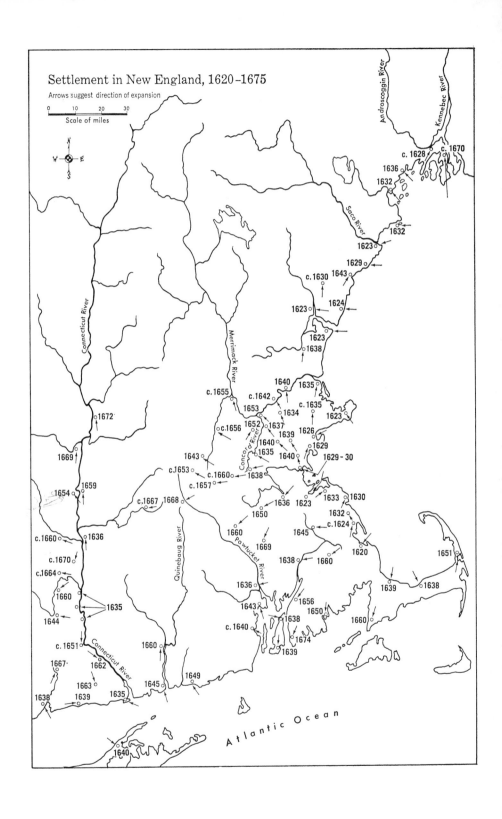

Settlement in New England, 1620–1675

Arrows suggest direction of expansion

0   10   20   30
Scale of miles

N
W   E
S

Androscoggin River
Kennebec River
Saco River
Connecticut River
Merrimack River
Concord River
Quinebaug River
Pawtucket River
Connecticut River

c. 1628
c. 1670
1636
1632
1632
1623
1629
c. 1630   1643
1623   1624
1623
1638
1640   1635
c. 1655   c. 1642   c. 1635
1653   1623
c. 1656   1652   1637   1634
1640   1626
1639
1643   1635   1629
c. 1653   c. 1660   1640   1629–30
c. 1657   1638
1672
1669
1654   1659   c. 1667   1668   1636   1623   1633   1630
c. 1660   1636   1650   1632
c. 1670   1660   c. 1624
c. 1664   1669   1645
1660   1638   1620
1644   1635   1639   1651
c. 1651   1638   1660   1639   1638
1667   1662   1636   1656   1660
1663   1643   1650
1638   1639   1635   c. 1640   1638
1674
1660   1639
1645   1649
1640

Atlantic Ocean

and other home seekers began a settlement nearby at Hingham. But a more significant advance came when a group of planters, led by the enterprising fur trader Simon Willard, in 1635 ventured sixteen miles into the interior, directly away from the seacoast, to establish a settlement at Concord. This new village was conveniently located on a stream which emptied into the Merrimack River, offering a route by which the furs of the Merrimack Valley might be intercepted before they came into the hands of other traders along the coast. This advance marked the real beginning of the inland push of the Massachusetts frontier and clearly demonstrated the strength and confidence achieved by the Puritan pioneers during their first five years on the coast. It was made possible by the relative weakness and docility of the local Indians.

For the next twenty-four years Willard's attention was largely oriented toward the north, where he sought to exploit the resources of the Merrimack area. In 1652 a new settlement was made at Chelmsford, much nearer the great south bend of the Merrimack, and in 1655 Willard established a residence there. Meanwhile, in the mid-1640s a young fur trader named Thomas King had built a trading post in the wilderness eighteen miles due west of Concord. King died shortly afterward, but in 1645 one of his associates, John Prescott, erected a trading house of his own at the same place. A few families began moving to this attractive area, which in time developed into the town of Lancaster. In 1659 Willard left the Merrimack Valley and established himself at Lancaster, where he acquired the business from Prescott's successor. Thus the pursuit of the lucrative fur trade in eastern Massachusetts resulted in the founding of three new towns—Concord, Chelmsford, and Lancaster.[6]

An upsurge of religious controversy in the Bay Colony quickly resulted in the founding of "heretical" Rhode Island in 1636–1638, and the town of Exeter, New Hampshire, at about the same time, as religious outcasts such as Roger Williams and Anne Hutchinson, with their followers, sought to establish havens in the wilderness. Each of these movements produced, in effect, a small new frontier, separate from the frontier of orthodox Massachusetts. With reference to the westward movement, however, the most significant offshoot of Massachusetts was a new frontier established in the valley of the lower Connecticut River in 1634–1636, when hundreds of settlers trekked overland through the forest or came around Cape Cod by ship to found the towns of Hartford, Wethersfield, and Windsor.

No river in southern New England offered better long-range prospects for the fur trade than the Connecticut. Until 1632 the Dutch traders from New Netherland had this area entirely to themselves, and with lively hopes of future success they built in 1633 a trading post at the place where Hartford was later to stand. Already, however, the seeds of competition were being sown, as Plymouth Colony sent a party led by William Holmes to begin trading on the river. Defying Dutch protests, Holmes proceeded upriver several miles past the recently established Dutch post, and set up a trading station for his own colony. Also in 1633 the Massachusetts trader John Oldham, following ancient Indian paths, pioneered the overland route from Massachusetts Bay to the Connecticut Valley in search of good sources of beaver. Two years later Oldham, with a small group of followers, again came to the Connecticut River. This time he began a settlement, later to become the town of Wethersfield, just five miles below the Dutch post.

Although Oldham was primarily interested in the fur trade, his move to the Connecticut Valley set in motion a migration of land-seeking Massachusetts farmers, who began to arrive in such numbers that neither the Dutch nor the Plymouth men were able to continue their trade in the vicinity for very long. By 1636 there were Puritan villages at Wethersfield, Hartford, and Windsor, containing some eight hundred settlers. Historians disagree as to whether this migration was stimulated primarily by economic, political, or religious conditions, but certain it is that the pioneers of Connecticut were seeking out a new frontier because they were highly dissatisfied with the opportunities afforded by the Boston area. Their venture was the first example of a great westward surge of population, bypassing less desirable intervening land, in a deliberate attempt to open a new frontier as a means of escape from disadvantageous conditions in the east.

Certainly the Puritan leaders of the Massachusetts Bay Colony had not anticipated such a vigorous expansion of the frontier as occurred in the years after 1630. Their original intention had been to plant a compact, closely regulated community of God's chosen few. When the great pressures of economic, political, and religious growth began to push the colonists farther into the wilderness, the Puritans knew that their holy experiment was in danger. Almost instinctively they realized that expansion meant inevitable weakening of the control and discipline so necessary if their original purpose was to be achieved. To this extent they already were grasping something of the significance of the frontier as a process.

Fortunately for the first settlers of Connecticut, the Indians of the immediate vicinity were friendly; in fact, as early as 1631 they had urged the white men to come and settle there for purposes of trade and, the Indians hoped, to protect them from their enemies the Pequots. This tribe, a relative newcomer to Connecticut, had migrated eastward from the upper Hudson, to the great grief of lesser tribes whom the warlike Pequots shoved aside as they advanced. In 1636 the Pequots constituted a serious threat to the peaceful local Indians and the newly arrived English pioneers as well. The result was a brief but fierce war of extermination in 1637 between the Pequots on the one hand and the combined forces of Massachusetts and the Connecticut River towns on the other.

The Pequot War was the first large-scale military conflict between the English and the Indians on the northern frontier, the first open explosion of animosities that had been gathering force during a decade or more of contact and friction. Its course, conduct, and conclusion were a sharp forewarning of what was in store for pioneers and Indians for decades to come. To inflict maximum suffering with total destruction seems to have been the order of the day. It is difficult to avoid the conclusion that many of the English welcomed an opportunity to teach the Indians a lesson they would never forget, and in truth they did exactly that. Pequot resistance came to an end after the great majority of the tribe had been ruthlessly tracked down and either killed or taken prisoner. The terms of peace to which the Indians submitted virtually put an end to the Pequots as a distinct tribe, for the survivors were parceled out among other tribes who had shown themselves friendly toward the English. Apparently the conscience of the Christians was untroubled, even as they wiped off their swords red with the blood of Indian women and children. Said one victorious participant, "We had sufficient light from the word of God for our proceedings."[7]

With the near-destruction of the Pequots, the way was opened for the continuing expansion of the Connecticut frontier, and in more populous Massachusetts the advance of settlement proceeded with seemingly relentless vigor. Some groups pushed deep into the area between Concord and the Connecticut Valley, founding such towns as Lancaster, Marlboro, and even isolated Brookfield. Others moved northward to plant new settlements along the lower Merrimack River and beyond to New Hampshire, or made their way into the growing communities along the coast of Maine. Still others crossed into Plymouth Colony and helped establish pioneering villages on Cape Cod and in the interior. For a generation after the conclusion of the bloody Pequot War this vigorous, optimistic expansion continued.

*T*HE SMASHING of one tribe in 1637 was anything but a solution to the long-range problem of Indian relations. Indeed, no really good solution to this complex problem has ever been devised and put into practice on a scale sufficient to overcome the great injustice and harm wrought by selfish and inept policies during three centuries.

On the northern frontier the colonists were confronted with the problem of Indian relations while still unprepared by experience or insight to deal with it effectively. Lacking unity as well as experience, lacking at first even the strength to pursue a bad policy to its conclusion, the colonies groped for an Indian policy that would be both consistent and effective. Through the fog of vacillation and uncertainty definite guiding principles began to emerge, principles that the colonial leaders soon accepted as fundamental in their dealings with the Indians. The first of these was unwavering firmness in all but the most hopeless situations, a principle well understood by any lion tamer who wishes to qualify for an old-age pension. This means an assumed boldness and a ready whip. At the same time it is essential that no irresponsible persons be allowed to torment the lions or otherwise irritate them, lest they forget their fear of the master's whip and in a blind fury leap upon him and the tormentors alike. Not only the instinct of self-preservation but the requirements of Christian ethics as well demanded that the Indians be dealt with justly and protected against fraud and other forms of mistreatment. These concepts, although not always clearly seen and followed, were ever present in colonial thinking on Indian policy.[8]

At the heart of all trouble between white men and Indians was the fact that the former were newcomers who were moving onto territory formerly occupied solely by the natives. Even though a transfer of land from Indian to colonist was sealed by mutual consent, the Indian was unable to foresee the full consequences of the transaction. He commonly assumed that he was merely sharing his territory with the white settler, a delusion that often led to a subsequent shock of realization and bitter resentment on the part of the Indian. Forcible ejection from home territory became for the natives a disillusioning experience.

As sincere moralists, the Puritans had to justify to themselves and the world their engaging in a process of dispossessing the Indians; they wrestled with the problem even while doing the very thing they were seeking to justify. How much of their theorizing was mere rationalization is difficult to determine. Apparently they never arrived at a complete, well-structured theory of displacement, but the general contour of Puritan thought on the question may be traced rather readily.

One begins with the medieval doctrine of Christian imperialism. According to this concept the whole earth was a legacy from God to His people, granted with the injunction to be fruitful, to multiply, and to subdue. The Indians, being pagans, were not among God's heirs and so were subject to displacement by the Christians.[9] This was quite in line with the Puritans' sense of a holy destiny. Whenever they appropriated Indian land by virtue of conquest, as in the time of the Pequot War, the Puritans rested easy in the knowledge that God's intentions for His chosen people were being carried out.

Supplementing this theological argument was the claim derived from royal dispensation. By virtue of discovery, the English monarch claimed lordship over a large segment of eastern America, with the right to grant portions of it to such of his subjects as he chose. In 1629 the Massachusetts Bay Company had been the recipient of one such royal grant, thereby acquiring in turn the legal right to make sub-grants within its area of jurisdiction. In theory, this could be done without the slightest regard to the native inhabitants; in practice, of course, the colonizers had to induce the Indians to acquiesce in their own displacement.

The Puritans further justified their actions by arguing that most American territory really was vacant anyway and therefore available for occupation. Were not the savages mere nomads, roaming over large areas but cultivating very little ground? They "ramble over much land without title or property: ther is more then enough for them & us," was the blunt comment of one theorist.[10] To English husbandmen, who thought of land in terms of well-tended farms, it was preposterous to suggest that valid title to thousands of acres of unimproved wilderness rested in the hands of mere roving savages. In 1652 the General Court of Massachusetts did go so far as to declare that the Indians were the rightful proprietors of land which they actually occupied and improved, but such land was considered to be a very small proportion of the whole.[11]

Even with all this theorizing, the Puritans, as a matter of justice and practical expediency, felt obliged to pay the Indians for land taken from them. Indeed, in most areas where the frontier advanced under circumstances other than war the process of bargaining for Indian land was generally prevalent. Cotton Mather even boasted:

> The good people of *New-England* have carried it with so much tenderness towards the tawny creatures among whom we live, that they would not own so much as one *foot of land* in the country, without a fair *purchase* and *consent* from the natives that laid claim unto it; albeit, we had a *royal charter* from the King of *Great-Britain,* to protect us in our settlement upon this continent.[12]

The statement, exaggerated as it is, contains a basic truth. At least the original intention and the usual practice, not only in New England but in New Netherland as well, was to obtain by fair purchase all land taken from the Indians. There are numerous cases in which the settlers paid for the same piece of land two or more times in order to satisfy all the Indian claimants and secure a clear title.

Generally speaking, no purchase of Indian land was considered fully valid until it had received the formal approval of the government. This was true not only in Massachusetts but also in Plymouth and Connecticut, and to some extent in Rhode Island and New York.[13] In frontier Maine, on the other hand, there was little or no attempt to regulate such purchases, and many a Maine landholder had no better evidence of title than a timeworn Indian deed bearing the crudely scratched marks of two or three sagamores. Even where the restrictive laws were fully in force, there was some evasion on the part of individual colonists, but on the whole the record of the colonial governments in this aspect of land policy was remarkably good.

With the Indians often quite willing to exchange tribal land for the products of European civilization, the time soon came when certain groups of Indians, especially those dwelling in areas where the English were settling in large numbers, were in danger of becoming virtually landless. As a means of solving this problem forever, with due attention to the needs of the Indians and the interests of the English, the colonial authorities began to set aside certain tracts of land as perpetual reservations for the dispossessed natives.[14] Almost inevitably this became little more than a device by which the white expansionists could rid themselves of the Indians with a clear conscience. And even the reservations were sometimes nibbled away by land-hungry colonists, while dilatory legislatures argued and investigated. An urgent complaint by the Pequot Indians, first voiced in 1713 because of alleged encroachments on their reservation, was still being heard as late as 1735. The dispute sometimes was carried on in language none too gentle. When the aggrieved Indians warned the neighboring farmers to respect their reservation, the whites threatened, the Indians said, "if wee done hold our tonge to beat our Brains out. . . ."[15] Woe to the weak!

Pious Puritans sometimes liked to theorize that regardless of any payment that might be given the Indians for their land, the heathen were receiving ample compensation anyway in the opportunity to hear the Gospel, for who could measure the value of salvation.[16] Usually, however, when an Indian was persuaded to part with a piece of real estate he preferred his pay in wampum and trading goods rather than Puritan preaching. In any event, the various theories of displacement enabled the Puritans to expand their control of land on the northern frontier, confident that removal of the heathen was being carried on under the smile of God. Only the Indians and a few radicals such as Roger Williams thought otherwise.

*W*HEREVER groups of Indians lived close to English communities there was a great possibility of interracial friction, rubbing raw the sensitive points of contact, heightening the tension that was to lead ultimately to open warfare and the consequent crushing of the Indians. There were numberless ways in which a white community might annoy a neighboring Indian community, and vice versa. In this matter, as in the problem of land acquisition, the English began with good intentions—to do justice to all parties without sacrificing the essential aspirations and interests of the settlers.[17]

One common form of annoyance was the damaging of Indian crops by roving cattle and hogs belonging to the colonists. English farming communities usually were careful to keep their planting fields well fenced as a protection against such animals; the Indians, on the other hand, were not accustomed to building fences around their cornfields, nor were they eager to alter their habits merely because they now had English farmers as near neighbors. The English felt that the Indians ought to take the precaution of protecting their fields, for with the farm animals allowed to roam at large in the woods, as was the custom, it was impossible to prevent them from straying onto unfenced land.

Some towns adopted a constructive approach to the problem. New Haven, for example, decided to confer with the local Indians about the possibility of fencing their fields and "to show them how, and to helpe them in their fencing, that so wee may not have such complaints from them of cattell & hoggs spoyling their corne, which they say makes their squaes & children cry."[18] Plymouth Colony had a law requiring all Indians who planted crops within the bounds of any township to fence their fields. Indians who planted on their own land outside of a township were either to be helped in their fencing by the English or else reimbursed for any damage done.[19] A New York law required that settlers in towns where English cattle might trespass on Indian planting grounds help the Indians protect their fields with proper fences.[20]

Despite all endeavors to lubricate the obvious points of friction between red man and white man on the frontier, the conditions under which the two races found themselves in close contact guaranteed the continuation of annoying incidents. Increasingly the Indians grew bolder as they lost their early awe of the English and their firearms. Irresponsible young braves, sometimes under the influence of the white man's liquor, committed malicious acts against neighboring settlers and their property. Under mounting provocations the temper of the colonists mounted too, until there was danger of an explosion. This was clearly evident in southern New England by about 1645. Connecticut authorized its magistrates to send parties of men into Indian villages where offenders were being sheltered and even to seize hostages in lieu of the actual culprits. Such hostages might then be turned over to the colonist whose property had been damaged, "either to serve or to bee shipped out and exchanged for neagers, as the case will justly beare."[21] This ugly twist well shows how sharp the irritation had become; as time went on and the provocations continued, it became sharper still.[22]

In cases of interracial crime the machinery of justice was entirely in the hands of the English. On the whole, the colonial authorities made a genuine attempt to see that justice was impartially administered. Indian offenders were tried and punished in accordance with the usual legal procedures, but it is not likely that the culprits or their fellow tribesmen really appreciated the fact or thanked the white men for it. What is more likely is that the Indians, whose concepts of property and social protection differed from those of the Europeans, as did their methods of dealing with offenders, misunderstood and resented the operation of English justice.

The records amply demonstrate that when the evidence warranted, the courts could and did rule in favor of Indians. For example, in a Massachusetts case certain Indians accused by a colonist of having stolen his money were acquitted by the court, with the accuser being ordered to pay the charges incurred by the defendants while in prison.[23] Still, the experience of a Massachusetts jail did nothing to sweeten the dispositions of the innocent victims of a white man's suspicion. More serious was the case in which four colonists robbed and murdered an Indian. The culprits were apprehended in Rhode Island, after which three of them were convicted in Plymouth Colony and executed for their crime. "Some have thought it great severity, to Hang three *English* for one *Indian*," commented Nathaniel Morton, "but the more Considerate will easily satisfie themselves for the Legality of it: and indeed, should we suffer their Murtherers to go unpunished, we might justly fear that God would suffer them to take a more sharp Revenge."[24]

There was always a strong temptation for the outraged frontiersman, contemptuous toward the Indian offender and impatient with the deliberate pace of judicial machinery, to take justice into his own hands. Connecticut early found it necessary to legislate against such private retribution.[25] But even in the courts, with their age-old procedures for protecting innocence and uncovering guilt, the accused Indian found himself at a great disadvantage. True, he had his opportunity to present evidence favorable to himself, but he was handicapped by language and personal appearance as well as the mere fact of belonging to a despised race. Moreover, Indian testimony, when directed against a white man, frequently was accorded little respect. The jury was comprised entirely of white men. This defect began to be partially remedied in the early 1670s by the introduction of mixed juries for cases in which both the criminal and his victim were Indians.[26]

For purposes of legal control the colonial authorities were eager to establish the status of neighboring Indians as subjects of the Crown and of the colony within which they resided. The assumption was easily made that because the Indians were residents of territory comprehended within a royal patent they were *ipso facto* subject to the jurisdiction there established and to the higher authority from which it sprang.[27] In many treaties the sachems were induced to acknowledge such a status, an acknowledgment that later could be employed against them whenever they resisted colonial authority. Thus an Indian uprising against the colonists was easily made to assume the character of a domestic insurrection, affording legal justification for treating the participants as traitors.

The flaws in this fabric of supposition were seen by only a few enlightened colonists, among them Roger Williams in the seventeenth century and the Massachusetts historian Thomas Hutchinson a century later. Williams put it bluntly in 1654 when he wrote, "I question whether any Indians in this country, remaining barbarous and pagan, may with truth or honor be called the English subjects."[28] Hutchinson developed the point further: "... if a view be taken of all the transactions between the English and them from the beginning, it will be difficult to say what sort of subjects they were, and it is not certain that they understood that they had promised any subjection at all.... When they call the King their Sovereign," continued Hutchinson, "perhaps they have no other idea than the Six Nations have when they call him Father." As for those Indians who had engaged in war against the English, "They are called Rebels and Murderers and treated as such. They knew not what was intended by Subjects...."[29] Hutchinson saw the problem clearly. It was another case of the Indians misunderstanding the real meaning of an English concept that was urged upon them by colonial authority. Here, as in the matter of transferring land, they failed to comprehend the actual force and effect of English terms quite foreign to their previous experience.

*F*ACED WITH unforeseen but irrepressible expansion, Massachusetts rather quickly evolved a policy designed to permit the inevitable while still maintaining control and cohesion in the holy experiment. This, in effect, bound the frontier process within certain definite rules and procedures to prevent the undesirable excesses of isolation, extreme individualism, and personal aggrandizement, which were already becoming recognized as characteristic of an uncontrolled frontier. If the authorities could prevent it, there would be in Massachusetts no lone pioneers beyond the reach of religious discipline, and no mighty landlords building personal power on their thousands of hoarded acres.

From the beginning, one important principle established in the Bay Colony was that land should be held by individuals in free tenure, as personal property, without the obligation of continuing payments to a landlord. Quitrents, so common elsewhere in the English colonies, were never an important feature of landholding in Massachusetts and were strongly opposed in other areas where Massachusetts traditions took root.[30] A second important ideal embedded in Massachusetts land policy was that landholding should be widespread among the population, that men should have land in amounts roughly proportional to their ability to make constructive use of it, and that engrossment of great tracts of land by ambitious individuals should be prevented. The Puritan leaders as well as the rank and file of the population recognized the inequities and disadvantages of conditions in England, where land was the basis of political power, with a few men having far too much for the general good and many men having far too little for their own well-being. Massachusetts was determined not to reproduce the conditions of the old country in a new country where land was plentiful.

This is not to say that grants of land to favored individuals were unknown in early Massachusetts, but compared with practices in areas outside southern New England such grants were relatively few. During the period from 1631 to 1656 they totaled a little more than a hundred, including a few as large as three thousand acres but for the most part much smaller in size. The largest number of individual grants were made in 1639; twenty-three, averaging 360 acres each, appear in the records for that year.[31] As one historian has explained, "The land policy of the New England colonies was democratic and far-sighted. Its guiding motive was not profit, but methodical occupation of . . . territory by actual settlers and the development of its great resources, not for the benefit of a few but in the interest of the whole community."[32] "Land," adds another scholar more succinctly, "was a socialized commodity."[33] The assumption was that only the General Court, consisting of the chosen representatives of the freemen, had the right to grant land, a right derived from the royal charter granted in 1629 to the Massachusetts Bay Company.[34]

In Puritan Massachusetts the frontier advanced not by bold forward thrusts of individual pioneers, but by controlled group enterprise in the planting of new towns. The process would begin when a few men of initiative in a town, feeling the pinch of land-hunger and lured by new land on the frontier, would band together to solve a mutual problem. They would persuade others in the town to join them, until the group would include perhaps a score of families. The leaders would make inquiries, and possibly do some actual exploring to discover a desirable tract of land with good soil, readily accessible by river or trail, and either already free of Indian claims or at least open to purchase at a reasonable price.

Then these men would approach the General Court with an outline of their project. If the group was composed of sound men of orthodox views and if the desired tract was available and not too remote from established towns, the General Court would be inclined to receive their petition with favor. First the Court would appoint a committee to investigate the situation. If the committee reported that the tract was free of prior claims, purchasable from the native proprietors, and generally suitable for a new town, the General Court would make a formal grant to the heads of families of the petitioning group, subject to proper extinguishment of the Indian title and accurate survey. The expense of these matters was borne by the petitioners; hence, their project already represented an investment on their part. The entire group of original grantees, heads of families, became known as the "proprietors" or "commoners" of the new town.

A grant from the General Court conveyed a tract of definite size and location, typically a block of land containing about thirty-six square miles. Certain conditions were attached which, if not satisfied, would cause the grant to be canceled. The group had to have a specified number of families, perhaps twenty, compactly settled on the land within a stated period of time, probably three years. This was to ensure that the land did not stand idle, depriving other men of its use. The inhabitants had to build a meetinghouse and call an orthodox minister to be their spiritual leader, paying him an appropriate salary. In at least one new plantation the General Court threatened to make the settlers return to civilization if they did not speedily acquire a clergyman.[35] But if there were heavy obligations, there were compensating encouragements. The infant community was granted exemption from colony taxes for a stated period of years.[36]

Having acquired their grant, the proprietors had to enter upon the land, select a site for their village, and stake it out. Accordingly, with the help of a surveyor, they would lay out a village street, reserving a central location for the meetinghouse. Along either side of the street they would mark off home lots which might be as small as a half acre, but were likely to be an acre or more in size, giving room for outbuildings and vegetable gardens as well as a dwelling. The home lots might be uniform in size and shape, or they might vary considerably. In any case, one of the choice ones, near the meetinghouse, would be reserved for the future minister. Later the home lots would be distributed among the settlers, one to each family, and each family would then construct its own house and outbuildings. In this way a nucleated village, compactly arranged for purposes of social control and defense, would quickly appear.

An example of legislative regulation is found in the *Records of the Governor and Company of the Massachusetts Bay in New England* where, with respect to the new plantation of Nashaway, the General Court authorized six men "to sett out lotts to all the planters, provided they sett not their howses to farr asunder; & the greater lotts to be proportionable to mens estates & chardges; & that no man shall have his lott confirmed to him before he hath taken the oath of fidellity before some magistrate."[37] This illustrates three important facts about the Massachusetts system of town planting. First, the government frowned upon scattered settlement with its attendant evils of isolation. Second, the quantities of land allotted to individuals in new towns were not necessarily equal; on the contrary, it was customary to grant lands roughly proportionate to the settler's contribution to the original cost of the plantation, the size of his family, and his wealth. Third, the Puritan leaders feared the frontier as a breeding ground of dissent. Consequently, they tried to prevent men whose political, social, or religious reliability was suspect from putting down roots in newly formed communities. It may be correct to say, as one historian has done, that "the Puritan colonies preserved orthodoxy by making the frontier a dumping ground on which the weeds of heresy were cast out and grew,"[38] but only if we understand that the procedure was an unintentional one. Certainly the Puritan leaders would have preferred to have Roger Williams and Anne Hutchinson back in England rather than in nearby Rhode Island.

The proprietors of a new town had to consider also the land available for agriculture. How should it be divided and arranged? Here much depended upon the nature of the terrain as well as the character and experience of the settlers. In England in the sixteenth and seventeenth centuries there was no single pattern of land use. Although in many parts of the country the prevalent form was an open-field type of agriculture with the husbandmen cultivating scattered strips in the various fields around a compact village, in other areas, most notably East Anglia, agricultural land was consolidated into unitary farms. Obviously, the two systems required quite different farming practices.

The settlers of Massachusetts were drawn from diverse areas of England, which meant that in newly formed frontier communities when the time came to decide how land should be allotted, there might well occur a sharp clash of traditions. Generally speaking, men preferred to carry on the kind of farming to which they were accustomed, but under the circumstances they sometimes found it imperative to compromise. Thus diverse traditions and practices were blended to produce new forms of land division and land use. In other words, frontier conditions, combined with the necessity for reconciling diverse habits brought from the Old World, gave birth to arrangements that were experimental, empirical, and novel.[39]

There might be considerable debate among the proprietors of a new town before an acceptable plan of land use would finally emerge. A typical arrangement would be to have two or more large planting fields and meadows laid out near the village. These would be divided into long narrow strips, which would be distributed among the proprietors—all who had a right to land in the new town. Typically, the distribution would be made by the drawing of lots, so that good land and bad land would fall to men by chance. Since any one settler would be entitled to several strips in each of the fields, the chances were that the good land and the bad land would be distributed fairly equitably. Each family would farm its own strips, growing crops in the planting fields and cutting hay in the meadows. But the planting fields were open except for a single fence around the circumference, and it was customary to allow cattle to graze within them after harvesttime, so there had to be community agreement on what crops were planted and when. Thus a large measure of group solidarity was essential, and the individual found himself necessarily subordinated to the group.

Even after a village had been built and the outlying fields divided, by far the greatest part of the overall grant would still be untouched. All the undivided land, mostly forest, would remain in the custody of the proprietors as common land (hence the term "commoners"), open to common use by all inhabitants of the town. Here they would gather firewood, berries, and nuts, or turn loose their pigs and cattle to roam for sustenance. Actually, the common land was a sort of reserve supply, held in the custody of the proprietors for future distribution among themselves, and for possible allotment to other persons who might later be admitted as residents of the town. Desirable newcomers might be granted land rights by the proprietors, but only the proprietors themselves had the right to distribute common land.[40] In time, as more and more non-commoners came to live in the town, their interests would diverge ever more sharply from the interests of the self-perpetuating group of proprietors, with consequent tension and strife, which in turn might drive the defeated and the dissatisfied to new frontiers.

The town meeting was instituted almost at the commencement of every town's existence. Here matters of common concern such as the laying out of roads, maintenance of fences, control of herds, and building of a meetinghouse might be discussed and decided. After 1647, and in some towns even before that date, all recognized adult male house-holders had the right to vote on town affairs. The New England town meeting was a practical solution to the problem of community living on the frontier of a new land and a most significant experiment in local self-government.

Isolated frontier communities sometimes found it necessary to act first and ask permission later, even in matters that normally fell within the jurisdiction of higher authority. The frontier village of Springfield on the Connecticut River early in 1639 found itself without a duly desig-nated magistrate to uphold the law. Accordingly,

> We the Inhabitantes . . . Beinge now by godes provedence fallen into the line of the Massachusete Jurisdiction: and it beinge farr of[f] to repayer thither in such cases of justice as may often fale out amonge us doe therefore thinke it meete by a generall consent and vote to ordaine (till we receive further directions from the generall court in the Massachuset Bay) mr William Pynchon to execute the office of a magistrate in this our plantation. . . .[41]

Such action speaks eloquently of the frontier spirit of self-reliance, combined with a responsible concern for law and order, that was already becoming manifest in expanding New England. Even more significant were the so-called plantation covenants, such as the Mayflower Compact and the Dover agreement of 1640, which may be described as primitive constitutions formulated as a basis for law and order by groups of pioneers who found themselves beyond the effective control and protection of duly constituted authority.[42] This, too, was evidence of a growing self-reliance, and the very experience of it helped to nourish the characteristic.

As more and more new inhabitants were admitted to a town, the number of home lots in the village would increase, and desirable meadow and cropland conveniently near the village would become more scarce. New fields would be opened up farther from the village, and in order to avoid long walks to and from work during the growing season, some men would build temporary or even permanent dwellings out near their farmland. These outlying farms were established in many towns at an early date, and represent an important breach in the Puritan ideal of social control by means of compact settlement. It was not uncommon for an outlying cluster of farmhouses, perhaps several miles from the mother village, to become a distinct village with its own problems and concerns. Such offshoots were under the jurisdiction of the township in which they were located, but the inconvenience of travel frequently caused them to seek separation from the parent town and official recognition as new towns in their own right, a request often granted with some reluctance by the General Court.[43]

If in the first days of a new settlement only the deliberate, measured chuck–chuck–chuck of the pioneer's ax told the listening Indians what was happening to their forest, it was not long before they might hear also the rumbling and splashing of rotating water wheels and the harsh rasp of water-driven saws. Every new village sought to have its own gristmill, sawmill, and smithy; consequently it was common practice for a newly established settlement to attract a miller and other specialized workers by offering land as an inducement. In this way the needed forms of colonial industry followed closely the advance of the Puritan frontier.[44]

At an early date the colonial authorities recognized the urgent need for a system of recording land transactions, but on the rapidly expanding frontier a system was more easily announced than enforced. Beginning in 1634 Massachusetts required that in every town the constable and a committee of the leading inhabitants view and record all landed property.[45] Three years later the Court was complaining of all-too-frequent neglect of the requirement, and as late as 1652 many men still transferred real estate without going through the formalities of registration.[46] Connecticut encountered a similar problem.[47] Such carelessness in procedure must be attributed primarily to the frontiersman's preoccupation with the immediate necessities of life, as well as his reluctance to pay a clerk's fee. Only when made to realize that his title to property might be jeopardized unless he complied, did the hard-pressed pioneering farmer succumb to the demands.

The Massachusetts system of controlled expansion had certain decided advantages. It provided order and stability in a process that in some other colonies, such as New York and Virginia, degenerated into frantic land-grabbing, with all the attendant evils of excessive accumulations, political graft, personal immorality, and interracial violence. In Massachusetts the towns themselves often placed severe restrictions on the right of their inhabitants to sell land, not only to prevent the introduction of undesirable newcomers, but also to make it difficult for wealthy individuals to buy up large amounts of land in the town. Under the Puritan system the advancing pioneer moved in accordance with a plan, quickly re-establishing and enjoying the order and security of a civilized community. Once organized and functioning, each new town could serve as a base from which the next advance might be made and supported. The typical Puritan pioneer was not a lone scout, but a member of a team.

*T*HE SYSTEMATIC, orderly advance of the frontier in early Massachusetts and Connecticut was not duplicated in the areas of settlement north of the Merrimack River or west of the Hudson, where interests other than that of Puritan state-building prevailed. The extensive territory comprising New Hampshire and Maine, which had been granted to John Mason and Sir Ferdinando Gorges by the Council for New England in 1622, saw a great variety of pioneering enterprises during the first three-quarters of the seventeenth century, under a multiplicity of conflicting claims and authorities. At first the great attractions that lured men to this coast were fishing and the fur trade. Soon, however, a third resource of the area began to be exploited—the magnificent forest. Seemingly endless miles of great sturdy trees provided the foundation for a lumbering industry that was to be the real driving force behind expansion in the area for years to come.[48] The abundance of good timber near tidal waters made possible the vigorous development of the New England ship-building industry, which drew upon what one contemporary enthusiast insisted was "the most incomparable timber for building shipps in the World."[49]

By 1640 there was a good scattering of small pioneering settlements along the coastal area from the Merrimack River north to the Kennebec and beyond.[50] These communities, all of them small and weak, had been established under a variety of circumstances. Many had begun as bases for fishing and the fur trade, gradually shifting their economic emphasis to lumbering and agriculture. Among the inhabitants were numerous servants and wage laborers employed in the hard toil of fishing or lumbering, young men highly susceptible to the temptations of an open frontier. Such a labor force proved difficult to control or even hold. "... Heare about these parts is neyther law nor goverment," complained one hard-pressed supervisor. "Yf any mans servant take a distast against his maister, away the[y] go to their pleasure."[51] The free air of the frontier, it would seem, was beginning to have its effect on restless men impatient with the restraints imposed by a system derived from an older age and an older continent.

By 1643 the Massachusetts Bay Colony had managed to extend its jurisdiction over the few small settlements in New Hampshire which previously had been governing themselves under their own plantation covenants. The continuing political turmoil and general disorder in the Maine settlements convinced the Massachusetts government that it must extend the blessings of Puritan discipline to that area as well. Although frontier particularism, local pride, and Church of England sentiment produced considerable opposition, by 1658 Maine was securely within the fold. Actually, many of the Maine settlers welcomed Massachusetts jurisdiction because it promised law and order, and the validation of land titles, in a frontier area that had seen far too much of lawlessness.

New England's mounting expansionism produced also an advance of the frontier southward as groups of Puritan pioneers took up land and founded new townships on Long Island and in East Jersey. By 1660 there were eleven Puritan settlements on Long Island, all formed on the New England model. Similar towns were founded in East Jersey during the 1660s by New Englanders, who held to their tradition of land tenure, making these new communities centers of opposition to the quitrent system of the proprietary regime.[52]

In New York, following the seizure of the colony from the Dutch in 1664, the new government lost little time in laying foundations for the continued advance of the English frontier. An agreement was made with the local Indians, including the Mohawk, which provided for the continuation of trade relations as they had been under the Dutch and for compensation when either race committed a wrong against the other.[53] The new governor, Richard Nicolls, also established definite procedures for the acquisition and settlement of new land. Purchasers first had to satisfy the appropriate sachem and have the purchase surveyed and recorded, paying a fee to the governor. Then they had to settle compactly by establishing a town. Each town was to have the right to choose its own officers and pass its own laws for the control of local affairs. As for the land itself, it was declared to be real property which the owner might sell or bequeath as he wished. In its main outlines this sounds much like the New England system. Quite foreign to the New England practice, however, was the requirement that in every town two lots be reserved for the governor's disposal.[54]

That New York failed to adhere strictly to the above regulations soon becomes apparent. The expansion of the New York frontier never became as closely controlled as that of Puritan New England. On the contrary, numerous grants to favored individuals continued to be made, while the feudal concept of manorial estates emerged from the ashes of the old Dutch patroonship system.[55]

*T*HE YEARS from 1630 to 1675, when the tidal wave of the English swept into America, were a period of impressive achievement on the expanding northern frontier. Amidst an almost infinite variety of circumstances and motives, substantial communities were established and the roots of European civilization were successfully transplanted to wilderness soil. The ugly aspects of the process—land-grabbing, interracial friction, ready violence—cannot obscure the significant fact that in less than five decades, with minimal assistance from the mother country, thousands of determined Englishmen made their way across the ocean, entered the wilderness, and created there a multitude of towns and farms. Even culture and education, especially in Puritan Massachusetts, were carefully transplanted and nurtured in the new environment, so that the blessings of many centuries of intellectual and moral development would not be lost in the struggle to overcome the wilderness. Here were laid important foundations, not only for the further advance of the frontier, but also for the building of a great nation.

◁ 4 ▷
War and Peace, 1675–1689

*F*rom the time of the Pequot War in 1637 and the Indian trouble under Kieft in New Netherland six years later, the fear of a general uprising of the tribes had hovered over the colonists of the northern frontier, casting its shadow upon the entire field of Indian relations. The colonists were never quite able to cast off suspicion about the intentions of their Indian neighbors, a feeling that was nourished throughout many years of uneasy peace by occasional offensive behavior, even sporadic violence, on the part of some Indians. In the earliest days of settlement the Europeans had been inclined to place much faith in the superiority of their weapons, tactics, and battle discipline, giving rise to a dangerous mood of overconfidence. But with further experience the colonists came to understand their weaknesses as well as their strengths, and to see that a sudden coordinated uprising of all the tribes could wipe the land clear of the white men.

In 1643 the four Puritan colonies of Massachusetts, Plymouth, Connecticut, and New Haven had banded together in a rather loose but moderately effective organization known as the New England Con-

53

federation, whose main purpose was to defend Puritan territory against the French to the north, the Dutch to the west, and the Indians in the midst. During the next thirty years the Confederation tried earnestly to cope with the complicated problem of Indian relations in a positive, systematic way. It was especially effective in bringing to bear upon any groups of troublesome Indians the combined frowns and, if necessary, knuckle-rappings of the Puritan colonies.

Fearing the possibility of a united Indian opposition, the New England colonies developed a strategy whose main objective was to keep the Indians divided. When it seemed advantageous, the colonial authorities did not hesitate to exploit intertribal animosities, lending their moral and sometimes their material support to those tribes whose interests and policies appeared to be most beneficial or least dangerous to the colonies. Sometimes, too, geography was a determining factor, the English according favors to a particular group of Indians because they were in a position to grant access to desirable land. Of course the consequence of such favoritism was corresponding resentment on the part of rival Indians, making them likely enemies of the English in any future war.

The colonies, being in a wilderness country an ocean removed from England, had to rely almost entirely on their own resources for defense against their enemies, both internal and external. That is why in most colonies, shortly after their founding, the authorities began to create a militia, gradually developing a system of training, organization, and leadership that was derived directly from experience in the mother country but modified and shaped to meet the special conditions and needs of a frontier society.[1]

The basic unit of the militia was the individual male citizen, who was subject to regular military training from the time he reached the age of sixteen until he withdrew to honorable retirement at the age of sixty. He was required to keep himself equipped with a musket and a specified quantity of powder and shot, ready for any emergency. Militiamen were organized into town companies known as trainbands, under local officers customarily elected by vote of their own men. This fostered a democratic spirit in military service but complicated the problem of maintaining good discipline. The practice of electing military leaders seems to be one significant modification of Old World practices brought about by the newness and isolation of frontier communities. Obviously the militia was a nonprofessional fighting force, equipped with such weapons as were available, and only partially trained for actual war.

In Plymouth the diminutive but courageous Captain Miles Standish was the original organizer of what little strength the settlers could muster for their own defense. Fortunately the colony enjoyed relative immunity from Indian trouble so long as Massasoit, the friend of the Pilgrims, ruled over the Wampanoag tribe. When Massasoit died about 1661, he was succeeded first by his son Alexander and after Alexander's untimely death by a second son known as King Philip. This proud, brooding sachem had long resented the constantly growing power of the English, with the consequent weakening of tribal autonomy and native culture. As tangible evidence he could point to the relentless expansionism of the English, who continued to acquire more and more land, until it seemed that soon none would be left for the red men. Likewise the powerful Narragansett tribe of Rhode Island, plagued by the same problem in its territory and vastly irritated by the obvious favoritism shown by the English toward the rival Mohegan tribe of eastern Connecticut, smouldered with resentment.[2] Gradually the Wampanoag and the Narragansett, former enemies though they were, discovered that they had a common interest in resisting the English encroachments and a common desire to make the white settlers pay dearly for their overbearing behavior. Other tribes also shared the sentiment. It is difficult now to see how under the circumstances a serious clash between the races could have been avoided indefinitely. All the tribes in direct contact with the colonists were in a worsening situation that could not be forever endured without striking back.

We have already mentioned such factors as English favoritism toward certain tribes and English insistence that the Indians obey colonial laws. Economically, too, the natives were sliding down the slippery path of subservience, unable to check their descent. Their ever-increasing dependence upon the hardware, textiles, and other manufactured products made available to them by the white traders, together with their growing addiction to strong drink, weakened the structure of Indian society. At the same time, sachems and powwows resented Puritan attempts to civilize and Christianize the Indians, viewing them as a threat to their own influence and power.

Indeed, the very way of life known and enjoyed by untold generations of Indians was threatened with obliteration as the complex, dynamic culture of western Europe imposed itself upon the simple, static culture of aboriginal New England. Retreat for the Indians was virtually out of the question as it would have brought with it subservience to the dreaded Iroquois Confederacy to the west. For proud and resentful Indians such as King Philip, then, the only answer was to hit back at the white men, in the desperate hope that destruction and terror would drive them back to the sea whence they had first appeared.

*K*ING PHILIP'S WAR broke out in June 1675, when Wampanoag warriors began looting houses in the frontier town of Swansea, some thirty miles west of Plymouth. Looting was followed by killing; both Plymouth and Massachusetts hurried militiamen to the scene; and the most bloody Indian war of the seventeenth century was underway. Fortunately for the colonies, most of the other tribes in southern New England either held back from joining the uprising until it became more apparent which side would win, or aligned themselves with the English. Both the Mohegan and the tattered Pequot remained faithful to the Connecticut Colony, while the watchful Narragansett teetered on the edge of uneasy neutrality. Clearly the Indians had not been able to achieve the unity so dreaded by the colonists.

In the first weeks of the uprising the colonial troops quickly drove the Wampanoag from their principal resort on the Mount Hope peninsula and nearly succeeded in trapping Philip and his warriors in a large, dismal swamp. If they had been able to collar him then and there, it is likely that Indian resistance would have collapsed as quickly as it arose. But Philip proved too slippery for the rather clumsy colonial forces, and made good his escape to the territory of the Nipmuck Indians in central Massachusetts. Catching the spirit of his defiance, tribe after tribe began to join the war of extermination against the white men, and soon the flames of deadly conflict were licking along the frontier from the Merrimack to the Connecticut Valley.

Most feared were the Narragansett, with their hundreds of fierce warriors.[3] It soon became apparent that their deepest sympathies were with the Wampanoag, and their eager young men were not always to be restrained. When the Narragansett failed to live up to the letter of their treaty agreements with the colonies, the Puritan leaders, drawing upon the theory of preventive war and not entirely unmindful of the potential market value of Narragansett land, in December 1675 sent a powerful expedition against the principal Narragansett stronghold. That of course brought the tribe into full and open belligerency, and from then on the conflict raged without restraint over much of southern New England. Soon, too, the war spread northward into New Hampshire and Maine, as still other tribes joined in against the white settlers. New England found itself literally fighting for its life.

The progress of the Indian war effort was signaled by columns of gray smoke rising above fields and forest as town after town fell victim to the sudden slashing raids at which the warriors proved so adept. Under this fierce and merciless assault, the entire frontier of New England reeled. Brookfield in central Massachusetts was burned by

Indians during a prolonged attack early in August 1675 and later had to be abandoned. Something of the ferocity of the assault is suggested by the testimony of a survivor:

> . . . they did roar against us like so many wild bulls, sending in their shot amongst us till towards the moon rising, which was about three of the clock; at which time they attempted to fire our house by hay and other combustible matter which they brought to one corner of the house, and set it on fire. . . . they continued shooting and shouting . . . scoffing at our prayers as they were sending in their shot upon all quarters. . . . there being in the house fifty women and children besides the men. . . .[4]

Squakeag (Northfield), at that time the northernmost settlement on the Connecticut River, was evacuated on September 6 and Deerfield less than a fortnight later. At about the same time an assault against Saco, on the coast of Maine, demonstrated the geographical spread of Indian hostility.

Each success elated the Indians, prompting them to new endeavors. Their strategic planning was elemental, such as might have been devised around a campfire by an assemblage of war chiefs, each the leader of a restless band. For long, dark weeks a primitive kind of warfare, consisting mainly of hit-and-run raids, hurled its defiant challenge at the colonial governments, with all their tradition and apparatus of European-style warfare. The warriors' skill in moving quietly and swiftly through the forest often enabled them to strike without warning, so that the English were hard put to provide any effective defense for their scattered frontier settlements. Moreover, when the militia, stung into action by a successful Indian raid, sortied from their villages to pursue the raiders, they exposed themselves to the danger of ambush, a tactic of which the Indians were masters. Many a soldier lost his life in such a trap before the English partially solved the problem by using friendly Indians as scouts to detect the hidden enemy.[5]

Increasingly, too, the colonial military leaders modified the formations and tactics brought over from the Old World, to meet the special conditions of forest warfare in the New. Thus the long, cumbersome pike, for centuries an important infantry weapon on the open battlefields of Europe, was abandoned in New England during the early stages of King Philip's War. Formations and evolutions of massed troops burdened with cumbersome equipment all too often provided the Indians with targets they could scarcely miss, or gave them opportunity to make good their retreat. During King Philip's War the colonial troops perforce learned something of the art of stalking and fighting Indian-style, but in the long run their most successful tactics developed from a blending of European order and discipline with Indian improvisation and individuality, and knowing when to emphasize each. Experience proved the best teacher. "A few months actual service against the Indian enemy in Philip's war," remarked one well-informed New England colonist, "made better soldiers, than all their exercise at home had done in forty years."[6]

Each frontier village designated one or more of its strongly built and conveniently located dwellings as garrison houses. In case of attack the villagers were to abandon their own homes and hasten to the designated garrison house where they would all join together in a common defense. This plan had the great disadvantage of leaving most of a town's dwellings and other property, including livestock, virtually undefended, with the result that the Indians had enormous opportunity to burn and pillage with relative impunity. During some periods of the war, when danger seemed constantly imminent, frontier families remained crammed into garrison houses for days at a time, not daring to venture more than a few rods from the protecting walls. In such cases little work could be done, crops were neglected, and shortage of food became a serious problem. Naturally the Indians sought to take every possible advantage of such difficulties, so the settlers scarcely knew how to protect themselves and their livelihood against their stealthy foe.

On February 10, 1676, painted warriors burned much of Lancaster and drove many of the frightened survivors into wilderness captivity.[7] Eleven days later half of the town of Medfield went up in flames during a fierce attack. Groton was burned on March 13 and abandoned soon after. At about the same time the government of Rhode Island recommended the evacuation of Providence and Warwick, and Connecticut ordered the abandonment of Simsbury. Massachusetts urged the people still clinging to their holdings along the upper Connecticut River to congregate in Hadley and partially burned Springfield. Marlboro suffered heavy losses on March 26, as did Rehoboth on the 28th and Providence on the 29th. Later that spring the rampaging Indians raided Andover, Woburn, Sudbury, Bridgewater, Hatfield, and Hadley.

Fearing the collapse of the frontier and the loss of heavy investments in land, the colonial authorities forbade unauthorized abandonment of frontier holdings, but in the face of the Indian fury many families turned their backs on home and fields to seek security elsewhere. The eastern towns found themselves increasingly burdened by the influx of refugees from war-stricken areas.[8]

During these difficult times, however, New England had been gathering its resources while absorbing the hard lessons of forest warfare. Military expeditions sent against the enemy began to score heavily. As colonial strength waxed, that of the Indians waned, and by the early summer of 1676 the doom of the Indian cause was becoming more certain. With large numbers of their best warriors killed and their food supplies severely diminished, the dejected, often terrified tribesmen began to sue for mercy in ever increasing numbers. "The Indeans are now in strayts for foode & dy much," reported one colonist. "Allsoe many come in to all places offering themselves to live or dy as the English will, they commonly kill theyr Chilldren, partly for crying wherby the English are derected to them, & partly for want of food for them. . . ."[9]

Philip himself, after watching his people die by the dozens under English musket fire or perish more slowly from hunger and disease, slipped back to his old headquarters in the western corner of Plymouth Colony, where the war had begun. There, on August 12, 1676, he was trapped and killed. Philip's demise marked the virtual end of Indian resistance in southern New England, but warfare blazed sporadically along the coastal frontier of Maine until 1677.

*K*ING PHILIP'S WAR was a decisive climax to forty years of Indian degradation. With Indian resistance broken, the English were to prove how ruthless they could be in victory. Considering the war as a civil insurrection fomented by subjects of the Crown (or at least of the various English colonies), the colonial authorities executed many of the male Indians known to have been active participants. Other captives, including some women, were sold as slaves in markets as far from their native forest as the West Indies, Spain, and the Mediterranean coasts. Still others were accepted as indentured servants by local residents, although the Indian's reputation for docility was not good.

Tribes that had been hostile to the English during the war emerged from the conflict as broken remnants, wholly at the mercy of the colonists. Even the tribes that had supported the English soon found themselves sharing the general degradation of their race, as they became increasingly dependent upon and subordinate to the colonists they had served. The Puritan colonies sought to guarantee their own future security by forcing the Indians to accept close and constant supervision, preferably on reservations. There had been some small beginnings of a reservation system in New England before King Philip's War, but the practice of moving the Indians onto special tracts really became general in the period after 1676.

If the Indians suffered mightily as a consequence of King Philip's War, so did the English, who were miserable even in their victory. The number of casualties in relation to the total population was high, in fact, among the highest of any war in American history. Probably close to a thousand colonists lost their lives as a direct result of enemy action. Many others—men, women, and children—died from causes related to the war. Hardest hit, of course, were the exposed frontier villages, a dozen of which now lay burned and abandoned. The advance edge of settlement had been driven back many miles, leaving hundreds of families uprooted and in many cases destitute. Homes and other buildings, as well as capital invested in tools, fences, cattle, and crops, were obliterated. Only the terrain itself remained, and for many a despairing pioneer family that was now scarcely worth claiming. So large were the numbers of refugees and so great the suffering that in faraway Ireland a collection was taken up in the churches of Dublin and the proceeds sent as charity to New England.[10]

Public confidence in the safety and future economic value of frontier land would have to be restored before the westward movement could be renewed. One serious threat to stability along the New England frontier was the continuing feud between the Algonquian tribes and the Mohawk. For several years the repeated incursions of Mohawk raiding parties terrorized the Algonquian tribes and alarmed the English settlers. Closely related to one such raid, but actually the work of hostile New England Indians, was the sudden, unprovoked attack on Hatfield in September 1677. After shooting down several of the inhabitants, the attackers took about twenty of the English as prisoners and drove them into captivity. Fortunately, most of these prisoners were later redeemed.[11] So far as southern New England is concerned, this raid may be considered a final afterclap of King Philip's War.

When it was seen that the attack on Hatfield was an isolated episode rather than a renewal of general warfare, the English again resumed the slow process of reclaiming lost lands and rebuilding the ruined villages along the ravaged frontier. Quite understandably, many families were hesitant to expose themselves again to the hazards of frontier living, but gradually the lure of land overcame all fears as the scattered populace regrouped and laid plans for reoccupation. The prevailing spirit is well illustrated by the order written into his will by a former resident of Warwick, "that upon the ground where I had a Corne & fulling mill standing... (before the Crewell indeans did destroy the said mill, together with my house,) ther be with all Expedition that may be, Another mill builded...."[12] Actually, however, it was many years before all of the territory lost in King Philip's War was resettled.

The usual practice was to rebuild a destroyed village on its previous site, often making use of old cellar holes and foundations. Both Connecticut and Massachusetts, in the interests of defense, sought to encourage compact rather than scattered settlement.[13] In spite of such official pressure, men gradually overcame their fears and built where good land happened to be available. As planting lands near the village centers became entirely appropriated, newcomers sought space at more remote locations. By 1688 Springfield, to cite only one case, included many outlying farms, with more than half of the town's population living some three miles or more from the village itself.[14]

Many of the colonists who had fought in King Philip's War had assumed that they were fighting not only to defend their homes but also to conquer desirable land then occupied by Indians. The breaking of Indian resistance after 1675 seemed to them ample justification for claiming frontier land as a reward for their services. Accordingly, in the years after the war the veterans formed organizations for the express purpose of persuading colony legislatures to grant special compensation in the form of frontier tracts. In this way there developed the first significant veteran problem in American politics. Despite this pressure, however, the legislatures were slow to act, so that in many cases it was not the veterans themselves but their heirs who finally received title. In many cases, too, the grantees quickly sold their rights to speculators. Actual settlement did get underway at last, and a number of new towns on the frontiers of Connecticut, Massachusetts, New Hampshire, and Maine had their beginnings as an outgrowth of King Philip's War.[15]

Especially important were the subtle but significant changes in New England's outlook and attitude wrought by the war. In fact, this desperate, destructive conflict must be considered a major turning point in the history of Puritan New England. Military expeditions and the abandonment of villages had taken many people far from their own localities, giving them an opportunity to see other places and mingle with other folk, not excepting "unorthodox" Maine and "heretical" Rhode Island. The result was a significant broadening of vision, even as the Puritan clergy labored mightily but in vain to shore up the communal integrity and discipline that had been the ideal in the quieter days before 1675. The shock of war had shattered many cherished illusions about the wilderness Zion. New Englanders now began to see the New World in all its stark reality, an arena where Indians and Englishmen—and Frenchmen too—were scheming and struggling for dominance. Even as the frontier slowly resumed its westward advance in the wake of Indian defeat, Puritan society was freeing itself from the narrow parochialism of the founding generation and preparing for a larger role in that arena.

*F*ROM THE Catskill Mountains the Delaware River moves generally southward toward the sea in a series of great zigzags. In colonial times, where it crosses the fall line at the site of Trenton, there was a two-mile stretch of rocky shallows which effectively barred the upper river to navigation, but below that stretch the river became a smooth highway, offering easy transportation to all who would come and go.[16]

To the east lay New Jersey, where numerous creeks afforded access to the interior. After the English conquest of New Netherland in 1664, a group of English Quakers, among them William Penn, acquired proprietary interests in New Jersey with a view to promoting settlement there. The Quakers, as a persecuted sect in Restoration England, needed a colony of their own to which they might emigrate; their situation was in some respects similar to that of the Puritans in the 1620s. To the Quaker proprietors, New Jersey seemed an excellent prospect, both as a place of refuge for their coreligionists and as an investment in real estate. Accordingly, they advertised their colony and welcomed immigrants.

From 1675, when the first group of settlers established themselves at Salem, New Jersey, until 1681, approximately 1400 new colonists, most of them Quakers, arrived in West Jersey.[17] Here they faced no grim prospect of Indian war. Not only were the Indians willing to accept them as neighbors, but the authorities adopted an Indian policy based on the concept that both races had rights deserving protection. Symptomatic of this was the rule that in legal cases involving Indians, the jury was to consist of six white men and six natives.[18] To some extent New Jersey served as a testing ground for enlightened policies which later, sometimes in modified form, were put into effect by William Penn in his own colony of Pennsylvania.

Little by little the Quaker pioneers fanned out to take up desirable farming land along the bulge of West Jersey, from just below the falls of the Delaware to Salem, about sixty miles to the south, enveloping the longer-established Scandinavian settlements in the process. As was so often the case during the expansion of the frontier, it was the quality of the soil that determined the direction and extent of the advance. These Quakers were farmers, for the most part, and had a farmer's eye for fertile soil. Avoiding the marshlands that lay along the edge of the Delaware River, they moved inland up the creeks until, within a mile or two, they began to find good ground. Later arrivals pushed the frontier of settlement toward the interior perhaps ten or fifteen miles more; after that they halted in the face of a discouraging belt of pine barrens. As more and more little clusters of population developed, the settlers laid out connecting roads, so that by the end of the century a rough highway extended from Salem to the falls of the Delaware, with the various settlements strung along it like beads. The area offered good opportunity; land could be bought from the proprietors for as little as £5 per hundred acres. Quickly the region became dotted with medium-sized farms, their prosperity evident from fine apple, peach, and cherry orchards and fields of corn, oats, rye, and wheat.[19]

Government was by elected assembly, in accordance with the remarkably liberal "Concessions and Agreements" issued by the Quaker proprietors early in 1677.[20] William Penn and his colleagues understood full well that without firm guarantees of individual liberty few European Quakers would emigrate to the New Jersey frontier and the land would remain in a wilderness condition, uncultivated and unprofitable. Thus the frontier yielded at the outset certain legal advantages for those willing to make the necessary personal sacrifices to venture there. In New Jersey these liberal concessions emerged quite readily, for they had been nourished in the social idealism of the Quaker leadership.

On a rapidly opening frontier one of the greatest problems is land distribution. Without proper restrictions land invariably will be engrossed in haphazard fashion, with overlapping boundaries, conflicting claims, irregular holdings, and monstrous accumulations in the hands of a few lucky or unscrupulous individuals. The proprietors of West Jersey early foresaw the problem and made plans to control it. The Concessions and Agreements included certain regulations governing the acquisition of land, including requirements that tracts be surveyed and formally registered. Later, in 1681, the assembly appointed a board known as the Commissioners for Settling and Regulation of Lands. This board promulgated a land code designed to ensure that the acquisition of land in the colony would be by methods both orderly and equitable, and in the best interests of all. One objective was to make it difficult for ambitious individuals to build up large compact estates that might be used for economic exploitation at the expense of small landholders or as a basis for the growth of a landed aristocracy.[21]

In spite of such favorable conditions, the growth of West Jersey during the first twenty-five years of settlement was not remarkably rapid. Quaker immigrants continued to arrive on the Delaware during these years, but after 1682 most of them turned westward into Pennsylvania rather than eastward into New Jersey.

As one of the leaders of the West Jersey enterprise, William Penn had learned much about the difficulties and advantages of founding a colony in the Delaware Valley and he began to develop plans for a colony of his own. He knew that west of the Delaware lay a vast territory, thought to be rich in natural resources, and still unoccupied. Through his excellent connections at Court, he received in 1681 a royal grant of this territory naming him as sole proprietor, with extensive powers both political and economic. No private person in all the history of colonial America was ever given a greater opportunity.

In contemplating the future of his magnificent private estate, named Pennsylvania, William Penn had two principal ideas in mind. For one thing, he looked upon Pennsylvania as an investment in real estate on a huge scale, a view quite in accord with the thinking of many ambitious Englishmen of the seventeenth century. He intended to derive a large and increasing revenue from land sales and quitrents. No less important, however, was his second idea, which was to create in Pennsylvania a commonwealth and a society grounded in Christian ethics, with brotherly love the keystone of human relations. In short, Penn wanted to put the Quaker way of life to a full and practical test in a new land where there were no ugly precedents to be swept away.[22]

Penn's liberalism and benevolence stood him in good stead when he began to seek settlers for his new colony. He promised personal freedom, good government, and reasonable prices for land. In addition, the Indians of the area were known to be receptive to Europeans and anxious to trade with them. Many a hard-pressed farmer, artisan, or shopkeeper in England and elsewhere in western Europe came to look upon Pennsylvania as the land of a golden future. With forthright honesty, Penn sought to allay excessive optimism. In a description of Pennsylvania published in London in 1681, he cautioned prospective emigrants that "they must look for a Winter before a Summer comes; and they must be willing to be two or three years without some of the conveniences they enjoy at home."[23] Pioneers on nearly every frontier America has ever known could say "Amen" to those words. Probably Penn already sensed the fact that colonists without false illusions would make the best pioneers.

A small advance group sent out by Penn reached the Delaware late in 1681. They disembarked at the angle formed by the Schuylkill and the Delaware, and housed themselves temporarily in caves dug into the riverbank. Few of the thousands who were to follow had to resort to such mean accommodations. Settlers in considerable numbers began arriving in 1682, bringing with them the usual clutter of tools, household effects, and other gear necessary to make a successful start in a new land. By now there had accumulated a half-century or more of good precedent upon which to build; wise pioneers drew upon the experience of predecessors who had tried it earlier—whether at Jamestown, Plymouth, New York, Boston, or New Jersey. The new arrivals in Pennsylvania found not a virgin land but a friendly, inviting area already partially occupied by hardy Scandinavian farmers. Overspreading much of the gentle landscape was the great American forest, not at all jungle-like, but consisting rather of well-spaced hardwoods. "The *Trees* grow but thin in most places, and very little under-Wood," remarked one observer.[24] This meant that the land was relatively easy to traverse and to clear for farming.

*L*IKE MOST STAGES of the westward movement, the coming of English pioneers to Pennsylvania was quickly followed by displacement of the Indians. It was the old story of Virginia, New Netherland, and New England, but with a difference. That difference is extremely important and merits the close attention of all students of the frontier. Penn knew what had happened elsewhere in America when white men settled where Indians had once held sway. The white men—at Jamestown, New Amsterdam, Boston—were Christians, but sooner or later they had got themselves into situations that made them fight like devils. Part of the trouble was that their religious understanding was not focused in such a way as to enable them to deal in a Christian manner with the natives. Many frontiersmen, repelled by the strange tastes and customs of the Indians, considered them scarcely human. William Penn viewed the matter in a different light. Long before he came to America he had assumed quite naturally that the natives of the New World were of the human species. As human beings they were children of God and brothers in Christ, even though presently in a state of heathenism. On this assumption Penn intended to act.

Furthermore, the special emphasis of Quakerism offered positive guidance in matters of human relations. The human heart understands benevolence and responds to love. This is true not only of civilized man but of the backward heathen as well. So the Christian of Quaker understanding would deal with the Indian both honestly and humbly, demonstrating genuine respect for the Indian as a person and love for him as a brother. He would not try to overawe the Indian by a display of might, for he deplored resort to violence as a means of settling issues among men. This was the essence of Penn's idealism in all matters of human relations; it was the foundation of his policy in dealing with the Indians.

The Puritans of New England, preoccupied as they were with formal theology and outward conformity, had not seen the matter in quite the same light. They believed themselves obligated to deal with the Indian honestly, but their thinking along this line was legalistic rather than humanistic. Certainly they did not approach the pagan savage in humility, but rather, proudly, in order to impress and overawe him. Deep down in their hearts they nourished contempt for the Indian because he was not civilized and fear of the Indian because he was potentially dangerous to their security. Penn believed that half-Christianity or warped Christianity was not capable of producing harmony between the races, but that pure Christianity, the Christianity of the Inner Light, would enable the white men and the red men to live side by side in peace. It is interesting to see how well this attitude of benevolence actually worked on the Pennsylvania frontier; we have little opportunity to study it on other frontiers, for it was seldom tested during the westward movement.

Legally, the royal charter gave Penn the right to dispose of Pennsylvania land as he wished. The Indians, being heathens, had no equal claim despite their prior occupancy. But Penn was not satisfied merely to stand upon his legal rights. The Puritans of New England had made the same decision, but primarily for reasons of equity and expediency. Penn did so as a matter of Christian principle. He insisted that land be acquired from its native proprietors only with their free consent and upon terms satisfactory to them. These two elements—consent and satisfaction—became in Pennsylvania the fundamental requirements in all official negotiations with the Indians for transfer of land.

The problem was complicated by the fact that Indian land usually belonged not to individuals but to groups, whose composition was not always thoroughly understood. This is one reason why the colonists often found themselves in the exasperating position of being dunned several times over by a sequence of Indian claimants after they had already bought a piece of land from its presumed owner. Penn, like many other purchasers, decided that the best thing to do was to pay for land as many times as necessary in order to obtain unchallenged title. This did not mean, of course, that he would toss money to any stray Indian who sought to extract it on the basis of a land claim, but it did mean that Penn or his agents were quite prepared to satisfy any *bona fide* groups of Indians who had a reasonable claim. Thus deed piled upon deed, often covering the same portions of land, with relatively little concern for precise delineation of boundaries.[25]

The first Indian deed transferring land to William Penn is dated July 15, 1682, three months before the proprietor actually arrived in Pennsylvania.[26] His agents had preceded him but, more important, he himself had taken the trouble to introduce himself by letter to the local Indians, advising them of his plans and soliciting their cooperation. No other colony inaugurated its Indian policy in such an open and honest fashion. In a letter dated October 18, 1681, Penn addressed the Indians as "My Friends," spoke of God's will that men should treat each other with kindness, and proceeded to explain his own intentions. The king of England, he said, has given Pennsylvania to me,

> but I desire to enjoy it with your love and consent, that we may always live together as neighbors and friends, . . . I am very sensible of the unkindness and injustice that hath been too much exercised toward you by the people of these parts of the world . . . which I hear hath been matter of trouble to you, and caused great grudgings and animosities, sometimes to the shedding of blood, . . . I have great love and regard towards you, and I desire to win and gain your love and friendship, by a kind, just, and peaceable life; and the people I send are of the same mind, and shall in all things behave themselves accordingly.

He then mentioned his commissioners who were being sent ahead to treat with the Indians about land and a covenant of peace. "Let me desire you to be kind to them and the people," Penn concluded, "and receive these presents and tokens which I have sent to you, as a testimony of my good will to you, and my resolution to live justly, peaceably, and friendly with you."[27] The letter was well designed to accomplish its purpose. It reveals not only a profound faith in the power of love, but also considerable knowledge of the techniques of Indian diplomacy.

Penn's benevolent approach won the confidence of the Delawares, ensuring that Pennsylvania would be able to continue its growth for many years without fear of Indian war. In its relations with the Indians Pennsylvania probably was the happiest of all the colonies. Penn and his agents bought tract after tract from the native proprietors in a way that left the Indians convinced that they were being treated fairly, although in the long run, as we now understand, their whole future was being bargained away.[28] At the time neither Penn nor the sachems foresaw the consequence. It would be easy, of course, to charge Penn with hypocrisy, but the Indians would eventually have detected any insincerity in matters so closely affecting their own well-being. Instead, they continued to hold William Penn in highest regard so long as he lived, and even long after his death they remembered him as a genuine friend entirely worthy of their trust. If later developments poisoned the good relations between the races in Pennsylvania, it was not the fault of William Penn.

*F*ROM THE BEGINNING Penn gave serious consideration to the problem of land distribution, a matter vital to the colony's growth and his own income. In order to encourage a rapid influx of settlers, he offered land unencumbered by Indian claims at easy terms—£2 per hundred acres, with a small annual quitrent. Penn firmly believed in the advantages of orderly settlement—he did not want his colony to consist of a ragged frontier of scattered individual holdings. Therefore his method, in theory at least, was to lay out townships consisting of 5000 acres, with the expectation that at least ten families would form a village near the center of each. Purchases of land had to be duly recorded within two months.[29] Penn also made an effort to prevent large individual holdings of vacant, unused land, and even attempted to promote conservation of forest resources by requiring that for every five acres of land cleared one acre of trees be left undisturbed.[30] Such regulations were not easy to enforce, and Penn's plans do not convey an accurate picture of how the colony actually developed. As in New Jersey, liberal guarantees of political rights proved attractive to prospective colonists, inducing many to undergo the sacrifices of a pioneering life in return for freedom from oppression and good opportunities for material success.

Penn welcomed to his colony people of diverse origins, with the result that the Pennsylvania frontier began at an early date to function as the proverbial melting pot, making Americans out of a great variety of Europeans. The process had begun earlier, with the Swedes, the Finns, and the Dutch, but it was greatly accelerated after the arrival of Penn. He deliberately advertised his colony not only in England, but in various parts of the Continent, especially Germany. A modern advertising executive in his office on Madison Avenue might envy the response to Penn's promotion campaign.

Welsh Quakers were among the first to reach Pennsylvania under Penn's direction. Wishing to preserve their identity as a distinct people, they did not settle among the English at Philadelphia but moved up the Schuylkill River to a large tract reserved for them. There, in the vicinity of modern Merion, Haverford, and Radnor, they planted their settlements and began to farm.[31] In time they spread out from that locality, while others of their nation, coming later, joined in the process.

Members of a German and Swiss religious sect, the Mennonites, formed another early and important element on the Pennsylvania frontier. Their leader, the cultured and well-educated Francis Daniel Pastorius, came to the colony in August 1683, and received a warm welcome from William Penn. As pacifistic and pietistic idealists, the two men had much in common. Soon Pastorius was joined by his followers, many of whom were skilled weavers from Crefeld in the Rhineland. They obtained a tract of land about six miles north of Philadelphia, where they founded a village known as Germantown. At first they experienced some of the deprivations and hardships of frontier living,

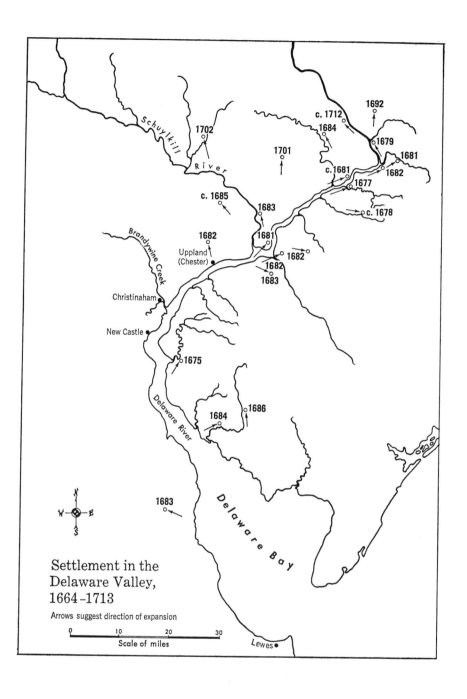

Schuylkill

1702

1701

c. 1712
1684

1692

1679

1681

c. 1681

1682

River

1677

c. 1685

1683

c. 1678

Brandywine Creek

1682

1681

Uppland
(Chester) •

1682

1682
1683

Christinaham •

New Castle •

1675

Delaware River

1684

1686

N
W ✦ E
S

1683

Delaware Bay

Settlement in the
Delaware Valley,
1664–1713

Arrows suggest direction of expansion

0	10	20	30

Scale of miles

Lewes •

but not with any extreme peril or suffering. Pastorius himself lived in a temporary dwelling thirty feet by fifteen feet in size, with windows of oil-soaked paper.[32] Before long the skill and industry of the Crefelders transformed a rough, pioneering settlement into a busy and prosperous little town, where the art of weaving fine linens was supplemented with agriculture, especially the growing of flax. Germantown was different from most frontier communities in that farming was secondary to handicrafts.

The rapidity with which land in Pennsylvania was parceled out is demonstrated by "A Map Of The Improved Part Of The Province Of Pennsilvania In America," drawn by Surveyor General Thomas Holme and published in London in 1687.[33] Only five years after the beginning of Quaker settlement much of the land from Brandywine Creek on the west to the great bend of the Delaware on the east and almost twenty miles upriver beyond that point had been assigned to groups and individuals. This does not mean that all the tracts were actually occupied, but it does suggest the scope and momentum of the proprietor's planning and his readiness to make land available. The welcome mat was prominently placed at Pennsylvania's doorway, and it is this more than anything else that made the Pennsylvania frontier the fastest growing of the eighteenth century.

Incorporated with Holme's map was "A General Description of the Province of Pennsylvania in America," consisting of passages culled from the promotional writings of William Penn. They depict a country both beautiful and inviting. "There is so great an encrease of Grain, by the diligent application of People to Husbandry, that within three Years some Plantations have got 20 Acres in Corn, some 40, some 50," asserted the proprietor.[34] "There are also *Peaches,* in great quantities, not an *Indian Plantation* without them. . . . they may be purchased by Bushels, very cheap." Included also was a brief description of the Indians and their way of life, with particular mention of their hospitable attitude toward the Europeans. Holme's map and the accompanying text were of a nature to make a favorable impression upon a European farmer or artisan wrestling with the question of whether or not to risk his whole future in a move to America. According to Penn and the map, the future was virtually assured, at least within a twenty-five mile radius of the City of Brotherly Love.

Tempered optimism was the tone of most responsible people who were familiar with actual conditions. To would-be settlers Penn himself offered this good advice: "Be moderate in Expectation, count on Labour before a Crop, and Cost before Gain, for such persons will best endure difficulties, if they come, and bear the Success, as well as find the Comfort that usually follow such considerate undertakings."[35] Similar caution marked the words of another Pennsylvania publicist, Thomas Budd: "It is rational to believe, that all considerate Persons will sit down and count the cost before they begin to build; for they must expect to pass through a Winter before a Summer, but not so troublesom a Winter as many have imagined."[36] Budd made little of the danger of Indians, wild animals, and rattlesnakes, but had the frankness to mention New Jersey mosquitoes!

By 1685 Penn was becoming interested in more distant land, especially the valley of the Susquehanna River as it arched down through the back country of Pennsylvania some seventy-five miles west of Philadelphia. "I have made a discovery of about a hundred Miles West," he wrote, "and find those back Lands richer in Soyl, Woods and Fountains, then that by Delaware; especially upon the Sasquehannah River."[37] Five years later, in 1690, he published *Some Proposals for a Second Settlement in the Province of Pennsylvania,* in which he revealed his plan for building a city on the banks of the Susquehanna.[38] He proposed to offer land at the rate of £100 per 3000 acres, with an annual quitrent of a shilling per hundred acres, the latter to be collected only after five years of actual settlement. Overland communication with the East "is as good as done already, a Way being laid out between the two Rivers very exactly and conveniently, at least three years ago," besides which there was the Indian trading path connecting a branch of the Susquehanna with a branch of the Schuylkill. Despite the proprietor's optimism, however, it would be many years before settlers in significant numbers would begin breaking the sod on the banks of the upper Susquehanna.

◁ 5 ▷

The Life of the Pioneer

What was it really like to be a pioneer on the northern frontier during the seventeenth or early eighteenth century? How did these frontier folk live from day to day? Such questions are not easy for a modern American to answer, for the technology of our century has transformed the American way of life so drastically that most of us have lost all acquaintance with the ways of even our grandfathers, to say nothing of our earlier pioneering forebears.

Take the matter of fire, for example. Whether in the seventeenth century or the nineteenth, a good wood fire—dancing, cheering, warming flames—was an essential feature of all pioneering. A fire served not only to cook food and give warmth in chilling weather but also to dry soaked clothing, keep wild animals at a respectful distance, help stragglers find their way, and hold off the somber cloak of darkness in a wilderness land. The campfire was the heart of every forest bivouac, whether of sailors ashore on the new-found coast of Maine, settlers just arrived on yet uncleared land in the back country of Pennsylvania, trappers and fur traders deep in Indian territory, or soldiers moving against the enemy along the shores of Lake George. Likewise in every pioneering dwelling, whether crude wigwam, log cabin, or substantial frame house, the well-kept fire on the hearth was the center of family life, the living symbol of survival in the wilderness. Fire was the great common denominator among all people of the wilderness because it was understood and used by all—Indians, Spanish *conquistadors*, French *coureurs de bois*, settlers, traders, soldiers.

What does fire mean to the modern American living on the very land where these pioneer campfires once were kindled? Usually little more than a pleasant convenience in the scientifically designed fireplace of a suburban ranch house, or a means of toasting marshmallows at the beach, or a method of clearing away fallen leaves in the autumn. But if we still have a little of the pioneering blood in our veins, we may yet feel a mystical sense of attraction to a good campfire, especially if it is deep in the woods far removed from the harsh pulsation of city life and the roar of motor vehicles along the highways. Then when darkness closes in and there are no sounds but the chirp of insects, the intermittent hooting of a distant owl, the low voices of a few companions—and the cheerful crackling of a good fire—we may sense in part something of the mood and spirit, the excitement and the awe, that attended the pioneers of old.

An understanding of the real nature of pioneering — the conditions under which the frontier folk lived — is important to an understanding of America today. The dangers, hardships, and satisfactions of frontier living contributed much to the attitudes, customs, and traditions of the American pioneers, and these in turn have entered the bloodstream of what we like to call "the American way of life." Generally speaking, the ways of the early settlers varied remarkably little from place to place and from decade to decade along the expanding northern frontier in colonial times. Their needs, the resources available to them, their methods of utilizing the resources, all remained fairly constant, so that it is possible to draw a general picture of pioneering life that is reasonably valid for all stages of frontier advance within the scope of this volume.

*T*HE EUROPEAN FAMILY that decided to try its hand at pioneering in America was confronted immediately with the problem of how to meet the initial costs, including the price of the voyage across the ocean and the equipment necessary to make a beginning in the New World. In 1685 overseas passage for a family of five persons cost about £25, and it was desirable, if at all possible, to invest another £5 in fresh provisions to supplement the coarse and meager shipboard fare.[1] The difficulty of meeting these expenses explains why so many immigrants came as indentured servants or redemptioners, with their passage paid.

A foresighted family with ample funds would try to accumulate a considerable stock of equipment in preparation for the great adventure, some of it being acquired prior to the ocean voyage and the remainder soon after arrival. The list might include a flintlock musket and a fowling piece; powder, lead, and a bullet mold; tools such as broad ax, felling ax, hatchet, spade, saw, grubbing hoe, weeding hoe, scythe, sickle, iron wedges, and a froe for cleaving shingles; harness for a draft animal; and utensils such as a frying pan and a cooking pot. In addition the family would buy and store up a quantity of provisions to sustain it during the first unproductive months on new land—a barrel or two of salt pork, some molasses and butter, several dozen bushels of Indian corn and other grain, peas and beans, a bushel of salt, some cheese, sugar, spices, and candles. Depending upon local circumstances and available funds, the new pioneering family might also invest in some livestock— possibly an ox, a cow, a bull, or a few pigs; these could be obtained in the colonies.[2]

After the long ocean voyage the first view of the American mainland filled the immigrant family with an unforgettable sensation, a mixture of anticipation and apprehension. From that moment until the day when the new pioneers settled upon their own piece of land, the wonders of the New World amazed them. The newcomers were almost certain to be curious about the wildlife inhabiting the American forest, and of course the descriptions of beasts and reptiles derived from old hands along the frontier often became inflated with retelling, so that America seemed to be almost a zoo of mythical wonders. Lions were heard roaring at night in early New England![3] But the actualities were interesting enough. The stately moose were admired for their size, and some colonists even speculated on the possibility of training them to become draft animals.[4] Wolves howled around frontier villages on moonlit nights, waiting for a chance at livestock. "One of them makes no more bones to runne away with a Pigge, than a Dogge to runne away with a Marrow bone," it was said.[5] Shaggy brown bears were sometimes glimpsed crashing off through the underbrush or sagely waiting for fish by a running stream, and deer were plentiful. In addition to these larger animals there were the smaller creatures of the forest—raccoons, skunks, and frisking squirrels for pioneer children to chase.

As for snakes, if the number of comments about them in the early accounts is any indication, they caused by far the greatest amount of shuddering fascination among Europeans. The death-dealing rattlesnake, then common along most of the northern frontier, was mentioned repeatedly, and often magnified into quite a horror. Rattlesnakes were described as being more than eighteen feet long, and it was even said that a person bitten by the reptile would turn "of the colour of the Snake, all over his body, blew, white, and greene spotted."[6] One correspondent, wishing to calm unnecessary fears, assured his readers that the rattlesnake cannot fly and is quite incapable of killing a man with his breath. On the contrary, he is "the most sleepie and unnimble creature that lives, never offering to leape or bite any man, if he be not troden on first . . . ."[7] That the settlers did not quickly lose their fear of the rattlesnake, however, is shown by the reluctance of colonial militia to pursue fleeing Indians through snake-infested swampland.[8]

Various remedies for snake bite were borrowed from the Indians. One suggestion was to chew snakeweed, swallowing the saliva and applying the residue to the wound.[9] Or one might prefer to try the juice of pennyroyal. A more drastic method was to gulp down the rattlesnake's own heart, or, somewhat less trying, to bruise the rattlesnake's liver (after first removing the gall) and then apply it to the wound.[10] Most effective of all was the Indian method of sucking out the poison by mouth.[11]

To the novice on the frontier the "wild" Indian was as great a curiosity as beast or reptile, and often more menacing. Few pioneer children could ever forget their first near view of a real, live, redskin. But soon the sight became familiar, for in many areas the Indians continued to dwell as near neighbors to the whites, often occupying land within the precincts of English townships. Some even took positions as servants in English households, and became familiar figures along the village streets. The settlers acquired a poor opinion of Indians in general, considering them indolent and slothful, given to lying, prone to irresponsible indebtedness, and incredibly addicted to strong drink. From the point of view of most colonists, they were dubious neighbors.

*T*HE PIONEER'S first big task upon arrival at his chosen homesite was to provide living quarters for himself and his family, making use of materials available on the spot. So he would set to work with spade and ax, first of all to clear a small piece of ground. This done, he was ready to begin construction.

There is a widespread impression that the pioneer of colonial times, with a beaverlike instinct, invariably hacked down the nearest trees and built himself a log cabin. Actually, although log construction was used by the Swedish pioneers along the Delaware River, it was virtually unknown to other Americans during much of the seventeenth century.[12]

The common practice was to build at first some sort of temporary dwelling whose style and manner of construction was either brought from the old country or borrowed from the Indians.

Four major types of temporary housing in the colonies have been identified.[13] The dugout, used in the earliest days of settlement in New England, New Netherland, and Pennsylvania, was a cavelike shelter dug into the side of a hill, or a pit dwelling consisting of a rectangular excavation roofed over with poles and slabs of bark. The Puritan historian Edward Johnson was referring to this type when he wrote that the earliest settlers "burrow themselves in the Earth for their first shelter under some Hill-side, casting the Earth aloft upon Timber; they make a smoaky fire against the Earth at the highest side, and thus these poore servants of Christ provide shelter for themselves, their Wives and little ones. . . ."[14] Similarly, in New Netherland they

> dig a square pit in the ground, cellar fashion, six or seven feet deep, as long and as broad as they think proper; case the earth all round the wall with timber, which they line with the bark of trees or something else to prevent the caving in of the earth; floor this cellar with plank, and wainscot it overhead for a ceiling; raise a roof of spars clear up, and cover the spars with bark or green sod so that they can live dry and warm in these houses with their entire families for two, three, or four years. . . .[15]

How comfortable or healthy a family might remain in such a dwelling during a long winter may best be left to the reader's own consideration. Certain it is that most pioneering families moved to other types of dwellings as quickly as feasible.

Another type of temporary shelter, often called a cabin, had walls of vertical stakes interwoven with flexible withes of willow or hazel and plastered with clay. The roof frame, slanting up on both sides to a central ridgepole, was covered with turf or thatch. More elaborate and sturdy was the cottage, which consisted of a simple frame made of squared timbers and covered on the outside with flat boards or overlapping clapboards. Some cottages may have had a filling of clay and chopped straw between the outer layer of boards and a crude form of interior wainscoting. Both of these types often had no floor other than the hard-beaten earth.

The *wigwam*, derived directly from the Indians, was in many ways the most practical answer to immediate needs in the wilderness. Sturdy poles cut from the woods were set into the ground at appropriate intervals to outline a rectangular floor plan. The opposite poles were then bent inward toward each other and fastened together so as to form a framework in the shape of a semicylinder. Bark, skins, or woven mats were used to cover the frame, leaving a hole in the roof as an exit for smoke from the cooking fire. The only floor was the hard earth itself, but bunks for sleeping were easily constructed Indian-fashion. A fireplace and chimney might be added, and perhaps even a crude swinging door. Such an abode was the first home remembered by more than one young American growing up on the northern frontier.

Wherever the forest grew thick, clearing the land for farming was a laborious task, to be accomplished a little at a time. The pioneer farmer had to get a crop started with as little delay as possible, so he usually tried to clear ground with a minimum of effort. One way was to chop down the trees with a felling ax, lop off and clear away the branches, and roll the logs off to one side for later use or for burning. This would leave a field of stumps, and the usual practice was to plant the crop in the clear spaces, putting off the hard job of rooting out the stumps until later. An easier method was to girdle the trees by cutting a ring all around the trunk. This caused the tree to die, so the foliage no longer blocked the sun, and crops would grow even among the dead trunks. In either case, final removal of the stumps was eventually accomplished with fire, ax, lever, and the muscle power of man or beast.

Some pioneers were so poor that they had to make their start in the wilderness with a bare minimum of equipment, perhaps even devising crude tools out of materials found on the spot. Wheels for a cart could be made by sawing slices from the end of a large hardwood log; many farmers had to make do with even less, and used crude sledges drawn by oxen or even by hand. Lacking a harrow to comb the ground after plowing, the pioneer might simply drag a large bush across his field. For smoothing and packing the soil, plenty of heavy logs were available to be used as rollers. A little ingenuity and resourcefulness, together with a strong back, could perform wonders.[16]

On the frontier, where life was primitive and survival sometimes a matter of raw competition, the gun was simply another tool in the hands of the pioneer.[17] It protected him against Indians, marauders, and wild animals; it brought to the family table venison, bear meat, and small game. By the middle of the seventeenth century the common firearm of the frontier was the flintlock musket, a smoothbore gun firing one or more leaden balls at a relatively low velocity. Although rather inaccurate at any range beyond fifty yards, at close quarters it was a deadly weapon. Pulling the trigger caused the hammer with its inserted flint to dart forward against a steel plate. The resulting spark ignited the powder in the pan, which in turn ignited the main charge in the barrel. Flints wore out and had to be replaced periodically, so the frontiersman on a long journey always had to carry a supply of new flints as well as powder and bullets. By the 1750s many frontiersmen were acquiring the newer, more accurate, long-barreled rifle, which also was fired by a flintlock mechanism.[18]

One of the great difficulties commonly encountered by new arrivals in America was the problem of adjusting to a new climate and diet. Some pioneers who experienced wilderness conditions such as crude housing immediately after completing their ocean voyage suffered extremely. The high mortality in such cases was probably as much the result of hardships endured during the long voyage as of climate and other conditions ashore.[19] Peter Kalm, the Swedish botanist, reported that newcomers in New Jersey often fell victim to chills and fever that gripped them during the late summer of their first or second year in the country. If they survived through the fall and winter, and recovered at the approach of spring, they usually gained an immunity to further attacks. It was a common saying among the local people that this malady served to accustom strangers to the New Jersey climate.[20] If so, it was a rugged initiation! With no trained physician within miles of a frontier settlement, remedies necessarily were traditional and home devised, or borrowed from the Indians. Pioneers endowed with rugged constitutions often managed to survive the hazards to health; all too many of the others, including a tragic multitude of women and children, were swept from the pages of history.

*O*FTEN the first crop planted by the pioneer on his new land proved to be scanty, and with supplies dwindling the family was forced, as Edward Johnson put it, to "cut their bread very thin for a long season."[21] After a year or so, however, when crops had started to come along nicely at last, the pioneer might consider building a more permanent and comfortable dwelling. He would by this time know the terrain well, and could choose a permanent site wisely. Usually this would be a piece of well-drained land, sheltered from the north wind, near a source of fresh water, and conveniently close to the planting fields and meadow.

A variety of house types were to be found along the frontier, the type most common in any locality depending largely upon the European background of the inhabitants, their experience in the colonies, and the materials available. Quite understandably, most people tried to reproduce as nearly as possible the kind of house to which they were accustomed in the old country. Thus many European practices and styles of construction were brought to the American frontier, but almost always with modifications to fit local conditions.

In New England the early settlers developed an eminently suitable type of frontier dwelling that was utilized over a wide area during the seventeenth century. First a rectangular cellar hole about sixteen by twenty-four feet was dug out and walled with field stones. Over this was erected a frame of oak timbers fastened together at the corners by means of skillfully contrived joints and wooden pins. Almost the whole of the north end of the house consisted of a massive field stone chimney with a large, deep fireplace opening onto the ground-floor level. Steep sloping rafters were added to the frame to support a roof of thatch or, as was common later, riven shingles of cedar. The floor was made with a double layer of boards for maximum warmth, the surface being of oak. Heavy hand-hewn beams barely six and a half feet above the floor supported the floor boards for the sleeping chamber above, which was reached by a ladder or a narrow stairway beside the chimney. Interior wainscoting of pine concealed a filling of clay and chopped straw packed between the members of the frame. The outer sheathing consisted of clapboards made of oak, cedar, or pine. Such a house contained only one room on the first floor and the single sleeping chamber above.[22]

In New Sweden houses were commonly made of peeled round logs, a type of construction imported from Scandinavia. At the four corners of the structure the logs were carefully interlocked by means of saddle notches, with all cracks and gaps in the walls being plugged with moss or clay. Such log houses could be constructed without the use of a single nail. In its simplest form this type of dwelling included a single room with an earthen floor, but later varieties included two or more rooms at ground level, with sleeping quarters above.[23]

In 1684 William Penn, drawing upon the experience of previous settlers, recommended that newcomers to his colony build for themselves "a House of thirty foot long and eighteen broad, with a partition neer the middle, and an other to divide one end of the House into two small Rooms."[24] This arrangement, known as the "Quaker plan," proved so practical for frontier living that it was widely adopted in Pennsylvania, whence it moved with the pioneers to other areas. It was used not only in frame and clapboard houses but in stone-built houses as well.

The Germans who came to Pennsylvania in the eighteenth century usually proceeded rapidly to their new lands without tarrying in the older districts. This gave little opportunity for them to be influenced by forms of construction evolved in America, so they tended to rely upon the style of architecture common in their homeland. When feasible, the Germans made good use of the abundant stone of the area. Sometimes they built frame houses, filling the space between the uprights with brick laid in patterns and left exposed. They were familiar also with log construction, and often built solid, substantial homes of hewn logs, skillfully jointed at the corners, and with gabled roofs.[25] The traditional log cabin of the American frontiersman was brought to the New World by Scandinavians in 1638, underwent considerable modification and elaboration in the hands of Pennsylvania Germans, and was finally adopted wholeheartedly in the eighteenth century by the practical-minded Scotch-Irish. These pioneers became masters of its construction all along the outer fringes of the frontier, thereby giving to America a symbol of proud poverty that was to have great political potency almost as long as the frontier remained.

In all pioneer homes, from dugouts to substantial frame dwellings, the fireplace was a feature of major importance. It may be described without exaggeration as the center of family living; on frosty winter mornings it attracted admirers like a warm-hearted coquette. The crudest of dwellings had only a hearth in the center of the earthen floor, but most frontier families, when able, devoted considerable time and effort to the construction of a good stone chimney with a fireplace. By modern standards colonial fireplaces were huge, often large enough to shelter a live cow, if one happened to wander in when the fire was out. A large lintel of oak or stone bridged the opening, serving also as a shelf on which might be kept flint, steel, and tinder. Hanging from a fixed horizontal trammel bar was an assortment of chains and pothooks for suspending iron cooking pots over the fire. Off to one side, also built into the stonework, was the oven for baking bread and puddings, heated by inserting live coals from the fireplace.[26]

Most of the light in a pioneer's home came from the fire on the hearth. For special illumination the early settlers ignited long splints of resinous pine, known as "candlewood," but this, as one observer noted, was "something sluttish, dropping a pitchie kinde of substance where it stands."[27] Greatly preferable were homemade candles of tallow or fragrant bayberry wax. Windows generally were small, for reasons of security. Because glass was expensive, many frontier homes had windows of oiled paper, which kept out the fresh air and admitted little light. Another common arrangement was to cover windows with sliding or swinging wooden shutters. Doors were made of solid, heavy planking and at night were secured against intruders by a horizontal crossbar. The typical pioneer home was a dark and smoky den, especially in wintertime.

Barns and other outbuildings were of secondary importance for the struggling pioneer. Livestock often had to fend pretty much for themselves. In time, however, the more successful farmers got around to building some sort of shelter for their animals. This might be nothing more than a crude lean-to, or it might be a fairly large barn such as the more prosperous Germans liked to build. In addition, fences were put up to keep cattle and swine from wandering among the crops.

Much of the furniture in a frontier home was made by the head of the household and his sons, for few pioneers could afford to carry bulky chairs and tables into the wilderness. The one material that was most plentiful in frontier regions was wood, and so the pioneers set about making their own stools, benches, settles, tables, chests, cupboards, and bunks or bedsteads—a good occupation for long winter evenings. Most of what they produced was simple and severely functional.

Fortification was another form of construction that occupied the settlers on the northern frontier from the earliest days, as they sought to protect themselves from actual or potential enemies, first the Indians and later the Indians in conjunction with the French. When the English settlers landed at Sagadahoc on the coast of Maine in 1607 they devised a rather elaborate plan of fortification for their settlement.[28] At Cape Cod a Pilgrim landing party in 1620, intending to pass the night ashore in strange territory, threw up a hasty barricade of logs and branches around their camp. Later, at Plymouth, the Pilgrims built a fortified meeting-house on a dominant position above their village.[29]

Along much of the northern frontier, especially in the eighteenth century, special forts of one kind or another were built, and sometimes garrisoned with soldiers. They varied in type from simple structures of squared logs surrounded by a palisade of vertical stakes to elaborate stone forts with carefully engineered walls and outworks. But through-out much of the colonial period, especially in New England, the fron-tiersman's principal answer to Indian raiders was the garrison house. This structure was both a fort and a dwelling. Essentially it was a dwell-ing that was specially constructed to withstand assault and furnish pro-tection for the people within. It might be surrounded by a palisade; it might have flankers at opposite corners; but almost invariably it was equipped with an unusually heavy door, wooden shutters at the win-dows, and walls sufficiently thick to stop bullets and arrows.[30] The colo-nial historian Thomas Hutchinson, speaking of Massachusetts in the 1690s, wrote that

> in every frontier settlement there were more or less garrison houses, some
> with a flankart at two opposite angles, others at each corner of the house;
> some houses surrounded with pallisadoes, others, which were smaller,
> built with square timber, one piece laid horizontally upon another, and
> loop holes in every side of the house; and, besides these, generally in any
> more considerable plantation, there was one principal garrison house,
> capable of containing soldiers sent for the defence of the plantation and
> the families near, whose houses were not fortified. It was thought justi-
> fiable and necessary, whatever the general rule of law might be, to erect
> such forts, castles, or bulwarks as these upon a man's own ground, without
> commission or special licence therefor.[31]

So it would appear that in matters of defensive construction the special perils of the frontier demanded a degree of improvisation and expedi-ency. The protection of human life took precedence over the fine points of law and the usual practices of more stable areas.

*M*OST PIONEERING FAMILIES depended largely upon agriculture for their subsistence, except in parts of Maine and New Hampshire where lumbering or fishing took precedence. Families tended to be large, for it was advantageous to have many hands to help with the farming. Some especially difficult or pressing tasks, such as building a house or gathering a harvest, were often completed through group cooperation, with a whole community coming together to help. Such occasions served also as social affairs, opportunities to meet with friends and have a good time together while achieving a useful purpose.

Secretary Van Tienhoven of New Netherland in 1650 wrote a report on pioneer agriculture, giving a useful picture of the practical business of farming. Newcomers in New Netherland, he said,

> must immediately set about preparing the soil, so as to be able, if possible to plant some winter grain, and to proceed the next winter to cut and clear the timber. The trees are usually felled from the stump, cut up and burnt in the field, unless such as are suitable for building, for palisades, posts and rails, which must be prepared during the winter, so as to be set up in the spring on the new made land which is intended to be sown, in order that the cattle may not in any wise injure the crops. In most lands is found a certain root, called red Wortel, which must before ploughing, be extirpated with a hoe, expressly made for that purpose. This being done in the winter, some plough right around the stumps, should time or circumstances not allow these to be removed; others plant tobacco, maize and beans, at first. The soil even thus becomes very mellow, and they sow winter grain the next fall. From tobacco, can be realized some of the expenses incurred in clearing the land. The maize and beans help to support both men and cattle. The farmer having thus begun, must endeavor, every year, to clear as much new land as he possibly can, and sow it with such seed as he considers most suitable.[32]

Maize, or Indian corn, was found to be an excellent crop in many areas. The pioneering farmer, without a plow and confronted with a field full of stumps, could resort to Indian-style agriculture, using a hoe. In the springtime he would dig small holes in the ground, spaced about five or six feet apart, anywhere he was able to do so among the stumps. He then dropped several grains of seed corn and perhaps a small fish into each hole, covering them with loose earth. In a few weeks green shoots began to appear. Then, as these grew taller, it became necessary to hill up the earth at the base of the tender stalks with the hoe, in order to give them support. The corn was ready for picking about four months after planting. On good land the farmer might expect a harvest of twenty or more bushels per acre—compared with the present-day yield of more than forty bushels. Some of the corn would be saved for seed, some would be ground into meal, and the remainder might help the livestock survive the next winter.[33]

Wheat was next to maize in importance as a crop. It grew particularly well in the rich soil of the Connecticut, Hudson, and Mohawk valleys, and in Pennsylvania. The ground was prepared for this grain first by plowing and then by combing the field with a harrow. The seed was planted broadcast. At harvest time the farmer and his helpers would move through the ripened grain with well-sharpened sickles in hand, rhythmically slicing close to the ground. Then the cut grain would be bound into sheaves and stored. Later, during the winter, the wheat would be threshed with flails and winnowed by being tossed into the air so that the breeze would carry off the light chaff.[34]

In addition to their basic grain crop, many farmers raised vegetables such as pumpkins, squashes, beans, and peas. During the eighteenth century immigrants from Ireland helped popularize the potato. Fruits thrived in many areas, but the development of a good orchard took considerable time. Other crops grown on pioneering farms included rye, barley, oats, tobacco, and flax.

Livestock was a most important resource in the pioneer's struggle for survival. Families that went to the frontier without livestock usually soon acquired some, either by purchase or by capturing wild strays.[35] Equipped with a pair of oxen or horses for plowing and other heavy work, a cow or some goats for milk, a few swine for meat, several sheep for wool, and some poultry for eggs, a frontier family could survive almost indefinitely, even if crops were slow to flourish. Unfortunately, the animals often had a hard time of it. Exposed to the extremes of weather, they wandered freely through the woods, seeking their own sustenance. Swine made out fairly well by rummaging for acorns, but the wild grasses often were insufficiently nourishing for cattle.

In some areas the raising of livestock grew into a highly successful enterprise, giving birth to what may be called a "cattle frontier," with rudimentary use of such techniques as the roundup and branding. The valley of the Piscataqua River in New Hampshire, for example, proved well suited for the production of good hay, and a thriving livestock industry developed there. Likewise in Hampshire County, Massachusetts, cattle raising became a specialty, with fine herds being driven to market at Boston. Rhode Island's Narragansett country, taken from the Indians in the seventeenth century, in the eighteenth became a noted center of cattle and sheep raising. In western Pennsylvania, too, large herds of cattle were raised for a growing eastern market. These developments suggest that the saga of the American cowboy was already beginning.[36]

Virtually all pioneers enlarged their supply of food by hunting or fishing. Some even made this kind of activity their principal means of support, having become highly skilled in the necessary techniques, with many borrowings from the Indians.[37] Certainly fish, fowl, and game animals were plentiful in the American forest, if one knew how to find them. Even allowing for some slight degree of enthusiastic exaggeration, the report of one resident of the Albany area in 1644 confirms the bounty of the wilderness:

> In the forests here there are also many partridges, heath-hens and pigeons that fly together in thousands, and sometimes ten, twenty, thirty and even forty and fifty are killed at one shot. We have here, too, a great number of all kinds of fowl, swans, geese, ducks, widgeons, teal, brant, which sport upon the river in thousands in the spring of the year, and again in the autumn fly away in flocks, so that in the morning and evening any one may stand ready with his gun before his house and shoot them as they fly past.[38]

Winter was a good time for turkey hunting. After a fresh fall of snow the big birds left tracks that could easily be followed by the hunter. In this way, said William Wood, some men in New England bagged as many as ten or a dozen turkeys in half a day. The colonists also learned that on moonlight nights the raccoons liked to rummage for clams on the beach. Hunting them there with dogs became a profitable diversion.[39] Bear, deer, raccoon, rabbit, squirrel, turkey, duck, goose—all were considered fair game and a welcome addition to the pioneer's rough board.

Catching fish was not so much a sport as a practical way of obtaining food; therefore nets and weirs were commonly used by pioneer fishermen. An experience described in a letter of 1680 is a good example of how the colonists learned from the Indians. Going to a stream to catch herring (alewives), the fishermen built in the shallow water a round trap about a foot high and two yards in diameter, with an entrance at one point. Then they cut down two birches and tied the tops together to make an extended barrier. This they took into the middle of the stream about a stone's throw above the trap, and holding it horizontal in the water, moved downstream, driving the fish ahead of them. At the right moment a bush was thrust into the entrance of the trap, and the fishermen found that they had enough good herring to fill a three-bushel sack.[40]

Most pioneering families, at least in the early stages of their frontier experience, had a simple, unvaried diet. Bread made from Indian meal, rye, or wheat was a staple. If the family had no oven, the loaf was baked in the ashes of the fire, Indian fashion. Game meat and fish were roasted over the open fire, fried in a skillet, or cooked in the iron stewpot along with whatever vegetables were on hand. Salted or pickled beef and pork from animals raised on the farm were an important part of the diet in many homes. Cows provided milk, butter, and cheese. Families that raised Indian corn consumed large amounts of corn meal porridge or pudding, often called *samp*. This was made by pounding Indian corn in a mortar, then sifting out the flour, and slowly boiling the residue in a pot of water.[41] It was often eaten with milk, as we eat hot cereal today, but without sugar. A porridge was made also of beans or peas.

How rapidly the settlers adopted native foods and Indian ways of cooking them is illustrated by the early use of the pumpkin in New England cookery. Sometimes the vegetable was baked, but a favorite colonial recipe for stewed pumpkin sounds especially tempting: Diced pumpkin was stewed slowly all day, with more pieces added from time to time as the volume diminished, but without adding more liquid. When thoroughly done, the stewed pumpkin was flavored with vinegar and ginger or spices, and a generous scoop of butter added. This piping hot delicacy often went to the table with meat or fish.[42] William Penn reported that in his colony the settlers liked to take sun-dried peaches preserved the previous summer and stew them with pieces of meat.[43]

Wild berries and nuts were gathered in the woods to enhance a pioneer meal, and even the lowly groundnut, which actually was a root tuber, was not to be scorned on lean days.[44] For sweetening, the backwoods settlers from New England to Pennsylvania relished the sugar derived from the sap of the sugar maple.[45]

Generally speaking, the early settlers did not drink water when other beverages were available. Beer was a favorite drink from Maine to the Delaware; in New England much of the barley crop was malted for the manufacture of beer. Other alcoholic beverages were derived from peaches, cherries, grapes, and corn. Apples went speedily to the cider press.[46]

There was much work to be done in addition to hunting, tending crops and livestock, and preparing food for the table. Pioneer women made a large proportion of the clothing worn by all members of the family, using mostly homespun and leather. Many frontier families supplemented their income by manufacturing potash and pearlash, used commercially in soapmaking and other processes. The method was a fairly simple one, requiring little special skill or equipment. The first step was to make a great fire of hardwood logs (often the very logs cleared from the farmer's planting field). Then the ashes were collected and leached in a barrel, and the resulting lye was boiled in a large iron kettle until there remained only a black residue known as potash. A further process, utilizing a sort of oven or furnace, converted the potash into the more valuable pearlash.[47] By selling pearlash the frontiersman could acquire cash or credit for the purchase of salt and other items that he himself could not produce.

Some backwoods settlers worked in certain types of organized frontier industry, such as lumbering, the production of naval stores, and milling. Whenever new territory began to be settled, sawmills and gristmills would early make their appearance; indeed, sometimes a mill served as the nucleus around which a settlement grew. Waterpower sites, at places on small streams where there was a fall or where the water could easily be channeled to create a fall, were eagerly sought by frontier capitalists.[48] The establishment of a sawmill in a frontier community was a tremendous boon to the inhabitants, freeing them from the laborious task of sawing lumber by hand.[49] A gristmill meant that home-grown grain could be ground into flour without tedious pounding in a mortar. For a pioneer lad and his father, carting the grain to the gristmill in the shady glen, and listening to the rumble and splash of the great waterwheel as it began its work, was a pleasant break in the routine of farming.

Probably one of the greatest faults of the American pioneer was his total indifference to the conservation of natural resources, an attitude spawned in the belief that the land and its bounty were virtually without limit. Early in his experience the colonial farmer became set in wasteful methods of cultivation. Later, when many of the settlers came to realize that the land they were farming was not inexhaustible, it was too late for them to change their habits. The depletion of the soil through wasteful, unscientific methods of farming was an additional stimulus for the westward movement, as discouraged farmers abandoned their declining acres and sought better land on new frontiers. All too often they repeated their old mistakes, exhausted the new land, and moved again. The colonial agriculturist Jared Eliot understood the problem well.

> When our fore-fathers settled here [he wrote], they entered a Land which probably never had been Ploughed since the Creation; the Land being new they depended upon the natural Fertility of the Ground, which served their purpose very well, and when they had worn out one piece they cleared another, without concern to amend their Land, except a little helped by the Fold and Cart-dung, . . . Our Lands being thus worn out, I suppose to be one Reason why so many are inclined to Remove to new Places. . . .[50]

Viewing the situation in Pennsylvania and New Jersey, Peter Kalm came to the same conclusion. The colonists, he said, becoming used to the abundance of rich land, had fallen into the same method of agriculture as the Indians; that is, to sow uncultivated grounds, as long as they will produce a crop without manuring, but to turn them into pastures as soon as they can bear no more, and to take on new spots of ground, covered since ancient times with woods, which have been spared by the fire or the hatchet ever since the Creation. . . . their eyes are fixed upon the present gain, and they are blind to the future.[51]

*T*RAVEL on the northern frontier was by foot or on horseback, or, if by water, in canoe or river boat. The first routes used by the pioneers were long-established Indian paths. Later these or similar trails were cleared and widened somewhat and called roads. Two-wheeled carts, drawn by horses or oxen, made their way slowly along such roads through the forest. Where roads did not exist, the relative absence of thick underbrush in many areas made overland travel still fairly easy for the man on horseback. In Pennsylvania it was said that even a cart could pass through the forest unhindered by obstructions.[52] The building and maintenance of roads was largely a responsibility of the local communities, much of the work being done by the inhabitants as a legal obligation. In New York, for example, residents were required to help clear land for roads "by Cutting or Stubing the Brush up pulling up the Stones that Can be Carried off the breadth of twelve foot and the Limbs of trees hanging over the Said Roads to be Lopt and Carried off. . . ."[53]

The extreme discomforts of overland travel in frontier regions need not be left to the imagination, for some of the early travelers who experienced the hardships have left vivid accounts which we may ponder as we cruise comfortably along our superhighways, perhaps in the very locations described. A good example is the experience of two travelers who were proceeding on horseback from the falls of the Delaware to Manhattan (modern Trenton to New York City). With evening coming on, they arrived at a creek, and having already covered some twenty-five miles that day, they gathered firewood, built a fire, ate supper, and settled down for the night. Before midnight it began to rain hard. As one of the men later recalled,

The rain continued so long and increased so that we could not sit down, because the place was so full of water. We had to take care and protect the fire from going out, which gave us enough to do. It was quite calm, or blew very little, the wind coming from all quarters; nevertheless, we could not dry ourselves, although we kept turning continually round towards the fire. We were wet through, and could do nothing better than to stand straight up, whereby from the length of time and the weight of our clothes we became very weary instead of having the repose we so much needed. Walk or sit, we could not, because it was too dark, and the land too full of water for the former, and for the other it was too wet. We were compelled to wait with patience in this position until daylight, which seemed to tarry, because we longed for it so much.[54]

For any modern traveler, this would be an unforgettable experience; for many hardened frontiersmen, it would have been little more than routine.

Oftentimes travel by water was preferable to travel overland. The settlers on the northern frontier quickly learned the advantages of native waterborne craft and adopted them for their own uses. As early as 1634 the inhabitants of Salem, Massachusetts, were using dugout canoes made from pine logs.[55] The Indian bark canoe, light to carry and swift in the water, became a great favorite of frontier explorers and travelers.[56] Frontiersmen living on major rivers such as the Connecticut had to build larger, more stable craft to carry heavy cargoes of bulky goods. They devised a type of shallow-draught, flat-bottomed boat made of planks, which could be propelled slowly upstream against the current by the use of long poles. Widely adopted during the course of the westward movement, the pole-boat became the work horse of pioneer river transportation.[57]

*I*NNOVATION, adaptation, change—these were the pulse beats of the frontier experience from the earliest days. The very language of the people was slowly reshaped to the needs of a new kind of living. Useful Indian words, such as powwow, wigwam, and tomahawk, denoting objects or conditions not known in the Old World began to fall readily from the lips of white pioneers. Likewise expressions borrowed from Dutch, French, German, or Swedish neighbors won a firm place in the everyday conversation of the English. Even well-established English words sometimes underwent a process of gradual change in the new environment. A good example is the word "lumber," which in England meant a sort of miscellaneous clutter, like trash. When the English pioneers cleared the land of trees, they caused the accumulation of great amounts of fallen timber which, until disposed of, was so much "lumber." Gradually the word was applied to usable wood, until it came to have its present American connotation.[58]

Immigrants who arrived on the northern frontier were entering upon a great adventure—not always romantic, but an adventure none-theless. They began a way of life that in many respects was markedly different from their previous experience. The physical environment of the new country—terrain, soil, natural resources, climate—often required a radical readjustment in the newcomer's way of doing things. New techniques offering the best chance of success had to be learned. And of course the restless shifting of people that was so much a part of the westward movement meant that personal associations were being drastically altered. People accustomed to close-knit European villages containing the same families generation after generation were surprised by the personal mobility made possible by the American frontier. Even those pioneers who came and settled as distinct groups eventually saw their grown children drifting off to better opportunities elsewhere and strangers arriving to take up vacated land among them. In this way traditions, attitudes, languages, and even blood began to blend together in the wonderful process that has produced a new nation on the American continent.

◁ 6 ▷

The Early Fur Trade, 1607–1689

*A*ll during the colonial period the business of acquiring animal skins and furs was a matter of great consequence in westward expansion. Peltry meant profits, because in Europe there was a growing demand for various kinds of skins and furs, to be used principally in wearing apparel. Moreover, the fur trade brought the Europeans and the Indians into economic conjunction in such a way that each of the groups became dependent upon the other. It was the one aspect of colonial endeavor in which the Indians had something so important to offer that they could command real consideration from the Europeans. Here, at least, the natives were more than mere obstacles to be shoved aside, for they were the ones who had access to the sources of peltry deep in the wilderness.

The continuing demand for furs, coupled with the inexorable advance of agricultural settlement, resulted in the rapid extermination of fur-bearing animals in areas adjacent to the advancing frontier. Consequently the profitable hunting grounds receded ever deeper into the interior. This was of the utmost concern to the various tribes, for it was not unusual for a tribe whose land lay near the coast to find itself without any accessible source of furs, as the animals in its territory retreated inland or became extinct. The consequence was bitter rivalry among the contending Indian groups, making it increasingly difficult for them to form a united front against white encroachments.

Similar divisions existed among the colonists. Group vied against group, colony against colony, for dominant positions in the valuable fur trade. The natural desire of ambitious traders and merchants to beat their rivals by getting closer to the sources was a strong factor in westward exploration, the establishment of new outposts in the wilderness, and the expansion of the frontier. As Frederick Jackson Turner and others have reminded us, the fur trader moved far in advance of the pioneering farmer, being often the first white man to enter new territory. Too, the competition for dominance in the fur trade became a matter of international rivalry, especially between the English colonies and the French. This development came about as they competed for the greatest sources of furs, which were found to lie deep in the heart of the continent, where neither country exercised unchallenged control and where both came to have important economic aspirations.

Before the coming of the Europeans, the Indians had made some use of skins and furs themselves, but the fact that fur-bearing animals were plentiful nearly everywhere in 1607 suggests that intensive hunting was a development directly related to the European market.[1] The Indians were quick to learn that furs brought desirable prizes from the white traders, and began to trade peltry for certain commodities that pleased them immensely and made life easier and more enjoyable— jewelry, mirrors, cosmetics, wearing apparel, blankets, cooking pots, tools, needles, knives, guns, and liquor.

All of this worked major changes in the Indian's way of life. He became economically, and sometimes politically, bound to a particular group of colonists. He became so accustomed to having and using certain items of European manufacture that he gradually lost his ability to get along without them. In this way he became a captive rather than a partner in the fur trade, much as a drug addict becomes bound to his supplier. The hunt for fur-bearing animals became an economic activity of central importance in his life and the life of his tribe. "It was much easier, and from an economic standpoint cheaper, for the Indian to exchange a few pelts and skins for European products of superior quality than to consume his time and energy in the production of an inferior grade," is the way one authority puts it. "But this means specialization in the hunt, the destruction of his means of subsistence and the loss of whatever technical aptitudes he once possessed, leaving him with much free time on his hands which was seldom put to productive use."[2] It is not difficult to argue that the Indian was the victim rather than the beneficiary of the colonial fur trade.

Pelts traded by the Indians included the skins or fur of the deer, moose, bear, otter, muskrat, marten, fox, raccoon, and above all the beaver. Unfortunately for the beaver, his hair was eminently suited for the felting process used in the manufacture of fur-napped hats, which in the seventeenth century graced every fashionable male head in western Europe. Close examination of a beaver skin will reveal two distinct layers of hair—a course outer layer known as the guard hairs and an under layer of shorter, softer hair. It was the silky under layer of "staple fur" that was so much in demand for felting.[3]

Because of its amphibious habits, the beaver can be an elusive quarry. "Their wisedome secures them from the *English*, who seldome, or never kills any of them," reported William Wood in the earliest days of Massachusetts settlement. Instead, "all the Beaver which the *English* have, comes first from the *Indians*, whose time and experience fits them for that imployment."[4] Indian beaver hunters used a variety of methods. Sometimes they broke beaver dams to lower the water in a pond and expose the quarry; sometimes they stalked the beaver with iron-tipped spear, bow and arrow, or gun; sometimes they set traps which they smeared with castoreum as a lure.[5] The beaver is not highly reproductive; consequently such diligent, systematic hunting rather quickly exterminated the species in areas where it was practiced. Furthermore, repopulation through migration from other areas was unlikely, because the beaver is not a rover by nature. This meant that as the nearer sources of beaver became exhausted, the hunters had to seek out new sources in the more remote interior.

Rivers were the key to the continental fur trade, first because the tributary streams and their ponds were the natural habitat of the beaver, and also because rivers gave access to the interior and served as highways down which the Indians transported their canoeloads of furs to be traded at the white men's outposts and settlements. Geography gave an initial advantage to the French, who settled along the St. Lawrence River, a route leading directly into the beaver country of the Great Lakes. In New England, by contrast, the rivers were relatively small, running generally north and south rather than east and west, so they were likely to be of diminishing importance as the sources of fur receded westward toward the country of the Great Lakes. In all the area of the northern frontier settled by the English, only the Mohawk Valley gave direct access to the Great Lakes region beyond the Appalachian barrier, and the Hudson-Mohawk route was controlled by the Five Nations of the Iroquois Confederacy. Farther south, the Delaware and Susquehanna rivers led northward toward the Iroquois country but did not penetrate the Appalachian barrier. So we see immediately that the Hudson-Mohawk route in particular, and the Iroquois tribes controlling that route, were destined to play a crucial role in the fur trade of the English colonies.

*T*HE EARLIEST fur traders on the northern frontier were the explorers and fishermen who frequented the coastal waters. During most of the sixteenth century European fishing vessels had been coming to North America for cod. Occasionally as they skirted the coast or landed to cure their catch, they came into contact with the natives and bartered European trinkets for the skins of animals. In this way the fur trade began. The seamen, of course, became increasingly aware of the profits to be made by such transactions, so as time went on the acquisition of furs became a lucrative side line. Many an English mariner about to sail for America stocked his sea chest with knives, mirrors, and hawk bells which later, on some piney shore, he would exchange for valuable skins and furs to take back to England.[6]

As soon as actual settlements began to be made, the business of trading for furs was intensified. Colonial planners realized early that settlements located on the major rivers down which the Indians would be likely to come in their canoes would possess a decided advantage in the competition for peltry. So river sites became of prime importance, and the trader who could establish his post upriver beyond his competitors would have the first opportunity at the furs. This could mean trouble. When a trader named John Hocking tried to force his way above a party of Plymouth traders on the Kennebec River, for example, a fight ensued in which Hocking was shot dead.[7]

Rivals in the fur trade seemed to be almost everywhere. The Dutch tried to monopolize the entire trade west of Cape Cod, and especially resented the establishment of a Pilgrim trading post on the Connecticut River in 1633. Earlier, the Pilgrims had been annoyed by the activities of Thomas Morton, an imprudent adventurer who operated a trading station near the south shore of Boston Harbor.[8] Likewise along the coast of Maine, especially on several of the important rivers of that area, the Pilgrims and others hastened to establish outposts of trade.[9]

One of the most imaginative of the early fur trading ventures was centered in New Hampshire. By 1629 the English had learned that the French in Canada were obtaining their furs from an interior region many miles to the south or west of Quebec, a region said to be dominated by a very large lake. What a stroke it would be if Englishmen should gain access to this wonderful source of furs and appropriate the region for themselves! The idea appealed to the business instincts of two ambitious English capitalists, John Mason and Sir Ferdinando Gorges, who with a number of other investors formed the Laconia Company.[10] This group was authorized to establish a base of operations on the coast of New Hampshire at the mouth of the Piscataqua River and to exploit a large tract in the remote interior near what was called the "Lake of the Iroquois," probably Lake Champlain. Identifying this region with the great source of French furs and believing that the Piscataqua River would give access to it, the Laconia Company set in motion its ambitious scheme for gaining control of the fur trade.

In 1630 the Company planted a settlement near the mouth of the Piscataqua River and made some attempt to explore the interior. Soon a trading post was established about six miles upriver and another some twenty-five miles inland on the Salmon Falls River. What the investors did not know was that their project was doomed from the outset by the facts of geography. The Piscataqua River does not lead to the great inland lake; in fact, a chain of mountains blocks the approach from the east. When the relatively limited fur trade of the Piscataqua region proved disappointing, the emphasis in the new colony shifted to fishing and agriculture. Later the Company suffered financial failure and dissolved. Its imaginative but impractical scheme for capturing the fur trade of the Northeast has been called "one of the first deliberate attempts by one of the rival fur-trading nations to outflank its opponents."[11]

The reasons why the coastal fur trade was in difficulty are suggested in a series of letters written in the mid-1630s by a factor stationed on Richmond's Island just below Casco Bay. From that vicinity south to the Piscataqua were few Indians, a diminishing supply of peltry, and far too many English traders competing with one another. Under these conditions profits tended to waste away. "Heare hath not bin to this Iland one Indian all this yeare, nor to the maine to our house, that brought Any skins to trade," complained the factor. "I sent out a boote twyse this last winter and got not on [one] ounce of bever from the Indians. . . ."[12] By this time the profitable coastal trading had moved to the area east of Casco Bay, where the Plymouth traders and many others were operating.

*T*HE MASSACHUSETTS BAY COLONY had its fingers in the fur trade very early, in fact, even before the arrival of the Winthrop migration in 1630.[13] The Puritan leaders of the colony viewed this particular form of economic enterprise, like every other, through the lens of religious purpose, and were concerned about the possible effects of the fur trade upon their Bible Commonwealth. Two aspects in particular commanded their attention. First, Winthrop and his colleagues were well aware of the financial advantages to be derived from the fur trade, and they wished to bolster the colony's economic strength by means of it. On the other hand, they were aware too that the fur trade tended to attract the peculiar talents of dishonest and disreputable characters. The Puritan leadership was determined to keep the fur trade under wholesome supervision and control, just as it sought to control the expansion of settlement. These two concerns—profit and integrity—lay at the heart of governmental policy with respect to the fur trade in Massachusetts during much of the seventeenth century.

The first important regulation was laid down in 1632, when the authorities decided that trading with the Indians would be permitted at only one designated house in each community. At the same time they levied a tax of 12*d.* per pound on all beaver traded.[14] The tax proved detrimental and was repealed early in 1635, after which the fur trade entered upon a period of expansion. In order to keep the business in responsible hands, the government found it necessary the following year to put it on a monopoly basis, granting three-year monopolies in designated areas to persons of good character who were willing to pay a yearly rent for the privilege.[15] This arrangement was modified in 1641 when Simon Willard and a group of associates chosen from the various towns were granted a three-year monopoly of the entire trade, with the right to establish their own regulations. Five per cent of all furs acquired were to go to the government; the remainder belonged to the traders themselves.[16] By 1647 the Bay Colony felt the need to derive a larger revenue from the fur trade and imposed a tax of twopence on every skin of beaver, otter, bear, and moose traded.[17]

The next ten years apparently saw a gradual breakdown of the system of control, for in 1657 the General Court, deploring the situation, appointed a six-man committee to let out the trade to responsible individuals on a contract basis.[18] The committee's report of the following year shows that a number of men in various parts of the colony had agreed to pay certain sums in return for monopoly privileges. Willard and three partners, for example, paid £25 for the fur trade of the Merrimack area. From these developments the Puritan line of approach to a troublesome and sometimes infamous business may be discerned. The aim was to encourage the trade enough to make it pay an income to the treasury, and at the same time to prevent abuses by keeping the business in the hands of a select group.

In Massachusetts the growth of the fur trade was rather closely linked with the expansion of settlement, as the Puritan authorities usually tried to discourage private individuals from going deep into the wilderness to set up lonely trading stations which could become centers of immorality as well as business. When an enterprising trader wished to advance his base of operations, he found it advantageous to invite a group of honest husbandmen to come and settle with him. Typically, most new trading posts in the Bay Colony quickly developed into commonplace agricultural towns.

After the founding of Hartford and the other towns on the lower Connecticut River, the only way to clench the fur trade of the Connecticut Valley was to go upriver well beyond the area of settlement. The man who had the foresight and the initiative to do this was a Massachusetts merchant named William Pynchon. This enterprising Puritan capitalist made a preliminary exploration of the area in 1635, and the next year established a trading post and settlement at Agawam, later renamed Springfield, a good twenty miles above Hartford.[19] In 1638 the government of the newly formed Connecticut Colony granted him a monopoly of the Indian trade at that place.[20] Pynchon, however, became involved in a bitter controversy with the authorities over the price of corn, and when opportunity presented, he attached his new settlement to Massachusetts rather than to Connecticut. The boundary between the two Puritan colonies remained in dispute for many years.

At first Pynchon followed the usual practice of contacting the Indians and inducing them to bring their peltry to his trading post. Soon, however, he began to extend the range of his operations, and in time developed a system of trading unusual for that period, and which worked so well that it was continued after 1652 by his son John. Holding a monopoly right leased from the Massachusetts government, the Pynchons in turn sublet certain rights to subsidiary traders. These men had to obtain all their trading goods from the Pynchon store at Springfield, at prices set by the Pynchons. They were also obligated to sell to the Pynchons all the peltry they obtained from the Indians. In effect, the central post at Springfield served as the heart and brain for an expanding network of outlying stations to the north and west, all contributing ultimately to the fortune of the Pynchon family. The town of Northampton, for example, had its first beginnings as a trading station run by one Joseph Parsons, under license from John Pynchon.[21]

The Pynchon family built its economic and political power in the upper Connecticut Valley largely upon a fortune made in frontier trading not only in peltry but also in agricultural products. Although shrewd and aggressive in business, both William Pynchon and his son John were men of integrity, examples of the frontier capitalist at his best. They treated the Indians with firm justice and in turn gained the respect of both the Indians and the frontiersmen. As for the fur trade itself, there can be no doubt that it was of great importance in opening the Connecticut Valley to settlement and in helping to sustain many of the early settlements during their first years.

*T*HE MOST IMPORTANT and significant fur trade of the northern frontier was developed by the Dutch in the valley of the Hudson River. To understand the great significance of this trade, especially its bearing upon Indian affairs and international relations, it is necessary to step back for a broad view of a much larger area. The French, who had established themselves on the St. Lawrence River as early as 1608, began drawing upon the great fur region lying to the north of the Great Lakes. Their trade was based upon friendly relations with the Huron, an important tribe inhabiting the area between Lake Ontario and Georgian Bay, who acquired furs from more remote tribes and brought them by way of the Ottawa River to the French posts on the St. Lawrence. So long as the Huron retained their position and the Ottawa-St. Lawrence route remained secure, this traffic could continue, to the great advantage of both the Huron and their allies, the French.

The Five Nations of the Iroquois Confederacy, dwelling in the area south and east of Lake Ontario, were enemies of the French and their Indian allies, especially the Algonquian tribes. Confronted with a combination of French-Huron-Algonquian power, the Iroquois were anxious to gain support from the Dutch on the Hudson. At first they were handicapped because the Mahican stood between them and the Dutch, but about 1628 the Mohawk defeated the Mahican and gained full access to the Dutch trading post at Fort Orange, thereby inaugurating a trade relationship that was to have momentous consequences for the future of the North American continent.[22]

Fort Orange, located on the west bank of the Hudson nine miles below the mouth of the Mohawk River, became the focal point of the Dutch fur trade. There the Indians came with their loads of peltry to sell them to the traders for clothing, blankets, hardware, guns, ammunition, and liquor. For the Iroquois this trade became almost a necessity; it was not only that ordinary trade goods had become important to their comfort, but only through their trade with the Dutch could they obtain European firearms with which to maintain themselves against their enemies. Inevitably, however, in their intensified hunt for furs to meet the demands of the Dutch traders, the Iroquois soon exhausted the supply of beaver in their own territory. Probably by 1640 few beavers remained in the country from the Hudson west to the Genessee River in the land of the Seneca.[23] This left the Iroquois threatened with ruin unless they could find some way to obtain furs elsewhere and continue their active part in the fur trade.

To the north, the Huron were busy and prosperous in their flourishing trade with the French. The Iroquois, blocked from direct access to good beaver country in the West by hostile tribes, found an apparent solution to their dilemma in the possibility of breaking in upon the Huron trade. They began sending well-armed parties northward beyond Lake Ontario to hunt beaver, or even to lie in wait for the Huron canoes, seize their valuable cargoes, and bring back the furs to be traded at Fort Orange. This activity proved highly successful, and the Iroquois warriors developed a mastery of the plundering game that made them a terror to French and Huron alike. So bold had they become by the spring of 1643 that they extended their operations close to the French settlement of Montreal itself.[24]

In 1647 the Huron lit a slow fuse at the back of the Iroquois country by making an alliance with the Susquehannock against the Five Nations. This signaled an intensification of the intertribal feud on the northern frontier. Two years later, in the winter of 1648–1649, the aroused Iroquois crept northward through the forest to the Huron country. There they suddenly pounced upon two Huron villages and destroyed them with such thoroughness that the terrorized Huron people abandoned many of their other villages and fled westward. Their precipitate flight brought to an end their economic value to the French, whose fur trade with the western tribes was now temporarily disrupted.

Flushed with victory and apparently about to become undisputed masters of the fur trade, the Iroquois next turned against their other enemies. They quickly overcame the Petun and the Neutrals, who lived west of Lake Ontario, and in the mid-1650s managed to subdue the Erie nation south of Lake Erie. Their struggle with the Susquehannock was more prolonged and less successful. Despite these victories, the Five Nations found themselves unable to grasp the entire fur trade of the northern frontier, for the Ottawa Indians of Lake Huron became interested in the old French trade that the Huron had so precipitately abandoned and succeeded to that profitable business. This arrangement was more than acceptable to the French, and so the old trade revived despite the remarkable upsurge of Iroquois power in the 1650s.

Through all this intertribal conflict the government of New Netherland had been warily treading a path of noncommitment, neither condoning nor condemning the Iroquois, and the Dutch traders at Fort Orange had continued to pursue their business much as before. In 1652 the village that had grown up at Fort Orange was given the name Beverwyck, acquiring at the same time important rights of local jurisdiction as a trading community. Henceforth the Indian trade at Beverwyck was under the supervision and control of the town officials, whose main concern was to protect the profits that were going to the local merchants.[25]

Keeping the trade fair and aboveboard was not an easy task. Almost anyone with a small amount of capital and initiative could get hold of some trading goods, encounter Indians with furs, and strike a profitable bargain. This made things difficult for the regular merchants and traders, who naturally wanted to keep the business at Beverwyck in their own hands. Their plan was to have the Indians bring their peltry to the town, where it could be traded in a regular and orderly manner under agreed-upon rules of procedure. But the competition for furs became so great that many traders were not willing to sit at Beverwyck and wait for the Indians to come to them. Instead, they sought to beat the competition by going out into the woods to intercept the Indians as they approached. With trader striving to outdo trader in this way, the orderly character of the business was in danger of breaking down altogether.

The colony government tried to control the situation by passing appropriate legislation. In 1647 a law had forbidden all inhabitants to go into the interior with trading goods, requiring them instead to wait for the Indians at the established trading posts. Apparently the law was not effective, for a similar restriction was laid down in 1652.[26] Still the interlopers flourished, and all too often they actually bullied the Indians into trading their furs. The Mohawk complained of Dutch traders "who run up and down on horseback, not only taking their Beavers by force and carrying them off, leaving the Indians to run after them, but also shove and beat them...."[27] Such behavior was a threat not only to the legitimate trade but also to the difficult and delicate field of Indian relations in general.

By the summer of 1662 the officials at Beverwyck had gone so far as to erect a post on a hill within sight of the fort, with strict orders that no trader was to venture beyond that point, but this did little to solve the problem. Complaining of a "ruined Trade" due to the irresponsible behavior of some traders, the town fathers excoriated the "many graceless and idle Loafers" who, "to the scandal and disgrace of the Christian name and Dutch nation, remain loitering near and about the erected Post, entire days from morning until night, even on the Lord's Sabbath and day of rest, in wait for the Indians...."[28] Even if the poor redskins with their bundles of furs were so lucky as to reach the town itself without mishap, they might then expect to be "assailed, taken by the arm and dragged with their Goods against their will into one house or the other," where they would be cajoled or intimidated into parting with their burden at dictated prices.[29] As a customer, the Indian was valued but certainly not respected.

*T*HE EUROPEANS who engaged in the fur trade along the northern frontier had a great variety of products to offer in exchange for peltry. Two were of special significance—firearms and liquor. When the Indians began to acquire guns and alcoholic beverages, both previously unknown in their culture, they sowed the seed of their ultimate ruin.

The native bow and arrow, despite its advantages of lightness, quietness, and rapidity of operation, was no match for the more efficient and deadly flintlock guns of the Europeans, especially in penetrating, shattering power.[30] Consequently, once the Indians had lost their first fear of explosions, they eagerly sought to obtain firearms, both for hunting and for intertribal warfare, and gave scant consideration to the fact that dependence on guns meant dependence on the white men for a continuing supply of powder and bullets.

Even before the first permanent settlements began, the occasional traders along the coast were exchanging guns for furs. The problem was mentioned in a royal proclamation of 1622; Sir Ferdinando Gorges spoke of it to Parliament in 1624; and in 1630 the Privy Council formally prohibited the trade in firearms in New England.[31] There was concern lest white settlers engaged in planting colonies in the wilderness lose the weapon superiority that made it possible for them to survive in the midst of hostile savages. One of the principal reasons why the men of Plymouth arrested and expelled Thomas Morton in 1628 was that he was supplying the local Indians with firearms, thereby endangering the Pilgrim community. When the Puritans settled at Boston, they acted speedily to prevent extension of the traffic, ordering one offender to be whipped and branded, and suggesting that henceforth the selling of firearms and ammunition to Indians should be a capital offense.[32] The suggestion was not adopted at the time, but in New Netherland the death penalty was actually prescribed as early as 1639 for colonists convicted of trading firearms to the natives. Plymouth formally prohibited the traffic in 1640, Connecticut two years later.[33]

Laws proved unequal to the temptation. The Indians had the furs, and the Indians wanted guns. If one trader obeyed the law and refused to sell guns, the Indians would take their furs to someone less scrupulous.

Actually, this practice eventually corroded the legislation itself, especially as the sources of beaver became more remote, because the colonies whose laws were most strict found that they were in danger of losing out in the fur trade. Bowing to what seemed an insoluble problem, one colony after another loosened its restrictions on the arms traffic.[34]

By 1675 the natives of New England not only possessed a fairly large supply of serviceable guns but had become quite adept in their use. Given the frequency of intertribal warfare, this was as much a threat to the Indians as to the white men. Indeed, the increasing destructiveness of forest warfare pointed to the ultimate ruin of all the tribes.

In a different way alcoholic beverages were as dangerous for the Indians as firearms. Once introduced to the sensations of intoxication the average Indian, having apparently a low constitutional resistance to alcohol and no comprehension of the long-range consequences, quickly became an avid tippler. He came to crave and demand liquor for just one purpose: to become thoroughly drunk. And he used his furs as a means of purchasing such drunkenness. Unfortunately, many white traders were perfectly willing to satisfy this craving in the interest of promoting business.

As in the matter of firearms, well-intended legislation proved of little avail. Looking back over more than a century of experience with the problem, the historian Thomas Hutchinson commented that as soon as the Indians obtained a taste of alcoholic beverages "they were bewitched with them, and by this means more have been destroyed than have fell by the sword."[35] A speech delivered by a sachem of the Delaware area outlined the problem with primitive eloquence:

> *The strong Liquors was first sold us by the* Dutch, *and they were blind, they had no Eyes, they did not see that it was for our hurt; and the next People that came amongst us, were the* Sweeds, *who continued the sale of those strong Liquors to us: they were also Blind, they had no Eyes, they did not see it to be hurtful to us to drink it, although we know it to be hurtful to us; but if People will sell it us, we are so in love with it, that we cannot forbear it; when we drink it, it makes us mad; we do not know what we do, we then abuse one another; we throw each other into the Fire, seven Score of our People have been killed, by reason of the drinking of it, since the time it was first sold us: Those People that sell it, they are blind, they have no Eyes. . . . We must put it down by mutual consent; the Cask must be sealed up, it must be made fast, it must not leak by Day nor by Night, in the Light, nor in the Dark. . . .*[36]

Following the example of the earlier colonies, Pennsylvania prohibited the indiscriminate sale of liquor to Indians, and with about the same result.[37]

All witnesses agree on the excesses of Indian intoxication; a drunken Indian was to be feared like a rabid dog. One observer called the Indians "beastly drunkards" who "Cry & howle extremely when they are drunk."[38] "If they are heated with Liquors," reported William Penn, "they are restless till they have enough to sleep; that is their cry, Some more, and I will go to sleep; but when Drunk, one of the most wretchedst Spectacles in the world."[39] Still another observer, this time in New York, wrote that once the fur-trading Indians tasted strong drink "they will never forbear, till they are inflamed and enraged, even to that degree, that I have seen Men and their Wives *Billingsgate* it, through the Streets of *New-York*, as if they were metamorphosed into the nature of those beasts whose Skins they bartered."[40] Not infrequently the drunken revels of the Indians resulted in the death or maiming of participants or bystanders.

Sometimes the sachems saw clearly the moral and physical damage that was being done to their people by the traffic in liquor and urged the colonial authorities to take more effective measures against it. But like guns and ammunition, alcohol had become a vital ingredient of the fur trade, and neither the profit-hungry traders nor their thirsty Indian customers were to be denied by mere laws. This is shown by the frequency with which the laws were reiterated. The General Assembly of Rhode Island even suggested that some unscrupulous traders had encouraged the passage of prohibitory laws in the expectation that many law-abiding traders would abandon the business, thereby leaving the field open for the lawbreakers.[41]

By 1686 the issue had invaded the arena of international politics, with English and French colonial authorities accusing each other of undermining the integrity of the Indians by allowing them to obtain alcoholic beverages. Wrote the Governor of New France to the Governor of New York, "Think you, Sir, that Religion will make any progress whilst your Merchants will supply, as they do, *Eau de Vie* in abundance which, as you ought to know, converts the Savages into Demons and their Cabins into counterparts and theatres of Hell." Replied the Governor of New York to the Governor of New France, with some pique, ". . . certainly our Rum doth as little hurt as your Brandy and in the opinion of Christians is much more wholesome; however to keep the Indians temperate and sober is a very good and Christian performance but to prohibit them all strong liquors seems a little hard and very turkish."[42] To alter an old saying, this exchange of views was a case of the keg calling the jug wet.

Certain it is that so long as the fur trade continued, the hunters would demand part of their pay in strong drink, a demand that most profit-minded traders stood ready to satisfy. There were positive reasons why the traders liked to dispense liquor in exchange for peltry: it kept the customers coming back for more; it was easy to cheapen by the addition of water; and its effects weakened the Indian's resistance to sharp bargaining. A dipperful given gratis at the start of negotiations could be counted on to speed the transaction—at the Indian's expense. Thus did the white men nourish a craving that was relentlessly corroding the moral stamina, the self-respect, the physical health, and the independence of the Indians.

*D*URING the second half of the seventeenth century the Iroquois fur trade, with its main base at Beverwyck, continued to hold first place on the northern frontier. When in 1664 the English took New Netherland from the Dutch and turned it into the English colony of New York, they hastened to establish close economic relations with the Iroquois tribes. In effect—and this was to be of major importance—the English became heirs to the old Dutch-Iroquois fur trade, which continued as before with little change.[43] Beverwyck became the town of Albany, but it remained predominantly a Dutch community, with most of its fur trading in the hands of the same Dutch merchants.

A visitor arriving at Albany by boat in 1680 would see before him a compact settlement sloping from the riverbank up to a palisaded fort.[44] A wall of vertical stakes completely surrounded Albany, reminding the visitor that this area still was frontier territory. Within this protecting wall were some eighty or ninety dwellings and two churches, arranged along the sides of regular streets. A short distance outside the gates, on both sides of the town, stood groups of lodges provided as living quarters for the Indians when they came to Albany to trade their furs. During the summer months, when this trading was at its height, Albany was a busy place, with Indians and traders visiting back and forth, examining bundles of furs and haggling over prices. Below the town, along the riverbank, the ketches and other small river craft waited to take on their cargoes of peltry destined for New York and the markets of Europe.[45] This was the principal fur-trading center of English North America.

The change from Dutch to English rule left Albany's long-standing trade policy intact. This policy, based on the facts of Indian relations, the growth of settlement, and the potential threat of the French fur trade, consisted essentially of two points: first, Albany was to continue to enjoy a protected monopoly of the fur trade; second, all trading was to take place at the town itself rather than at various Indian villages or elsewhere in the wilderness. Accordingly, the town officials, as in Dutch days, resisted with adamantine constancy every attempt by any other New York town or by groups of merchants from outside the province to siphon off any of the Iroquois trade. At the same time, they did everything they could to prevent individual traders from going into the woods to establish contact with the Indians.[46] In 1672 a group of enterprising Massachusetts merchants tried to intrude upon the New York fur trade, under a thin pretext of helping to forestall French advances. Their real motive was to establish a relationship with the Mohawk Indians in order to exert leverage against the restive New England tribes, while at the same time enlarging their own fortunes. As always, the unswerving opposition of the New Yorkers proved to be more than a match for such a scheme.[47]

Albany's virtual *de facto* monopoly of the Iroquois trade in New York was given official sanction in 1678 by Governor Edmund Andros, who decreed that no other settlement in the province should participate in the trade. At the same time, however, he granted to the town of New York a monopoly of the colony's overseas trade, which meant that the Albany fur traders had to receive their trading goods and export their peltry by way of Manhattan. In this way a pattern of commerce developed that was to remain in effect through the remainder of the colonial period, with the town of New York serving as the entrepôt for the Albany fur trade. The province derived considerable income from duties levied upon both the imported trading goods and the exported furs.[48]

The Albany fur trade remained of great importance to the prosperity and security of the Five Nations. Not only was English support a vital factor in their struggle against other tribes, but the English were able to furnish them with manufactured goods at prices that the French were unable to meet. This prevailing price advantage, caused by the more advanced development of English manufacturing industry, English domination of the sea lanes, the high import duties levied on trading goods by the Canadian authorities, and the fact that the St. Lawrence River remained frozen during the long Canadian winters, was to be a major factor in the struggle between England and France for the fur trade of North America. An Indian with peltry to trade knew that he could obtain a gun, powder, a good knife, or a woolen blanket, for fewer beaver skins at Albany than would be required for the same items at Montreal. That is why Albany attracted furs as a magnet attracts iron.

The advantageous Albany trade, more than any other factor, kept the Iroquois tribes attached to the English interest, and every informed colonist knew that the collapse of this relationship might well be disastrous for New York and the other English colonies. At the same time, virtually all the Algonquian tribes from northern New England to Delaware Bay feared the Iroquois, and not without reason. The Five Nations continued to extend their dominion by conquering and absorbing weaker tribes, as they had done earlier with the Petun, the Neutrals, and the Erie. By 1675 even the Susquehannock, themselves an Iroquoian people, had succumbed.[49] It is no wonder, then, that the Algonkins readily inclined toward the French, who appeared as the opponents of both the dreaded Iroquois and the English landgrabbers.

The French were determined to retain a large share of the fur trade in their own hands, and if possible to exclude the English entirely. Somehow they had to keep the Iroquois from interfering with the Ottawa–St. Lawrence trade and at the same time find ways to overcome the handicap of higher prices on French trading goods. At times they tried to seduce the Iroquois with prospects of profits to be made at Montreal. They sent courageous Roman Catholic missionaries to dwell among the Iroquois and plant in their minds not only the faith but also the idea that France was the country to be trusted and followed. Under such persuasion some of the Mohawk and Oneida actually moved to Canada as converts, settled down under French supervision, and became known as the Caughnawaga Indians.[50]

At other times the French employed force, or the threat of force, to cow the Five Nations. In 1673 the new governor of Canada built Fort Frontenac, named after himself, at the northern end of Lake Ontario near the entrance of the St. Lawrence River. This stronghold was intended to prevent the Iroquois from coming north of the lake to hunt beaver or to interfere with the passage of French furs. Although experience was to prove that Fort Frontenac could not possibly choke off this activity entirely, the fort did serve a useful purpose, if only by helping to impress both the French Indians and the Five Nations with the determination of Governor Frontenac to protect his own.[51] Six years after the construction of Fort Frontenac, the French erected a fortified post at Niagara to guard the important route between Lake Erie and Lake Ontario.

Not all the French peltry that reached Albany came as a result of Iroquois plundering. A considerable amount in the years after 1671 was brought to Albany by French *coureurs de bois*, outlaw traders who, like the Indians, were attracted by favorable English prices. In short, the French fur trade was suffering a serious leakage of peltry caused by the activities of both Iroquois raiders and renegade French traders. Only French military power, combined with extensive French influence among the western tribes, preserved for the time a rather uneasy equilibrium on the fur-trading frontier.

*T*HE DECADE of the 1680s brought a sharp renewal and dangerous intensification of French-English rivalry in the fur trade. In the late 1670s the Iroquois had taken pains to revitalize their alliance with Albany, and then, having done this, in 1680 they abruptly ended a period of relative peace in the forest by launching an attack upon the Illinois tribe in the distant west. This violent outbreak was the beginning of a renewed struggle for domination of the western fur trade.[52]

When Colonel Thomas Dongan became governor of New York in 1683 he brought with him an aggressive determination and a capacity for imperial vision such as only the French had previously known. Dongan quickly grasped the elements of the great power struggle now commencing, and in particular he saw clearly that the Anglo-Iroquois axis, so closely bound up with the Albany fur trade, was the hinge upon which turned the whole future of the English and the French in North America. During his five eventful years as New York's governor, Dongan developed a dynamic imperial policy whose ultimate goal was the capture of the entire fur trade of the northern frontier and the eclipse of France in North America. The policy was soundly based upon past experience, borrowing much from Dutch precedent in Iroquois relations, but it was remarkable also for the way in which it looked to the future, seeming to anticipate the great struggle with France that was to dominate the next three-quarters of a century of colonial history.

The bedrock of Dongan's policy was to keep the Five Nations firmly attached to the English interest. Whenever opportunity presented, he took pains to warn the Iroquois of the sinister character of French intentions, urging them to reject every French attempt to extend influence among them. Dongan even tried to regain the allegiance of the Caughnawaga Indians. To this end he offered land at Saratoga where the Caughnawaga might settle and promised to provide them with Catholic priests and a church, but his efforts failed and the converted Indians remained under French supervision.[53] The Five Nations, however, reasserted their allegiance to the English and continued to gnaw like beavers at the foundations of French power and influence in the West.

Another aspect of Dongan's policy was to uphold and even strengthen the traditional Albany monopoly of the Iroquois fur trade. Early in his administration, he had to deal with a challenge to that monopoly coming from an unusual direction. With the founding of Pennsylvania in 1682, agents of William Penn sought to acquire from the Iroquois tracts of land on the upper Susquehanna River, in order to attract Iroquois furs in that direction. In fact, to the alarm of the

Albany merchants, a significant amount of peltry did find its way down the Susquehanna, the Schuylkill, and the Delaware. But officially the Iroquois resisted the blandishments of the Pennsylvania agents and declined to sell them the territory they needed as a base for trading. Likewise New York's royal proprietor, the Duke of York, when apprised of the situation made clear his intention "to preserve the Indian Trade as entire as I can for the benefitt of the Inhabits and traders of New Yorke preferably to all others."[54] His hand strengthened by such firm backing, Dongan did all in his power to prevent encroachments from the south. Furthermore, in 1686 he granted to the town of Albany a charter of incorporation confirming the exclusive trading privileges of the inhabitants and strengthening the long-standing custom by which the Albany magistrates virtually controlled New York's relations with the Iroquois tribes.[55]

The French had already recognized the importance of strategically located forts in the West as a means of controlling the wilderness routes, and now Dongan began to argue that the English would do well to build some forts of their own. A well-designed, well-maintained fort located at a point where several important routes converged could serve both as a control station for the Indian trade and a defense against foreign encroachment; but if the English failed to act in this matter, they might wake up one morning to find the West and its vital fur trade seized and held in a network of French forts. Accordingly, Dongan urged that New York undertake the building of wilderness forts, especially one on the near side of Lake Ontario to counteract the influence of Fort Frontenac.[56] This proposal, however, remained in embryo until more than a quarter of a century later, while the French proceeded with their own plans.

Dongan also saw clearly that the old Albany policy of making the fur trade come to the town, rather than sending aggressive traders far into the interior to seek it out, was not an adequate answer to French initiative. Certainly the Iroquois alone could not be depended upon to win the lion's share of the trade for Albany. But until the coming of Dongan the Albany merchants and the Iroquois stood firmly on the old policy of trade only at Albany. Dongan performed the rather remarkable feat not only of inaugurating a significant change in the policy but of gaining considerable Albany and Iroquois backing for his plan.

Pursuing the new policy, the governor sought to encourage the remote tribes of the Great Lakes region to bring their supplies of peltry directly to Albany, where they could sell them at the advantageous English prices. The Iroquois agreed not to block the approach of such Indians. More important, Dongan began sending groups of English traders, escorted by Indians, far into the interior to establish contact with remote tribes and acquire their supplies of furs. Beginning in 1685 enterprising traders from Albany, under authorization from the governor, probed to the heart of the Great Lakes trading area, even to Michilimackinac. They traded with the Huron, Ottawa, and other distant Indians, impressed upon them the advantages of dealing with the English rather than the French, and brought back peltry to make the eyes of the merchants glisten.[57]

Soon the French regime in Canada began to feel the complex structure of its own system of Indian alliances trembling underfoot as though by the prolonged shock of an earth tremor. Alarmed, the authorities at Quebec reacted with all the resources at their command. English traders who dared invade the French sphere of influence were tracked down and arrested. Such was the fate of Major Patrick Magregory, who was leading a party toward Michilimackinac in 1687.[58] Already military reinforcements had arrived in New France, and in the summer of 1687 a strong French force advanced into the country of the Seneca, burning Iroquois villages as it went. This was a clear warning of French determination.

By this time the first faint outlines of the impending struggle between England and France in North America were becoming clear. Even the English king, James II, was becoming aware of the importance of the Five Nations, for he ordered Dongan to claim them as subjects of the Crown entitled to the protection of English arms. It was the fur trade more than anything else which had lured both the French and the English deep into the wilderness during the seventeenth century. And it was ambition to dominate the fur trade through favorable alliances with important groups of Indians which now was pushing the two rival colonial blocks toward the brink of war.

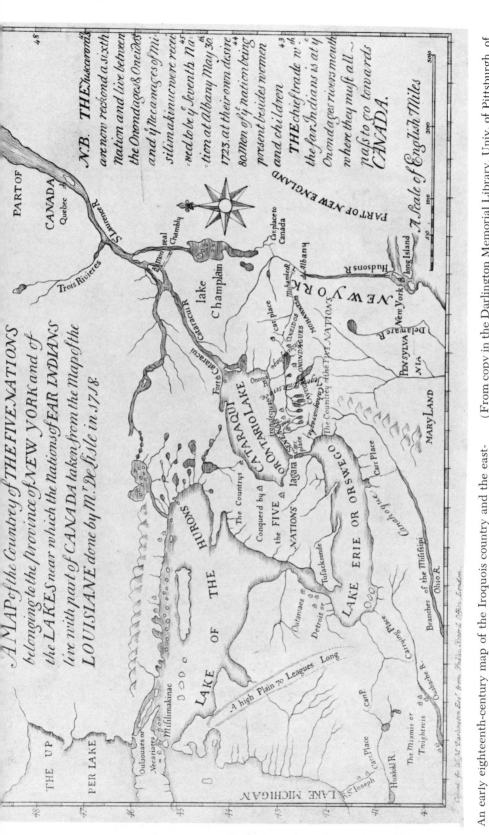

An early eighteenth-century map of the Iroquois country and the eastern Great Lakes. Important portages on the river routes are shown.

(From copy in the Darlington Memorial Library, Univ. of Pittsburgh, of maps in Public Record Office, London, and Crown copyright)

A MAP of the Countrey of THE FIVE NATIONS belonging to the Province of NEW YORK and of the LAKES near which the Nations of FAR INDIANS live with part of CANADA taken from the Map of the LOUISIANE done by Mr. De lisle in 1718.

N.B. THE Tuscaronts are now reconnd a sixth Nation and live between the Onondagos & Oneids and ye Necariages of Missilimakinac were received ye seventh Nation at Albany May 30 1723. at their own desire 80 Men of ye nation being present besides women and children

THE chief trade wth the far Indians is at ye Onondaga rivers mouth where they must all past to go towards CANADA.

PART OF NEW ENGLAND

PART OF CANADA
Quebec
Trois Rivieres
St. Laurence R.
Montreal
Chambly
lake Champlain
Cataracui R.
Fort Cataracui
CATARAQUI or ORONTARIO LAKE
The Countrys Conquered by the FIVE NATIONS
LAKE OF THE HURONS
THE UP PER LAKE
Outlaouacs or Necariages
Michilimakinac
LAKE MICHIGAN
Rr. St. Joseph
Huakil R.
The Miamis or Twightwis
Ouabache R.
Branches of the Missisipi
Ohio R.
Canahogue
LAKE ERIE OR ORSWEGO
Tufackrondie
Detroit or
Outanaes
A high Plain 70 Leagues Long
Niagara
carr place
Onondago
Onnontagues Sonnonthouans Cayugos Oneidos Onondagues
The Countrey of the FIVE NATIONS
Mohawk R.
Schenectady
Albany
New York
Long Island
Hudsons R.
NEW YORK
PENSYLVANIA
MARYLAND
Delaware R.
carr place to Canada

A Scale of English Miles

Copied for W. M. Darlington Esq. from Public Record Office, London.

Diorama of an Iroquois hunting group. Note the construction of the hunting lodge at left and the venison drying on the rack at right. In the center a deerskin is being skived. (N.Y. State Museum and Science Service)

Interior of an Algonquian wigwam, as reconstructed at Plimoth Plantation. Many a trail-weary frontiersman found hospitality in such a dwelling. (Plimoth Plantation Photo)

Great Captain   Fort Richmond Feb.ry 11 1742

Loron Speakes in the name of the rest

This Winter when our two men went to Boston and came back
again they told us what you said to them which is allong as if
had rec.d a Letter You know there is no body understands Indian
Georges and that was the reason we could not send an answer to
what you sent us — and now we come to Richmond where our lang
is understood ————————— Our hearts are towards you ever since
you have bin in Government ———— The men that came from Boston
told us you designed to see us at Georges we should all be much
rejoyced to see you there for we cannot conveniently meet you farth
Westward —— We much like your promise to comply with Govern
Dummers agreement with us ———— One thing we don't like (whi
we agreed uppon with Gov.r Dummer) we apprehend is not comp
with which was that if any goods rise our furrs were to rise w
them we solemly agreed with Gov.r Dummer that we should ha
for our furrs at Georges truckhouse as they then sold for at
Boston Your Excel.cy may please to inquire of Govern.t Dumm
the Treasurer and other Merch.t who buye furrs whether we hav
justice done us on this head ——— the truck matter here gives
8/ for Saples 16/ for Spring bever 18/ for Otters 20/ for Cat van
We now are kept much in the dark as to our trade the man that
mannages it understand very little as to our Language or trad
his being a Minister we a little wonder at his comming to trade hi
It was also agreed at Casco that we should allwayes have a full
Supply of Provisions and other things we need — now we want
all sorts of Provisions and many other nessesarys and have alon
time bin without them and in the middle of Winter the most
nessesary time we could want them in ——— We should be
glad there was a man at Georges that understood trading w
us and the Language. Our men mentioned Jabez Bradbu
unto your Excel.cy we like him well ———————

438

for want of Provission and through a mistake we have kild three horses
at Sagadahock on Small Point side we understod they were wild and
free for any body accordingly we dryd the flesh openly, two dayes after we
sold them fix men came to us with thier guns cockt demanding satisfac-
ppon thier appearing in such a hostile manner we flew to our guns one
of our men being wise told us we had better surrender our armes then
begin a quarrell which might be attended with such ill consiquences
and not understanding what these men said to us we delivered them four
guns and two hatchets, as a pledge for pay for the horses they intimating
we understod them to take them by violence if we did not resign them
promisse pay for the horses in the Spring uppon the delivery of our guns
are all in good health & give our Love and Service to your Excel-

Indian Marks

Sauess
Hannellas
Uxawaramet
Pau
Messer
Josph Mare
Ambaroes
Espeguant

Loron
Pemmorawet
Nemquid
Lewagem
Quuebenuit
Margaret

etter from the Eastern Indians to the Governor of Massachusetts concerning the fur
ade. Note how the signatories made their individual marks at the end. The letter is
uoted on page 148. (Secretary of the Commonwealth of Massachusetts)

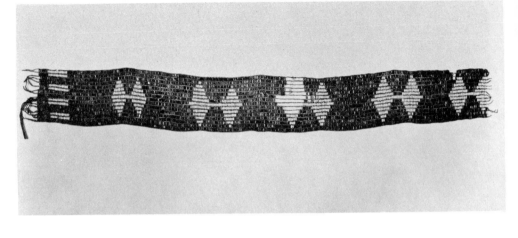

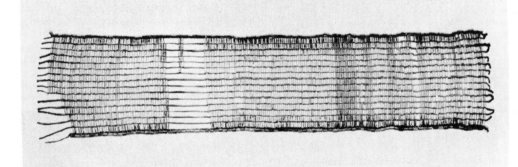

(Upper) Five Nations war wampum belt, 38 inches long. Wampum consists of cylindrical beads cut from shells and drilled lengthwise through the center. Dark wampum and white wampum were strung to form meaningful patterns. *(Lower)* Mohawk wampum belt, 25 inches long. Belts such as this were used in Indian diplomacy. *(Opposite)* A string of wampum such as was used in the Indian trade. This particular string is 112 inches long. (Museum of the American Indian, Heye Foundation)

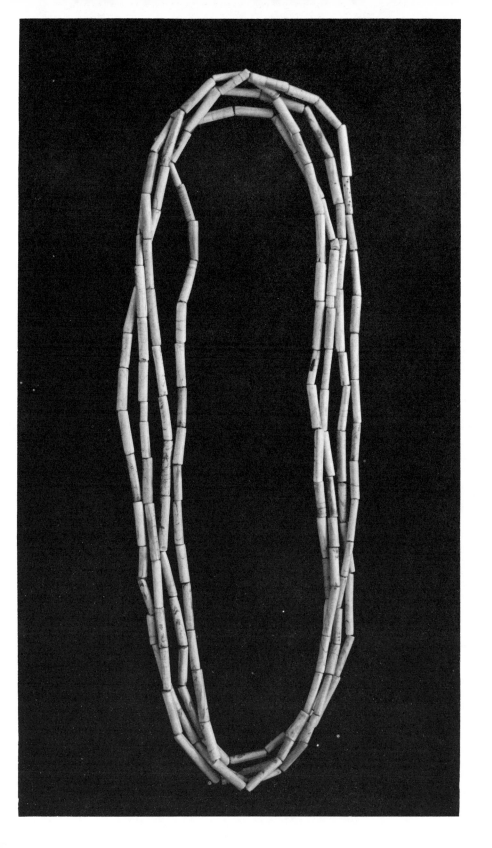

A pioneer housewife husking corn, as in the mid-seventeenth century. Indian corn, or maize, was a staple along much of the northern frontier. (Plimoth Plantation Photo)

The main street in a well-ordered frontier village, as seen at reconstructed Plimoth Plantation. Not all pioneering settlements were so neatly arranged or well maintained. (Plimoth Plantation Photo)

(*Opposite*) Tools and implements used by the pioneer farmer. Note especially the wooden plow, the A-shaped harrow, the scythe, the ox yoke, and the crude pitchforks. The two-wheeled cart was a luxury not all pioneers could afford. (New York State Historical Association, Cooperstown, N.Y.) (*Above*) A Palatine plow, dated 1759. (New York State Historical Association, Cooperstown, N.Y.)

New England pioneers erecting a dwelling. Note the frame construction and the way in which the vertical sheathing is being pegged in place. The man at the extreme left is making shingles with a mallet and frow. (Plimoth Plantation Photo)

A thatch-roofed cottage, such as was built by the Pilgrims at Plymouth.
(Plimoth Plantation Photo)

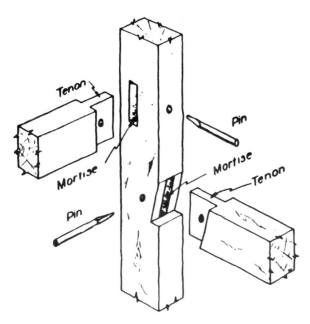

(Left) Mortise and tenon construction, a method employed on the frontier for joining timbers to form the frame of a house without using metal bolts or spikes. *(Below)* Using a broadax to square-hew a log. (Hugh Morrison)

A log being turned into planks at the saw pit. This is hard work, especially for the man in the pit. (Plimoth Plantation Photo)

Pioneer tools. On the wall may be seen three variants of the broadax, and on the chopping block is a typical felling ax. (New York State Historical Association, Cooperstown, N.Y.)

◁ **7** ▷

English-French Imperial Rivalry, 1689–1713

*E*arly in the history of English settlement along the northern frontier perceptive men began to view with apprehension the creeping approach of French power from the north. Prophetic were the words of Edward Trelawny who, writing from New England early in 1636, predicted that unless some effective measures were taken to check the French advance, "there will bee butt small hopes in Continuing our *plantations* so neere them who daylye drawe towards us, whose neighbourhood (I much feare) will prove very prejudiciall unto us."[1]

When King Philip was spreading ruin over New England with lavish hand in 1675, many of the colonists believed that French priests and traders were instigating and supplying the Indians as part of a plan to oust the English from the area.[2] In Maine the French coveted the land as far south as the Kennebec River and enjoyed increasing influence among the Abnaki Indians. To the west, in the area between Lake Champlain and Lake Erie, where valuable land and the lucrative fur trade were at stake, the French were even beginning to challenge the special relationship of the English with the Iroquois tribes. From the point of view of the English colonists, especially those interested in frontier land and trade, all this was extremely menacing. France was seen as the hovering, stalking, advancing enemy, seducing the savage nations to further its own ambitious ends.

In reality, the English too were expanding their area of occupation, so that the French had just as much reason for apprehension. As both sides enlarged their respective zones of activity, the great unoccupied buffer region in between was reduced, and the confrontation of French and English expansion became direct and dangerous. Unfortunately, there was no mutually recognized boundary between English and French territory on the northern frontier. Where rival claims overlapped, each side tried to hold its position or advance its claim by gaining the support of strategically located groups of Indians. By 1688 the danger of open conflict had become acute.

The first serious trouble occurred in Maine during the summer of 1688, after the English governor Edmund Andros confiscated the goods of Saint-Castin, a French trader on the Penobscot River. The Indians of Maine considered this action an affront to them and began to demonstrate their resentment in ways that quickly led to bloodshed. The spread of Indian anger was made clear the following June when a band of Pennacook suddenly attacked Dover, New Hampshire, killing almost two dozen colonists and carrying twenty-nine into captivity.[3]

While these alarming developments were taking place in northern New England, the Five Nations were burning with resentment against the French, who in 1687 had chastised them for hostile activity by ravaging the country of the Seneca. Adding to their anger was the treacherous act of the French governor in abducting some innocent kinsmen of the New York Indians and sending them to row in the galleys of Louis XIV. Now the Five Nations began taking their revenge. In August 1689 a large Iroquois war party pounced upon the French village of La Chine, near Montreal, and wrought fearful destruction, slaying the terror-stricken inhabitants without regard to age or sex.

Not long after this devastating blow the indomitable Frontenac, now seventy years old but still tough and vigorous, arrived in New France to begin a second administration as governor. His coming roughly coincided with the commencement of a major European conflict, the War of the League of Augsburg (or King William's War, as it was known in the English colonies). Frontenac's objective was to drive back the rising Anglo-Iroquois threat and if possible conquer the province of New York, thereby acquiring for New France an ice-free outlet to the sea and the richest portion of the English fur trade. Frontenac did not shrink from using the most deadly force available to him—mixed raiding parties of woods-wise *coureurs de bois* and fierce with defiance. Thereupon he landed his troops and opened fire. The operation was conducted with a notable lack of skill, and the army quickly became disheartened. Soon the attack had to be called off, the troops scrambled back to their ships, and the entire fleet withdrew. Thus ended in a humiliating sputter the first major attempt by colonial forces to wrest the key town of Quebec from the hands of the French.[8]

After 1690 the war settled down into a pattern of retaliation and counterretaliation which inflicted much suffering on frontier communities but contributed little toward a meaningful victory for either side. French raiding parties of *coureurs de bois* and Indians, usually led by experienced French officers, continued to spread terror among the isolated inhabitants of the frontier. Except for a few small forts at important locations, the English had no fixed defenses against these incursions other than the privately owned garrison houses. For offensive operations the colonies relied upon the militia, sending out patrols to watch for enemy warriors, or killer groups to track down and slay them in the woods. As a means of encouraging the troops in their pursuit of Indian raiders, the colony governments adopted the practice of paying bounties for enemy scalps, just as they might offer a reward for the heads of wolves or other predatory beasts.[9]

Some frontier communities came dangerously close to panic, the settlers threatening to abandon their holdings and rush pell-mell to safer ground. Should this happen, it could mean the collapse of the frontier, with woeful consequence for everyone who had invested capital in frontier lands, if not for the entire population. To prevent such a calamity, the General Court of Massachusetts passed an act in March 1695 forbidding residents in certain frontier towns to move elsewhere without prior permission from authority, on pain of forfeiture of their property. Those who had already moved were ordered back, unless they could hire a substitute to carry out their obligations to the town.[10] The reason behind this emergency decree is clear: every able-bodied male who quitted an exposed town weakened its defensive power and made more difficult the task of those who remained.

The terror that impelled families and even whole communities to abandon the frontier was not without justification. Frontier living in a time of Indian warfare carried with it the distinct possibility of violent death or frightful captivity. Back in 1682 all New England had thrilled to Mary Rowlandson's published account of her ordeal as a prisoner of the Indians during King Philip's War. Such captivities became almost commonplace during the subsequent intercolonial wars. Usually prisoners taken during Indian raids were forced to accompany their captors on a long hard march through the wilderness to Canada. In wintertime this in itself could be a terrible ordeal; captives too weak to stagger on were

Indian warriors. This meant that all the horrors of savage warfare would be loosed upon the English frontiersmen, for whenever those two breeds were brought together as a combat team in the wilderness, the restraints of civilization quickly gave way.

Such a team made its way south down the Champlain Valley in January 1689/90, snowshoes plocking through the snow with a resolute rhythm born of long experience and grim determination. Finally, on the night of February 8, they sighted the palisades of Schenectady. Pouring through the unguarded gate, the French and Indians quickly seized control of the village. Terrorized inhabitants were dragged from their houses to be slain by the tomahawk or held as prisoners. Almost every dwelling in Schenectady was burned, after which the exulting raiders disappeared into the forest, taking with them twenty-seven captives and considerable booty.[4] Behind them they left a mounting wave of panic that swept through the countryside to the very precincts of Albany. Frightened families began packing their belongings and hastening down the river to greater security at Manhattan.[5]

In March another war party made a highly successful raid on the frontier settlement of Salmon Falls in New Hampshire. Still later in the spring the combined French forces besieged the fort at Casco Bay and forced its surrender. Despite the stunning success of these operations, the French found their major objective, control of the Hudson River, beyond their immediate grasp. At the same time, their ruthless assaults upon the civilian populace infuriated the English and invited counterattack.

"Courage! Courage!" had been the counsel of an Iroquois orator. "In the Spring to Quebeck, take that Place, and you'll have your Feet on the Necks of the French, and all their Friends in America."[6] Considering that both New England and New York were still rent by internal divisions stemming from the Glorious Revolution, it is remarkable that they were able to undertake as ambitious a campaign as they did. The English plan was to strike to the very heart of New France, the fortified towns of Quebec and Montreal. For this purpose an expeditionary force was assembled at Albany, and a still larger force embarked in a fleet at Boston. Because of delays and hardships, the Albany force was able to advance no farther than Lake Champlain before giving up and turning back. Subsequently a small but determined raiding party led by John Schuyler did make an attack upon the French settlement of La Prairie across the river from Montreal, but this effort was of little strategic importance.[7]

The Boston expedition under the command of Sir William Phips, made its way up the St. Lawrence River. Arriving before the promontory of Quebec, Phips called upon the town to surrender, but was answered dispatched with a blow of the tomahawk. Some survivors lived with the Indians for months or even years, working for them as slaves, subject to their capricious whims and drunken rages. Others were fortunate enough to be purchased by the French, and either held in prison or allowed to assume the role of servant in a Canadian household, with the possibility of eventual return to the English colonies.

Even in the purgatory of Indian captivity there were some dauntless souls who made the best of hard circumstances. One much-admired New England heroine, who well demonstrates both the desperation and the murderous vengefulness that such a war could arouse in the human heart, was Hannah Duston of Haverhill, Massachusetts. This woman, accompanied by two companions, escaped from her captors, and not empty-handed at that—she took with her ten dripping Indian scalps![11] James Alexander, a captive with a flair for the practical joke, took his revenge in a different fashion. One dark night, being sent out by the Indians to fetch water, Alexander left the empty kettle on a piece of sloping ground and ran back to the Indian camp. Puffing and wide-eyed, he blurted out that he had seen some Mohawk warriors lurking near the spring. His master went to see for himself, with Alexander showing the way. Coming again to the place where he had left the kettle, the prankster gave it a good kick, sending it clattering down the slope among the dark shapes of tree stumps, which served very nicely as pseudo-Mohawk. Instantly the frightened Indian "could see a *Mohawk* in every Stump on motion, *and turn'd Tail to,* and he was the best Man that could run fastest."[12] The stunt was carried off so well that the entire village hastily decamped.

Frontier dwellers experiencing the dangers of Indian warfare sometimes felt that the colony government was not doing enough to protect them from the enemy. While it is true that in many cases the responsible authorities were slow to act and niggardly when they did act, the deeper truth is that none of the colonies had the means to erect an airtight system of defense for its entire frontier. The zone of settlement was too extensive and the populace too thinly spread to block the enemy at every point, especially an enemy as mobile as the French and Indians. As Thomas Hutchinson later explained,

> The settlement of a new country could never be effected, if the inhabitants should confine themselves to cities or walled towns. A frontier there must be, and nothing less than making every house a fort, and furnishing every traveller with a strong guard, could have been an effectual security against an enemy, as greedy after their prey as a wolf, and to whom the woods were equally natural and familiar.[13]

In other words, a man who undertook to be a pioneer had to accept as an occupational hazard the possibility of being scalped.

On July 11, 1691, Governor Henry Sloughter of New York sent an important message to the governors of some of the other English colonies, reminding them of the supreme strategic importance of Albany, "the only bulwark and safe guard of all Their Majestys plantacons on the main of America...."[14] The loss of Albany, the governor pointed out, would destroy the Anglo-Iroquois alliance, without which the English could not hope to retain their colonies in North America. Sloughter then went on to appeal for better intercolonial cooperation in a common war effort. In particular he proposed that the various colonies "agree to a certain fund to be levyed amongst us all in proporcon, for the raising and paying of men dureing this warr, that if possible the memory of the French might be rooted out of America; all which by a hearty union, amongst our selves and due deliberation may be easily effected." There was ample precedent for such an arrangement in the New England Confederation, which had brought King Philip's War to a victorious conclusion, but Sloughter's proposal evoked little enthusiasm from the colonies. Each government was jealous of its own prerogatives and fearful that it might be required to make some contribution detrimental to its own well-being.

The inability of the English colonies to subordinate their individual concerns to a unified effort against the common enemy was a major weakness that persisted throughout the succession of colonial wars. It might well have been a fatal flaw. Typically, the colonies nearest to the danger were most ardent for united action, while colonies not immediately threatened showed a marked reluctance to commit themselves. In Pennsylvania, Quaker pacifism prevented that colony from offering to its hard-pressed neighbors much more than pious advice, until Pennsylvania itself began to feel the lash of Indian fury during the last of the French and Indian wars.

The Five Nations, upon whom the English relied so heavily whenever there was bloody work to be done, soon took notice of the divisions among the English. To them it seemed strange that the various colonies, all supposedly one people under one great king, did not give wholehearted support to each other in time of war. It was a Mohawk sachem who put the matter most bluntly:

> . . . you Sett us on dayly to fight & destroy your Enemies, & bidd us goe on with Courage, but wee See not that you doe anything to it yourSelfs, neither doe wee See any great Strenth you have to oppose them if they Enemy should breake out upon you; we hear of no great matter is like to be done at Sea, we hear nothing of itt; The warr must also be hottly Pursued on your Sides, what is it that our neighbors of n: England and the Rest of the English that are in Covenant with us doe, they all Stay att home & Sett us on to doe the worke. . . .[15]

The Mohawk charge stung because it was true. But the English might well have reminded the sachem that the Five Nations themselves did not always act in perfect unity, even in time of war, a fact that was to become more apparent as the years went by.

*A*FTER EIGHT YEARS of desultory raiding back and forth across a wilderness borderland, King William's War was brought to an indecisive conclusion by the Treaty of Ryswick in September 1697. In virtually every respect the situation as it had existed before 1689 was left unchanged, and the boundaries between French and English territory in North America remained in dispute. One did not need the gift of prophecy to foretell the early resumption of hostilities; indeed, the years following the Peace of Ryswick were no more than a breathing-space between wars. During this uneasy interval the northern frontier was confronted with three problems—resettlement of areas abandoned during the war, recementing of Indian relations, and preparations for future emergencies.

With the future so uncertain it is no wonder that the majority of colonists, remembering all too well the bloody fate of many unfortunate pioneering families during the war, felt no compelling urge to move to the remote frontier. The greatest enthusiasts for resettlement were the men who had made investments in frontier real estate as a speculative venture, for the value of such property was closely linked with the progress of settlement. Pioneering families who had sunk every scrap of their wealth in a frontier farm often had little choice but to trek back into the wilderness, start rebuilding, and hope that the future would bring a larger measure of security. In general, the process of resettlement proved hesitant and uncertain; the frontier gradually restabilized, but showed little inclination to advance.

The tribal groups of Maine, usually called simply the "Eastern Indians" by the government of Massachusetts, found it expedient to get back into the good graces of the English, at least for the time being. Although many of them were still strongly under the influence of the French, they longed for the advantages of English trade, which had been denied them during the war. Covenants were renewed in January 1698/99, September 1699, and June 1701, affording some small degree of comfort to the English and certain minor concessions to the Indians.[16] Neither side felt any real confidence in the other, however, and the Indians made clear their intention to remain neutral in any future conflict, a position that the English had to accept even though they considered it the next thing to being pro-French.

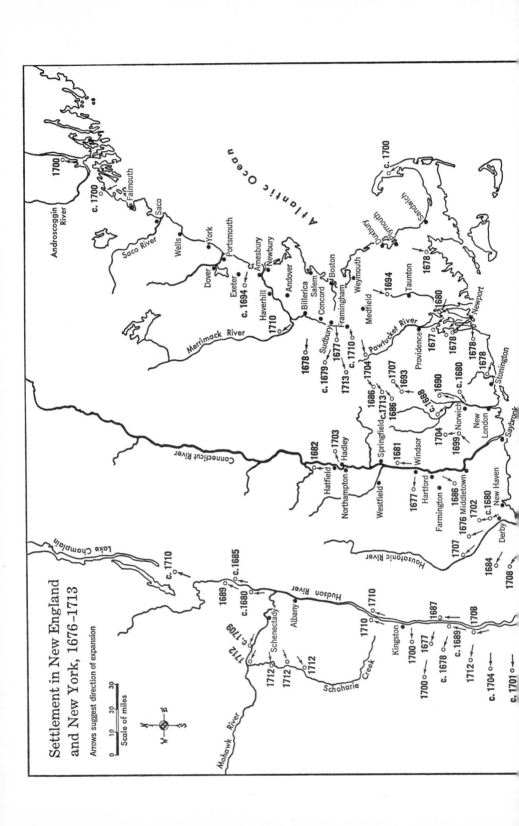

Settlement in New England and New York, 1676–1713

Arrows suggest direction of expansion

Scale of miles
0   10   20   30

Atlantic Ocean

Lake Champlain

Androscoggin River

Saco River

Saco

Merrimack River

Connecticut River

Hudson River

Mohawk River

Schoharie Creek

Housatonic River

Pawtucket River

1700

c. 1700
Falmouth

Wells

York

Dover

Portsmouth

Exeter
c. 1694

Haverhill

Amesbury
Newbury

Andover

Billerica

Concord
Salem

Boston

Framingham

Weymouth

Medfield

Taunton
1694

Duxbury
Plymouth

Sandwich
c. 1700

Newport
1678

1680

Providence
1677

1678

1678

1678

Stonington

c. 1680

1690

Norwich
1704

New London
1699

Saybrook

1693

1707

1686
c. 1713

c. 1685

1686

Springfield
1681

Windsor

Hatfield
1682

Hadley
1703

Northampton

Westfield

Hartford
1677

Farmington

Middletown
1686

1676

New Haven
c. 1680

Derby
1702

1684

1708

1707

c. 1710

1689
c. 1680

c. 1685

1712
c. 1709
Schenectady

Albany

1712
1712

1712

1710

1710

Kingston

1700
1700

1677
c. 1678

1687

c. 1689
1708

1712
c. 1704

c. 1701

1710

Sudbury
c. 1679

1677
1713

1710

Billerica
1710

1678

As for the Iroquois of New York, they emerged from King William's War appreciably reduced in strength and not a little disenchanted with their friends the English. Governor Bellomont reported that the population of the Five Nations during the period 1689–1700 (probably counting only the warriors) dropped from 3500 to about 1100, with the Mohawk reduced almost to nothing.[17] These losses were partly the result of casualties in war and partly the consequence of defections to the French. In a spirit of disillusionment the Iroquois Confederacy was beginning to reassess its traditional policy of support for the English and antagonism toward the French. Within the villages of the Five Nations a sharp factional split developed, one faction preferring the traditional policy and the other, under the influence of French priests and converted Indians, seeking to establish connections with Canada. It is easy to understand why the province of New York viewed this development with profound concern.

Basically, the Iroquois were impressed with French strength in the West and alarmed by the mounting English appetite for more wilderness land. They now realized that if either the French or the English should become supreme in America, their own future would be seriously threatened. Sensing that they themselves might constitute a balance of power in the imperial rivalry, the Iroquois began feeling their way toward a position of neutrality that would permit them to continue their profitable economic relationship with the English and yet stand clear of war's destruction. This new posture the English were powerless to prevent, at least for the present.

During the summer of 1701 the Five Nations made two diplomatic moves of great importance. They renewed their friendship with the English, even going so far as to place large portions of their vast hunting grounds under the protection of the king of England; they also came to an agreement at Montreal with the French and the French Indians, promising to remain neutral in future wars in return for a French promise to respect their neutrality.[18] The agreement with the French is of special significance for it marks a definite turning point in Iroquois policy, the beginnings of a strategy consisting largely of an attempt to play the English and the French off against each other, with a view to preventing either from becoming dominant. This new policy had marked effects upon the future development of the northern frontier, while helping the Five Nations survive the intercolonial wars of the eighteenth century.

In fort building as well as in diplomacy the French were making significant progress. They were able to establish a fortified outpost at Detroit, guarding the important water route between Lake Erie and Lake Huron, and another at Mackinac, where Lake Huron joins Lake Michigan. Together with Fort Frontenac and the outpost at Niagara, these new forts were important links in the chain of posts designed to guarantee French domination of the Great Lakes and the Indian trade of the surrounding area. The English had no comparable network.

In 1700 Governor Bellomont of New York ruefully informed the authorities in London that the forts on the frontier of his province "are in so Ruinous a Condition that they will now scarse bear the firing of a Gun upon them." In particular, the forts at Albany and Schenectady "are not only scandalously weak but do us unspeakable Mischeif with our Indians, Who conceive a proportionable Idea of the Kings Power and Greatness."[19]

Bellomont, who was alert to the future importance of the West, made some positive proposals for strengthening the northern frontier. The forts at Albany and Schenectady should be reconstructed of stone, he said, and the others put in a state of repair. In addition, he suggested that two new forts be erected, one at the southern end of Lake George to guard the entrance to the Champlain Valley and the other in the Onondaga country near the southeastern shore of Lake Ontario to counteract the effect of Fort Frontenac. Just as in Dongan's day, New York was reluctant to appropriate funds for such expensive projects, and the neighboring colonies were not inclined to contribute, even though the forts might benefit them indirectly. Consequently, little was done, and the disunited English colonies slid into the next great war in a state of confused and feverish unpreparedness.

*Q*UEEN ANNE'S WAR began in 1702 over an issue of dynastic power in Europe, but as late as the summer of 1703 an uneasy quiet prevailed along the length of the northern frontier. The first blow from the north came in August of that year when bands of Abnaki warriors, led by a few Frenchmen, descended upon the coastal village of Wells, Maine, and other isolated settlements in the vicinity. The attacks conformed to a pattern already well established along a blood-stained frontier—stealthy approach, sudden assault, indiscriminate slaughter, destruction by fire, hasty retreat with plunder and prisoners. As one contemporary historian lamented, ". . . there was no safety to him that went out, nor him that came in, but dreadful calamity on every side."[20] So war came again to the northern frontier, with the prizes exactly the same as before—opportunity for further expansion, and domination of the Indian trade.

Ever since the end of the previous war, the Albany merchants had been busily trying to reconstruct their fur trade, not only with the

Iroquois and other Indians but even indirectly with the French. There is clear evidence that an undercover trade between Montreal and Albany, profitable to both parties, had come into being. Most of the Albany merchants were of Dutch background, men who were scarcely subject to the stirrings of English patriotism. Furthermore, so great was the influence of these merchants in their own colony that governmental policy tended to follow rather closely upon their heels. Therefore New York, relying upon the pledge made by New France not to invade the Iroquois country if the Five Nations remained neutral, saw no good reason why it should become involved in this new war to the jeopardy of its own frontier and the disruption of the valuable fur trade.[21] With the onset of Queen Anne's War, then, New England was left to battle the French and their Indians virtually alone.

One of the most exposed settlements on the New England frontier was Deerfield in the upper Connecticut Valley, a town already well acquainted with the horrors of wilderness warfare. Deerfield's condition in the autumn of 1703 was depicted in stark outline by the local pastor, the Reverend John Williams, who wrote,

> We have been driven from our houses & home lots into the fort . . . . we have in the alarms several times been wholey taken off from any business, the whole town kept in our children of 12 or 13 years & under we have been afraid to improve in the feild for fear of the enemy. (our town plat & meadows all lay exposed to the veiw of an enemy if they come at any time on the mountains.) We have been crowded to gather into houses to the preventing indoor affairs being carryed on to any advantage . . . . strangers tell us they would not live where we do for twenty times as much as we do the enemy having such an advantage of the river to come down upon us . . . . the fronteir difficulties of a place so remote from others & so exposed as ours are more then can be known if not felt.[22]

Shortly before dawn on the last day of February 1703/4 Mr. Williams was startled out of his sleep by the battering of hatchets on the door and shutters of his house, a thundering overture to another in the long series of frontier tragedies. Earlier that night a war party of about two hundred and fifty Frenchmen and Indians had made its stealthy approach while the weary watch on the walls, bored by long days of uneventful waiting, retired to sleep. The deep snow had drifted high against the palisades, forming a sort of ramp for the pack of shadowy figures that swarmed over the walls into the area of habitation. Within a matter of minutes the place was at their mercy.[23]

What this kind of warfare could mean to a frontier family is well illustrated by the experience of Deerfield's minister. At the moment when the Indian hatchets began hammering on the door, the members of the

Williams family then at home included father, mother, and seven children. Two of the children, a six-year-old boy and a new baby, were killed outright by the attackers. Williams, his wife, and the remaining five children were led into the wintry wilderness as captives. When Mrs. Williams proved unable to keep up with the party, an Indian killed her with a tomahawk. Later the father and his children were separated as the Indians broke up into diverse bands. Mr. Williams eventually reached the vicinity of Quebec, where he lived until exchanged more than two years later. Four of the five Williams children also were eventually released, and returned to New England. The fifth, Eunice, was converted to Roman Catholicism, remained among the Indians by her own choice, and married a Caughnawaga Indian. Many years after her capture, Eunice and her Indian husband visited the scenes of her childhood. But by this time she was above all other considerations a Canadian Catholic squaw, and could not be persuaded to remain among the white Protestants, her own kin.[24] Actually, during the Indian wars there were quite a few cases of English prisoners, especially children, who adopted the Indian way of life, losing all interest in their former homes. This certainly suggests that the Indians could be hospitable as well as cruel to those they held in their power.

The daily perils of life on the frontier constantly wove their influence into the warp and woof of pioneer existence, coloring the pattern of pioneer character. During those times of great fear and stress, French and English alike learned to despise and hate each other and the Indians who opposed them. For a century now the frontiersmen and the Indians had been clawing at each other sporadically and sometimes viciously. This tragic interracial conflict was already becoming central in the story of the westward movement, destined to color the tale with blood until almost the opening of our own century. Where must we lay the blame for this great tragedy? Historians of long ago assumed, as did many of the colonists, that the Indians were nothing more than ignorant savages, motivated solely by primitive instincts that made them crafty, cruel, and treacherous—in short, little better than wild beasts. Other writers, seeking to overcome such unfair prejudice, have gone to the opposite extreme in picturing the Indians as noble children of nature, endowed with all the simple virtues uncorrupted by the taint of civilization. Neither interpretation is satisfactory, for both ignore some of the evidence upon which a valid judgment must be based, and both fail to recognize the great complexity of the problem.

The tides of history carried the Europeans to America; it is quite unreasonable to argue that the Europeans had no right to come without invitation from the natives. The first arrivals came believing that they had at least as much right to the land as did the Indians, and they came with good intentions of dealing justly. The trouble was that an irreversible process had been started, challenging the Indians with the dynamic power of a civilization with which their relatively simple culture could not compete. In this developing confrontation, selfish and even vicious attitudes began to bubble to the surface among both races, amid growing misinterpretation and mistrust. Both sides committed wrongs against the other; both retaliated. Sometimes these episodes were petty, sometimes serious, but each one added to the antipathy that was spawning the interracial wars. To what extent the story might have been a happier one if there had been more Massasoits, more Roger Williamses, and more William Penns in the American wilderness, we can only surmise.

There is no denying that the Indians were victimized, just as there is no denying that well-intentioned frontier folk were cruelly mistreated, even slaughtered, by Indians. To try to lay the blame for violence and ruthless cruelty on one side or the other is futile, for neither was wholly at fault or completely innocent. Point a finger at the cold-blooded massacre of the Pequot tribe by Christian Puritans in 1637, and you must then consider the slaughter of white settlers by Virginia Indians in 1622, an episode well-known to the New Englanders. And before that there was the kidnaping of innocent Indians by English sea captains.

In a sense the Indians were the unwitting victims of European power politics, as Europe's age-old quarrels began to spread around the world. Every major war came to have its counterpart in the colonies, and the geographical location of the Indians between the colonial rivals inevitably involved them in the strife. Intertribal antagonisms were readily exploited by the Europeans for their own advantage, while at the same time the vigorous expansionism of the colonies drove the Indians to violent measures of resistance. All this put the problem of Indian-white relations beyond any real possibility of a simple, peaceful solution, and so the tragedy of interracial warfare continued to spread its ugly blot across the land.

Even as the unfolding of frontier rivalries promoted bitter hostility toward the French, or the English, or the Indians, so too there began to appear among the English themselves early traces of sectional antagonism. New Englanders despised New Yorkers for their reluctance to join in hostilities against a common foe. In Massachusetts it was even said that some of the plunder from ravaged frontier homes had a way of turning up in the markets of Albany. Pacifistic Pennsylvanians were charged with callous indifference to the plight of fellow countrymen in areas where warfare raged. And along much of the exposed frontier there was rising resentment against fellow colonists who resided comfortably far from the danger zone, back in some prospering eastern town, resisting every attempt to provide more adequate defenses for the frontier people because it would mean higher taxes. This nascent sectionalism, as yet fairly weak and only vaguely oriented, may be traced back at least as far as the time of King Philip's War, but not until the eighteenth century did it begin to assume a role of major significance in the growth of America.

Most frontiersmen accepted the French and Indian wars as a bitter condition of life in America and simply tried to carry on as best they could under difficult circumstances. Whenever possible they continued their routine work on the land. Occasionally they joined a major military expedition, or helped patrol the woods, or spent long hours on guard duty at garrison house or fort. We "have our Hands much taken from Our Labours by Watching, Warding, Frequent Alarms," was a typical frontier complaint in those bloody years. "Many of Us are driven from Our Homes. Much of Our stock is killed by the Heathen: Many Of Our able Men removed from Us, And Many thinking of Moveing if they knew whither to goe. . . . And Wee daily grow more & more feeble and deplorable: daily Walking and working with fear, Trembling & Jeopardy of life."[25]

At times the deprivation and suffering inflicted by enemy raiding parties came close to breaking the morale of the people. Numerous petitions sent from afflicted communities to the governmental authorities, describing their plight and pleading for an abatement of taxes or other forms of assistance, indicate how fragile was the spirit of rugged self-reliance in these early years. Seldom did hard-pressed frontier communities show reluctance to accept almost any form of aid that could be wheedled from the government.[26] The following complaint from one discouraged Massachusetts town, in the form of a petition to the General Court, reveals much about the mood of the frontier in those days:

> Broockfield   October 23   1710
>
> The humbel petisian of you[r] poar Destresed people Heear caleth aloud for pity & help Therefor we Adres the Gieneral Coart that They would consider us and set us in sum way or othr where By we may have a subsistance so long as you shall se ca[u]se to continue us heere we Did not com heear with out order neiter are wee wiling To goe away wit out order There Fore wee Are wiling to leave our selves with you to Doe for and with us as you think Best you knowe our Dificaltyes as to the comman enenye and Besides That our mill Dam is Broakn so y^t we have neither Bread nor meal But what we Fetch 30 miles which is intolirable to Bar either For Hors or man which puteth us upon in Deavering to rebuilding of it which is inposibel For us to Doe with out your pity and Helpe winter is so neear y^t we must intreat you to Doe sumthing as sone as may bee nomore But are your pooar Destresed Begers[27]

In this particular case the General Court appropriated £10 to help the town rebuild its dam. The truth of the matter is that the pioneers, in colonial times at least, living on an exposed frontier in time of great danger, never deceived themselves into believing that they were self-sufficient. Instead, they looked eastward for support and sometimes wished fervently that their ambition or poverty had not carried them so far away from comfort and security.

On the other hand, moments of great peril sometimes challenged the settlers to amazing heights of heroism. The stories of such occasions are many, forming a significant part of our national folk tradition. There was the April day at Oyster River (Durham), New Hampshire, for example, when the Indian enemy struck without warning. All the men were at work some distance from their dwellings, but the women of the settlement were congregated in a single garrison house, and upon that one building the Indians concentrated their attack. Believing that their only hope lay in concealing the fact that no men were present to defend the house, the undaunted women rearranged their hair and donned their husbands' jackets and hats. Then, seizing muskets, they poured such a hot fire upon the Indians that eventually the attack was abandoned and the people were saved.[28] In all justice, the husbands should have served supper to their womenfolk that evening!

*F*OR NEW ENGLAND, the high points of Queen Anne's War were the occasional offensive operations that provided the angry and frustrated settlers some opportunity to strike a telling blow against the enemy. The first such expedition was led by Benjamin Church, the old hero of King Philip's War, who in 1704 secured the coast of eastern Maine and burned down the French settlement at Grand Pré in Acadia.[29] More ambitious was the campaign of 1709, directed against the French strongholds on the St. Lawrence. An army of some fifteen hundred men, under the command of Colonel Francis Nicholson, advanced from Albany to Wood Creek near the southern end of Lake Champlain, in anticipation of strong support in the St. Lawrence by a fleet to be sent from England. Soon, however, Nicholson's army began to weaken through disease and desertion, and the endless task of conveying bulky supplies from the rear bases up along the wilderness routes proved more formidable than the enemy. The seal of total failure was put on the campaign when the English fleet was diverted to other duties. Nicholson's weary and discouraged men had no choice but to withdraw and disband.[30] The following year Colonel Nicholson led an expedition that seized Port Royal in Acadia, a minor triumph that left the major target of the St. Lawrence Valley still firmly under French control. Quebec continued to glitter remotely as the supreme prize whose capture would signal the dissolution of the French menace along the entire northern frontier.[31]

It was in 1711 that all circumstances, from London to the northern frontier, finally fitted together for a supreme attempt against the bastion of the St. Lawrence. England sent a powerful fleet under Sir Hovenden Walker, with six thousand regular troops. This armada arrived at Boston in June, where it was further strengthened by the addition of more than a thousand colonial troops commanded by Samuel Vetch. At Albany a force of more than two thousand men, colonists and Indians, was being assembled by Colonel Nicholson for an advance up the Champlain Valley. The various colonies contributed men and money to the endeavor with remarkably little grumbling, for all were eager to taste the fruits of victory. Qualified support came even from Pennsylvania which, although it declined to send soldiers, did appropriate £2000 for the campaign. Several sachems of the Five Nations journeyed to Boston, where they were treated as dignitaries and shown the might of the combined land and naval forces, to convince them that this time the English had both the means and the will to beat the French.[32]

With the highest of hopes the expedition sailed out of Boston Harbor at the end of July, destined for one of the most ignominious and unnecessary failures of all. Due largely to the timidity and incompetence of the naval commander, nine of the ships were wrecked on the rocky north shore of the St. Lawrence nearly three hundred miles short of the objective. Thereupon the fleet withdrew without making any further attempt to reach Quebec. Nicholson and his army had gone as far as Wood Creek when the news of Walker's failure arrived. Furious, the Colonel hurled his wig to the ground and stamped on it; then in bitter disappointment he again led most of his army back to Albany.[33] Quebec, as the nucleus of French power in North America, remained a continuing threat to the northern frontier of the English.

In the spring of 1713 Queen Anne's War was brought to an end by the Treaty of Utrecht. For the northern frontier the most significant portion of the treaty was the transfer of Acadia, now called Nova Scotia, from French to British rule. The arrangement was far from perfect, however, for the boundary of Nova Scotia remained in dispute, and the French acquired great opportunity for future intrigue among the local populace, both French and Indian. But for the moment, at least, the clouds of warfare were dispersed, and the frontier folk basked in the unaccustomed sunshine of peace and relative security.

*W*HAT THE PERIOD of warfare from 1689 to 1713 meant to the development of the northern frontier may be perceived by a comparative study of maps showing population distribution for the years 1675, 1700, and 1720.[34] During this period of hostilities three spearheads of frontier advance pointed north toward Canada—one along the coast of Maine, a second along the Connecticut River, and a third along the Hudson. Each was located in 1720 at about the same place as in 1675 and 1700. In Maine, English settlements stretched to the mouth of the Kennebec River, with only a few daring souls residing precariously in the region beyond; on the upper Connecticut River English settlement barely reached across the northern boundary of Massachusetts; in New York there were few pioneers at any great distance beyond Schenectady, either in 1675 or in 1720. Most of the expansion that did take place during the period was lateral, a process of filling in the spaces between the spearheads. But farther south, where the wars were little felt, the frontier advanced with vigor, especially westward from Philadelphia in the years between 1700 and 1720.

By the end of Queen Anne's War the northern frontier was completing its first century of growth. During this time the population of the northern English colonies had increased from a mere handful to about two hundred thousand. It was the continuing growth of this population, vigorous and assertive, that was creating most of the force behind the expansion of the frontier. Throughout the period these colonists, still essentially Europeans, had been absorbed in the life-and-death business of learning how to cope successfully with the wilderness environment. Their conflicts with the Indians had grown from limited, local affairs to complex and widespread struggles, closely intertwined with the wars of the rival European powers.

As a result of all their experiences, good and bad, the settlers were developing ways and attitudes more American than European, although the transformation, so intriguing to students of history, certainly was a gradual and subtle one. On the other hand, there is little evidence to indicate that the first century of frontier experience was sufficient to produce in remoter regions a kind of American distinctly different from the colonist who resided in or near the large coastal towns, even with the sectional antagonism that had begun to intrude upon the scene. The truth of the matter is that in 1713 virtually the entire area of settlement still remained so close to the frontier experience that no significant distinction can be made. If there was to be in America a meaningful dichotomy between East and West, it would appear later among a more diversified people.

◁ 8 ▷

The Expanding Frontier, 1713–1743

*T*he Peace of Utrecht in 1713 brought to an end the first phase of intense Anglo-French rivalry in North America and introduced thirty years of uneasy peace along the northern frontier. Both sides were able to advance into the wilderness with a greater degree of assurance. While the French continued their attempts at deep penetration of the continent, the swarming populace of the English colonies resumed its pressure against the adjacent wilderness, signaling the start of a new period of expansion. Although Anglo-French rivalry was still focused most actively on the fur trade, there was increasing emphasis upon Indian alliances and the effective control of territory. Both sides had come to realize the great importance of Indian support, especially that of the Iroquois Confederacy, and sought to strengthen their influence with the various tribes.

The astonishing growth of population in the English colonies after 1713, most notably in Pennsylvania but to some degree in all the colonies, increased the demand for new land. It has been estimated that between 1710 and 1740 the population of Pennsylvania increased from

24,450 to 85,637, while that of all the northern colonies together increased from 184,686 to 510,249. The population of New Hampshire, which had long remained small because of wartime dangers, increased from 5,681 to 23,256 during this period.[1] As thousands upon thousands of immigrants poured into the colonies following the Peace of Utrecht, men with capital to invest became keenly aware of the profits to be made by catering to the mounting demand for new land. Speculation in frontier tracts developed into something of a mania.

Although England continued to provide considerable numbers of immigrants, the most important groups of newcomers after 1713 were the Germans and the Ulster Scots, or Scotch-Irish. Many came as indentured servants or redemptioners, willing to exchange temporary loss of freedom and years of hard labor for the chance to make a new life for themselves in America. Upon completing their terms of service these poor folk often gathered their few possessions and took up land at the far edge of settlement. In this way the frontier was constantly being reinforced with new blood.

A rather unusual group of immigrant pioneers were the nearly 2500 refugees from the German Palatinate who were transported to the province of New York at the expense of the British government in 1710.[2] These unfortunate, destitute people had agreed to work in the production of much-needed naval stores until they had compensated the government for its expense in transporting and settling them. The Palatines began their hard new life on the Hudson River tracts that had been selected for the project, working as unfree men at a job for which they had little inclination or experience. Within a little more than two years the undertaking collapsed because of mismanagement and inadequate financing, whereupon many of the Palatines, now free of an onerous obligation but unhappily without a livelihood, removed themselves to Albany and Schenectady.

Thirty-five miles to the west of the Hudson, beyond a wilderness area of forested hills, the small but turbulent Schoharie River flows northward from the Catskill Mountains to enter the Mohawk twenty miles west of Schenectady. The valley of this little river was known to the Palatines, who believed that the British government had promised the place to them. Indeed, they looked upon Schoharie as a veritable vale of opportunity. Some fifty or sixty families were so impatient to begin a new life that they would not wait even for the passage of winter, but late in 1712 made their way overland through the snow and settled along the Schoharie River about twenty miles from its mouth. Other Palatine families joined them there the following spring.

Doggedly determined to succeed, the Schoharie pioneers were pitifully unprepared for the conditions confronting them. Because of their previous status as unfree laborers, they lacked even the most essential tools for clearing and working the land. Some men made crude tools from forest material and in one way or another began to till the soil. Fortunately the local Indians were friendly, and the assistance they gave the settlers during the difficult early months was partly responsible for their survival.

The Schoharie land had not been officially allotted to the Palatines, which meant that they were occupying it as squatters, without title. In 1714 Governor Hunter issued grants in the area to other persons, thereby making them the legal owners, but the Palatines stubbornly declined to buy or lease their holdings from the grantees or to evacuate the territory. Their argument was the classic one resorted to by frontier squatters everywhere: we are the ones who have suffered the hardships of first settlement; it is our labor that has improved the land; we now have homes and cultivated fields in what used to be only a wilderness; we will not now give up all this to men whose only right to the land is a scrap of paper. When the provincial authorities sent an officer to eject the squatters, the Schoharie pioneers gave him such a hot reception that he found it expedient to withdraw in undignified haste. He was not the last of his kind to learn that on the remote frontier a lawbook is no match for a cocked gun.[3]

During this period there was also a growing interest in the Mohawk Valley, the ancient passageway leading from the upper Hudson to Lake Ontario. Men who had occasion to make their way along the Mohawk River could not help but be impressed by the wild beauty of the valley. Not far above the river's mouth was Cohoes Falls, whose sound of plunging waters was "like the roar of a Storm at Sea heard from the Land in the dead of night."[4] It was this formidable barrier that forced westbound travelers to enter upon the river by means of an overland route from Albany rather than by boat at the river's mouth. Above the falls the Mohawk wound for a hundred miles through wooded hills, leading eventually to a portage from which other waterways led still farther west to Lake Ontario. Along the banks of the Mohawk, especially at places where tributary streams made their entrance, were sizable flats of rich bottom land, eminently suited to farming, and on the higher reaches above the river was much good grazing land.

In 1712, the year in which the Palatines entered the Schoharie Valley, a fort was established at the place where the Schoharie enters the Mohawk, to protect the few farmers who had dared settle west of Schenectady.[5] This fort, named after Governor Hunter, gave some slight assurance to the pioneers, but even after the coming of peace in 1713 colonists showed little enthusiasm for settling west of the Schoharie. As always, too, the Albany fur interests were opposed to any advance of the farming frontier that might threaten their hold on the Indian trade, and the Iroquois likewise grumbled at the prospect of a renewed westward movement. For about ten years, therefore, little progress was made, although the discovery of how well the Mohawk lands were suited to the growing of wheat aroused the interest of potential settlers.[6]

Governor Hunter was succeeded by William Burnet, who inherited the troublesome problem of the Palatines. Recognizing that what the Palatines needed above all was a secure title to good land and viewing them as a possible barrier against future Indian attacks, Burnet granted them two tracts in the upper Mohawk Valley: Stone Arabia and Burnetsfield, some twenty and forty miles west of Fort Hunter, respectively. Here some of the Palatines from Schoharie and others who had remained in the Hudson Valley settled in the mid-1720s. Once more these sturdy folk underwent the hardships of pioneering on newly opened land; their success meant a significant expansion of the Mohawk Valley frontier, with farms now located more than fifty miles west of Schenectady.

When in 1727 New York established a fortified outpost on the eastern shore of Lake Ontario, guarding the western entrance to the Mohawk Valley route, still other potential settlers became actively interested in the region. But men of great influence had the inside track, and especially in the 1730s much of the desirable land along the Mohawk River was granted in large portions to various speculators. These investors were still to some extent under the influence of the old patroonship concept of landholding, preferring to people their land with tenants rather than divide and sell it to independent farmers. Since few ambitious, active men wanted to become tenants, the system had the effect of retarding frontier expansion in New York. Only gradually during the 1730s did pioneering farmers move upriver beyond Fort Hunter to occupy the vacant lands. By the end of the decade the German colony at Burnetsfield still marked the farthest point of regular agricultural settlement in the Mohawk Valley.

Attractive land was discovered also in Cherry Valley, fifteen miles west of the Schoharie. In 1738 a Scot named John Lindesay acquired a grant to the area, with the intention of planting a settlement of Scotch-Irish pioneers. Lindesay took his family and some servants to Cherry Valley in 1740. During their first winter they came close to starvation, but were saved from such a fate by a friendly Indian who supplied them with food. The following year a group of about thirty Scotch-Irish settlers, attracted from the New Hampshire frontier, joined the Lindesays at Cherry Valley, and the isolated little community slowly began to take on a look of permanence.[7] By 1743 the line of advanced settlement in New York reached from Saratoga on the Hudson River

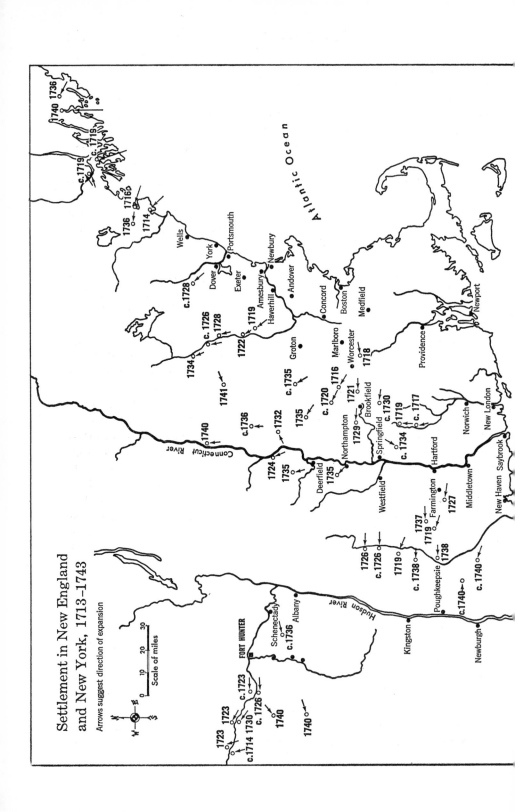

Settlement in New England and New York, 1713–1743

Arrows suggest direction of expansion

Scale of miles
W E
N S
0 10 20 30

Atlantic Ocean

Connecticut River

Hudson River

FORT HUNTER
Schenectady
Albany
c.1736
Kingston
Newburgh

1723
1723
c.1714 1730
c.1726
1740
1740 o
c.1723

1726
c.1726
1719 o
c.1738
Poughkeepsie
c.1740 o
c.1740 o
1737
1719 o
1738

Wells
York
Portsmouth
Dover
Exeter
Amesbury
Haverhill
Newbury
Andover
Concord
Boston
Medfield
Newport

1740 1736
c.1719
c.1719
1716
1736
1714

c.1728
c.1726
1728
1719
1722
1734
1741 o

Groton
Marlboro
Worcester
Providence
1718

c.1735
1720
1716
1721
Brookfield
c.1730
c.1719
c.1717
Northampton
1729
Springfield
c.1734
Hartford
Norwich
New London
1735
1735
c.1736
1732
1740
1724
1735
Deerfield
1735
Westfield
Farmington
1727
Middletown
New Haven Saybrook
1719 o

west along the north side of the Mohawk as far as Burnetsfield, and then south to Cherry Valley and the Schoharie villages, forming a rough perimeter based on Albany, with a radius of from twenty-five to seventy miles.

*N*EW ENGLAND saw the Peace of Utrecht as an opportunity to regain lost ground by resettling abandoned towns, perhaps even to extend the area of settlement far beyond its pre-1689 limits. The Eastern Indians had accepted the verdict of war, having made their peace with the government of Massachusetts in July 1713, and could be expected to refrain from intimidating the frontier settlers as they straggled back to their burned houses and neglected fields. Numerous investors, their heads full of grandiose plans for peopling the wilderness at a profit, were busy lining up the necessary political and economic support for their projects.[8]

A large part in the subsequent advance of the New England frontier was played by hundreds of Scotch-Irish immigrants who arrived at Boston in 1718 under the encouragement of certain prominent land speculators. The newcomers spread out in several directions. Some settled in Worcester, Massachusetts, and from there fanned out to found other towns such as Rutland, Pelham, Warren, Blandford, and Colerain. Later the vigorous Scotch-Irish stream moved farther up the Connecticut Valley into New Hampshire and Vermont.[9] Another contingent of the 1718 migration advanced across the Merrimack River to a tract of land granted them by the General Court, where in 1719 they constructed the new village of Londonderry.[10] Still others succumbed to the blandishments of investors in the Kennebec area of Maine, who were promising one hundred acres free to each family and free transportation from Boston to the site. In this way the towns of Brunswick and Topsham on the Androscoggin River were begun, while at the same time other pioneering families were settling on the lower Kennebec. By 1720 the eastern extremity of the frontier was firmly anchored at the Kennebec River, and some ambitious men were even dreaming of exploiting the area between the Kennebec and the St. Croix.[11]

The French, of course, were well aware of the English activity on the Kennebec and viewed it as a threat to their own position. Their immediate hope for stopping it was embodied in the person of a devoted and courageous priest named Sebastian Rale, who presided over a mission post among the Abnaki Indians at a place called Norridgewock, many miles up the Kennebec River. Rale's influence upon the natives was in proportion to his courage; the English, who were painfully aware of his presence on the Kennebec, charged that he was inciting his Indians to acts of open hostility against the settlers. One New England leader described Rale as "a constant & Notorious Fomenter & Incendiary to the Indians to kill, burn, & destroy. . . ."[12]

If Rale was indeed stirring up the Abnaki against the English, as the evidence indicates, his task was made easier because of Indian resentment against the sharp practices of the New England traders and the determined advance of the pioneering farmers. There could be no doubt that the Indians would, if they could, force the frontier back to the vicinity of Saco and Wells, which would mean a retreat of about forty miles. English conferences with the Indian leaders in 1717 and again in 1719 did little to resolve the problem; clearly Rale, as an agent of the French regime at Quebec, was convincing the tribesmen that French power could give decisive backing to their resistance against English encroachments.[13]

Matters came to a head in 1722 when the Indians, alarmed by a Massachusetts attempt to seize Father Rale, retaliated with an attack upon the new settlements, setting fire to a large number of houses at Brunswick and carrying off several of the inhabitants. The government of Massachusetts thereupon declared war against the Eastern Indians.[14] The ensuing conflict, which lasted for more than three years, is usually known as Dummer's War, being named after the governor of the Bay Colony. Neither France nor England was directly involved.

In August 1724 the colonists struck a fatal blow when a special raiding force of New England men surprised Rale's fortified mission station, killing not only a number of Indian leaders but also the fighting priest himself.[15] As a result of this devastating attack the scattered Indians were greatly weakened and offered little more than sporadic resistance to the English.

In order to encourage frontiersmen to continue harrassing the enemy, the government of Massachusetts offered large bounties for scalps. Indian hunting took on the appearance of a potentially profitable business venture. A group of hardy frontiersmen would band together under a recognized leader for the express purpose of hunting down Indians and sharing the proceeds. The most famous of these bands was that of Captain John Lovewell of Dunstable. In 1725, after one or two fairly successful forays, Lovewell led his men northward to a place known as Pigwacket, in what is now Fryeburg, Maine. There on May 8 they engaged a strong party of Indians in what quickly developed into a furious fight. Lovewell soon realized that he was up against more warriors than he could comfortably handle; in fact, the badly mauled scalp hunters were lucky to make an escape with the loss of only about a third of their number. Left at the scene of battle was the body of Lovewell himself.

What frontier warfare could be like is illustrated by the case of one of Lovewell's party who because of his wounds was unable to join the retreat. At his request his departing comrades left him a loaded gun so that when the Indians came to take his scalp he might kill one more of them first. During the retreat another man, dying of his wounds, urged that his fleeing comrades go on without him, and this was done.[16]

After Lovewell's defeat, popular enthusiasm for scalp hunting diminished noticeably in Massachusetts. Finally, however, when the Indians saw that further hostilities would be unavailing and would at the same time deprive them of much-needed English trading goods, they buried their pride and sent a delegation to Boston to arrange a peace. An agreement was formally reached on December 15, 1725, bringing Dummer's War to an end.[17]

The pacification of the Indians was followed by a new spurt of activity on the part of settlers and speculators. From Falmouth to the Kennebec, and west to the Connecticut River, pioneer houses once more were being raised. A resident of Falmouth noted in his journal on October 27, 1726, that "There is a considerable number of people down here, to look out for farms, designing to settle here."[18] When people were convinced that the Indian menace had abated, even the abandoned settlements on the Androscoggin began to be reoccupied.

In New Hampshire, too, advance parties of pioneers began to clear land and plant new settlements beyond the zone of the old frontier, which before 1713 had remained fairly close to the lower reaches of the Piscataqua River. After the establishment of the Scotch-Irish town of Londonderry in 1719, other townships were laid out beyond that settlement and gradually occupied by pioneers coming up from older communities in Massachusetts and southern New Hampshire.[19]

Farther to the west, in the upper Connecticut Valley, the government of Massachusetts in 1724 built Fort Dummer on the west bank of the river eleven miles above Northfield. Constructed of great squared logs of yellow pine laid horizontally, this strong outpost lent additional confidence to pioneers seeking to establish homes in that region.[20] By 1736 there was a settlement at Upper Ashuelot (now Keene, New Hampshire), and four years later a few hardy pioneers had established themselves as far north as Number Four, where Charlestown now stands.[21] All during these years of renewed frontier advance in New England the Indians remained watchful—and sullen.

*D*URING the seventeenth century the lumber industry of northern New England had developed rapidly, hacking away at the apparently limitless miles of pine forest with such complete disregard for conservation that the lower reaches of the Piscataqua and other such rivers became almost stripped of good trees. Gradually the lumbermen extended their activities eastward toward the Kennebec, especially after 1713. It is no exaggeration to say that in the early decades of the eighteenth century lumbering took precedence over agriculture along the Maine frontier, with many of the pioneers looking for good stands of sound, straight trees rather than plots of fertile soil, and spending most of their energy felling and processing timber rather than cultivating crops. All along the lower reaches of the rivers was to be heard the monotonous rasp of water-driven sawmills.[22]

As early as 1691 the English government had signified its concern for a future supply of masts for the Royal Navy by including in the new charter for Massachusetts a provision reserving to the Crown "all trees of the diameter of twenty-four inches and upwards at twelve inches from the ground" standing on land not privately owned.[23] Responsibility for enforcing the royal policy rested with the surveyor of the woods, an official whose duties were certain to make him highly unpopular with the lumbermen. Starting in 1705 the post was held by John Bridger, who had to cope with a hostile attitude that extended all the way from lumber camps to the paneled chamber of the House of Representatives in Boston. Pure economic interest—the desire of an important frontier industry and the host of people dependent upon it to remain untrammeled in their exploitation of natural resources—formed the basis of opposition. Evasion of the law by men who could think of dozens of ways to conceal or disguise their acts became for Bridger a constant problem.

In 1711 Parliament extended the restrictive policy to cover the entire area from Maine to New Jersey, but the new law received about as much deference from the frontiersmen as the old. No doubt the violators—lumbermen who actually chopped down the reserved trees, and others who took care to see that no plank wider than twenty-four inches emerged from a sawmill to arouse the suspicion of government inspectors—would not have been so bold in their defiance of the law if they had not enjoyed the powerful backing of colonial leaders. Dr. Elisha Cooke and other prominent Massachusetts men who had a stake in the lumber industry maneuvered adroitly to foil the surveyor of the woods and his agents. One tactic which they tried was to lay out townships spreading over much of Maine's accessible forest land, without any intention of immediate settlement but merely to claim that a township was private property and hence exempt from the forest law. The same maneuver was tried in New Hampshire.

England's increasing concern for her sources of timber was revealed by two enactments of Parliament in 1721. Lumber was placed on the list of enumerated commodities, which meant that American lumber was not to be shipped from the colonies to non-British ports, and a forest law even more stringent than the act of 1711 was passed, forbidding the felling of any pine tree on land not included within the bounds of a township. Still the lumbermen showed their contempt for such legislation by wholesale evasion. The deep forest of northern New England proved a difficult place for royal officials to teach rough frontiersmen the principle of strict adherence to law. In 1729 Parliament acted again, placing on the books a comprehensive statute reiterating the basic provisions of previous forest legislation and authorizing the royal surveyors to mark all reserved trees with the Broad Arrow. Shaped like a crow's foot, this symbol of royal prerogative was made by three swift blows of a hatchet. From 1729 on, the surest way to start an argument in a lumber town was to utter the words "Broad Arrow."

The job of the surveyor and his deputies was not an easy one, but it had its compensations. There were splendid opportunities for graft, and it was not unusual for the king's men to accept bribes for permitting favored individuals to ignore the Broad Arrow policy. The whole lumber industry knew that this sort of bribery was going on, which only helped to intensify the general contempt for the law. Royal deputies who did attempt to prevent the cutting of reserved timber were in danger of rough treatment at the hands of angry lumbermen; at Exeter, New Hampshire, resistance reached the proportions of a riot.[24] For many New Englanders the spirit of resistance to royal authority had its first beginnings in their resentment against the Broad Arrow, mark of the mother country's apparent determination to interfere with the American economy.

There can be no doubt that the quest for timber was a major factor in the expansion of the New England frontier, especially in Maine and New Hampshire. The seventy sawmills on the Piscataqua River alone produced in one year approximately six million feet of planks, shingles, and staves.[25] Just how many men were directly involved in lumbering is impossible to determine, but there must have been hundreds of them, laboriously chipping away at the edges of the great forest. The ring of their axes signaled the advance of a distinctly different type of pioneer.

During the years from 1713 to 1743 the zone of settlement in New England was expanding in several directions, haltingly it is true but with a persistence that boded ill for the native tribes and for the French as well. Eastward along the coast of Maine, northward through New Hampshire and up the Connecticut Valley, westward into the area of the Berkshires and northwestern Connecticut, rumbled the ox-drawn carts of the pioneers. At the same time, many localities that had previously been bypassed in favor of more promising land were now gradually being settled, so that the whole area was becoming more solidly populated. Likewise in New York the zone of settlement advanced not only northward up the Hudson River, but also westward through the Mohawk Valley and along the Schoharie, while farther to the south, in New Jersey, a constantly increasing population of farmers was busily changing wilderness into cultivated land.

*T*HE MOST DYNAMIC expansion of all was taking place in Pennsylvania, where the Peace of Utrecht nearly coincided with the beginnings of a large-scale influx of Germans and Ulster Scots. Especially after 1717 the Scotch-Irish poured into Penn's Quaker colony, not because they were averse to fighting (which they definitely were not) but because that colony seemed to offer them the best opportunity to acquire land and begin the pursuit of happiness in a tolerant society. According to one observer in Philadelphia, the summer of 1717 saw the arrival of "12 or 13 sayle of ships from the North of Ireland with a swarm of people."[26] They continued to arrive year after year, with occasional great spurts of immigration. In Pennsylvania the Indians were peaceful; soil and climate were known to be of the best; and there was plenty of available land stretching in a great arc from the falls of the Delaware to the lower reaches of the Susquehanna.

So well did Pennsylvania advertise its advantages that all too many naïve and hopeful toilers from Europe arrived at Philadelphia with anticipation to match the sentiments expressed in the following lines of poetry, published in the *Pennsylvania Gazette* for January 21, 1728/9:

> Hail *Pennsylvania*! hail! thou happy Land,
> Where Plenty scatters with a lavish Hand:
> Amidst the Woods we view the Friendly Vine,
> With Purple Pride, spontaniously entwine;
> Where various Cates arise without the Toil
> Of labouring Hind, to cleave the stubborn Soil;
> The skipping Deer in wild Meanders sport,
> And *Ceres*, with *Pomona*, keep their Court:

A Thousand winged Choristers delight
At once the list'ning Ear, and ravish'd Sight:
Where free from Clouds we breath Aetherial Air,
And *Sol* keeps Holiday throught the Year:

Nothing there of sweat and blisters, rattlesnakes and wolves, or even Indian marauders, with all of which the Pennsylvania pioneers would have to contend. More realistic is the description given by a modern historian, who depicts the lonely, somber setting of the deep wilderness: "Darkness, gloom, silence—these were conditions of the western forest. Song birds progressed into the woods only as clearings became common; at first the sole sounds were the cries of eagles or ravens and at night the hooting of owls, the howling of wolves, and the occasional wild scream of a panther launching itself on its prey."[27]

Pennsylvania's German and Scotch-Irish pioneers advanced into the wilderness much as water creeps over uneven ground, spreading into diverse rivulets that in turn subdivide as they probe and seek the easiest routes, sometimes diverted by obstacles in their path, but never brought to a full stop so long as more water keeps up the pressure in the rear. In Pennsylvania that pressure was always there, as more and more immigrants continued to arrive, anxious to establish homes for themselves. They came mostly in groups, with the predominant Scotch-Irish and Germans offering an interesting contrast. Both nationalities were on the move in Pennsylvania at the same time, often advancing along the same routes into the same valleys, but almost never did they intermingle. Germans would take up land in one part of a valley and Scotch-Irish in another.[28] While the Germans usually settled down permanently and devoted all their energy to a meticulous and thrifty husbanding of the soil, the more venturesome Scotch-Irish were inclined to light in one place for awhile and then move on. Later arrivals usually filtered on through the settled areas until they reached virgin land. For these reasons the Scotch-Irish soon became recognized as the toughest, most adventurous pioneers on the northern frontier, and in Pennsylvania at least, the ones most active in expanding the area of settlement toward the west.

Most of the people who moved into the back country of Pennsylvania had arrived originally at one of three ports—Lewes, Newcastle, or Philadelphia. From the west bank of the Delaware three major routes led north and northwest into the wilderness. The easiest route was the easternmost, up the valley of the Delaware River beyond Philadelphia. The second was up the Schuylkill toward the Blue Mountains. Farther to the west lay the third route, the most challenging of all, up the valley of the Susquehanna River. Whichever route was chosen, the practice of the pioneers was to move up the main river until they came to unoccupied fertile land, usually along the banks of a tributary stream or creek where good water was available to drive millwheels and slake the thirst of man and beast. At such places they settled down, often several families in the same neighborhood, and began to clear the land for farming.

Fifteen miles northeast of Philadelphia, Neshaminy Creek enters the Delaware River from the north. Along this inviting stream numbers of Scotch-Irish families began to settle during the early 1720s, perhaps even earlier. By 1728 there were settlers as far north as Easton, where the Lehigh River joins the Delaware, and within no more than two or three years Scotch-Irish pioneers were to be found at a number of places in what is now Northampton County. In 1740 and 1741 industrious Moravians established religious communities at Nazareth and Bethlehem.

Although the entrance to the Schuylkill route to the interior was conveniently located at Philadelphia, that river was less inviting to the pioneers than the Delaware because of its rocks and shoals. Nevertheless, it did lead in the right direction—toward frontier land—and so it served as an avenue for many. Settlements were made along Skippack and Perkiomen creeks, both of which flow into the Schuylkill from the north. By about 1740 there were Amish folk living in the northwestern part of the present Berks County, along the Northkill Creek. Earlier, during the 1720s, some discontented Palatine families from the Schoharie Valley in New York had migrated down the Susquehanna River and established homes along Tulpehocken Creek, a tributary of the Schuylkill. Among these families was that of Conrad Weiser, a young man soon to play a leading role in the Indian affairs of Pennsylvania.

The principal surge toward the frontier was from Newcastle and Philadelphia west to the Susquehanna and then north to the many tributary streams flowing in from both sides. In this movement the Scotch-Irish were definitely predominant. Beginning in 1710, Scotch-Irish settlers founded a number of communities in what is now the western portion of Chester County, some forty miles west of Philadelphia. From this region the restless stream of pioneers continued onward until the waters of the Susquehanna diverted them toward the north. In the meantime they were being joined by other land seekers moving up from Maryland. By about 1725 there were pioneering settlements in the Pequea Valley, along Chickies Creek, and at Derry, Donegal, and Paxtang. Within the next few years other land was taken up along Conewago, Swatara, Monda, and Paxtang creeks, which are eastern tributaries of the Susquehanna. So rapidly had settlement progressed that in 1729 the region was organized as Lancaster County.[29]

While these developments were taking place on the eastern side

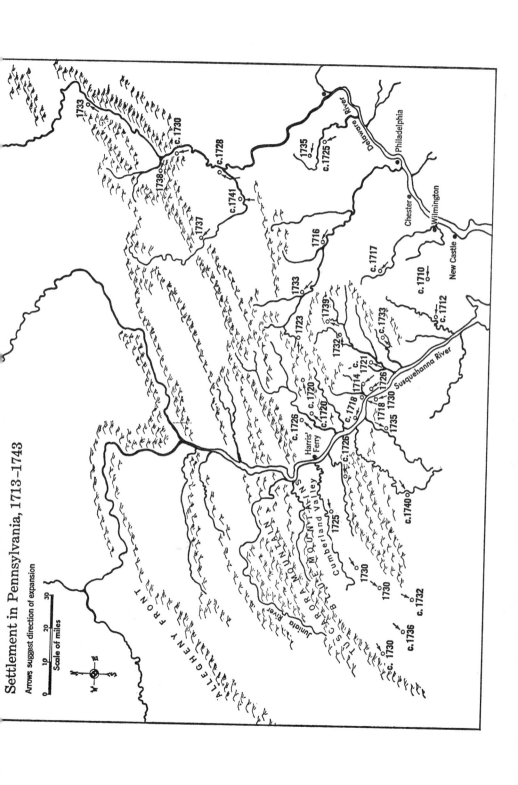

Settlement in Pennsylvania, 1713–1743

Arrows suggest direction of expansion

Scale of miles

0 10 20 30

of the Susquehanna, other pioneers were discovering the good land lying along the streams to the west. Some frontier families were moving directly up the western side of the river from Maryland, but the main Pennsylvania migration crossed the river at Harris' Ferry, where there had been a trading post since about 1705, and then moved southwestward down the fertile and inviting Cumberland Valley. As early as 1725 there was at least one enterprising settler not far from the present Carlisle, a good fifteen miles west of the Susquehanna. It has been estimated that by 1731 there were some four hundred families living in the Cumberland Valley.[30] About 1736, Scotch-Irish pioneers founded the present Mercersburg, and five years later a few settlers were beginning to enter what is now Fulton County. The movement southwestward from the Susquehanna was the beginning of a momentous parade of pioneers into one of the most important avenues of frontier advance, the Great Valley of the Appalachians.

*F*ROM THE TIME when William Penn first invited settlers to his proprietary province there had existed, at least in theory, an orderly process for the acquisition of land in Pennsylvania. By the terms of the royal charter, all land belonged to the proprietor. In time a land office was established as the agency for selling proprietary land to those who wished to settle upon it. Prior to 1719 the established price for land was £5 per 100 acres, with an annual quitrent of one shilling to be paid to the proprietor. Then the price was doubled. In 1732 there was a further increase to £15 per 100 acres.[31] Increases in the price of land vexed the Indians; they had originally sold out for relatively small payment, and the higher prices made them suspect that they had been cheated. James Logan, the provincial secretary, tried to reassure the Indians by explaining that land was like iron, of little worth in its natural state but increasingly valuable as developed and utilized. In the case of Indian land, said Logan, "the English make it of Value by using it."[32]

It is true that the value of Pennsylvania real estate was enhanced by the increasing demand for good land, a demand constantly fed by the continuing stream of immigration. It is equally true that the proprietors, the heirs of William Penn, were eager to obtain as much revenue as possible from their province. At about the same time that the price of land was increased in 1732, the westward movement had reached the first range of the Appalachians and was beginning to turn southward into the Cumberland Valley. That valley, in turn, was an avenue leading toward the back country of Virginia, where good land could be obtained at much lower cost than in proprietary Pennsylvania. No wonder, then, that thousands of frontier folk during the next three or four decades moved southward from the back country of Pennsylvania, following the Great Valley of the Appalachians, until they came to land that could be had almost for the taking. Later some would begin venturing westward into Kentucky and Tennessee.

Many of the Scotch-Irish in Pennsylvania, being poor, simply ignored the niceties of legal purchase and settled on land to which they had no title. These squatters often remained unmolested by the authorities for a number of years, during which time they would labor hard to clear the land, erect buildings, and cultivate fields. When the rightful owner did finally show up to challenge their possession, demanding a price commensurate with the improved condition of the property, the squatters were understandably resentful and even fierce in their resistance. The investment of their own labor, they believed, gave them a right more valid than his. In cases where squatters had settled on unassigned land the authorities sometimes accorded them the right of preemption, that is, first priority as purchasers when the land was put up for sale, at a price commensurate with the condition of the land before it was improved.[33]

More and more, as time went on, the Indians in Pennsylvania became uneasy about the rapid spread of settlement across the land which had once been theirs. They were resentful, in particular, about English appropriation of land at the forks of the Delaware, the Palatine migration to Tulpehocken Creek, and English claims to land along the upper Susquehanna River.[34] The problem was complicated by the fact that the Iroquois Confederacy exercised jurisdiction over the Indians of Pennsylvania, including the Delawares, and claimed much of the land toward which the frontier of settlement was moving. For some years now, the valley of the Susquehanna River had been used by the Five Nations as an area of Indian colonization, a region to which they invited various displaced groups of Indians to live under Iroquois supervision.[35]

In the 1720s some of the Delawares and other Indians in eastern Pennsylvania, disturbed by the apparently relentless forward thrust of European settlement, began migrating westward. For a time they established their camps in the area around the forks of the Susquehanna, but many of them continued their migration until they were settled along the Allegheny and upper Ohio rivers. There, by 1731, they began to come under the influence of the French, a development that caused mounting alarm in Pennsylvania.

The faith of the Pennsylvania Indians in the integrity of the English was further undermined by the so-called Walking Purchase of 1737. Many years earlier the Indians had deeded to William Penn a parcel of land along the west bank of the Delaware. Apparently the terms of the grant were deliberately vague, for at that time there was plenty of land to be had and Penn's main interest in the tract was its frontage along the river. In any event, nothing much was done about the grant until 1734, when the son of William Penn reactivated the claim and demanded the land. By this time land in that region had become much more valuable, and so, in a spirit quite different from that of either the first proprietor or the Indians who had made the original grant, the English laid careful plans to squeeze from the vague terms of the deed as many thousands of acres as they possibly could. In partial justification, it might be said that the Delawares themselves had not been entirely fair in their dealings with the English, sometimes repudiating agreements already made and demanding additional compensation for land previously sold. But two wrongs never make a right, and what was done by the English in the Walking Purchase of 1737 was a good cut less than fair.[36]

As defined in the old deed, the boundary of the tract in question was to extend from a certain point on the bank of the Delaware River inland as far as a man could go on foot in a day and a half, and then back to the river again. With these peculiar terms in mind, the proprietors' agents began careful preparation, which included a preliminary survey of the route to be followed by the "walkers" and the clearing of a path along that route so that there would be no obstacles to slow their progress. With this advantage, certainly never contemplated by the original parties to the bargain, a special team of "walkers" was able in the specified day and a half to cover "a prodigious Extent of Country," to be exact, sixty-four miles in a straight line.[37] Then, to compound the flimflam, the surveyors laid the return line not the shortest way to the Delaware, as the Indians might have expected, but at an angle of more than ninety degrees from the walking line, which made it run parallel to the river for many miles. In this way a huge tract was included within the terms of the old Indian deed, to the outrage of the Delawares, who saw themselves openly gulled and helpless to prevent the consequences.

The Walking Purchase of 1737 reveals quite clearly the growing contempt for the local Indians felt by the provincial authorities, who saw the Delawares as a disunited rabble, not capable of adhering to a consistent policy and hence not worthy of regard. In fact, during the early 1730s Pennsylvania had been forging a new Indian policy, based upon recognition of Iroquois jurisdiction over the various tribal groups within the colony. Henceforth the colonial authorities would pay less direct attention to the local groups and instead deal directly with the Iroquois, relying upon them to make the local Indians behave themselves and honor their commitments.[38] None of the tribes then living in Pennsylvania dared resist the Iroquois, so the transition was made without serious difficulty.

The role that the Iroquois Confederacy was coming to play in the Indian affairs of Pennsylvania is well demonstrated by the great Indian conference held at Philadelphia in July 1742. That was nearly five years after the completion of the Walking Purchase, which supposedly had conveyed to the English the land at the forks of the Delaware. Pennsylvania now complained that a stubborn remnant of the Delaware tribe still remained on that land, refusing to give way before the advance of English settlement. The Iroquois leaders heard the charge, gave it due consideration, and then in the presence of all the delegates from the various tribes administered to the Delawares a never-to-be-forgotten tongue-lashing, ordering them to quit the area and betake themselves to the upper reaches of the Susquehanna. There was no doubt who was boss. The Delawares did as they were told, but they took with them in their westward trek a smouldering resentment of their treatment at the hands of the white men, a resentment that helped open their ears to the cajolery of the French. Delaware animosity was to exact a heavy price from the frontier settlers of Pennsylvania for the land they had obtained, honestly or otherwise.[39]

*T*HE TECHNIQUES of successful pioneering in the eastern woodlands, learned through hard experience during the seventeenth century, were utilized by an ever-increasing army of frontiersmen from Maine to Pennsylvania in the years following the Peace of Utrecht. Many of these people had been born and raised under frontier conditions, and were hardened to meet the severe demands made upon them. Others were trying it for the first time, often with the help of experienced friends and neighbors. The frontier of the eighteenth century attracted many types—family men and confirmed bachelors, saintly Christians and crass materialists, honest farmers and scheming fakers, good team men and lone wolves. By 1743 the northern frontier was far-flung and diverse, peopled by men of various nationalities and sects, pursuing their fortunes in a variety of ways. The experience of the past had convinced them, or most of them, that America had a future in the west, a future that could be realized only by a continuing struggle to overcome the two major obstacles, geographical and human. The former they were mastering by experience; the latter, they now realized, included not only the Indians, whom most frontiersmen feared or despised, but also the French of Canada, recognized as a persistent, often daring, sometimes deadly, foe. The French and the Indians together constituted a threat that no settler on the northern frontier and no responsible colonial official could afford to minimize or ignore.

◁ 9 ▷

The Fur Trade and English-French Rivalry

$\mathcal{T}$he year 1689 opened a period of warfare between England and France in North America that was to continue, with occasional intervals of uneasy peace, until the conquest of Canada in 1760. During this period the two rival empires maneuvered and pushed for domination of the great fur trade of the continent, not so much because it was essential for their economic prosperity, although the income from the trade was indeed considerable, but because it was so closely identified with Indian relations. The various tribes, having become utterly dependent upon European trading goods, gravitated toward whichever colony was able to trade most regularly and effectively with them. Both the English and the French recognized that alliances with the Indians, especially with key groups such as the Iroquois Confederacy, were essential to the expansion of their colonies.

The Board of Trade, Britain's governmental committee of imperial administration, in a noteworthy report of 1721 showed its own awareness of the close relationship between the Indian trade and Indian alignment when it recommended that new forts be built "in such places where they may best serve to secure and inlarge Our Trade, and Interest with the Indians, & break the Designs of the French in these parts."[1] Noting that the future growth of the English colonies was dependent upon the success of trade relations with the Indians, the Board deplored the "unreasonable avarice of our Indian Traders" and urged the adoption of effective regulations to protect the Indians from unfair practices tending to alienate them from the English.

By its very nature the Indian trade constantly bred avarice, corruption, degradation, and violence. The competition for profits was becoming ever more intense. With much of the actual trading being carried on in the remote wilderness through hasty bargaining between profit-hungry white traders and naïve, often ignorant Indians, all kinds of abuses were rampant. Effective control of trade practices to prevent alienation of the Indians was constantly attempted and seldom achieved. Even a superficial scanning of the records of nearly any English colony on the northern frontier will disclose repeated attempts to suppress the abuses in the fur trade; the frequent reiteration of rules and regulations indicates how ineffective such attempts usually were.

Many traders saw no wrong in taking advantage of an Indian. Cadwallader Colden, the eighteenth-century authority on Indian affairs in New York, tells of one prominent merchant who defrauded a whole group of Indians by selling them kegs filled with water rather than rum. Anticipating that the kegs would not be opened until his customers were hundreds of miles away in their own country, he concealed his fraud by rum-soaking the rags that were used to make the bung-stoppers tight, so that a sniffing Indian nose would have no cause for suspicion. As it happened, however, the Indians discovered the fraud before they had gone very far, and hastened back to complain against the cheating merchant. Their complaints were in vain. The citizens of the area sent the culprit to sit not in jail but in the provincial legislature, and the attempt to prosecute him for his fraud was conveniently dropped.[2] Nor was he the only one to sell water in place of rum. A New York law of 1735 suggests that adulteration was a fairly common practice among the traders.[3] No wonder that, as Colden remarked, "The Indians . . . will on no occasion trust an Albany man. . . ."[4]

There is not the slightest reason to suppose that the New York traders as a group were appreciably more grasping or dishonest than those of New England or Pennsylvania. Everywhere that the trade was practiced there were unscrupulous men who tricked and cheated the Indians, thereby threatening the stability of Anglo-Indian relations. Again and again the Indians lodged complaints about such behavior, but colonial authorities were either unwilling or unable to bring the trade under strict and effective control.

Charles Thomson, a Pennsylvanian who was well acquainted with the Indians and their problems, was outspoken in his condemnation of the traders. By "suffering a Parcel of Banditti, under the Character of Traders, to run up and down from one *Indian* Town to another, cheating and debauching the *Indians*," he said, "we have given them an ill Opinion of our Religion and Manners, and lost their Esteem and Friendship."[5] This situation played into the hands of the French, who were not slow to exploit the anger and chagrin of the natives. It is paradoxical that the English, in order to extend their political influence among the tribes, had to build up a trade among them, a trade which invariably bred abuses whose effect was to alienate the Indians. As a rule, however, the lure of relatively inexpensive English trading goods was sufficient to overcome Indian resentment, making it possible for English influence to creep forward ever farther into the west.

Rum and other alcoholic beverages, always an important ingredient in the Indian trade, continued their demoralizing course among the Indians. Their long-range effects upon the health, morals, and general well-being of every tribe that participated were little short of disastrous. Missionaries seeking to uplift the Indians joined governors and other responsible officials in denouncing the excesses, and even some of the traders themselves, at least the more perceptive and humane ones, added their voices to the chorus of protest. Governor George Thomas of Pennsylvania solemnly expressed his apprehension that

> the Indian Trade as it is now carry'd on will involve us in some fatal Quarrel with the Indians. Our Traders in Defiance of the Law carry Spirituous Liquors amongst them, and take the Advantage of their inordinate Appetite for it to cheat them of their Skins and their Wampum . . . and often to debauch their Wives into the Bargain. Is it to be wondered at then, if when they Recover from the Drunken fit they should take severe Revenges.[6]

Three Pennsylvania commissioners, of whom Benjamin Franklin was one, advised the provincial government that liquor obtained from traders had caused the Indians to become "dissolute, enfeebled and indolent when sober, and untractable and mischievous in their Liquor, always quarrelling, and often murdering one another."[7] All this suggests that the white man's beverages were probably as deadly to the Indians as the white man's guns and bullets.

In their sober moments the Indians themselves, or their chiefs, begged the colonial authorities to bring the liquor traffic under control so as to prevent the utter degradation and ruin of the Indians. At the great Indian conference held at Carlisle, Pennsylvania, in October 1753, the Oneida sachem Scaroyady said to the English delegates, in all frankness,

. . . Rum ruins us. We beg you would prevent its coming in such Quantities, by regulating the Traders. . . . We desire it may be forbidden, and none sold in the Indian Country; but that if the Indians will have any, they may go among the Inhabitants, and deal with them for it. When these Whiskey Traders come, they bring thirty or forty Cags, and put them down before us, and make us Drink; and get all the skins that should go to pay the Debts we have contracted for Goods bought of the Fair Traders; and by this Means, we not only ruin ourselves, but them too. These Wicked Whiskey Sellers, when they have once got the Indians in Liquor, make them sell their very Cloaths from their Backs—In short if this practice be continued, we must be inevitably ruined. We most earnestly therefore beseech you to remedy it.[8]

The temptation and dilemma of the Indians were well illustrated by Scaroyady himself who, after completing his speech, made a gift to the English, saying, "Our Women and Young People present you with this Bundle of skins, desiring some Spirits to make them chearful in their own Country; not to drink here." The English granted the request.

*F*ROM AN EARLY DATE, Puritan Massachusetts recognized the importance of bringing the Indian trade under effective governmental control.[9] The various experimental attempts of the seventeenth century, usually based upon the granting of monopolies to selected individuals or groups, culminated during the last decade of the century in a program of strict government monopoly that was to form the basis of the colony's policy during the entire first half of the eighteenth century. In spite of some difficulties, the Massachusetts program was remarkably successful, especially if measured in terms of its long-range effect upon Indian relations.

In 1699, following the re-establishment of peace after King William's War, the General Court of Massachusetts announced the basic principles upon which the trade with the Eastern Indians was to be reconstructed. Government-operated trading posts, or truck houses, were to be established, each under the command of a designated truckmaster. These posts would enjoy a monopoly of the Indian trade on the Nashaway River, the Merrimack River, and the entire area east of the Piscataqua River. In addition, there was to be a government-operated trading vessel, which would range along the coast. By this closely regulated system of government trade at prices deliberately kept low, it was hoped that the private English traders, and the French traders as well, would be unable to remain in the competition. This, in time, would eliminate the abuses commonly associated with the private trade and at the same time wean the Eastern Indians away from French influence.[10]

Hardly had the system been established when it was blasted, first by Queen Anne's War and later by Dummer's War, but after each setback the program was renewed.[11] From 1726 until the outbreak of King George's War in the 1740s the Massachusetts truck-house system completely dominated Eastern trade. From time to time additional posts were established, not only in Maine but also on the upper Connecticut River. The appointed truckmasters were oath-bound to maintain the standards established for the trade, with fair treatment for the Indians. That this did not eliminate all difficulties is clear from the following Indian letter in the Massachusetts Archives, vol. XXXI:

Fort Richmond   Feb^{ry} 11th 1742

Great Captain

Loron Speakes in the name of the Rest—This Winter when our two men went to Boston and came back again they told us what you said to them which is all one as if we had rece^d a Letter You know there is no body understands Indian at Georges and that was the reason we could not send an answer to what you sent us—and now we come to Richmond where our language is understod—Our hearts are towards you ever since you have bin in Government—The men that came from Boston told us you designd to see us at Georges We should all be much Rejoyc'd to see you there for we cannot conveniently meet you farther Westward—We much like your promise to comply with Govern^r Dummers agreement with us—One thing we dont like (which we agreed uppon with Govr Dummer) we apprehend is not complyd with which was that if any goods rise our furrs were to Rise with them—We Solemly agreed with Govr Dummer that we should have for our furrs at Georges Truckhouse as they then sold for at Boston Your Excel^y may please to inquire of Govern^r Dummer the Treasurer and other Merch^{ts} who bye furrs whether we have justice done us on this head—The Truckmaster here gives us 8/ for Saples 16/ for Spring bever 18/ for Otters 20/ for Cat[ ]s We now are kept much in the dark as to our trade the man that mannages it understands verry little as to our Language or trade his being a Minester we alittle wonder at his comming to trade here It was also agreed at Casco that we Should allwayes have afull Supply of Provissions and other things we need—now we want all sorts of Provissions and many other nessesaryes and have along time bin without them and in the midelle of Winter the most nessesary time we could want them in—We should be glad there was a man at Georges that understod trading wth us and the Language Our men mentioned Jabez Bradbury unto your Excel^y we like him well—for want of Provissions and thro^{ugh} amistake we have kild three horses at Sacadahock on Small Point side we understod they were wild and free for any body accordingly we dryd the flesh openly. Two dayes after we kild them six men came to us with their guns cockt demanding Satisfacti[on] uppon their appearing in such a hostile manner we flew to our guns one of our men being wise told us we had better surrender our armes then to begin aquarrell which might be attended with such ill consiquences and not well understanding what these men said to us we delivered them four guns and two hatchets as a pledge for pay for the horses they insisting (as we understod them) to taike them by violence if we did not resign them we promise pay for the horses in the Spring uppon the delivery of our guns We are all in good health & give our Love and Service to your Excel^y

[Indian Marks]

The Massachusetts system of control, nevertheless, gave the authorities some effective means of suppressing the worst abuses, and in general the Indians were gratified. One modern authority has called the Massachusetts truck-house system "the most striking innovation in the conduct of the fur trade in colonial New England."[12]

Massachusetts did not maintain the system for any profits it brought into the colony treasury. The principal objective was diplomatic, not economic. Under the system the truckmasters paid the Indians for their peltry at whatever rates prevailed in Boston and sold trading goods to the Indians at low prices. Whatever small profits might be made in such transactions were swallowed up in the costs of building and maintaining the official trading posts.[13] The program actually showed a financial deficit, which helps explain why it was unpopular with the lower house of the legislature. It was opposed also, of course, by the private traders who found themselves crowded out of the picture. The Indians who traded with the truckmasters were often baffled or annoyed by some aspects of the system, especially the fluctuations in the prices paid for furs (not always matched with corresponding fluctuations in the prices of English goods), but there can be no doubt that over a period of many years the truck-house system was popular with the Eastern Indians and was largely responsible for luring many of them away from their previous French connections.[14]

*F*OR SOME YEARS after the French and Indian terror-raid on Schenectady in 1690, Albany and its fur trade were in a period of serious decline. Even the coming of peace in 1697 did not bring with it a full restoration of prosperity, as the French intensified their efforts to undermine the allegiance of the Five Nations. By 1701, the Iroquois had traveled so far along the path of expedient noncommitment that in the same year they could both proclaim allegiance to the French monarchy and place much of their beaver ground under the protection of the English sovereign.[15] In that year too the French established an important outpost at Detroit, guarding the passage between Lake Erie and Lake Huron. "... What will become of us at this rate," was now the cry of the Five Nations. "Where shall We hunt a Beaver, if the French of Canada take possession of our Beaver Country."[16]

New York's policy of noninvolvement in Queen Anne's War was a conscious attempt to protect the Albany fur trade from the buffetings of international conflict. New England, whose own frontier territory was laced with blood during this second conflict with France, quite accurately attributed New York's policy to its commercial interests.[17] After the Peace of Utrecht in 1713, New York began to give even more serious consideration to the rebuilding of its Indian trade, but it was not until William Burnet assumed the governorship in 1720 that truly decisive measures were undertaken.[18] Burnet arrived none too soon. At that very time the French were establishing themselves in a strong position at Niagara, guarding the water route between Lake Ontario and Lake Erie. With this, both the eastern and the western exits from Lake Ontario were controlled by Quebec.

Governor Burnet learned much about the problems besetting New York's fur trade from Robert Livingston, who became his confidential adviser.[19] With Livingston's assistance, Burnet formulated a triple policy designed to wrest the great fur trade of the West from the hands of the French and thereby establish British hegemony over all the tribes west of the Iroquois country and south of the Great Lakes. In brief, Burnet proposed to encourage direct trade between the remote Western tribes and New York, stop the exchange of French peltry and English trading goods between Albany and Montreal that was enabling the French to continue their successful pursuit of the western trade, and establish one or more fortified trading posts on the Great Lakes to counteract the influence of the French forts already built there.

In the 1680s, Governor Dongan had inaugurated a policy of sending parties of traders far into the Western wilderness to seek out the Indian trade, a policy representing a sharp departure from the long-standing practice of limiting all trading to the confines of Albany. With some misgivings both the Iroquois and the Albany merchants had consented to the new policy, in the interests of an expanded trade. An enterprising Dutchman, Arnout Viele, between 1692 and 1694 had journeyed all the way from Albany to the lower Ohio Valley to establish trading relations with the distant Shawnee and even to persuade them to bring their furs to Albany. At that time an Onondaga sachem was moved to remark, perhaps with an undertone of apprehension, that "when those farr Indians come then this place [Albany] will be desireable like a fair maid that has many lovers so all people will flock heither."[20] Thus there was ample precedent for Burnet's attempt to attract the Western tribes.

At a conference held at Albany in 1721, Governor Burnet asked the Iroquois sachems "to keep an open path and so sweep itt clean for all the far Indians to pass freely through their country to albany to trade. . . ."[21] The Indians acquiesced. A year later Burnet dispatched Major Abraham Schuyler and a party of men to the Seneca country with instructions to make contact with remote Indians and try to establish a trading base somewhere on the shores of Lake Ontario. If possible, Schuyler was even to purchase land at Niagara Falls and along the shore of Lake Erie, thereby cutting in behind the French position at Niagara. Cooperating with Burnet, the provincial legislature decided to raise a total of £500 to promote the trade with the Western tribes and help keep the Iroquois attached to the English.[22]

There had long existed two divergent factions among the Albany fur merchants. One group favored the policy of actively promoting a direct trade with the Western Indians; the other preferred to forget about the West and continue trading with the French merchants of Montreal. The latter trade, engaged in by many of Albany's leading citizens, required little effort or risk, but produced good profits. No wonder it was popular in the mercantile community. The basis for the trade with Montreal was the inability of the French to acquire within their own system the excellent trading goods that the Western Indians desired, especially the kind of woolen blanketing known as strouds. Using the Catholic Iroquois of Caughnawaga as go-betweens, the French merchants of Montreal sent bundles of fine furs to Albany and received in exchange good English woolens. The woolens, in turn, were sent from Montreal into the West, where they obtained still more furs.[23]

The Iroquois disliked the Albany-Montreal trade because it by-passed them completely. French officialdom disliked the trade because it diverted valuable furs to the English colonies and seemed to enhance the economic position of the English. Some imperial-minded English colonial officials such as Robert Livingston, Cadwallader Colden, and Governor Burnet disliked the trade because it enabled the French to continue dealing directly with the Western tribes, thereby preventing the growth of English influence in the West and keeping the tribes oriented toward Montreal rather than Albany. With so many of the interested parties opposed to the Albany-Montreal trade, it seems remarkable that the exchange of goods through the Champlain Valley was able to continue, but continue it did in spite of all official opposition. Good profits were being made from this trade both in Montreal and Albany, so the respective imperial interests of France and Britain were ignored by those who profited.[24]

Governor Burnet had become convinced that the Albany-Montreal trade was seriously undermining British prestige among the Indians and threatening the future of the northern frontier. Only by denying to the

French merchants the superior British trading goods they so desperately needed could England break the French grip on the fur trade of the West. At the urging of both Livingston and Burnet, the legislature of New York in 1720 laid an absolute prohibition on the sale of all Indian trading goods to subjects of the French Crown. The law was renewed and strengthened in 1722, 1724, and 1725 in an effort to stifle evasion.[25]

The interdiction of the profitable Albany-Montreal trade immediately brought into the open the great factional differences that divided New York's mercantile community. Many of the Dutch fur merchants of Albany and their business associates in the town of New York, who were satisfied with the easy and regular profits of the Canadian trade, growled about the new law and continued to deal with the French surreptitiously. But other prominent men, led by Robert Livingston and Cadwallader Colden, convinced that Britain's future in the West was threatened by French domination of the Western Indians, wholeheartedly supported the governor's program. The opposing factions made such contradictory statements about the effects of the prohibition that a bystander would scarcely believe they were talking about the same thing. "I assure you that this act is a great Deterement to our Province," complained Cornelis Cuyler, one of the Albany merchants.[26] On the contrary, asserted a Council committee of which Colden was a prominent member, the prohibition is so beneficial to New York, "that we know not one Person that now opens his Mouth against the Act."[27] No doubt there was a measure of truth on both sides. When the Western Indians discovered that the French were no longer able to supply them with the desired trading goods, they began to welcome the British traders, some of whom were now moving into the region of the Great Lakes. By 1725 the French were beginning to complain that the English were gobbling up the Indian trade from one end of Lake Ontario to the other.[28]

Nevertheless, the opponents of Burnet's program at Albany and Manhattan quickly organized and began to work for repeal of the prohibitory legislation. Unable to move the governor and his supporters, they turned to their business associates in England, the powerful merchants from whom they purchased their Indian trading goods and to whom they sold their peltry, urging them to make an appeal to the Board of Trade. Under the resulting pressure New York in 1726 repealed its absolute prohibition but at the same time burdened the renewed Albany-Montreal trade with double duties levied upon all Indian trading goods destined for Canada. For example, strouds traded directly with Western Indians were taxed 15 shillings, while those sent northward from Albany were assessed 30 shillings. Interestingly enough, one of the men who contracted to collect these duties was Cornelis Cuyler, the outspoken opponent of the prohibitory law.[29]

The problem of administering and enforcing the new regulations proved a difficult one, and was finally solved in a way not pleasing to Colden. In 1729 the Crown, hearkening to the continued protests of the London merchants, disallowed all New York legislation aimed at the trade with Canada. From then until 1760, when Montreal fell to the British, French furs and English trading goods passed easily through the Champlain Valley, despite official French attempts to prevent the traffic.[30]

Another aspect of Burnet's program was to establish British posts at strategic locations in the West for the purpose of attracting the Indian trade and affording protection for the frontier. As early as 1708 a French observer had remarked, "It is of very great consequence to prevent the English from making any posts on Lake Ontario, for if they were once established there they would impede our communication with the Iroquois, which would be very prejudicial to the Colony."[31] He was not exaggerating. The Board of Trade thoroughly agreed with this part of Burnet's program, as shown by its report of 1721 recommending the construction of fortified posts on both Lake Ontario and Lake Erie.[32]

About 1722 one of Burnet's exploring parties apparently set up a crude trading post at Irondequoit Bay, on the southern shore of Lake Ontario.[33] A more important site, however, was at the mouth of the Oswego River, the western end of the Mohawk Valley trade route. Here in 1725 New York established a trading post that was to become an important center for the fur trade and a major threat to the economic well-being of New France. Oswego was well situated to interrupt the flow of furs along the southern shore of Lake Ontario toward Fort Frontenac and the St. Lawrence River. In 1727, to protect this key position, Burnet constructed a strong fort, with walls four feet thick.[34] Henceforth Fort Oswego stood as a bold challenge to the French fur trade and French ambitions in general, south of the Great Lakes. For one thing, it helped counteract the influence of French missionaries among the Iroquois by impressing the Six Nations with the British will to prevail in the West. In addition, Fort Oswego served to encourage the westward expansion of settlement in the Mohawk Valley, for now the vulnerable back door to the area was effectively guarded.[35]

Although the locale of their activity was changing, New York's fur traders remained much the same as they had always been. The provincial government found it necessary to pass a law prohibiting any Oswego trader from setting up his hut more than three hundred yards from the trading post and "using any manner of Arts or Compulsion to Engage and forestall the Trade of the Indians."[36] It sounded like Albany all over again. One exasperated Albany merchant characterized the Oswego traders as "a parcell young wild brutes who for the most part have no breeding nor Education, no honour nor honesty and are governd only by an unruly passion of getting money by fair or foul means."[37] At a somewhat later date an observer on the scene at Oswego predicted the utter ruin of the trade, "for their is such a Number of Traders here and such Vile Steps taken to undermine each other in his trade that it consequently cant hold Long; and the little low means used in the Trade to hurt each other must give even the Savages a Damn'd mean Opinion of us; especially our Honesty &c."[38]

In spite of Fort Oswego's importance, Albany continued to function as the main depot for the New York fur trade. A merchant in Albany received his peltry from the Caughnawaga Indians, who brought it down from Canada, or from subsidiary traders, who obtained it from the Iroquois and the Western Indians at Oswego. This peltry, consisting mostly of beaver but including many other types as well, was then shipped down the Hudson to Manhattan and from there to some firm in England. Subject to the vagaries of a fluctuating market, the furs were sold by the English agent, who in turn purchased trading goods as specified by the Albany merchant, sending them on to him for his further use in the trade. The merchant, of course, had to bear all the expenses of transportation both ways, including fees and insurance. In many respects the commercial structure of the fur trade bears a close resemblance to that of the tobacco trade in the Southern colonies.

Business letters from the London agents Samuel and William Baker to Albany fur merchant Johannes Bleecker reveal much about the actual workings of the transatlantic traffic.[39] Bleecker shipped to his agent beaver, raccoon, fox (both red and gray), muskrat, marten, otter, mink, wolf, wildcat, bear, and dressed deerskins. The agent's commission for marketing the peltry was 2½ percent of the proceeds. In addition Bleecker had to pay the custom and entry fees and all charges for freightage, lighterage, wharfage, porterage, cooperage, cartage, and storage. For example, a shipment of peltry in 1743 was sold for £60 14s. 6d. From this was deducted the agent's commission of £1 10s. 4d. and additional expenses amounting to £8 6s. 8d., leaving Bleecker a credit of £50 17s. 6d. Bleecker also had to pay his agent a commission amounting to 2½ percent of the cost of all trading goods obtained including, in addition to the actual price of the goods, such charges as entry and cocket, carriage, and bills of lading. Finally there was the matter of insurance, optional with the Albany merchant. In 1741 the cost of insuring a consignment of trading goods valued at £25 on the voyage from London to America was £1 7s., including stamps and the agent's commission.

At such a distance, there was certain to be some misunderstanding and distrust between the Albany men and their London factors. "It seems to me you are Resolved to serve me always Wrong and never to observe my orders," grumbled Cornelis Cuyler to his agent. "The strouds which you have now sent me are Course Refuse old musty strouds, good for nothing. . . . Concerning my skins, I never send you Refuse skins but you always Complain over them when you sell em Less as you ought to Do."[40] A little later we find the same agent explaining to another Albany client the reason why he had had to make a large deduction for wastage; it seems that some of the beaver skins arrived in London with feet still attached, and these appendages had to be amputated before the skins could be weighed on the scales.[41]

In addition to rum, imported from the West Indies or manufactured in the colonies, a major commodity employed in the New York fur trade was English woolens. These consisted mainly of strouds, together with duffels, which were finer and more expensive. The Indians had become extremely particular about such woolen goods, favoring only certain types, with the result that the purchasing agents in England had to be extremely careful to meet specifications. Strouds of a dark blue color, for example, were greatly preferred to those of a lighter blue, which tended to fade. Complained Cornelis Cuyler to his London agent, "as for the four Blankets, which I have Received by Capt. Stephens . . . the Indians Dont Like them Beter then other new fashon Blankets, Because they are to Narrow for their Lenght [sic], Neither is the stripe good, and no Markes as the french blankets have, and not thick enough."[42] William Johnson reported to his agent that some blankets previously sent him "were woven too Cloose, & the Wool too Short & Coarse. besides the letters, and other marks, Selvage &ca were not exactly the Same of the Pattern, nor so neat, all which the Indians are verry curious In."[43] Philip Livingston summed up the problem when he remarked that the Indians were "a strange wimsecall people" who "will have good Choise goods, and do understand them to perfection."[44] In this respect, at least, the traders had to take great care if they wanted to succeed.

The Indian bead money known as wampum continued at this later period to play an important part in the fur trade, but under greatly altered circumstances. These small cylindrical shell beads had originally been manufactured only by certain tribes living along the coast, but the industrious Europeans soon acquired the skill. By the eighteenth century the manufacture of wampum for the fur trade had become a specialized business practiced by certain recognized craftsmen in the colonial towns, especially Albany where busy-fingered Dutchmen drilled the beads with "a well tempered needle dipt in wax and tallow. . . ."[45] James Simpson of New York was referred to specifically as a wampum maker.[46] Something of the scope of the business can be grasped from an order sent by Cornelis Cuyler for 40,000 best clam shells and 500 best conch shells "for to make white wampon."[47] But perhaps most astonishing of all is Philip Livingston's letter ordering both black and white wampum beads from England. To be sure of getting beads with all the appearance of authenticity ("made in America by native Americans"), Livingston sent samples of the beads along with his order, urging his agent to obtain "the same Collour & biggness even & smooth pray gett them made if possible."[48] So the New York trade was pursued, by whatever means were thought necessary for success.

*T*HERE HAD BEEN a fur trade on the Delaware River, carried on by the Dutch and the Swedes, before William Penn was born. The arrival of Penn and his settlers in the 1680s merely intensified a business already well established if not highly organized, and for many years thereafter the peaceful Delawares came each year to Philadelphia to trade their peltry for the products of European manufacture. Penn himself was quick to recognize the potentialities of the Indian trade in Pennsylvania. Both the Delaware and the Susquehanna rivers led northward toward the Iroquois country, and there is little reason to doubt that his early interest in lands along the upper Susquehanna was prompted in part by the prospect of tapping the great sources of furs to the north.

During the seventeenth century a vast territory stretching from the Allegheny River on the east to the Maumee and Wabash rivers on the west had been largely emptied of Indians as a result of Iroquois warfare. By the early decades of the eighteenth century this region was abounding with game and hence was very attractive to Indians living elsewhere, as a source of both food and peltry. Since the Iroquois Confederacy now claimed the area by virtue of conquest, any tribes desiring to move in had to submit to Iroquois jurisdiction if they cared to avoid trouble. Soon various groups of Indians began to enter and settle in the region—Delawares from Pennsylvania, Iroquois from New York (henceforth known as Mingoes), Shawnee from the south and east. Farther to the west, from Detroit along the Maumee-Wabash water route and beyond, dwelt other tribes who were inclined toward the French.[49]

When some of Pennsylvania's Delawares moved west to the Allegheny River about 1724 in search of game, the white traders who had been accustomed to dealing with them in the East quite naturally followed along also, in order to continue a profitable trade relationship.

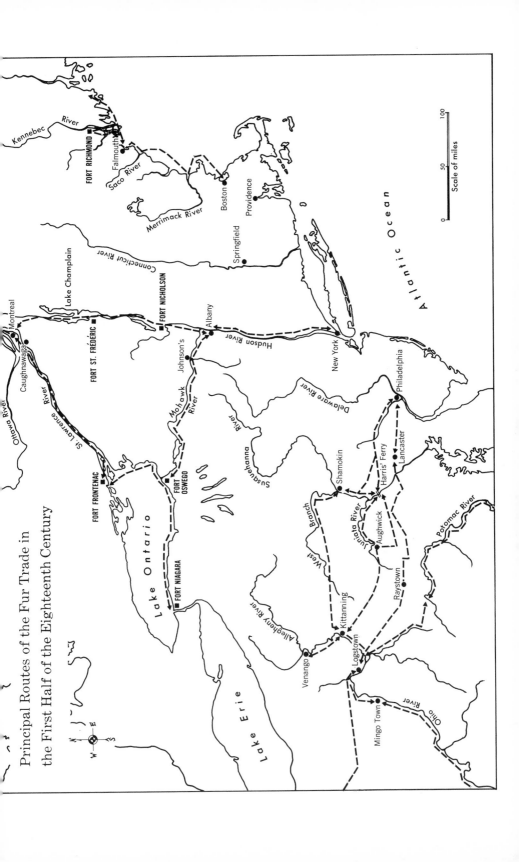

Principal Routes of the Fur Trade in
the First Half of the Eighteenth Century

The ranges of mountains separating the Susquehanna Valley from the upper Ohio Valley were not a formidable barrier to hardy men on horseback, and a number of feasible routes for the fur trade were scouted out and developed. These became the wilderness highways for the traders and their trains of heavily laden, plodding pack horses. Three routes were of special importance. The first, known as the Shamokin Path, led from the forks of the Susquehanna up the west branch of that river, across the mountains to Mahoning Creek, and thence to the Allegheny. Roughly parallel to this route but some distance to the south was the second trail, known as the Frankstown or Kittanning Path. This much-used route led from the Susquehanna River up the Juniata and through Kittanning Gap to the Indian village of Kittanning on the Allegheny River. Still farther to the south was the third route, the Raystown Path, which led westward from Harris' Ferry. Sixteen miles west of the Susquehanna, at what is now Carlisle, an auxiliary path branched off to join the Kittanning Path at Aughwick. The Raystown Path itself dropped southwest to pass through what is now Shippensburg, and then proceeded west through Raystown (Bedford) and across the Laurel Ridge to the junction of the Allegheny and Monongahela rivers, the forks of the Ohio.[50]

As the Pennsylvania traders extended their activity beyond the mountains, their trade with the various Indian groups enlarged year by year, thanks to their aggressive pursuit of business and their ability to outbid the French competition. Especially during King George's War in the 1740s, when New France was subjected to a British naval blockade that greatly diminished the flow of trading goods through Quebec, did the Pennsylvanians extend the scope of their activities in the trans-Allegheny region, trading along the south shore of Lake Erie almost as far as Detroit itself. This, in turn, meant that British influence among the Western tribes was on the increase.[51]

In 1748 a portion of the powerful Miami tribe (known to the British as Twightwees), under the leadership of a pro-English chief nicknamed Old Briton, established the town of Pickawillany, nearly a hundred miles up the Miami River and almost five hundred miles due west of Philadelphia. Here Pennsylvania traders were welcomed by the Indians, and Pickawillany immediately became a center of British influence in the West.[52] Leaders of various Indian groups living beyond the mountain barrier, including the Miami, the Delawares, the Shawnee, the Mingoes, and the Wyandot (Huron), were easily induced to align their people with the British pattern of trade. Pennsylvania's annual export of peltry reached a value of about £40,000 sterling.[53] Such volume spelled success; by 1748 France seemed about to lose its last chance to play a controlling part in the development of the strategically located Ohio Valley.

In many ways the Pennsylvania fur trade resembled that of New York, except that in Pennsylvania the wilderness end of the business was carried on not at one or two government-established posts such as Oswego but in dozens of Indian villages, wherever stores of peltry were to be found. A large part of the trade was in deerskins, together with mink, raccoon, bear, fox, wildcat, muskrat, otter, and some beaver. So common were buckskins in the Pennsylvania trade that their value became a standard measure, a common way of expressing worth. From this we derive the slang term for one dollar, a "buck."[54]

Certain mercantile companies in Philadelphia, such as Shippen and Lawrence, Baynton and Wharton, and Levy, Franks and Simon, imported trading goods from England and had them carried by wagon to company storehouses in the frontier town of Lancaster. Here the traders, many of whom were organized in groups and partnerships, obtained the rum, woolens, and hardware which they then conveyed on sturdy pack horses to their own bases of operation deep in the interior. The peltry obtained from the Indians was brought back to the company storehouses, where it was credited to the trader's account and later carted to Philadelphia for shipment to England. Much of this business, from London all the way to the Ohio Valley and back, was conducted on a credit basis, which meant that unforeseen circumstances, such as Indian defection or malfeasance on the part of an employee, constituted a rather serious risk.[55]

The best way to gain an understanding of how the Pennsylvania fur trade actually worked is to study the early career of George Croghan, an Irish immigrant who entered the colony in 1741, moved to the western frontier, and quickly rose to become the leading Indian trader of the area. He established a trading base on Condogwinet Creek, a short distance west of Harris' Ferry, with easy access to the major routes to the West. Gradually he extended his operations, building outposts with storehouses and living quarters on the Youghiogheny, the Allegheny, at Logstown on the upper Ohio, on the Muskingum, at Sandusky on Lake Erie, and at the Miami village of Pickawillany. Croghan learned to speak both the Delaware and the Iroquois tongues. He came to have an excellent understanding of the Indians, was respected by them, and was instrumental in extending British influence among the Western tribes at the expense of the French.[56] By 1748 the government of Pennsylvania was beginning to look to George Croghan as a man able to carry out important missions in the tricky field of Indian diplomacy.

The year 1748, when many tribes seemed to be attaching themselves to the British interest, marked a high peak of British influence in the upper Ohio Valley. Immediately ahead lay a sudden and precipitous decline. Pennsylvania traders were alarmed by increasing signs of Virginia's determination to make good its territorial claims at the forks of the Ohio, thereby breaking in upon the profitable fur trade of the area.[57] From the north came a far more serious threat. New France, thoroughly aroused by the extension of British influence in the West as a result of success in the fur trade, was making one more attempt to regain the support of the Indians and chase the British out of the trans-Allegheny region. In 1749 Captain Céloron de Blainville led a military expedition on a circular tour of the disputed area, traveling by way of the Allegheny, Ohio, Miami, and Maumee rivers, warning off British traders wherever he found them.[58]

Three years later an unofficial raiding party of Chippewa and Ottawa warriors, under the leadership of a French trader named Charles Michel Langlade, attacked the Miami village of Pickawillany, where George Croghan and other Pennsylvania traders were accustomed to carry on their business. The attacking force dispersed the villagers, burned the cabins of the British traders, and took a small number of English prisoners.[59] This blow put an end to Pennsylvania's trading activity on the Miami River. In fact, by 1753 the British fur trade in the West lay in ruins, with traders and their Indian customers alike overawed by the sudden display of French might. The trend of the previous two decades was being reversed, as the Miami and other tribes began to waver in their attachment to the British, looking instead to the advantage of a French connection.[60]

In Pennsylvania, as elsewhere, there were traders who habitually cheated and abused the Indians. Now, with French prestige once again on the rise, it was more than ever imperative for the government of Pennsylvania to bring order into its Indian trade lest the bad influence of unscrupulous traders alienate the tribesmen still further. In theory, the only persons allowed to engage in the trade were those who had obtained licenses from the government, but actually many frontiersmen traded without ever bothering to apply for a license. Probably it was these unlicensed operators who most flagrantly flouted the rules, abused the Indians, and in general gave the fur trade in Pennsylvania its bad reputation.[61]

Indians and law-abiding traders alike appealed to the authorities for a more effective system of control.[62] In 1753 Benjamin Franklin, immediately after attending a conference with the Indians at Carlisle, wrote a letter to James Bowdoin of Boston inquiring about the Massachusetts system of government-operated truck houses. Bowdoin replied with a copy of the basic law and an enthusiastic endorsement of the system as a means of preventing the bad consequences that always seemed to arise when the Indian trade was left open to private enterprise.[63] Thereupon Franklin became a strong advocate of legislation to establish a similar system in Pennsylvania.

A bill that would involve the government directly in the fur-trading business was duly introduced, but it quickly became entangled in a dispute between the Assembly and the governor over control of the colony's Indian affairs. After a long period of wrangling between the two branches of government, a basic law was enacted in 1758, providing for a government commission to lay down the rules by which the trade was to be carried on, including fixed prices.[64] Beyond the Alleghenies only the government itself was to have the right to exchange goods with the Indians. In this way a policy of strict regulation of the Indian trade by means of a government monopoly, first successfully developed for the eastern frontier of Massachusetts, was transplanted to the western frontier of Pennsylvania.

*T*HE FUR TRADE was an inseparable component of the westward movement, for peltry was the one valuable commodity that the Indians not only controlled but could convey to the Europeans on a continuing basis that brought profits to both parties. For white men of an enterprising nature, the fur trade offered the possibility of large, quick profits, and perhaps even fabulous wealth. But because the business was conducted with unsophisticated natives, often in remote parts of the wilderness, there were great temptations for all who participated. Especially tempting were the many opportunities to cheat the Indians by getting them drunk and then inducing them to part with their furs at ridiculously low prices. This tactic was practiced everywhere by unscrupulous traders. It is not difficult to see why the fur trade attracted some of the worst men who came to the colonies, and corrupted others who started out as honest, conscientious Christians.

Obviously, the way in which the fur trade was conducted had a direct bearing on Indian-white relations. Abused, disgruntled Indians were inclined to welcome opportunities for vengeance, including vandalism against traders and pioneering farmers. A disrupted, irregular, and trouble-ridden fur trade, moreover, was detrimental to the interests of the traders and merchants who sought to conduct the business in a regular and fair way. Worse still, the abuses played directly into the hands of the French, who were anxious to convince the Indians that the English were not to be trusted. Conversely, a healthy, well-conducted fur trade was the most effective means of gaining and holding the loyalty of the Indian tribes, and this in turn was crucial to the future of the colonies in the American West. Clearly, then, the fur trade was a special kind of business, one whose conduct was a matter of great concern to the public in general.

Apparently nobody in the colonies, with the notable exception of the irresponsible, exploiting traders, seriously questioned the need for some degree of governmental regulation and control of the Indian trade. Experience had taught that unregulated free enterprise in the fur trade was corrosive to good relations with the Indians, and hence potentially disastrous for the entire colonial population, to say nothing of the imperial concerns of the mother country. Consequently, the colony governments began to experiment with various forms of control, culminating in the Massachusetts truck-house law and its offspring, the Pennsylvania act of 1758. This legislation deliberately and with malice aforethought killed free-enterprise trading in designated areas, where the government assumed the exclusive right to engage in the Indian trade.[65]

On every part of the northern frontier the quest for furs carried white men deeper and deeper into the wilderness, giving them a growing confidence in their ability to master the environment of forested America while making the natives contribute heavily to a growing colonial prosperity. Compared to the general population the men actually engaged in the fur trade were few, but their influence on the expansion of the frontier was enormous. It was they who dealt most frequently with the Indian tribes, thereby molding the character of Indian relations for good or ill, and it was they who unintentionally but quite effectively cleared the way for the continuing advance of the farming frontier toward the setting sun.

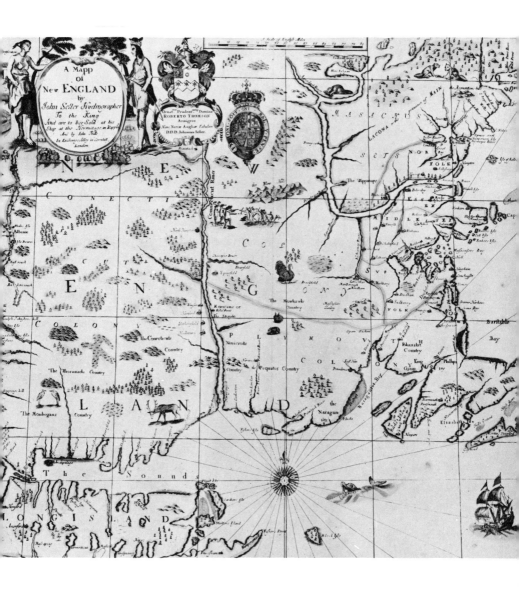

John Seller's map of a portion of the northern colonial frontier, *ca.* 1680. Note the palisaded Indian village in the upper left corner and the skirmish between colonists and Indians just east of the Connecticut River. The gnawing beaver, top center, symbolizes the importance of the fur trade. (From the Map Collection of the Yale University Library)

Surveyor's plan of a new frontier village, 1750. At the main intersection
are the lots reserved for the as yet undesignated minister, the meetinghouse, and a school. (The New York Public Library)

Broockfield October 23 1710   582

The humbel petisian of yor poor bestresed people
Heear caleth alovd for pity & help Therefor we
Advres the Gienerall Coart that They would con
sider vs and set vs in sum way or other where
by we may have a svbsistance so long as yov sh
all se case to continve vs heere we did not com
heear with ovt order neiter are wee wiling
To goe away wit ovt order There fore wee
Are wiling to leave ovr selves with yov to
with Doe for and with vs as yov think best
yov knowe ovr dificaltyes as to the com
man enemye and Besides That ovr mill that
is Broakn so y we have neither Bread nor
meal byt what we ofetch 30 miles which is in
tolerable to bar either for Hors or man
which pvteth vs vpon in beavering to rebvild
ing of it which is imposibel for vs to Doe wi
th ovt yovr pity and Helpe winter is so
neear y we most intreat yov to Doe svmt
hing as sone as maybee nomore byt are
yovr povar Bestresed Begers
                                    Henry Gilb
                                    Phillip Gos
                                    Josph Banister
                                    Jammett oover
                                    Thomas Barns
                                    inf Behlf of the
                                    resto of the inha
                                    bitance

                    Vartey

Letter from a frontier village in distress, 1710. It is quoted on page 122.
(Secretary of the Commonwealth of Massachusetts)

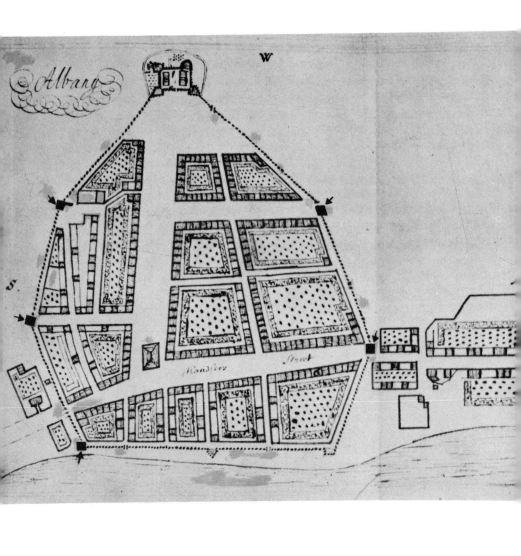

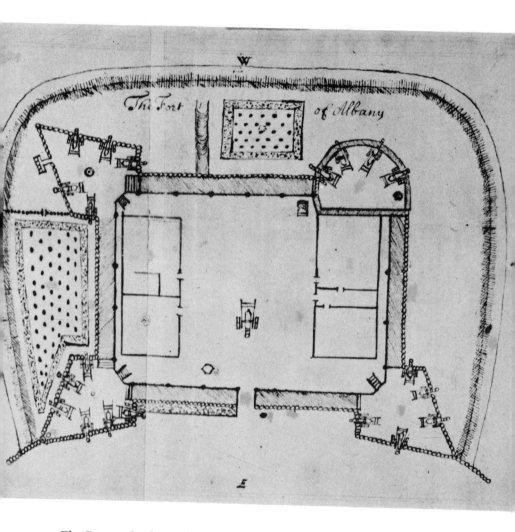

The Reverend John Miller's plan of Albany, 1695. Opposite is shown all of the town included within the palisade, extending from the Hudson River up the hill to the fort. There are six gates. Blockhouses at intervals along the palisade are indicated by arrows. The building standing at the junction of the two main streets is the Dutch church. Running north (right) from this church is Handlers Street, whose name refers to the Dutch *handlaers*, or merchants of the fur trade. Albany was the greatest fur-trading center of the northern frontier. An enlargement of the fort appears above. (From copy in New York State Library, Albany, N.Y.)

A General Rule for the Prices of goods supplyed to the
Eastern Indians by the Several Truckmasters & of the
Peltry received by ye Truckmasters of the Indians.

One Beavr. in Season is Viz

1. yd bro. Cloth 3. Beavr. Skins in Season	1. Otte. Skin in Season is one Beavr
1. yd 2 Gingerline 1. Ditto in Season	1. Bear Skin in Season is one Ditto
1. yd Red or blew Kersey 2. Do. in Season	2. halfe Skins in Season is one Ditto
1. yd good Duffells 1. Do. in Season	4. pappoose ditto in Season is one Ditto
1. yd 2 bro. fine Cotton 1. Do. in Season	2. foxes in Season is one Ditto
2. yd of Cotton. 1. Do. . in Season	2. woodchucks in Season is one Ditto
2 yd 2 of halfe thicks 1. Do. in Season	4. martins in Season is one Ditto
5. Pecks Indian Corn. 1. Do. in Season	8. minckes in Season is one Ditto
5. Pecks Indian Meale 1. Do. in Season	5. pounds of feathers is one Ditto
4. Pecks Peass. 1. Do. in Season	4. Raccoones in Season is one Ditto
2: pound of Powder. 1. Do. in Season	4. Seal Skins large is one Ditto
2 Pint of Shot 1. Do. in Season	1. Moose Hide is two Ditto
6. fatham of Tobacco 1. Do. in Season	1. Pound of Castorium is one Ditto
40. Biskets 1. Do. in Season	
10. Do of Pork 1. Do. in Season	
6. Knives 1. Do. in Season	
6. Combes. 1. Do. in Season	
20. Seamds Thread 1. Do. in Season	
1. Hatt 2. Do. in Season	
1. Hatt with hattband 3. Do. in Season	
2 large Kittles 1. Do. in Season	
1 small Do. 1. Do. in Season	
1. Shirt 1. Do. in Season . . .	
1. Shirt with Ruffells 2. Do. in Season	
2. smal Axe's 1. Do. in Season	
2. small Hoes 1. Do. in Season	
3. do. midling Hookes 1. Do. in Season	
1. Sword Blade 1. Vi 2 Do. in Season	

John Phillips prsid
of the Comitte

In Council
July. 14 1703.
Read and approved
Is. Addington Secry

(*Opposite*) This document, dated 1703, indicates how the beaver pelt was used as a standard of value in the trade carried on between the government of Massachusetts Bay and the Eastern Indians. For example, one beaver pelt in season could be exchanged for any of the following: a yard of good duffel, five pecks of Indian corn, two pints of gunpowder, six fathoms of tobacco, forty biscuits, a half dozen knives, a shirt, or two small axes. Likewise the beaver was considered equivalent to one otter, one bear, two foxes, two woodchucks, four martens, four raccoons, or eight minks. (Secretary of the Commonwealth of Massachusetts) (*Above*) Modern reconstruction of the Pilgrim trading post at Aptucxet, near the head of Buzzards Bay. The size of the structure suggests the importance of the trade. (Samuel Chamberlain)

A frontier blockhouse at Fort Halifax, Winslow, Maine, dating from the mid-eighteenth century. Compare with the painting opposite, presumably of the same structure. (Library of Congress)

Blockhouse at Fort Halifax, Winslow, Maine. From an oil painting by James Henry Shegogue in 1853. Both this illustration and the photograph opposite show that the blockhouse was constructed of squared logs dovetailed at the corners. Note also the overhanging second story and shingled roof. At the time this painting was made the blockhouse was approximately a hundred years old. (Maine Historical Society)

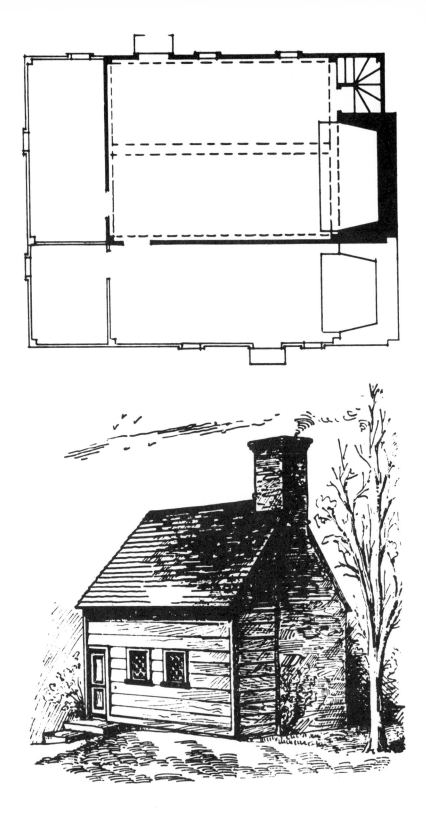

(Opposite, above) Plan of a typical seventeenth-century New England dwelling. Note how the original structure (dark lines) could be expanded as the family grew and prospered. *(Below)* Roger Mowry House (1653), Providence, Rhode Island. This is an excellent example of simple but substantial pioneer housing. (Both John H. Cady and the Rhode Island Historical Society) *(Above)* Thomas Clemence House, Manton, Rhode Island, dating from the late seventeenth century (restored). (Library of Congress)

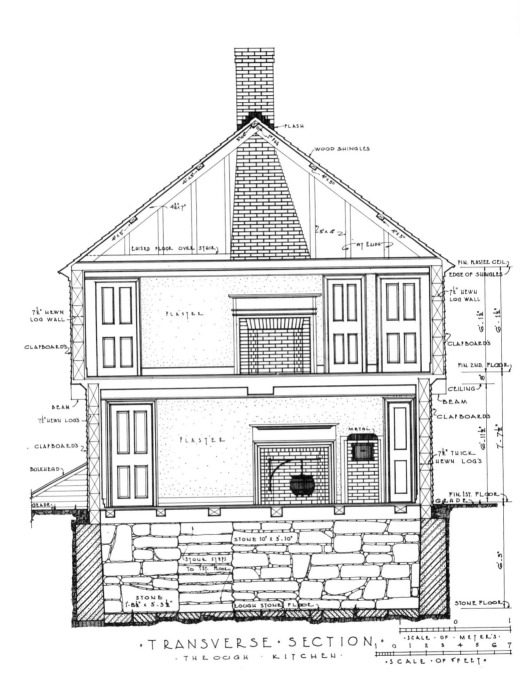

FLASH

WOOD SHINGLES

3"×6" 1"×14"

4"×5"

4"×5"

4½"×7"

3"×4"

4"×5"

4"×5"

4"×5"

RAISED FLOOR OVER STAIR

AT ENDS

FIN. PLASTER CEIL.

EDGE OF SHINGLES

7½" HEWN LOG WALL

7½" HEWN LOG WALL

PLASTER

CLAPBOARD'S

CLAPBOARD'S

FIN. 2ND. FLOOR

CEILING

BEAM

CLAPBOARD'S

BEAM 7½" HEWN LOGS

PLASTER

METAL

7½" THICK HEWN LOG'S

CLAPBOARD'S

BULKHEAD

FIN. 1ST. FLOOR

GRADE

GRADE

STONE 10' × 5'-10"

STONE STEPS TO 1ST. FLOOR

STONE 1'-8½" × 5'-3½"

ROUGH STONE FLOOR

STONE FLOOR

6'-1½"   6'-1½"

6'-11½"   7'-7½"

6'-5"

·TRANSVERSE·SECTION·

·THROUGH·KITCHEN·

SCALE·OF·METERS

0   1

SCALE·OF·FEET

0 1 2 3 4 5 6 7

(Opposite) Drawing of the McIntire Garrison House, near North Berwick, Maine, dating from the mid-seventeenth century. It shows that
frontier architecture was not always simple and crude. Note the thick-
ness of the walls, consisting of hewn logs faced with clapboards. The
overhang of the second story did not serve any useful purpose, but was
traditional in construction of this kind. *(Above)* Exterior view of the
McIntire Garrison House. (Library of Congress)

William Damme Garrison House, Dover, New Hampshire, *ca.* 1698. Note the square-hewn logs. (The Society for the Preservation of New England Antiquities, Boston)

Kitchen of the Parson Capen House, Topsfield, Massachusetts, dating from the late seventeenth century. (Samuel Chamberlain)

Kitchen of the Ogden House, Fairfield, Connecticut, dating from the
early eighteenth century. (Samuel Chamberlain)

◁ 10 ▷

Land Speculation

*T*he Europeans who invested their lives or their fortunes in the English colonies in America came from a continent where land was a scarce and valuable commodity. In fact, the actual proprietorship of land, generally speaking, was limited to a privileged aristocracy of wealth and power, so that land itself was recognized as a symbol of status. The acquisition of land was traditionally the first step in the difficult climb toward not only economic and social standing, but political power as well. America, on the other hand, was a place where land was plentiful and easy to acquire. Is it any wonder, then, that transplanted Europeans with economic, social, and political ambitions were eager to grasp as much American land as possible in the belief that wilderness acres were the key to a golden future?

Investment in real estate, or the acquisition of undeveloped land in the expectation of increasing value and subsequent profit, is one of America's oldest, most firmly established forms of business. In colonial times it developed along fairly simple lines. The investor obtained at low cost a large tract of wilderness land, either by purchase from the

Indians, or by grant from colonial authorities, or both. Because the property was located on the remote frontier far from centers of population, and because it lay covered with virgin forest, it was not in immediate demand and hence cheap. The costs the investor had to bear included some or all of the following: expenses related to finding and exploring the tract prior to purchase, satisfaction to the Indians, charges for having the tract surveyed and recorded, various legal fees, bribes to colonial officials when necessary, annual quitrents to Crown or proprietor.

The initial expenses were justified by the expectation of later profits—speculation in land was a little like fishing in a well-stocked pond. Invariably, wilderness land increased in value as it became absorbed by the frontier of settlement. The continuing growth of the colonial population constantly fed the fires of land fever; newcomers and younger sons trudged westward in search of farmland; and what had once been cheap, undeveloped, wilderness land became increasingly attractive property. The speculator rejoiced when the tide of the westward movement approached his tract; in fact, a shrewd investor would do everything possible to attract settlers. His efforts might include advertising the merits of his property in the public press, influencing legislators to have a road built into the area or a fort constructed nearby as protection against the Indians, offering free land to the earliest arrivals, and even rounding up a shipload of emigrants in Europe and paying their way to the land of opportunity.

If the Indians remained peaceful, the investor, once the tide of settlement had set strongly in his direction, could expect to watch the value of his property mount. Bit by bit he would sell it off in farm-size chunks or larger portions until it was all gone and his fortune made. By then he would be an influential and respected man in his colony, possibly with a magnificent estate of his own. He could rejoice in having lined his own pockets while at the same time helping to win a wilderness land for his country—land speculation and patriotism often held hands under the table. Only in Puritan New England, where the founders feared the rampant power of land wealth as they had known it in the Old World, was a consistent, systematic attempt made to prevent large-scale engrossment of land by ambitious individuals.[1]

*I*N NEW YORK after the English conquest in 1664, the Dutch concept of patroonships lingered like a faint odor from the dead past, reinforced by the age-old English aspiration for the wealth and power associated with an estate in the country. The decade of the 1690s brought to the province a governor who was more than willing to gratify his suitors with truly baronial grants. Governor Benjamin Fletcher, during the six years of his rule (1692 to 1698), issued to land speculators patents for hundreds of thousands of acres of frontier land, and of course profited personally by the transactions. Much of this land was virtually given away by the governor under terms requiring only negligible quitrents, and even these were commonly ignored. Since the cost of holding unimproved land in New York was trivial, the grantee often was in no great hurry to bring actual settlers to his tract. In time he would see that portions of it were cleared and farmed by tenants, whose labor would add to the value of the property. Later, perhaps many years later, the original grantee might sell out for a princely sum, or bequeath to his descendants a magnificent landed estate forming the basis of family power for generations to come.

Fletcher made several grants that were especially flagrant. One was based on an Indian purchase procured by Domine Godfrey Dellius, minister of the Dutch church at Albany, under conditions that reek of fraud. The Mohawk sachems later charged that Dellius had induced some of their people to sign a deed of sale for a huge tract "under Colour of preserving their Land to them, & told them it was a deed of Trust to him & some others to prevent some Designing People from getting Grants of their Land." It seems in retrospect that the "Designing People" were none other than Dellius himself and his associates, for the transaction became the basis of a grant from Governor Fletcher of a fifty-mile stretch of land on both sides of the Mohawk River at an annual quitrent of one beaver skin. Peter Wraxall, the Secretary of Indian Affairs, was probably quite correct when he commented that the whole business "appears from the Records to be an Infamous Cheat & most iniquitous Imposition."[2] Another Fletcher grant to Dellius extended some seventy miles in length and twelve in breadth on the east side of Lake Champlain. For this tidy piece of property the specified annual quitrent was the hide of one raccoon.

Fletcher's successor as governor, the Earl of Bellomont, was shocked to find that the greater part of the province had fallen into the hands of less than a dozen great speculators. This condition he considered deplorable for two reasons: it alienated the Indians, who saw their future endangered, and it deflected free settlers to other colonies where the best land was not already engrossed by mighty magnates. Bellomont set about to cure the malady by drastic surgery. Backed by the Albany merchants, who were alarmed about Indian defection, and by the common people of the colony, Bellomont in 1699 induced the legislature to annul eight of Fletcher's major grants, including the two in which Dellius was involved.[3] The reform governor also established a minimum quitrent

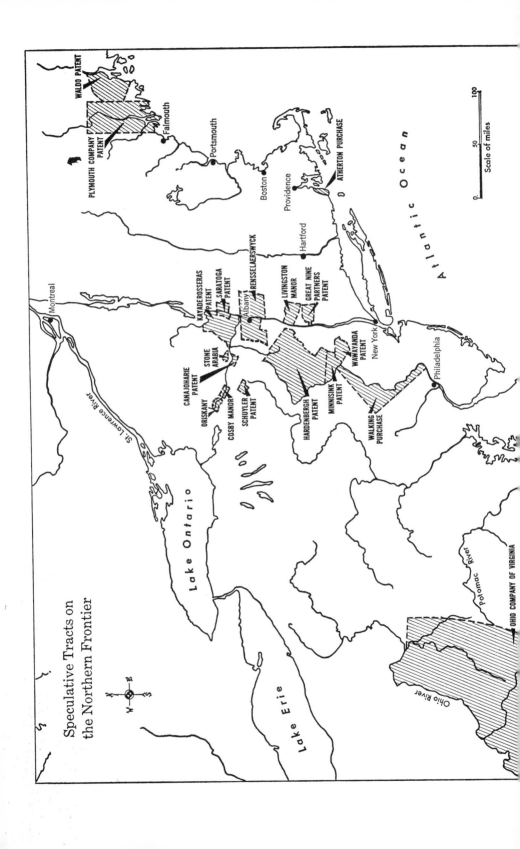

Speculative Tracts on
the Northern Frontier

of 2*s*. 6*d*. per 100 acres, which in theory, at least, greatly reduced the temptation for landholders to retain vast tracts of land in an unimproved condition.[4] That the problem was not entirely solved, however, was made perfectly evident by the behavior of Bellomont's successor, the ill-favored Lord Cornbury.

Like Fletcher before him, Cornbury distributed frontier tracts with a lavish hand, as one of the perquisites of his office. Much of the restraint that Bellomont had sought to impose was quickly swept away. In 1705 Cornbury granted to five prominent men of speculative bent more than thirty thousand acres at the place where the Mohawk River approaches the Wood Creek waterway leading toward Lake Ontario. This was twenty years before the founding of Fort Oswego, but during most of the seventeenth century the Mohawk Valley had been a major fur route, and these investors were anticipating the possibility of controlling the vital portage on that route. Their grant, known as the Oriskany Patent, lay seventy-five miles to the west of the settled frontier, affording little promise that pioneering farmers would come there in the near future. The five speculators must have been counting heavily on the continued importance of the Mohawk Valley as a highway of commerce, much as a modern investor might buy up land for a restaurant and motel at a place he has learned is scheduled to be the junction of two major highways. Viewed from another angle, the Oriskany Patent was a wager that the French would not gain full control of Lake Ontario and that the Iroquois Confederacy would not turn against the English.[5]

The Oriskany Patent was a trifle compared to some of Cornbury's other grants. In 1708, for example, he issued a patent to thirteen persons for a gigantic tract called Kayaderosseras, occupying a large part of the angle formed by the junction of the upper Hudson River and the Mohawk.[6] But by far the most extensive of Cornbury's grants was the Hardenbergh Patent of the same year. Sixty years later it was still a subject of legal controversy, at which time some of the underhanded maneuvering required to obtain a grant of such enormous size was disclosed. Originally, Johannes Hardenbergh and a group of associates had petitioned for permission to buy from the Indians a small tract in one specified county of New York. From that seemingly innocent beginning grew a tract spreading over more than a million acres between the upper Delaware River and the Hudson, just west of Kingston, New York. Legal counsel for a contending claimant suggested that both Cornbury and the Indians had been misled by the unscrupulous speculators. "My Lord Cornbury was well known both in Britain & America as a Gentleman remarkably unattentive to Business and therefore very liable to be deceived," was the way the barrister put it. Later in his argument he touched upon a crucial point in the game of land speculation, when he remarked,

To what an enormous Extent patents will grow if the proprietors are permitted to explain their Bounds by Indian deeds taken near fifty years after their dates, Your Lordship & this Honorable Board will readily conceive. In proportion as Lands rise in Value such Deeds which can always be procured at the Expense of a few Gallons of Spirits will multiply & descendants from the first patentees will by such means be able to reap at the Expense & to the prejudice of the Crown what their forefathers never sowed.[7]

By 1738 practically all the land along both sides of the Mohawk as far west as the Oriskany Patent was in private hands, although much of it remained unoccupied and unimproved. This advance was achieved, unfortunately, only at the cost of further worsening of relations with the annoyed and resentful Iroquois.[8]

*O*NE OF THE most ambitious of the Mohawk speculators was Philip Livingston, younger son of Robert Livingston, the noted Secretary of Indian Affairs. In April 1732, eight Mohawk sachems bitterly complained of Livingston's activity and vowed "never to sell him a foot of Land."[9] Nothing daunted by this rebuff, Livingston plowed ahead with his plans. Preserved for the prying eyes of the twentieth-century historian are many letters written by Philip Livingston relating to a speculative scheme for obtaining a large tract along the Mohawk River west of Schenectady. This land, it was thought, could be made to yield excellent profits through the selling or leasing of farms and the production of naval stores. More important still, it was so located as to suggest the possibility of capturing most if not all of the fur trade of the Mohawk Valley. Livingston even hoped that a second tract north of Albany might be acquired, enabling him to intercept the Canadian trade as well.[10]

New York's governor at the time was William Cosby, who had plans and favorites of his own, so Livingston adopted the tactic of working behind the governor's back to obtain the desired grant directly from the king. As an additional precaution against his opponents in the colony, Livingston remained concealed in the background, while his son Peter, together with Samuel Storke, his London agent in the fur trade, approached the throne as the actual petitioners. They were prepared to unlimber a battery of arguments in favor of their request, arguments shrewdly calculated to gain the support of various influential interests, including English merchants and manufacturers, imperialists, and patriots in general. If the Mohawk tract were granted to them, they argued, it would help revitalize New York's declining fur trade, thereby increasing the demand for English woolens. In addition, the traders at Oswego and other remote places might obtain needed supplies of grain from this tract at a relatively modest cost. And the petitioners did not hesitate to insist that all of this would serve to attach the Indians more firmly to the English cause, while blocking French expansionism in the West. How could any red-blooded British businessman or government official resist such an appeal?

Alas, the surveyor whom Livingston had approached to lay out the tract disclosed the scheme to Governor Cosby. "I never expected he would have been guilty of such a base act," Livingston grumbled with a disgust known only to the pure in heart.[11] But the unfortunate disclosure did not end the project, for Livingston and his colleagues had seen the flash of gold and were persistent. In 1734 Livingston was urging his London partners to make utmost haste in winning the support of the royal authorities, at the same time instructing them that if the plan finally collapsed, his name should remain concealed. That Livingston understood full well the *modus operandi* of English politics is demonstrated by his warning to Samuel Storke that success was not likely "unless you can gett one of the Lords of trade and Mr Walpole in to be Concernd which Last supported by Sir Robert might be of great Service."[12] In other words, the best way to move the plan along through the clogged channels of British officialdom was to offer shares to influential politicians, a common form of bribery.

Exactly how large an extent of land Philip Livingston really hoped to acquire is not easy to determine. He spoke of a tract with very large dimensions; yet when the actual petition was submitted to the Crown by Samuel Storke and Peter Livingston, the dimensions were given as approximately six miles. This much is clear—the petitioners were trying to obtain the royal grant prior to purchasing the land from the Indians, a reversal of ordinary procedure. We may assume, on the face of the evidence, that Livingston's intention was to gain royal assent for a fairly limited purchase and then multiply the size many times over when extinguishing the Indian title, in the hope that any subsequent legal challenge could be braved out. Something of this sort seems to be implied in Livingston's letter of November 13, 1735, in which he advised Storke to take into the venture one or two of the leading Lords of Trade, and a member of the Council, or even the Duke of Newcastle himself, "& then the boundaries may the easier be enlargd. . . ." If only we can pull it off, asserted the enthusiastic Livingston, it will be for us as good as "a glorious Eastindia voyage."[13]

Still the affair hung fire, while opposition built up among rival speculators and among Albany merchants who feared that such land-grabbing would drive the Iroquois into the waiting arms of the French.

The persistent Livingston lashed his colleagues on to renewed efforts including, of course, the usual bribery. "Do not Scurple [sic] to advance what money may be nesessary," he urged.[14] Later, in the spring of 1736, he took another tack. Since New York was about to gain a new governor, he suggested that it might be helpful "to make him privy to the affair with offer to be concernd for ¼ or ⅕ or less in said Lands...."[15]

The adverse forces proved in the end too powerful for Livingston's grandiose scheme. George Clarke, acting governor after the death of Cosby, and himself an avid collector of frontier lands, was a major obstacle, along with other prominent men who coveted Mohawk lands for themselves. Cadwallader Colden, the surveyor general, submitted to Clarke an adverse report on the Livingston proposal, pointing out that it embraced land already patented to others and that the proposed boundaries were not clearly defined. The Common Council of Albany and the Commissioners for Indian Affairs also expressed their firm opposition.[16] So the scheme foundered. Its tortuous and camouflaged course has been described in some detail because it shows so well the grasping spirit, political intrigue, and general trickiness that had become so much a part of land speculation on the northern frontier.

The feverish speculative activity in New York during the middle decades of the eighteenth century was in many respects a natural phenomenon. Men with capital to invest found that no other field offered such tempting opportunities as did speculation in frontier lands. Royal officials, inadequately compensated by the home government and the provincial assembly, turned to land speculation as a means of rewarding themselves for the troubles and responsibilities of their office. Finding it sometimes prudent to conceal their activity, the big speculators adopted the practice of having names other than their own appear on the necessary documents. Political supporters and other trucklers were quite willing to let their names be used as a "front" for some politician's acquisitive planning. Later, of course, when the desired tract was firmly in hand, these "proxies" would quietly drop out of the picture. By this method what had appeared to be a grant of 200,000 acres to twenty persons might actually convey that much land to only one large speculator.[17]

One outspoken critic of the feverish land-grabbing, especially because of its adverse effects upon Indian relations and the healthy development of the frontier, was Peter Wraxall, the Secretary of Indian Affairs. Said Wraxall, with unconcealed scorn,

> The injustice the Indians have suffered with regard to their Lands, has contributed to drive Numbers to the French in Canada, & in general very much weakened the Attachment of our Indians to us. this hunger after Land seems very early to have taken rise in this Province, & is become

now a kind of Epidemical Madness, every Body being eager to accumulate vast Tracts without having an intention or taking measures to settle or improve it, & Landjobbing here is as refind an Art as Stock jobbing in Change Alley . . . . hence the Country is kept unpeopled produces little or nothing in proportion to its Extent and the Possessors in perpetual Law suits & inveterate Quarrels about their Boundaries & Contest & Hatred transmitted thro their Families.[18]

*T*HROUGHOUT most of the seventeenth century New England's system of settlement by townships, with the size of individual allotments very closely tied to the grantee's actual need for land and ability to use it, had kept large-scale land speculation at a remarkably low level. In most cases the proprietors of a grant became actual residents of the new township, serving as trustees of the undivided land. The General Court was cautious in making grants and almost invariably imposed strict conditions requiring actual settlement and improvement of the land within a stated period of time. In this way the Puritan leadership had hoped to maintain a close-knit, disciplined society, impervious to the disintegrating influence of the frontier. But time, actual conditions in America, and human nature were all against them. In a country of amazingly rapid growth, where new land was plentiful and the far edge of the frontier constantly beckoned to men of adventurous spirit, the inhabitants would not forever remain satisfied with a confining and controlled system of landholding. One important development was the gradual consolidation of family holdings within the agricultural township, resulting in the establishment of unitary farms in place of the old medieval arrangement of scattered strips in open fields. More and more pioneering families, too, were taking up land and building dwellings out in the countryside, away from the nucleated villages.

The last decades of the seventeenth century witnessed also the gradual erosion of the entire power structure through which the Puritan oligarchy had exercised its control, as a new generation of leaders, many of them as much oriented toward business and commerce as toward religion, arose to challenge the ideas and ways of the old order. Some of these men, in fact quite a few of them, became interested in frontier land as an investment. Moving into the legislatures of the New England colonies, they began to loosen some of the old restrictions on land grants. It became possible for a group of investors to obtain from the colony government the grant of a new township somewhere in the wilderness, without committing themselves to reside there. Instead, their plan would be to sell real estate at a profit, with the value of their holdings increasing as more and more settlers came to the area. Such investors became, in other words, absentee proprietors, who risked only their capital and derived their gain from the labor of other men. Between them and the actual settlers there frequently arose considerable antagonism and resentment.[19]

Since Maine was under the jurisdiction of Massachusetts, and the financial center of Massachusetts was Boston, it is not surprising that the majority of the principal speculators in Maine lands were members of the Boston mercantile community. Many of them, too, were active in politics, holding important positions in the colony government. Governor Jonathan Belcher advised a correspondent to put his money into "uncultivated wilderness lands in this Province" which will "advance your estate three times faster than money put to interest."[20] To another he remarked that the Casco Bay area "settles apace, and the lands will accordingly grow in value."[21] That Belcher was experienced in the process of turning frontier land into comfortable profits is shown by his generous advice on the subject. Replying to an inquiry from the Duke of Chandos as to the best method for promoting settlement on wilderness property, Belcher wrote:

> . . . I take the freedom to inclose to your Grace a copy of one of my leases, the charge whereof to me was about £ 80 sterling; but some settlements I am now designing to bring forward will be thus,—A farm of 200 acres, with only a small house & barn (no living stock or utensils), and such a house & barn may cost about £ 30 sterling, & I wou'd make a lease of 14 years. The tenant to be oblig'd in the term thorrôly to subdue & bring to English grass (fit for the scythe) 40 acres of land. . . . The first tenants we get to our wild lands are commonly poor and often unfaithfull, and turn the quick stock put into their hands into money, & make off; that of late . . . I settle none but in the manner I now mention, and generally look for a man with a wife & children, who are able to go thorrô such a lease. . . . [22]

The first speculative group to get itself organized and functioning after the Peace of Utrecht was the Pejepscot Company, a small band of investors including Thomas Hutchinson (father of the governor-historian). The Pejepscot lands in which Hutchinson and his associates were interested comprised an area lying along the lower Androscoggin and Kennebec rivers, south to Casco Bay. About 1628 a trader named Thomas Purchase had established himself in that region, and in 1632 he and George Way had received from the Council for New England a patent to the land. The Indian war of 1675 cleared the land of settlers, including Purchase, but although the Pejepscot area remained vacant for a number of years thereafter, the owners and their heirs kept their rights alive. In the early 1680s a Boston merchant and land speculator, Richard Wharton, began buying up those rights, until he had title to the entire area, a tract of some half a million acres.[23] Political opposition prevented immediate development, and Wharton died insolvent in 1689.

Two wars later, in the fall of 1714, the government of Massachusetts set up a committee to oversee the re-establishment of the frontier in Maine, while at the very same time Thomas Hutchinson and the other Pejepscot investors purchased the Wharton lands from the executor of Wharton's estate at a price of £40. Now the door to effective development of the area stood wide open, for some members of the speculating group also were members of the newly appointed governmental committee. The following May the General Court heard the committee's favorable report on the Pejepscot venture and in June authorized the establishment of two towns on the Androscoggin River.[24]

Unlike many speculators in New York, the Pejepscot proprietors were eager to introduce pioneering farmers onto their lands, as shown by the Company's advertisement published at Boston on June 24, 1715.[25] Promising free transportation by ship to the site, the Company also offered one hundred acres of land free to each of the first one hundred families to build and occupy a house there. Prospective settlers were advised that by vote of the General Court the stone fort near the falls on the Androscoggin River was to be put back into service for their protection; in addition, they would enjoy a five-year exemption from colony taxes. This was encouragement indeed.

Soon beginnings were made at three towns—Augusta (not to be confused with the present capital of Maine), Brunswick, and Topsham. Dummer's War in the 1720s erased these early endeavors, but during the following decade settlement proceeded anew. Because the members of the Pejepscot Company were absentee proprietors, their interests tended to diverge from those of the pioneering settlers, with consequent friction and difficulty. In general, however, the Company enjoyed a fair measure of success, while contributing measurably to the expansion of New England's Eastern frontier.

Starting in 1727 the General Court of Massachusetts further gratified the growing pack of speculators by inaugurating a policy by which new townships were authorized not singly as in the prudent past but in groups. Various reasons underlay this new practice, among them the urge to create a barrier zone against the Indians, the need to meet the insistent demands for frontier land being voiced by organized veterans of the colonial wars, the desire to strengthen Massachusetts' hold on territory claimed also by New Hampshire, and the inclination to furnish the colony's business community with choice opportunities for investment. Accordingly, between 1727 and 1738 a galaxy of new townships was created extending from the Presumpscot River in Maine to the border of New Hampshire, and from the Merrimack to the Connecticut River across the southern part of the present State of New Hampshire.[26]

Many of these townships were specifically designated for the veterans of King Philip's War and King William's War, or their heirs, but the actual grantees in many cases had no desire to move to the frontier, and simply sold their rights to speculators.[27] In this way it became easy for an investor with plenty of capital to turn over a large amount of land at considerable profit. This alone shows how far the Bay Colony had retreated from the rigid policy of the seventeenth century. The government still attached to such grants a condition that actual settlement be achieved within a designated time, but the requirement proved difficult to enforce. The fact of the matter was that there were not enough willing pioneers to provide each of the new towns with its quota of inhabitants. Actual settlement proceeded at a slow pace, and the disruption of the Massachusetts community tradition was not as great as might have been expected. In fact, the families that did brave the wilderness tended to take with them an ideal of social order, which they nurtured in their new location. As one historian has well observed, "The frontiersmen of New England, like the Plain People of Pennsylvania, continued without much change the social institutions of their fathers."[28]

It was also in the 1730s that Connecticut, partly at the behest of speculators, opened to settlement its last large area of desirable vacant land, along the upper Housatonic River in the northwestern corner of the colony.[29] As a result a number of new townships were established, including Kent, whose beginnings have been studied intensively. The findings contradict or at least bring into doubt some of the traditional views about the eighteenth-century frontier in New England.[30] It has commonly been assumed that frontier dwellers usually were victimized by the eastern bigwigs who dominated both government and business. Settlers in frontier communities, according to this view, were the hapless debtors of the affluent merchants and absentee proprietors, who further increased their advantage by denying to the western townships proportionate representation in the legislature.

It has now been shown that the Connecticut town of Kent, although at first unrepresented in the colony legislature, also was not required to pay colony taxes. Later, when Kent did begin to send representatives to the assembly at Hartford, the town actually was over-represented relative to its population. Moreover, the early settlers did not find themselves cast as underdogs in a conflict with eastern creditors and absentee proprietors; instead, a large proportion of the pioneering townsmen were themselves speculating in land, often with good success. The picture that unfolds is of a reasonably prosperous frontier community that in its way of life and its way of thinking was scarcely to be distinguished from the older towns of Connecticut. Certainly in this case there was no sharp line of antagonism between west and east, and it is likely that similar studies of other frontier towns will reveal a somewhat similar pattern.

The advance of the frontier was retarded during King George's War in the 1740s, but with the return of peace in 1748 the business of speculating in frontier land once again became attractive. Along the banks of the Kennebec River in Maine appeared new forts and new dwellings, under the encouragement of a determined group of Massachusetts speculators known as the Plymouth Proprietors, whose claims to the region brought them into conflict with rival speculators such as the Pejepscot Company and with settlers already on the land. Nevertheless, as was so often the case in land speculation, influence in high places enabled them to proceed with their plans. Governor Shirley welcomed the opportunity to checkmate French claims by pushing ahead with English settlement, and so was inclined to favor the program of the Plymouth Proprietors. Later, as inducement and reward, he was given eight shares in the company.[31] The local Indians objected strenuously to the northward advance of the English up the Kennebec, but their protests were unavailing. Consequently the Indian mood in this region grew ominously sullen, with deep foreshadowing of trouble yet to come.[32]

At the same time there was a renewed thrust northward up the Connecticut River. Governor Benning Wentworth of New Hampshire, an avid speculator, was granting numerous patents in what is now Vermont. It was his practice to reserve for himself 500 acres of choice land in each new township granted. Although actual settlement proceeded slowly, there developed a bitter controversy between New Hampshire and New York over jurisdiction in the area. The New Englanders managed to establish several new settlements west of the Connecticut River in the southeastern corner of Vermont. Some men even laid plans to plant a township on each bank of the Connecticut River at the Coos meadows, some eighty miles above the Massachusetts border, but strenuous objections by the St. Francis Indians, who threatened to resist by force if the project were pursued, brought an end to the attempt.[33]

The activities of many other prominent land speculators, such as the Connecticut promoters who formed the Susquehanna Company in 1753, and Dr. Elisha Cooke of Boston who steered the Muscongus Company through the troubled waters of Massachusetts politics, emphasize what we have already observed, that land speculation was big business on the eighteenth-century frontier, with the lure of profits often beclouding the lamp of principle. That the anticipated profits did not always materialize only increased the excitement of the game.

*S*O FAR as the development of the northern frontier is concerned, land speculation produced effects both good and bad. In some instances speculators created the conditions that made it possible for pioneering farmers to enter a desirable tract and begin transforming it into productive farmland. They offered attractive inducements to settlers, enabling them to make a start, and, above all, they provided essential capital for quieting Indian claims, surveying the land, constructing defensive works, and even building roads. It is only fair to point out that without the planning and promotion furnished by land speculators, many parts of the frontier would have remained in a wilderness condition much longer than they did. As with the fur trade, however, speculating in land coincided most closely with the common weal when it was subject to some measure of regulation and control by the representatives of the people. Uncontrolled, it often ran wild, to the danger and damage of the populace.

On the other hand, there is much evidence to show that in many instances large-scale engrossment of land delayed and discouraged actual settlement of frontier areas. This was especially true when the speculator retained his tract in its virgin condition without making any attempt to attract free settlers. Governor Hunter of New York testified that nothing had contributed more to keeping his province sparsely populated that "single men's possessing vast tracts of Land to the extent of some 20 and some 30 miles square which they keep in their own hands, in hopes of Planting them with Tenants of their own, which is never to be expected in a Country where the Property may be had at so easy Rates."[34] A similar problem existed in parts of Maine, where, as a committee of the General Court stated, regular settlement was impeded "by reason of some Persons claiming Large Quantities of Land, which they are not capable themselves to settle, as the Law directs, nor are willing to part with to others, that offer to settle on them."[35]

Land speculation was often a contributing factor in the deterioration of Indian relations. Many of the speculators developed such a monstrous appetite for land that they would employ almost any means to get it. In their dealings with the Indians they frequently resorted to low trickery, showing little regard for the sentiments of the natives and scarcely more for the future safety of the frontiersmen. Again and again the tribes signed away huge portions of their territory, only to discover later the real extent of their loss. As one sachem complained, "when a Small parcell of Land is bought of us a Large Quantity is taken instead of it."[36] The lust for land, which was the driving force of land speculation, contributed much to the dangerous friction between the races on the frontier.

Land acquisition was a double process. Not only did the Indian proprietors have to be bought off, but the colony government had to be induced to give its consent through a grant or patent. This, of course, immediately threw land speculation into the arena of politics. Added to the low standards of political morality prevalent in eighteenth-century England, the temptation of the large profits to be made by land-jobbing was a corrupting influence in American government. Men who otherwise maintained an ideal of integrity in their personal lives succumbed to the expedience of dishonest deception and downright lying when frontier tracts were at stake.

A widely held attitude toward frontier land is clearly demonstrated in a letter from one of Pennsylvania's leading citizens. Claiming to own a tract of unsurveyed land near Shippensburg "by right of Possession," this gentleman gave instructions that it be appropriately marked so that there might be no mistake about its ownership. But as an added precaution he suggested that a tree on the property be cut down for staves "and then the Surveyor, & others will think I have actually got a Patent for it."[37] It would seem that some of the cunning of the fox had entered the character of the American colonist.

It is said that every man has his price, and apparently in land speculation the price was rather easily found. The use of trickery in matters of government was a habit readily formed, but hardly broken. So the ways of the land speculators, both in and out of government, fostered and nourished political corruption in American life.

In studying the problems of the frontier, one becomes aware of the divisive effect of land speculation. It was a game that almost anybody with capital could play, but the advantage was always with the small minority that had influence and power. The seemingly limitless land of America was up for grabs, and some men had a tremendous grasp. Inevitably the ordinary people found themselves left with little. In the Old World this would have seemed perfectly natural, and might have been accepted by all as one of the hard facts of life. But in the land of plenty, with land more plentiful than anything else, frontier folk struggling to get their roots into the good earth resented the fact that the wealthy were waxing more wealthy still by acquiring huge amounts of land, at little cost, through political influence. The elements of class resentment and class conflict began to appear, especially during the eighteenth century, as a by-product of land speculation.

One other unfortunate concomitant was the spirit of exploitation that ballooned into a national characteristic. This spirit was fathered by the wonder that Europeans felt when they first contemplated America's incredible bounty. There seemed to be plenty for all forever, so why be concerned with conservation. The vast extents of vacant land, so attractive to the eyes of the land speculator, contributed to this sense of limitless plenty, causing men to grow heedless of moderation and propriety. Many of the schemes devised by ambitious men with a little capital and a huge amount of self-assurance can only be described as downright greedy. In some cases such men aspired to the kind of power and wealth associated with the aristocracy of a feudal system; in others they merely thirsted for princely profits such as any good Renaissance capitalist might hope to make. But underlying it all was the burgeoning spirit of exploitation that was destined to advance all the way across the continent with the successive waves of pioneers, nearly consuming the best of our natural resources until, in the first half of the twentieth century, an aroused public finally asserted its own rights.

◁ 11 ▷

Christianity on the Northern Frontier

*P*ossibly the most important geographical advance ever made by the Christian religion was from Europe to America during the age of discovery and colonization. The New World, lying three thousand miles or more from the Old, was virgin territory of vast scope, hitherto unknown to Europeans; more, it was inhabited by a race of people completely untouched by the legacy of Greco-Roman culture or the influence of Judeo-Christian concepts. For European Christianity, America became at once a great challenge and a testing ground. The Roman Catholic form of Christianity responded to the challenge in Canada, Mexico, and Central and South America. The various branches of Protestantism met their challenge in what is now the eastern part of the United States, including the northern frontier.

Virtually all the Europeans who migrated to the English colonies were of the Christian faith, coming from lands where some branch of Christianity was the official religion of the state and where forms of religious observance were customarily followed by the great majority of the people. Each newcomer brought with him to the northern frontier

179

not only a bundle of material possessions but also a spiritual heritage that included an acquaintance with the Bible, certain concepts of prayer and worship, and some awareness of moral standards with a religious sanction. What that heritage came to mean on the frontier and how it was affected by the frontier are questions most pertinent to our study.

Geography itself had a great influence. The very size of the new land, partitioned as it was with various natural barriers such as rivers and mountains, meant the isolation of whole communities and even single families. This in itself posed a serious problem to organized religion. Cohesion was an important element in church discipline; a widely scattered flock was difficult to shepherd. Yet frontier conditions tended to foster a high degree of mobility, with families moving from place to place as opportunity occurred. This, combined with the influx of immigrants from a variety of lands, caused an intermixing of peoples and a consequent mingling of traditions and practices. Thus an Anglican family might find itself not only far removed from the nearest Anglican church and priest, but with a Baptist family and a Quaker family as nearest neighbors. Religious beliefs and practices, as well as language and social customs, began to intermingle in the melting pot. This did not necessarily result in the rapid breakdown or blending of religious observances. On the contrary, many homogeneous pioneering groups clung tenaciously to their own ways, but the very experience of being exposed to other customs and concepts, under pioneering conditions, inevitably broadened the attitude of European sectarians.

Meeting the challenge of the frontier experience developed in many people such qualities as courage, simplicity, self-reliance. But for others the results were not so favorable. The isolation and hardships of frontier life could be corrosive, gradually wearing down the thin surface of civilization, laying bare the ugly core of sloth, selfishness, and even depravity underneath. Wherever the control normally exercised by state, society, and church was weakened because of distance, there the relative independence of frontier life could test severely the morality and piety of the settlers. Often, too, the frontier attracted the very people who by nature were rebellious against generally accepted standards.[1] Contemporary observers of frontier life made frequent mention of declining morality and loose living among the pioneers. Although many of these writers viewed the frontier with a negative bias, the information they present leaves no room to doubt that the older standards of Europe and the colonial seaboard were undergoing some modification in the wilderness.

Along the coast of Maine, especially in the more remote settlements dominated by horny-handed fishermen and lumbermen, there developed a way of life shocking to the Puritans of Massachusetts. In 1665 three royal commissioners reported that the plantations beyond the Kennebec River were inhabited by "the worst of men. They have had hitherto noe government and are made up of such as to avoid paying of debts and being punished have fled thither: for the most part they are fishermen, and share in their wives as they do in their boats."[2] The Reverend Cotton Mather, Puritan among Puritans, was outraged by the fact that in some frontier towns, mostly in Maine, the settlers were slow to undertake the burden of supporting an orthodox church. When King William's War began, Mather observed that the first blows fell upon "the more Pagan Skirts of *New England,* where no *Minister* of God was countenanced." Salmon Falls in particular, a frontier settlement that was destroyed by the enemy in March 1690, was noted for its "most Heathenish Disrespect unto a *Ministry,*" according to Mather.[3] Actually, such towns probably were characterized not so much by heathenism as by poverty and the religious indifference of men who had become preoccupied with material gain. Many of the inhabitants doubtless preferred no minister to one of Mather's kind.

Frequent contact with Indians and their way of life had a demoralizing effect upon some of the colonists, just as the character of the Indians sometimes was undermined through association with the worst elements in the white community. Fur traders, especially, found in the depths of the forest an easy escape from the restraints imposed by organized society and reveled in the freedom of Indian ways. Some became almost Indians themselves in costume, manner, and personal conduct. In 1623 one of Thomas Weston's unruly crew at Wessagusset, twenty-five miles north of Plymouth, was reported to have slipped the cables of civilization and turned savage.[4] Peter Kalm was told that a similar tendency had appeared among the early Swedish settlers on the Delaware, so that by the time the English began to arrive, "the Swedes to a large extent were not much better than savages."[5] Even in Puritan Connecticut the problem was not unknown, for in 1642 the legislature, alarmed because "divers persons departe from amongst us, and take up their abode with the Indeans in a prophane course of life," set a penalty of at least three years' imprisonment for such libertines.[6] Admittedly these fears and reports may have been exaggerated—they certainly display an ingrained bias against the Indians—but there is no reason to doubt that isolation in the wilderness did offer a tempting outlet for suppressed appetites and emotions.

On Pennsylvania's frontier in the 1740s the Reverend David Brainerd encountered many colonists who were living beyond the immediate influence of church and clergy. One winter's day at the forks of the Delaware this itinerant minister "Preached to the ... people ... upon the sunny side of a hill; had a considerable assembly, consisting of people who lived, at least many of them, not less than thirty miles asunder; some of them came near twenty miles."[7] On another occasion in the same area Brainerd

> Preach'd to a small Assembly of *High Dutch* People, who had seldom heard the Gospel preach'd, and were (some of them at least) very Ignorant. . . . They requested me to tarry with them, or come again and preach to them. And it grieved me that I could not comply with their Request, . . . they being as *Sheep not having a Shepherd*. . . .[8]

Far up the Susquehanna River Brainerd lodged at a house where he was "much afflicted in the evening, with an ungodly crew, drinking, swearing, &c." Later he came upon a pioneer family that to him seemed quite devoid of religion. Concerned, he tried "to discourse with the man about the life of religion, but found him very artful in evading such conversation. . . ." The next night the rebuffed missionary, pondering the problems of religion on the rough frontier, was glad to camp out in the open woods among converted Indians, where he "slept with more comfort than while among an ungodly company of white people."[9]

Gottlieb Mittelberger, who did some traveling along the Pennsylvania frontier in the 1750s, found similar evidence of a falling away from godly ways. Many of the country people, he asserted, "lead a rather wild and heathenish life," which he attributed to the lack of opportunities for schooling in the frontier areas. Some frontiersmen actually scorned and ridiculed well-meaning clergymen who sought to interfere. "Such outrageous coarseness and rudeness," Mittelberger argued, "result from the excessive freedom in that country, and from the blind zeal of the many sects. Liberty in Pennsylvania does more harm than good to many people, both in soul and in body." He found that "Sunday is very badly kept, especially in the rural districts, where most country folk pay little attention to it."[10]

In the interest of accuracy, however, it should be pointed out that many pioneers held firm to the highest standards of conduct, and cherished their religion in the wilderness. To such people the rough frontier was merely one of God's testing grounds for the proving of the faithful. They took the Bible with them into the wilderness and, if separated from an organized church, held regular worship in their own homes until such time as a congregation could be formed.[11]

Some religious groups, fearing the corrosive effects of the frontier experience yet wishing to take advantage of frontier opportunity, migrated to the American wilderness as a flock. A good example is the communal pioneering of the Moravians in Pennsylvania. These devout Germans, like the Puritans before them, not only came to America in groups, but settled together in tightly organized communities. During the 1740s they founded two settlements, Bethlehem and Nazareth, near the junction of the Delaware and Lehigh rivers. The Moravians organized themselves into a tightly knit religious community with all buildings and even tools owned by the church. Each member worked for the community and received from the community, in a spirit of religious consecration.[12] From simple beginnings the Moravian towns developed into flourishing centers of industry and agriculture, at the same time preserving in the wilderness a strong tradition of culture.

No religious tenet was more severely tested on the northern frontier than the Christian pacifism of the Quakers. Declining to take up arms against hostile Indians and sometimes even refusing to seek the shelter of the local garrison house, earnest Quakers tried with almost incredible persistence to show to their fellow colonists a higher way of dealing with the aroused natives. In times of Indian warfare, Quaker pioneers were confronted with a tormenting dilemma. When all around them the frontier folk were hastily preparing to defend their settlement or else were retreating to safer ground, the Quakers had to answer for themselves this question: Should they remain in the place of danger, unarmed, and expose themselves and their children to violent death, or should they withdraw and save their lives for further service, at the cost of weakening their spiritual witness? The question was answered sometimes one way, sometimes the other.[13]

Certainly the conditions of frontier life confronted organized religion with challenging new problems, which sometimes placed the churches under great strain. Such testing was not an entirely unfamiliar process in the long history of Christianity, a religion distinguished by its capacity to adjust to changing conditions and new times, but the American wilderness did present a challenge of unusual dimensions because of its relative isolation from the old centers of religious authority. With varying degrees of success the churches met that challenge and made the necessary adjustments. Probably the greatest single effect was the loosening of ecclesiastical control over the individual, attended by a gradual weakening of denominational rigidity.

*F*ROM THE TIME OF its founding, the Christian Church has felt an obligation to expand its fellowship by the conversion of nonbelievers. England became Christianized through the efforts of missionaries, and in turn sent missionaries of its own to attempt the conversion of other areas. So it is not surprising that when Englishmen began to contemplate the founding of colonies in America, they cited as one of their main objectives the Christianization of the heathen natives. Indeed, the very seal of the Massachusetts Bay Colony depicted an Indian uttering the appeal, "Come over and help us," a reminder of the cry that came from Macedonia to the apostle Paul.[14]

In the earliest days of colonization there was a certain amount of unwarranted optimism about the conversion of the Indians, optimism soon dispelled by hard experience. Most Indians, it was found, did not welcome the Gospel as though they had been waiting for it all through the long centuries of pagan darkness. Indeed, there were many thorny barriers standing in the way of the missionaries. Language was one. The tribal dialects proved difficult for Europeans to master, and even when learned they were found to be ill-suited to the explanation of concepts and doctrines that had evolved in a totally different culture. Frequently the missionary preachers tried to work through Indian interpreters who had developed some proficiency in the English language, but even then it was difficult to know whether a message had been correctly transmitted and comprehended. As the Indians did not have a true written language, it was necessary to devise one, using the English alphabet, so that the Bible might be made available to them.

Another difficulty arose from the huge gulf that separated the culture of the European from that of the native American. Complexity of thought and belief confronted a primitive simplicity, with results often baffling to both. This in itself constituted a major handicap when the missionaries tried to share their religious heritage with the primitive people of the forest. Some of the most sincere colonists who were concerned with the Indians came to the conclusion that before the natives could be converted to Christianity they would have to adopt some of the elements of civilized living.[15] In other words, civilization would have to precede Christianization.

Still another barrier was the glowering hostility of sachems and medicine men, who saw in the Christian religion a challenge to their own power and influence. Many of these native leaders set themselves firmly against the activities of the missionaries, resisting them in every way possible short of actual violence. It was reported from Connecticut, for example, that the sachems at first seemed receptive to preaching but soon discerned that "religion would not consist with a mere receiving of the word; and that practical religion will throw down their heathenish idols, and the sachem's tyrannical monarchy:" whereupon they "did not only go away, but drew off their people, some by flatteries, and others by threatenings: and they would not suffer them to give so much as an outward attendance to the ministry of the word of God."[16] When possible, the missionaries usually tried to work through the native leaders rather than against them; the best chance for success was to persuade an entire community of Indians to submit to instruction together.[17]

Everywhere that devoted men of God labored to inject into the consciousness of the Indians the ethical ideals of Christianity, they were embarrassed by the contrary behavior of white men who called themselves Christians. The Indians were not slow to detect the vast difference between Christian professions and Christian conduct, and did not hesitate to confront the missionaries with the discrepancy. Often they used this discrepancy as an excuse for rejecting the white man's religion. A Dutch pastor in New Netherland reported that sometimes a group of Indians would stand and watch him preach to his white congregation and afterward would ask him what it was all about. "I am admonishing the Christians, that they must not steal, nor commit lewdness, nor get drunk, nor commit murder, . . ." he would reply. "Then they say I do well to teach the Christians; but immediately add, *Diatennon jawi j Assirioni, hagiouisk*, that is, 'Why do so many Christians do these things?' "[18] A century later the question was still being asked. One missionary found that the Indians he encountered were constantly being misled by "the ill Examples of *nominal Christians*," which made it "unspeakably Difficult to treat with them about Christianity."[19] He told how an Indian with whom he was discoursing

> inquired why I desired the Indians to become *Christians*, seeing the Christians were so much worse than the Indians are in their present state. The Christians, he said, would lie, steal, and drink, worse than the Indians. It was *they* first taught the Indians to be drunk: and *they* stole from one another . . . . and he supposed that if the Indians should become Christians, they would then be as bad as these. And hereupon he said, they would live as their *fathers* lived, and go where their *fathers* were when they died.[20]

There is a fairly obvious element of hypocrisy in these and similar Indian comments, for Indian behavior was far from perfect. The assumed pose of innocence was not beyond the skill of a people such as the Iroquois, for example, who were accomplished in dramatic presentation, oratory, and statecraft. Yet the criticism carried with it the sting of unpleasant truth, and was rightly recognized by the missionaries as one of their major problems.

Viewing the whole period of settlement on the northern frontier down to 1763, and considering the clear imperative of missions in Christian thought, one is surprised that so little was actually attempted toward the conversion of the Indians. This was partly the result of early difficulties and discouragements, which convinced many colonists that the savages were beyond the pale of God's mercy, at least for some time to come. But the most important reason for neglect was simply that the colonists and their European backers became so involved in the business of conquering the wilderness and pursuing material success on the frontier that they had neither time nor interest to spare for the support of Christian missions. Indifference hardened into reluctance and bitter opposition, as wilderness warfare made the Indians seem like vicious beasts rather than human beings. In troubled times the missionaries and other men who demonstrated a spirit of concern for the natives became objects of scorn, even violent hostility, on the part of the frontiersmen.

Sometimes a missionary made his way into the wilderness only to discover rather quickly that his strength was not equal to the obstinacy of the heathen and the hardships of living among them. Such a man usually hastened back to civilization as soon as he decently could and took a civilized pastorate in some well-established town. But there were others whose faith was so intense and whose concern for the Indians was so deep that they endured ridicule, hostility, cold, hunger, fatigue, and even profound disgust, to go on living among the primitive people of the forest for the salvation of their souls. The magnificent devotion and heroism of the Jesuit missionaries in New France is well known, that of the Protestant missionaries in New England and the Middle Colonies less so.

Puritan Massachusetts produced one of the first great missionaries to the Indians in the person of the Reverend John Eliot. It was in 1646 that this "man of simplicity, directness, and strength" began his practice of making frequent visits to nearby Indian villages to preach and teach, having first learned how to communicate in the local Algonquian dialect.[21] During the remainder of his long life, Eliot played the double role of minister of the church at Roxbury and shepherd to the Indians of eastern Massachusetts. He came to believe firmly in the importance of civilizing as well as converting the natives, and gave them practical encouragement in the development of stable community living, industry, agriculture, and education.

In 1651 the General Court designated a special tract of land on the upper Charles River as the site of a new community where Eliot's converts might come together to live under his supervision.[22] Natick, as this village was called, was soon well established, with its own meetinghouse, native dwellings, and cultivated fields. Later other such Christian villages were formed in other parts of the colony. Eliot took pains to develop native leadership, and succeeded in training a number of Indians to be pastors and teachers among their countrymen. Perhaps the greatest monument to this man's devotion was a volume published at Cambridge in 1663, entitled *Mamusse Wunneetupanatamwe Up-Biblum God.* It was the entire Bible translated into the Algonquian tongue.[23]

The Dutch and English inhabitants of New York seem to have been largely indifferent to the possibility of converting the Iroquois until the mounting success of French missionary priests among these tribes raised the specter of Canadian domination. That prospect startled the province, causing merchants and politicians to endorse missionary enterprise as a means of counteracting French influence.[24] The two most noteworthy missionaries in New York after 1712 were William Andrews and Henry Barclay. By about 1742 a large proportion of the Mohawk tribe had submitted to Christian baptism.[25] The other nations of the Iroquois Confederacy remained less susceptible, wavering between the triple magnets of French Catholicism, English Protestantism, and paganism.

Many of the missionaries of English background, Puritan and Anglican alike, unconsciously repelled the Indians by their obvious attitude of patronizing superiority. This was a handicap not shared by the Moravians, who were more like William Penn and his Quaker contemporaries, never doubting that the natives were human beings worthy of their deepest concern. As missionaries the Moravians made excellent progress in the region of the upper Delaware River. Individual Indians, impressed by their sincerity and good will, began to accept Christianity and present themselves for baptism. To overcome one of the greatest barriers to effective communication between the races, a school for the study of Indian languages was established at Bethlehem in 1744. A few years later the Moravians planted a mission station at Gnadenhütten on the Lehigh River. Here many converts were gathered, until the settlement was attacked and destroyed in the French and Indian War.[26]

Some of the organized churches saw greater need and opportunity for missionaries among the frontiersmen than among the Indians. This was especially true in the eighteenth century, as Puritan discipline weakened and the old pattern of migration by congregations was superseded by family migration. The rapid expansion of the frontier caused the severing of many church ties; families caught up in the hustle of the westward movement were swept beyond the immediate influence of the established churches, and a new generation began to grow up without congregational experience. The scattering of population often made it difficult, if not impossible, for the frontier folk to organize and maintain churches of their own.

Attempting to counter these conditions, the churches of the East, in particular the Anglican and the Presbyterian, fostered missionary activity in frontier areas. The Society for the Propagation of the Gospel in Foreign Parts, an Anglican organization chartered in 1701, maintained evangelists in New York and other colonies. In general, however, these missionaries were more active and more successful in well-established communities than on the frontier. The Presbyterians were somewhat more effective in providing religious guidance to the frontier folk. In

Pennsylvania the Presbyterian pastors of eastern churches were expected to make occasional journeys to newly settled areas, helping the people to form themselves into congregations that would eventually be self-sustaining.

The demands and hardships of the frontier experience caused some men to forget their religion, but made others cherish it the more. Much has been written about the lawlessness of the frontier. In many places where the power of law had not yet become effective only the benign influence of religion, nurtured in the hearts of the people, acted to restrain selfish ambition and maintain the peace. Thus Christianity served as a preservative of human values in the difficult transition from wilderness to civilization.

*T*HE VARIOUS RIPTIDES and crosscurrents of religious development along the northern frontier converged in the 1730s in the movement known as the Great Awakening. Recent research and reinterpretation has shown that this first great American religious revival was not primarily a frontier phenomenon, although much of its early strength did seem to come from the newer communities of New England and the Middle Colonies.[27] The fervent, emotional appeal of the revival preachers stirred the hearts of frontier folk; it also proved extremely effective among the people of the older towns. In fact, the Great Awakening defies simple classification as either a class or a sectional movement. The error of attempting to bind it too closely to the frontier becomes immediately apparent when we recall that a similar revival, indeed, a sort of parent movement, was under way in Europe at the same time.

By placing renewed emphasis upon the supreme importance of saving unregenerate souls, the Great Awakening produced a fresh upsurge of interest in the possibility of Christianizing the Indians. A group of Massachusetts clergymen and other leaders, including the Reverend Jonathan Edwards, decided to inaugurate a new Indian mission in the far western part of the colony.[28] The local Indian leader and his people gave their consent, and a young tutor at Yale, John Sergeant, assumed the post of missionary in 1734. Taking his departure from the village of Westfield, Sergeant journeyed toward the site through "a most doleful Wilderness," along "the worst Road, perhaps, that ever was rid."[29] The new station was located on the Housatonic River, at a place to be known as Stockbridge. There the Indians set up a village, with a central building to serve as meetinghouse and schoolhouse.

Progress was fairly steady, although there was the usual difficulty with the traders and the supplies of liquor they made available to the Indians. By 1747 nearly fifty Indian families were in residence.[30] Sergeant was a firm believer in the importance of training the Indians in the useful arts to enable them to make their way in the civilized world; he and his helpers devoted much time to that kind of education. "The *Indians* are a very difficult People to deal with," Sergeant once remarked. "Whoever undertakes to have much to do with them, had need to fortify himself with an obstinate Patience."[31]

In 1743 Sergeant began teaching the Indian tongue to a young colleague in the ministry, David Brainerd, who was serving as missionary to a group of Indians at Kaunaumeek, an outlying station nearly twenty miles from Stockbridge. If saintly devotion is the criterion, Brainerd was to become probably the greatest of all missionaries to the Indians anywhere in the English colonies. After his brief but rugged introduction to the calling at Kaunaumeek, Brainerd transferred to the upper Delaware River to work among the Indians of that area. For most of the remainder of his short life, he poured out his small store of health and strength to carry the Gospel to the Indians of Pennsylvania and New Jersey. He made long, difficult journeys on horseback through the wilderness, as far west as the upper Susquehanna River, traveling hundreds of miles, sometimes sleeping in the open woods in wet, cold weather, lashing his frail constitution on in the service of God. To those Indians who placed themselves under his care, Brainerd became a beloved shepherd. There is no telling how far his good influence might have reached if his physical health had matched his spiritual devotion. He sank slowly—in fact, with astonishing slowness considering the way he drove himself in his labor—and died in the home of Jonathan Edwards in 1747, before his thirtieth birthday.[32]

*M*OST STUDENTS of history are well aware that contact with the ways of European civilization started the Indians down a slippery path of degeneration. Less clearly understood is the extent to which Christian missionaries combated the trend and tried to rescue their charges from the worst consequences of European greed and exploitation. A simple example of this was the attempt to protect the Indians from the constant temptation of liquor, an enormous factor in their slide to ruin. More complex but equally important was the missionaries' emphasis on practical education for the Indians, including not only elementary book learning but also vocational training in agriculture and industry. The significance of these early attempts has not been widely recognized, probably because they were sporadic and conducted on a small scale. Nevertheless, they did point the way toward more highly organized and supported programs that have proved to be extremely beneficial. The movement grew out of Christian concern with a practical problem.

A historian of a previous generation once wrote that "the attempt to subdue the Indian by love, charity and non-resistance would have meant not so much the disappearance of evil as the disappearance of the colonists."[33] Perhaps attractive as an epigram, this statement represents a judgment that is open to serious criticism, mainly for what it does not say. After all, genuine love and charity for the Indian, in the Christian sense, prevailed in the hearts of only a handful of the many colonists who had dealings with him, and was seldom evident in the behavior of governments or the mass of frontiersmen. The few unusual Christians, such as Roger Williams, William Penn, and David Brainerd, enjoyed marked success in their personal relations with the Indians. It is just possible that the tragic history of Indian relations in this country might have been drastically different if the great majority of the colonists had viewed the native people in the same light.

Certain it is that a considerable part of the white population distrusted and even opposed the missionary endeavor. In times of Indian warfare, for example, some colonists accused the missionaries of being "soft on Indians." But the most consistent opposition apparently came from men who had a selfish interest in land or who thrived on the cheap trickery of the Indian trade. Such people, virtually all of whom must have been at least nominal Christians, had no real interest in the welfare of the Indians, either material or spiritual, and feared that the missionaries somehow would insulate the natives against their activities. So they resorted to all kinds of underhanded methods to hamper the missionaries and destroy the Indians' confidence in their spiritual benefactors. Eliot, Andrews, Barclay, Brainerd, and many others were confronted with this kind of opposition.

One of the stark realities of frontier history is that the Indian way of life, being confronted with the more dynamic and powerful forces of Western civilization, had to submit to a transformation or become extinct. Survival of the Indian depended upon his ability to make a difficult transition to a way of life that would harmonize with the evolving culture of the whites. In colonial times the most sincere, and at the same time the most constructive, approach to the problem was made by the missionaries of various denominations—Puritans, Anglicans, Moravians, Presbyterians, and others—who saw at first hand the enormous difficulties facing the Indians and in the name of Christ tried to take these people by the hand and lead them to an acceptable solution.

◁ 12 ▷

The Overthrow of New France

*F*or many years prior to the outbreak of King George's War in the spring of 1744, the British and the French in America had been eying each other with mounting suspicion and apprehension. Each side had reason to suspect that the other represented a threat to its future, especially along the sparsely settled zones of the frontier and in the great trans-Appalachian West. As early as the 1730s far-visioned British colonial leaders had begun to contemplate the prospects of expansion beyond the Appalachians into territory vital to French imperial interests.[1] As we have already noted, the increasing success of the British traders, with their advantageous price differential, was undermining Quebec's intricate structure of Indian alliances. And the French were painfully aware that each passing year widened the already vast discrepancy in numbers between the few thousands of *habitants* and soldiers under the *fleur-de-lis,* and the hundreds of thousands of settlers in the British mainland colonies.

At the same time, the British colonists were equally apprehensive when they contemplated the activities of their French rivals. It seemed

191

that the royal regime at Quebec was pursuing a definite program of territorial acquisition whose purpose was to block further English expansion in the West, confining the British to the coastal area east of the mountains. Had not the French established a far-flung network of wilderness forts—Frontenac, Niagara, Detroit, and others—controlling the vital routes of communication and trade in the trans-Appalachian region? Moreover, in 1731 the industrious French had erected a new fort at Crown Point on the western shore of Lake Champlain, to prevent any future British advance toward the St. Lawrence along the most convenient interior route. Crown Point was like the tip of a warning finger pointing toward the back country of New England and the upper Hudson Valley. It could serve very well as a base for offensive operations against those regions.

Equally ominous was the progress being made by French missionaries in exploiting Iroquois dissatisfaction with the British. French influence was increasing especially among the Onondaga and the Seneca, to the alarm of New York's frontier leaders.[2] The ambiguity of Iroquois policy at this time was made manifest in June and July of 1744. At Albany a delegation of sachems from the Six Nations expressed their earnest desire to avoid hostilities with the French but promised to engage actively in the British war effort if the French should attack the colonists. Shortly after making this commitment, delegates from the same Confederacy met with colonial officials at Lancaster, Pennsylvania, and solemnly committed the Iroquois to a position of neutrality.[3] This left everything uncertain except the fact that the Iroquois no longer had any genuine enthusiasm for warlike adventures on behalf of their traditional allies. It seemed that the old pattern of Indian alignment throughout the West was becoming like a bog of quicksand, shifting and treacherous, with some groups being lured into the British orbit of trade, others being enticed by French persuasion and power, still others wavering somewhere in between.

*W*ITH ENGLAND AND FRANCE both laying claim to a huge interior region between the zones of effective settlement and each seeking to advance its own interests in the area as best it could, violent conflict was almost inevitable. Declarations of war by the mother countries in the spring of 1744 served as an invitation for the renewal of open hostilities in the American wilderness. All through the exposed back parts of the colonies the settlers braced themselves for the blows that were sure to come. For the next sixteen years, through the trying times of King George's War and the great French and Indian War, the frontier was to be a battleground for the conflicting imperial ambitions of the British and the French, with colonists and Indians alike fighting and suffering through the last agonies of this epic rivalry.

New England, feeling itself directly threatened by the power of the enemy from the north, began making preparations for the fray. New York, on the other hand, wavered between active participation and a nebulous neutrality, with the influential fur merchants of Albany quite unwilling to sacrifice their business for the sake of British imperialism. Although prominent leaders such as Governor George Clinton and Cadwallader Colden were eager for the province to assume its military responsibilities, their influence was scarcely sufficient to overcome the indifference of many New Yorkers, to say nothing of the neutrality-minded Six Nations. As for Pennsylvania, the Quaker leadership of that booming colony smugly clung to the notion that previous benevolence in dealing with the Indians would continue to be rewarded by exemption from Indian warfare, and showed little interest in matters of military import.

The French in Canada at first seemed inclined to let matters develop further before committing themselves to large-scale operations against the British colonies. Thus for a time there was little to report along the northern frontier except the activities of occasional Indian raiding parties. In June 1745 New England militia, with the invaluable assistance of the Royal Navy, scored the greatest single achievement of the war by seizing the great French fortress of Louisbourg on the east coast of Cape Breton Island, a stronghold that long had threatened the security of colonial shipping. The victory set the bells ringing in Boston, cannons blasting off joyously in Maine, and bonfires flaring in London.[4] After that, warfare along the frontiers developed with greater intensity, as the French and Indians addressed themselves to the congenial task of punishing the exposed settlements of the English.

Toward the end of November 1745 a raiding party from Crown Point descended upon Saratoga, the northernmost English village in the Hudson Valley, and left it in ruins. More than a hundred colonists were killed or taken captive in this surprise raid. Fear ran like quicksilver through the settlements below, with the inhabitants hastily making preparations for withdrawal to safer ground. Soon few English or Dutch faces were to be seen in the whole valley north of Albany; even Albany itself lost some of its population to Manhattan.[5] The following spring the Eastern Indians threw off all restraint and turned their wrath upon the feeble young settlements of the Kennebec. Waldoboro was erased from the map with frightening thoroughness, and from that moment the villages as far south as Falmouth lived under a cloud of dread. The kind of warfare against which there was no sure defense was spreading its dark shadow across the face of the land.

As King George's War dragged on, the colonial authorities grew increasingly impatient with the neutrality of the Iroquois, for their active assistance was sorely needed in beating back the raiding parties of the enemy. Still the Six Nations, burning with resentment over English practices in land acquisition and the fur trade, angry especially at the high-handed tactics of the Dutch leaders in Albany, refused to become openly involved. Although they still professed loyalty to the English, their ears remained open to subtle enticement from Canada. At the same time, the frontier ambitions of both Massachusetts and Pennsylvania prompted the leaders of those colonies to attempt the enlargement of their own influence among the Iroquois, contrary to the wishes of New York. All this made for a complex and difficult situation in a time of war and worked to the advantage of the French.

The problem very nearly came to violence in January 1745 when a rumor of mysterious origin, to the effect that the colonists at Albany and Schenectady were plotting a sudden massacre of the neighboring Indians, spread among the Mohawk.[6] Only with considerable difficulty were the Indians quieted, and many of them continued to nourish deep suspicions of Anglo-Dutch intentions. One of the Mohawk leaders, in a conversation with Conrad Weiser of Pennsylvania, reasserted Iroquois fidelity to the British in general but ruled out any further friendship with Albany men. "We could see Albany burnt to the Ground, Or every Soul taken away by the Great King, & other people planted there," he added bitterly.[7] This attitude among the Mohawk, to say nothing of the more remote nations of the Confederacy, was a serious handicap for the English colonies in the struggle against New France.

Briefly in late 1746 and early 1747 the Iroquois were induced to go on active service against the enemy, under the skillful prodding of the Mohawk Valley trader William Johnson.[8] But their enthusiasm for such adventures proved transitory, being weakened by continued French enticement and the failure of the British to develop a vigorous and concerted war effort. If the Iroquois do not receive from us all the supplies they expect, warned Governor Shirley, "it is more than probable that they will be disgusted at their being left in the lurch by us, and will fall entirely into the interests of the French, which will be more fatal to these colonies than any thing that has yet befallen us."[9] Shirley's fears were not without foundation. The Six Nations contributed little to the colonial war effort, leaving the settlers along the frontier to fight their own battles against the dreaded raiders from the north.

Far more important in the long run, however, was the British naval blockade, which prevented all but a trickle of trading goods from reaching Canada, thereby forcing still higher the prices at which the hard-pressed French fur traders had to sell to the Indians. These traders found themselves operating under an increasing handicap at the very time when their aggressive competitors from Pennsylvania, loaded with seemingly endless quantities of good inexpensive English textiles and hardware, were pushing ever farther into the West.[10] As a consequence, the Western Indians now were drifting rapidly into the economic orbit of the British, a trend which, if continued, would surely result in the collapse of French influence and power everywhere south of the Great Lakes, including the Ohio Valley. As though to emphasize this prospect, a Wyandot chief known as Nicolas, probably instigated by the Pennsylvania trader George Croghan, in 1747 attempted to organize a general Indian uprising against the French traders.[11] That the plot proved abortive was of little comfort to the French, whose position in the area remained precarious throughout the remainder of the war.

In 1748 King George's War was brought to an indecisive conclusion by the Treaty of Aix-la-Chapelle, and for the time being the bloody raids along the northern frontier ceased. All territory, even Cape Breton Island, reverted to its prewar status. In actuality none of the issues had been settled; both sides held intently to their imperial ambitions.

*F*OR THE NEXT seven years every frontiersman who pondered the future had to figure on the prospects of a new war. The French and their fierce Indian allies remained an everpresent menace, certain to come pouring in upon the back country whenever England and France again came to blows. Under this threat, few settlers could contemplate with serenity a resumption of pioneering along the exposed frontier. Nevertheless, the constant hunger for fresh, cheap land, and the enticing possibilities of profits to be made in land speculation and the fur trade, again impelled large numbers of colonists to venture into the remote interior. Slowly and hesitantly, almost with an air of weary resignation, the pioneers resumed their struggle with the wilderness. Bit by bit the line of settlement edged forward to regain lost ground and even venture into virgin territory.[12]

In New England, pioneering families moved northward up the valleys of the Kennebec and the Connecticut rivers. Likewise on the upper Hudson River many farmers drifted back into an area made desolate by the recent war. Often they found their old homes entirely destroyed and had to shelter themselves for the time being in crude huts made of boards.[13]

Unlike New England and New York, Pennsylvania suffered little in King George's War, so there was almost no interruption in the apparently tireless push of the Scotch-Irish up the spreading network of rivers and creeks. A new wave of immigration, beginning about 1749, added strength to the movement. Along the upper reaches of the Delaware, Lehigh, and Schuylkill rivers, and especially along the western tributaries of the Susquehanna, the spreading tide of humanity crept forward. Reading and Carlisle both had their beginnings in 1751. Two years later a visitor described Carlisle as a community of about sixty dwellings, mostly inhabited by Ulstermen.[14]

Many Pennsylvania frontiersmen were staking out claims for themselves in territory still owned by the Indians and therefore officially closed to white settlement. The principal center of intrusion was the winding valley of the Juniata River, which enters the Susquehanna from the west. Such unauthorized settlements along the Juniata and its numerous branches caused great concern to the government of Pennsylvania because of their adverse effect on Indian relations. During the spring of 1750 an official party led by the provincial secretary, Richard Peters, went out and ejected some of the squatters, even burning their cabins to discourage a later return. But return they did, in defiance of orders and disregarding Indian resentment. Not until the region was purchased from the Indians in 1754 was the problem erased, and then just in time for the next outbreak of frontier warfare.[15]

*C*ÉLORON DE BLAINVILLE'S military excursion through the upper Ohio Valley in the summer of 1749 was interpreted by the British colonies as clear evidence of a Gallic determination to prevail in America. The French, wrote one colonist, "Intend to prevent the English spreading any farther on the Continent—and to be Masters of the whole as soon as may be."[16] This gloomy deduction was reinforced by the testimony of several Pennsylvania traders who as captives among the French had had opportunity to observe their military preparations in the West.[17] Indians who previously had aligned themselves with the British now were becoming fearful of imminent French retaliation. Not only the tribes of the upper Ohio but the Iroquois as well dreaded what the immediate future might bring, and wondered whether the English had the will and the stamina to hold back the menace.[18] That the French were equally apprehensive of British expansion beyond the mountains, especially in the form of extended trading operations by Pennsylvania and Virginia, and correspondingly fearful for their own future in the West, was largely overlooked even by the most perceptive of the colonial leaders. Possessing man power and other resources vastly superior to those of the enemy, the British nevertheless cast themselves in the role of the mouse awaiting the pounce of a crafty and very hungry French cat.

Numbers of the Iroquois had drifted southward into the upper Ohio Valley, where they mingled with Shawnee, Delawares, and other Indians, forming a heterogeneous population susceptible to French influence. Their resentment against the English was heightened by the mounting activity of such speculating groups as the newly formed Ohio Company of Virginia, an organization dedicated to the furtherance of British trade and settlement in the transmontane West.[19] At the same time, French influence continued to make significant inroads in the home territory of the Iroquois Confederacy, especially among the Onondaga, Cayuga, and Seneca. Conrad Weiser in 1750 noticed many French Indians in the Onondaga country seeking to cultivate a pro-French attitude among their New York cousins. Apparently, too, there had been a significant turnover in the membership of the Iroquois Council, largely through death, with the new members "devout to the French," as Weiser put it.[20] The Seneca in particular were under the pervading influence of Canadian missionaries, whose goal was to bring the entire Confederacy over to the French side. Only the counterinfluence of William Johnson was of comparable strength in this crucial game, and Johnson was handicapped by his own involvement in the factional strife of New York politics. Moderate Iroquois opinion wavered in bewilderment. As one Indian spokesman said in 1753,

> we dont know what you Christians French and English together intend we are so hemm'd in by both, that we have hardly a Hunting place left, in a little while, if we find a Bear in a Tree, there will immediately Appear an owner for the Land to Challenge the Property, and hinder us from killing it which is our livelyhood, we are so Perplexed, between both, that we hardly know what to say or to think.[21]

Beginning in 1752 the French put on a dazzling demonstration of the advantages to be gained by determination and speedy action. The humiliating lesson opened with the destruction of the trading center of Pickawillany on the Miami River by a raiding party of French Indians led by the French trader Charles Langlade.[22] The following year a strong French military expedition began constructing a chain of forts that was to connect Lake Erie and the Forks of the Ohio, in order to make good the claim put forth by Céloron in 1749. The English were to be excluded, by force if necessary, from *la belle rivière*.

Among the colonial leaders who saw the French program as a

serious threat to Britain's future in America was Governor William Shirley of Massachusetts. An ardent imperialist, Shirley favored a policy of bold action best described as "beating the enemy to the punch." When he received intelligence that the French were occupying territory near the headwaters of the Kennebec River, with the prospect of building forts along the river itself, he took appropriate countermeasures and notified the General Court of his forebodings. French policy, Shirley warned, included both an attempt to win the allegiance of all Indians west of the Appalachian Mountains, with the consequent ruin of English trade, and the forging of an iron barrier all along the back of the British colonies to keep the settlers forever confined to the seaboard. "The French," he concluded, "seem to have advanced further towards making themselves Masters of this Continent within these last 5 or 6 Years, than they have done ever since the first Beginning of their Settlements upon it...."[23]

Shirley was a leader in the movement for colonial unity that culminated in the Albany Congress of 1754, an intercolonial conference whose immediate purpose was to mend the tattered alliance with the Six Nations. The Iroquois came dragging into the conference with an obvious air of resentment, grumbling over a long list of grievances. As always, they complained of bad treatment in the fur trade and deplored the continuing traffic along the Champlain Valley between Albany and Montreal. They blamed the colonial governments for the lack of adequate defenses along the frontier, a weakness that left the Indians exposed to the first strokes of the enemy. They objected to encroachments being made, especially by Pennsylvania and Virginia, on territory supposedly under Iroquois jurisdiction. And most bitterly they condemned the activities of New York land speculators, who continued to deprive them of important segments of their domain.[24]

Obviously, there would have to be a drastic alteration in colonial attitudes and policies if the Iroquois and their subsidiary tribes were to be convinced of the faithfulness and benevolence of the English. Yet even as these important matters were under consideration at Albany, the English showed their true colors, quite unchanged and perhaps unchangeable. A Connecticut land company, working through a New York agent whose tactics were questionable, purchased from the Iroquois a large tract of land along the upper Susquehanna River, including the Juniata Valley. At the same time, also employing dubious methods, proprietary agents from Pennsylvania induced the Iroquois to sell the same territory to their colony. These disreputable transactions occurred during a conference intended to impress the Indians with the unity, to say nothing of the good will and integrity, of the English.[25] The Iroquois sachems went away from Albany only partially satisfied with a patched-up alliance; later, as they became more fully aware of the real nature of the land transactions, their resentment boiled again. Other Indian groups such as the Delawares and the Shawnee, who were dwelling on portions of the land that had been sold, also cursed the perfidy of the English, and became increasingly receptive to French influence as it spread through the transmontane region. A new grievance had been added to the old "Walking Purchase" of 1737.

In April 1754, two months before the beginning of the Albany Congress, a strong French force had expelled a working party of Virginians from the Forks of the Ohio and begun to build a wilderness stronghold at that strategic point. To counter this important move, Colonel George Washington led forth a small expedition of Virginia militia, only to be defeated by the French early in July at Fort Necessity. Now the ambitious plans of the Ohio Company for the development of the upper Ohio Valley lay shattered. The new French stronghold at the Forks, named Fort Duquesne after the governor of New France, stood as unmistakable evidence of French determination and success.

Not only was French power now firmly planted at the Forks of the Ohio, to block the westward aspirations of Virginia and Pennsylvania, but nearly everywhere the Indians were showing signs of hostile intentions. In New England, Colonel Israel Williams noted the "universal Terror" being felt by the frontier folk. "Its now open War," he remarked grimly, "and a very dark & distressing scene opening. . . ."[26] Asserting that French plans included the capture of Albany and the winning of the Six Nations to their cause, Williams warned that if this should be accomplished, ". . . farewell Peace & Prosperity to New England, Yea to North America." William Johnson saw equally ominous signs in his area. Writing to Governor Shirley, he reported that

> imediately on the news of Washington's defeat, above two Hundred of the Six Nations went to Canada . . . I fear many of them will be prevailed on to join the French & go to Ohio, as Severall of them have done last Summer. and those who may return will be so corrupted, & poisoned that they Seduce the rest. . . . we are for the most part Spending our time in squabbles & Chit, Chat, while the French are indefatigable in their endeavours, and spare nothing at this Critical point of time to pervert them, which I am Sorry to See them Succeed in beyond expectation & the more so, as it might be prevented.[27]

Johnson strongly urged the speedy redress of Indian grievances, but the best time for that was already past. The English colonies were actually engaged in open hostilities with their French antagonists; the opening shots of the momentous Seven Years War had already been fired in the American wilderness.

*A*WAKENED to the mounting danger in America, England dispatched General Edward Braddock with two regiments of regulars to drive the French from the Forks of the Ohio and make the West safe for British trade and settlement. Braddock reinforced his little army in the colonies and then began to move it westward toward the distant mountains. Much of the route lay through wilderness terrain, and it was necessary for the army to cut its own road as it went. Finally, on July 9, 1755, when less than ten miles from Fort Duquesne, the British unexpectedly ran into a well-prepared force of French and Indians. The next few hours were little short of disastrous for the British colonies. Braddock was killed and his army sent reeling back the way it had come, in precipitous retreat. This was a victory for wilderness terrain and wilderness men.

Word of the stunning defeat spread like the shock wave of an underground tremor. Lancaster heard of it on the evening of July 15; Albany got the news six days later; on July 23 the government at Boston received notice, whereupon "The Good Secretary upon reading the Melancholy Tidings fainted."[28] For understatement we have the word of one frontiersman, who wrote that ". . . general *Braddock's* defeat greatly increased the gloom, which sat on the countenances of the *Americans*."[29] In many a frontier cabin there was more than deep gloom; there was stark fear.

For many months after that fateful July day, the back-country settlements in Virginia and Pennsylvania staggered under the hatchet blows of French and Indian raiders. The scalping knife and the fiery torch carried their message of hate and vengeance from village to village, dwelling to dwelling. Faced with such horror and with scarcely a hope of successful resistance, hundreds of frontier families abandoned their farms and with precipitate haste straggled along the trails and roads toward the East. One Pennsylvanian reported that "Almost all the women & children over Sasquehannah have left their habitations, & the roads are full of starved, naked, indigent multitudes. . . . Not one twentieth man has arms."[30] A member of a Pennsylvania expedition that pushed its way up the Lehigh Valley to the stricken Moravian settlement of Gnadenhütten reported, after arrival,

> Here allround appears Nothing but One continued scene of Horror & destruction where lately flourished a happy & peaceful Village is now all silent and desolate the Houses burnt the Inhabitants butchered in the most shocking Manner their mangled Bodies for want of Funerals exposd to Birds & Beasts of Prey & all Kinds of Mischief perpetrated that wanton Cruelty can invent.[31]

Furious at the savages who could wreak such destruction, this nonpacifistic Pennsylvanian concluded, "I for my Part am determind to scalp all I lay my Hands on with unrelenting Rage. . . ." What made the situation increasingly dangerous was the growing inclination of Indians all along the frontier to join in with the French, now that things were going their way. In New York even Sir William Johnson, recently appointed superintendant of Indian affairs for most of the northern frontier, was having difficulty keeping the skittish Iroquois under saddle and reins.

On August 14, 1756, the English post at Oswego, guardian of the Mohawk Valley, surrendered to the French and was left in ruins. News of this calamity evoked fresh wails of despair. "Ill Success in the War!" wrote one New Englander in his diary. "*Mahon & Oswego* lost, either thro' Treachery, or Cowardice; or rather our Sins! The Sword of the destroying Angel unsheath'd! And God departed!"[32] Frontier forts seemed almost useless in preventing the incursions of Indian raiders, for the garrison troops often dared not venture forth against the passing enemy for fear of being ambushed. Expressing his disillusionment concerning the effectiveness of such outposts, one colonist asserted bitterly that if he were a raider "I'd pull off my Hat if I pleased and pass them knowing you can make no Salleys and make what Spoil I pleased and return the way I came or any Other."[33] Indeed, that is nearly what the Indians were able to do during this unhappy time. ". . . I look upon it a question of more Serious consideration than many imagine," concluded the same observer, "Who will be Masters of America The French or the English." The fall of Fort William Henry at the southern end of Lake George in August 1757 and a ravaging attack on the German Flats in the Mohawk Valley later the same year revealed only too clearly the southward reach of French power. The Hudson Valley itself was directly threatened, as was much of New England.

In the meantime Pennsylvania, hard hit for the first time in its history, was beginning to reassess its traditional policy of pacifism. Until 1756 the Quaker minority completely dominated the government, thanks to a deliberate system of underrepresentation for the frontier counties, and even after that date Quaker influence remained powerful in the colony. Quaker pacifism shunned all preparations for war, which explains why the outbreak of hostilities found the Pennsylvania frontier totally unprepared. The resulting terror and destruction suggest that no matter how suitable a policy of nonviolence may be for a well-integrated group thoroughly devoted to its ideal, such a policy is impractical if not actually immoral when imposed by a minority upon an entire state in a time of international violence. It was the frontier that was most directly threatened by the French and Indians, and the frontier had no faith in Quaker pacifism.

To the outrage of the suffering frontiersmen, many Quakers continued to blame the defection of the local Indians upon proprietary policy and frontier greed, and talked as though resistance to attack were nothing but another provocation. The frontiersmen, burned out of their homes in the wilderness, thought otherwise. One modern historian has made the interesting assertion that

> Happier would have been the history of Pennsylvania in this period, it would seem, had the Quakers occupied the frontier regions. No doubt all Friends soon would have acknowledged a defense policy inescapable, and perhaps they might have contributed a more sound Indian policy based upon stark realism, but retaining a solvent of fairness and regard for the rights of the Indians.[34]

Benjamin Franklin, who had some understanding of frontier problems and the relationship between Indian affairs and the imperial struggle for North America, led a movement to break the pacifist grip on Pennsylvania policy. Starting in the winter of 1755–1756, the province did begin to construct a long protecting shield of frontier forts stretching across the backcountry from the Delaware Water Gap south to the Maryland border beyond Carlisle.[35] Still the Indian depredations continued, while the Quakers and their political opponents fought a seemingly endless battle of propaganda in a prolonged struggle for control of provincial policy.

*A*FTER THREE YEARS of gloom and defeat for the British, the tide of war at last began to turn in 1758, thanks largely to the strategic vision and imaginative leadership of the new prime minister, William Pitt. The northern frontier first saw the products of Pitt's planning in the shape of substantially increased military support, including new and able commanders. By this time, too, individual boldness was beginning to reappear among the frontiersmen, producing a few daring heroes and a much larger number of reasonably courageous followers. Here was the stuff out of which victory might be shaped. Among the heroes was New Hampshire's Robert Rogers, who organized and trained a band of fighting rangers and led them on many a perilous foray against the French and Indians.

Scalp bounties offered by colonial governments encouraged small groups of frontiersmen to comb the woods for likely victims. It was a dangerous way to make a living, as James Cargill could testify. He and his partner were scalp hunting in Maine and were about a quarter of a mile apart when Cargill spotted two Indians. As he was watching them, a Frenchman in concealment took aim at him and fired, shattering his powder horn. Almost before Cargill knew what had happened the

Frenchman was upon him, fighting like a wildcat. The New Englander managed to tear himself loose, recovered his gun, and broke it over the Frenchman's head. Then he took off in the direction of his partner, pursued by two Indians who gave up the chase only when their quarry shouted for his partner and received an answer in return. Reunited, the scalp hunters wasted no time in getting back to base.[36]

One development important to British victory in the war would be a reconciliation between the colonies and certain tribes nominally subordinate to the Six Nations, such as the Delawares. Primary responsibility for achieving this objective rested with Sir William Johnson, by virtue of his office as Indian superintendant. But Johnson found himself at loggerheads with the Pennsylvania Quakers, who had their own way of handling such matters. They gave their backing to the besotted Delaware chieftain Teedyuscung, while Johnson preferred to conciliate the Iroquois, in the expectation that they in turn would bring the Delawares to heel.

The two opposite policies came face-to-face at the frontier town of Easton, Pennsylvania, in October 1758, when Johnson's personal representative, George Croghan, met with the Pennsylvanians and the sachems of the Iroquois and Delaware tribes. The issue was finally resolved when the Iroquois successfully reasserted their right to dictate policy to the Delawares, overriding Teedyuscung, and proclaimed an end to hostilities between the Delawares and the English. As compensation, the agents of the Pennsylvania proprietors gave back to the Iroquois the great tract they had purchased from them at the time of the Albany Congress.[37]

The meeting at Easton has been called "the most important Indian conference ever held in Pennsylvania," for it signalized a very significant shifting of Indian strength away from the French and toward the English.[38] This, together with the mounting power of British forces in America, accelerated the decline of French strength and helped produce an impressive series of victories in the field. The last major defeat for British arms had occurred on July 8, 1758, when the French commander, the Marquis de Montcalm, repulsed General James Abercromby's army at Ticonderoga. After that, the increasing resources of the British began to tell. Louisbourg fell to General Jeffrey Amherst on July 26, 1758, opening the eastern approaches to the St. Lawrence River. A month later the opposite end of the great river also was stripped of its guardian outpost as the British forced the surrender of Fort Frontenac. In November, thanks to the realignment of the Delawares and other groups of Indians, General John Forbes, who led a British army westward from Philadelphia along a newly constructed road across the mountains, was able to seize the Forks of the Ohio without serious opposition.

Shortly prior to Forbes's arrival at Fort Duquesne, the French garrison had blown up their stronghold and withdrawn toward the north. By the opening days of 1759 the upper Ohio Valley was firmly in British hands, and all eyes were turning toward the remaining centers of French power along the chain of the Great Lakes and the St. Lawrence Valley.

The thundering climax of the long struggle came the following summer, as strong British forces, including considerable numbers of American frontiersmen, advanced against the French positions. On July 25 the important French post at Niagara surrendered to a mixed force of British and Indians commanded by Sir William Johnson. This victory undermined the entire structure of French power west of Montreal. The strategic significance of the event was seen clearly by one of the participants, who wrote,

> The possession of the important Fortification of Niagara, is of the utmost consequence to the English, as it gives us the happy opportunity of commencing & cultivating a friendship with those numerous tribes of Indians who inhabit the Borders of *Lake Erie, Huron, Michigan* & even *Lake Superiour;* And the Fur trade which is carried on by these tribes, which all centers at Niagara, is so very considerable, that I am told by very able judges that the French look upon Canada [as] of very little importance without the possession of this important Pass; it certainly is so and must appear obvious to any one who understands the geography of this country. It cuts off & renders their Communication with their Southern Settlements impracticable.[39]

Detroit was left to rot on the vine, being finally plucked by the frontier ranger, Major Robert Rogers, in 1760. The downfall of Niagara left little room for doubt in the minds of the Western Indians that the French were doomed.

Even as the troops of William Johnson were rejoicing in their success at Niagara, the French were pulling out of Ticonderoga and Crown Point, and retreating along the Richelieu River toward Montreal. Already the able young British general, James Wolfe, having advanced up the St. Lawrence River from the sea with a powerful fleet and army, was lurking before the bastion of Quebec. On September 18, 1759, soon after both Wolfe and his worthy opponent Montcalm had lost their lives in the decisive battle on the Plains of Abraham, Quebec fell into British hands. News of the victory brought wild joy into the hearts of the British colonists, especially the frontier folk of New England, who for generations had deemed Quebec the principal source of their woe. From the pulpit Jonathan Mayhew voiced the feelings of many:

> Quebec, after repeated struggles and efforts is at length reduced: *Quebec,* I had almost called it that Pandora's box, from whence unnumber'd

plagues have issued for more than an hundred years, to distress, to enfeeble, to lay waste, these northern colonies; and which might, perhaps in the end have proved fatal to them![40]

The subsequent downfall of Montreal and the surrender of Canada were almost anticlimactic. By the end of 1760, British forces were in effective control from Cape Breton Island to the upper Mississippi River. The terms of the Treaty of Paris of 1763, officially ending the last of the great intercolonial wars in North America, brought all of France's mainland territory east of the Mississippi, including Canada, under British rule. A truly vast area had become potentially available for further expansion of the British colonies.

*S*CARCELY had the French abandoned the Forks of the Ohio and surrendered Quebec before traders, speculators, and pioneering farmers began to venture back into the remote frontier areas, poking among the ruins of their former dwellings or seeking out fresh ground to exploit. The Forks of the Ohio, where a new fort named after the great prime minister William Pitt was soon under construction, quickly became a center for Pennsylvania traders, anxious to beat out their Virginia rivals in the rapidly reviving Indian trade of the trans-Appalachian West. Their single-minded pursuit of profits meant a resumption of all the old objectionable practices, despite the new regulatory law of 1758. As before, the Indians were the dupes and victims. Likewise the Albany merchants gathered together the remnants of their old trade, including the exchange of furs and trading goods between Albany and Montreal. At least as early as November 1760 one prominent Albany businessman recorded the receipt of otter and marten pelts from Canada, even though France and England were still at war.[41] *Mercatura omnia vincit.*

At the same time land speculators, singly and in organized groups, were busy promoting new settlement. The swarming pioneers, convinced that at last the West was reasonably safe, readily fell in with their schemes. New Englanders began to venture onto the lands vacated by the displaced Acadian peasants, bringing new vigor to Nova Scotia. On the coast of Maine and up the Kennebec River, too, saws and hammers were busy on new construction, much of it on land controlled by hard-headed groups of investors such as the Plymouth Company.[42]

Governor Wentworth of New Hampshire, always alert to the scent of profits in land grants, looked again to the wilderness area between the Connecticut River and Lake Champlain. His lavish hand signed township charters by the dozen—sixty-three in 1761 alone, with forty-six more in the next two years, not counting other such grants east of the Connecticut. "The rapid progress of these grants filled the coffers of the governor," was the straightforward comment of an alert contemporary.[43] Pioneers began moving into the area, many of them coming north from Connecticut, whose last frontier was already being heavily settled. A whole company of pioneers from the Massachusetts town of Hardwick migrated to new land at Bennington.[44] Not to be outdone, New York's John Henry Lydius, a man of acquisitive instinct, was promoting settlement on Otter Creek southeast of Crown Point.[45]

The Indian district of Wyoming, far up the Susquehanna River in northern Pennsylvania, also was the scene of new pioneering activity. An ambitious group of Connecticut speculators known as the Susquehanna Company claimed the area and, despite outraged protests from the Iroquois and Delawares, sent in advance parties in 1762. The local Indians, led by Teedyuscung, remained sullen. One night, in some fashion still unexplained, the Indian village caught fire and was destroyed. Teedyuscung himself died in the flames.[46] Quite naturally, the Indians arrived at certain obvious conclusions as to the cause of the fire and awaited an opportunity for revenge. In the meantime, settlement of Wyoming continued.

Many miles to the west, beyond the mountains, other pioneers were advancing into the area just east of the Monongahela River and southeast of Fort Pitt. By 1760 there were about 150 settlers, other than soldiers, residing in the vicinity of Fort Pitt itself, the nucleus of the modern city of Pittsburgh.[47] The routes used by Braddock and Forbes in their approaches to the Forks had been made into usable roads, providing reasonably good access to the new area of settlement in southwestern Pennsylvania.[48] Indeed, almost everywhere along the northern frontier, from Maine to Pennsylvania, there was renewed advance by traders, speculators, and settlers. For increasing thousands, the great West was an irresistible lure, the threshold of promise.

With white settlers advancing into the wilderness in ever-growing numbers, the British government was confronted with the immediate problem of protecting and quieting the Indians whose lands and rights were being threatened. Late in 1761 the Crown issued a special admonition to the governors of certain royal colonies, reminding them of "the fatal Effects which would attend a discontent amongst the Indians in the present situation," and ordering them to see that the tribes were not deprived of their lands by unlawful means.[49] Henceforth all applications to the governors for permission to purchase land from the Indians were to be referred to London for review. This restriction proved to be only the first installment of a royal policy that was to bring the westward movement almost to a halt. But before that could be accomplished

Indian resentment boiled up into a widespread resistance movement, usually known as Pontiac's Rebellion. Fierce and bloody warfare raged along the western frontier during much of 1763.

In the meantime, on October 7, 1763, the British government issued an order forbidding all settlement beyond a line drawn along the crest of the Appalachian Mountains, as a temporary means of preventing future hordes of eager pioneers from goading the Indians into further retaliation. In this way the Crown erected an invisible barrier across the pathways of a massive folk migration that had been gathering strength and momentum for nearly 150 years. Whether the policy was wise, or even practical, only the future could show.

*M*ANY YEARS AGO Frederick Jackson Turner, the great historian of the American frontier, went over much the same ground that we have explored in this volume. Having already formulated the main outlines of his hypothesis concerning the relationship between the frontier experience and the character of modern America, based partly upon his experience with trans-Appalachian frontiers, Turner quite naturally sought and expected to find in the period before 1763 ample confirmation of his concepts. After all, between Gosnold's first view of the two great barriers in 1602 and the signing of the Treaty of Paris in 1763 stretched more than a century and a half of pioneering along the northern frontier, or slightly more than half the total span of American frontier experience. So it is not surprising that Turner found what he was looking for.

In summing up his conclusions about one portion of the northern frontier, Turner wrote,

> . . . we find many of the traits of later frontiers in this early prototype, the Massachusetts frontier. It lies at the edge of the Indian country and tends to advance. It calls out militant qualities and reveals the imprint of wilderness conditions upon the psychology and morals as well as upon the institutions of the people. It demands common defense and thus becomes a factor for consolidation. It is built on the basis of a preliminary fur trade, and is settled by the combined and sometimes antagonistic forces of eastern men of property (the absentee proprietors) and the democratic pioneers. The East attempted to regulate and control it. Individualistic and democratic tendencies were emphasized both by the wilderness conditions and, probably, by the prior contentions between the proprietors and nonproprietors of the towns from which settlers moved to the frontier. Removal away from the control of the customary usages of the older communities and from the conservative influence of the body of the clergy, increased the innovating tendency.[50]

Turner's assertions about the frontier experience prior to 1763 were backed with an impressive array of evidence culled from the colonial records, apparently revealing almost in full bloom the same characteristics of democratic individualism, self-reliant ingenuity, pugnacity, and sectional particularism that he had found in flourishing profusion on later frontiers beyond the Appalachians.

Much of the evidence that Turner gathered on the colonial frontier was exceptional rather than typical, selected for the very reason that it did seem to sustain his hypothesis. What Turner probably realized but failed to emphasize was the fact that a distinct frontier society with its significant characteristics was very slow to emerge out of the seedbed of a transplanted European culture. Not until well into the eighteenth century do we begin to find a fairly sharp differentiation between society in general and the peculiar society of the frontier. Indeed, virtually all of the settled region from the Atlantic beaches to the most remote cabin on the slopes of the mountains, with the exception of a handful of urban centers such as Boston and New York, was frontier. The farmer on the outskirts of Philadelphia still had much in common with the farmer of the Juniata Valley. The same problems and the same responses to them were remarkably widespread throughout the colonies, so that during most of our period there was little cause for the appearance of the kind of sectionalism usually associated with the Turnerian frontier. This community of interests prevailed so long as the pioneers and the Easterners both remained on the same side of the Appalachian barrier, a fact recognized by Turner when he wrote that "The settlements from the sea to the mountains kept connection with the rear and had a certain solidarity."[51] Furthermore, the almost continuous arrival of new settlers from Europe, the majority of whom found their way rather readily to the regions where land was available, had the effect of extending the prevalence of Old World ways in America. The persistence of European culture in the American wilderness was greater than many historians have been willing to allow.

Nevertheless, the frontier experience was having its effect, however gradually. Turner was on firm ground when he asserted, "Our early history is the study of European germs developing in an American environment. . . . The frontier is the line of most rapid and effective Americanization."[52] Quite clearly the very experience of coping with a new environment and taming the wilderness was transforming Europeans into Americans. The elements in this gradual, almost imperceptible, yet fascinating process are numerous and diverse.

The sheer necessity of adapting to new conditions, of finding new ways to solve new problems, worked profound changes. Sometimes the frontier folk met these demands with ingenuity and inventiveness. Not infrequently, however, they borrowed the techniques of the native Americans, thereby absorbing to some extent the most useful elements of Indian culture. In addition, there was much intermingling of nationalities on the frontier, fostered by the mobility so common in regions where the zone of settlement is undergoing rapid expansion. This meant an intermixture of folkways that in itself contributed greatly to the development of an American way of life.

Turner placed great emphasis upon frontier "traits." By this he meant those qualities of mind and character that seemed to evolve through the frontier experience, producing men easily recognized as pioneer types, such as Robert Rogers, Daniel Boone, and Davy Crockett. Again, in the colonial period we do not find this process fully developed, for older influences were tenacious. This is not to say, however, that there is no evidence of early beginnings. Indeed, the vast opportunities offered to traders, speculators, lumbermen, cattlemen, and pioneering farmers by an apparently limitless hinterland did foster the growth of an exploitive spirit that was becoming increasingly noticeable during the first half of the eighteenth century. Big thinking, accompanied by the evolution of appropriate techniques of exploitation, was a significant development in colonial America, where the frontier entrepreneur of one kind or another had become a familiar figure.

Likewise we can hardly fail to notice the early growth of self-reliance as a pioneer response to the challenge of frontier conditions. Sometimes this self-reliance grew with amazing rapidity in favorable seasons, only to wither when conditions became unusually difficult, as in a time of Indian warfare. But those frontier folk who survived the hardest rigors cherished the trait, for it gave them self-respect. A man was proud of what he could do for himself. This self-reliance, in turn, helped nourish early sprouts of a democratic spirit that first took the form of a certain impatience with authority imposed from above. Prior to 1763 this spirit was yet feeble, and hardly sectional in character. Its period of burgeoning growth lay in the immediate future. Despite the colonial pioneer's occasional combativeness, as shown in his attitude toward Indians, proprietors' agents, and sometimes sheriffs, he believed in law and order, and endeavored to establish some form of regular authority wherever he settled. In most cases this was taken care of by extension from older communities.

Inevitably, of course, differences did arise between newly settled areas on the frontier and more firmly established regions near the coast. A good example of this, found in many colonies, was the question of whether the government should levy additional taxes in order to provide military defenses for exposed frontier communities. Since many frontier areas were denied proportionate representation in colony legislatures, as in Pennsylvania, the seaboard regions, which dominated government, were able to ignore frontier demands of this nature. Certainly by the middle decades of the eighteenth century, sectional issues were beginning to intrude upon the American political scene.

In general, however, all these various consequences of the frontier experience are only dimly apparent before 1763, and we must avoid the error of reading into the colonial period what we have already found clearly delineated in a later, more thoroughly developed era. What we are justified in concluding is that the frontier was an ever-present reality from the very first days of settlement and that its influence was pervasive. This influence, working its way slowly but surely into the American character all during the first hundred and fifty years of our history, helped lay the foundations for a continued westward movement across the continent, forming the basis for the phenomenal growth of the United States.

NOTES

Chapter 1: The Challenge of the Unknown Wilderness

[1] Henry S. Burrage, ed., *Early English and French Voyages . . . 1534–1608* (J. Franklin Jameson, ed., *Original Narratives of Early American History Series*, n.p., 1906), p. 330. For another account of Gosnold's voyage, see the Massachusetts Historical Society *Collections*, 3d ser., VIII (1843), pp. 72–81.

[2] William Wood, *New Englands Prospect* (Prince Society *Publications*, I, Boston, 1865), p. 17.

[3] Albert C. Myers, ed., *Narratives of Early Pennsylvania, West New Jersey, and Delaware, 1630–1707* (J. Franklin Jameson, ed., *Original Narratives of Early American History Series*, New York, 1912), p. 229.

[4] Thomas Pownall, *A Topographical Description of the Dominions of the United States of America*, Lois Mulkearn, ed. (Pittsburgh, 1949), p. 31.

[5] Samuel Penhallow, *The History of the Wars of New-England with the Eastern Indians* (New Hampshire Historical Society *Collections*, I, Concord, N.H., 1824), pp. 18–19.

[6] Myers, *Narratives of Early Pennsylvania*, p. 236.

[7] *Ibid.*, pp. 384–385.

[8] [Philip Vincent], *A True Relation of the Late Battell fought in New England, between the English, and the Salvages* (London, 1637), p. 14. Additional information on Indian dwellings may be found in Dwight B. Heath, ed., *A Journal of the Pilgrims at Plymouth* [*Mourt's Relation*] (New York, 1963), pp. 28–29; Charles C. Willoughby, *Antiquities of the New England Indians* (Cambridge, Mass., 1935), pp. 244–260, 289–295; Clark Wissler, *The American Indian: An Introduction to the Anthropology of the New World* (3d ed., New York, 1938), p. 110; Clark Wissler, *Indians of the United States* (New York, 1940), p. 58.

[9] Harold E. Driver, *Indians of North America* (Chicago, 1961), pp. 49–53, 320–321; Wissler, *The American Indian*, pp. 12–14, 21–23.

[10] John Gyles, *Memoirs of Odd Adventures, Strange Deliverances, &c. In the Captivity of John Gyles, Esq.* (Boston, 1736), p. 25.

[11] Driver, *Indians of North America*, pp. 246–248, 254–255; Wissler, *The American Indian*, pp. 185–186; John M. Cooper, "Land Tenure Among the Indians of Eastern and Northern North America," *Pennsylvania Archaeologist*, VIII (1938), pp. 55–59.

[12] Adolph B. Benson, ed., *Peter Kalm's Travels in North America* (New York, 1937), p. 561. See also J. Franklin Jameson, ed., *Narratives of New Netherland, 1609–1664* (J. Franklin Jameson, ed., *Original Narratives of Early American History Series*, New York, 1909), p. 72; Myers, *Narratives of Early Pennsylvania*, p. 230. Good descriptions of Indian life are to be found in E[dward] W[inslow], *Good Newes from New England* (London, 1624), pp. 52–61; Roger Williams, *A Key into the Language of America* (Narragansett Club *Publications*, I, Providence, R.I., 1866), *passim;* Thomas Lechford, *Plaine Dealing: Or, Newes from New-England* (Massachusetts Historical Society *Collections*, 3d ser., III, 1833), pp. 102–105; Thomas Hutchinson, *The History of the Colony and Province of Massachusetts-Bay*, Lawrence Shaw Mayo, ed. (Cambridge, Mass., 1936), I, 384–402.

[13] Christopher Levett, *A Voyage into New England Begun in 1623. and ended in 1624* (London, 1628), p. 21.

[14] Samuel Lee to Nehemiah Grew, June 25, 1690 (Massachusetts Historical Society, Gay Transcripts, Miscellaneous Papers, I, 85–98).

[15] Samuel Hopkins, *Historical memoirs, relating to the Housatunnuk Indians* (Boston, 1753), pp. 22–23.

[16] For a description of the appearance and clothing of Indian women in New England, see John Josselyn, *New-Englands Rarities Discovered* (London, 1672), pp. 99–101.

[17] Driver, *Indians of North America*, pp. 116–117, contains an excellent description of the longhouse.

[18] It has been suggested, but not proved, that scalping was an innovation introduced by the Europeans. This seems to me highly doubtful. It is true, however, that at various times the colonial authorities did offer bounties for the scalps of enemy Indians, thereby encouraging the practice. See above, pp. 132–133, 202–203.

[19] Williams, *A Key into the Language of America*, p. 264.

[20] Cadwallader Colden, *The History of the Five Indian Nations Depending on the Province of New-York in America* (Ithaca, N.Y., 1958), p. 8.

[21] Nathaniel Knowles, "The Torture of Captives by the Indians of Eastern North America," American Philosophical Society *Proceedings*, LXXXII (1940), pp. 186–190.

Chapter 2: The Coastal Pioneers: Plymouth and New Netherland, 1620–1664

[1] Burrage, *Early English and French Voyages*, p. 419. See also Henry S. Burrage, *The Beginnings of Colonial Maine, 1602–1658* (Portland, Me., 1914), pp. 63–99; Charles M. Andrews, *The Colonial Period of American History* (New Haven, Conn., 1934–1938), I, chap. 4.

[2] Richard Arthur Preston, *Gorges of Plymouth Fort: A life of Sir Ferdinando Gorges . . .* (Toronto, 1953), p. 161.

[3] J. Franklin Jameson, ed., *Johnson's Wonder-Working Providence, 1628–1651* (J. Franklin Jameson, ed., *Original Narratives of Early American History Series*, New York, 1910), pp. 40–42.

[4] The text of the Mayflower Compact is to be found in William Bradford, *Of Plymouth Plantation*, Samuel Eliot Morison, ed. (New York, 1953), pp. 75–76.

[5] Later, when time and energy permitted, the earliest dwellings were replaced with small frame houses, covered on the outside with clapboards and roofed with thatch. There has been much discussion about this matter. The most authoritative accounts are Harold R. Shurtleff, *The Log Cabin Myth: A Study of the Early Dwellings of the English Colonists in North America* (Cambridge, Mass., 1939), pp. 101–110; Thomas Tileston Waterman, *The Dwellings of Colonial America* (Chapel Hill, N.C., 1950), p. 239; and Hugh Morrison, *Early American Architecture, From the First Colonial Settlements to the National Period* (New York, 1952), pp. 9–12. Certainly the log cabin of the later frontier was not to be seen at Plymouth.

[6] Heath, *A Journal of the Pilgrims at Plymouth*, pp. 45–46.

[7] [Robert Cushman], *A Sermon Preached at Plimmoth in New-England December 9. 1621* (London, 1622), Epistle Dedicatory.

[8] Bradford, *Of Plymouth Plantation*, p. 81.

[9] *Ibid.*, pp. 96–97; W[inslow], *Good Newes from New England*, pp. 2–4.

[10] W[inslow], *Good Newes from New England*, pp. 42–43.

[11] Lois K. Mathews, *The Expansion of New England* (Boston, 1909), p. 14, lists the settlements in New England made prior to 1630. They include besides Plymouth: Hull, Weymouth, Braintree, Quincy, Salem, Lynn, Marblehead, Strawberry Bank, Durham, Dover, Cape Porpoise, Damariscotta, South Berwick, York, Saco, Portland, and several others. Many of these were sponsored or authorized by the Council for New England, a group of prominent Englishmen.

[12] Allen W. Trelease, *Indian Affairs in Colonial New York: The Seventeenth Century* (Ithaca, N.Y., 1960), pp. 37–38, 40; Clarence W. Rife, "Land Tenure in New Netherland," *Essays in Colonial History Presented to Charles McLean Andrews by his Students* (New Haven, 1931), pp. 48–49.

[13] E. B. O'Callaghan and Berthold Fernow, eds., *Documents Relative to the Colonial History of the State of New-York* (Albany, 1856–1887), I, 37–38; Jameson, *Narratives of New Netherland,* p. 83.

[14] Jameson, *Narratives of New Netherland,* p. 87.

[15] S. G. Nissenson, *The Patroon's Domain* (New York, 1937), pp. 21, 81. A somewhat different interpretation, emphasizing agricultural development as the major objective, is presented in Rife, "Land Tenure in New Netherland," p. 45; Alexander C. Flick, ed., *History of the State of New York* (New York, 1933–1937), I, 266; and Emory R. Johnson *et al., History of Domestic and Foreign Commerce of the United States* (Washington, 1915), I, 29.

[16] The text has been published in E. B. O'Callaghan, comp., *Laws and Ordinances of New Netherland, 1638–1674* (Albany, 1868), pp. 1–10; and Jameson, *Narratives of New Netherland,* pp. 90–96.

[17] Flick, *History of the State of New York,* I, 267; Morrison, *Early American Architecture,* p. 103.

[18] Percy W. Bidwell and John I. Falconer, *History of Agriculture in the Northern United States, 1620–1860* (Washington, 1925), p. 63.

[19] Nissenson, *The Patroon's Domain,* p. 16.

[20] O'Callaghan and Fernow, *Documents Relative to the Colonial History of the State of New-York,* I, 210.

[21] An excellent discussion of Indian affairs under Kieft, utilizing the results of recent research on the subject, is contained in Trelease, *Indian Affairs in Colonial New York: The Seventeenth Century,* chap. 3.

[22] *Ibid.,* pp. 72–73; Flick, *History of the State of New York,* I, 288–289.

[23] Ellis Lawrence Raesly, *Portrait of New Netherland* (New York, 1945), p. 175.

[24] Ruth L. Higgins, *Expansion in New York, with Especial Reference to the Eighteenth Century* (Columbus, Ohio, 1931), pp. 1–10; Flick, *History of the State of New York,* I, 314–315.

[25] O'Callaghan, *Laws and Ordinances of New Netherland,* pp. 442–443.

[26] O'Callaghan and Fernow, *Documents Relative to the Colonial History of the State of New-York,* I, 551.

[27] Flick, *History of the State of New York,* II, 59–60; John E. Pomfret, *The Province of West New Jersey, 1609–1702: A History of the Origins of an American Colony* (Princeton, N. J., 1956), pp. 5, 9–10.

[28] Myers, *Narratives of Early Pennsylvania,* p. 100n.

[29] Benson, *Peter Kalm's Travels in North America,* pp. 710–715.

[30] Christopher Ward, *New Sweden on the Delaware* (Philadelphia, 1938), *passim.*

[31] Evarts B. Greene and Virginia D. Harrington, *American Population Before the Federal Census of 1790* (New York, 1932), p. 88.

[32] Bradford, *Of Plymouth Plantation,* pp. 113–119.

[33] *Ibid.,* pp. 120–121, 144–145.

34 [Cushman], *A Sermon Preached at Plimmoth*, p. 17.

35 Raesly, *Portrait of New Netherland*, pp. 102–103.

36 *Ibid.*, pp. 138–140, 155–156.

37 Jameson, *Narratives of New Netherland*, p. 398.

Chapter 3: The Tidal Wave of the English, 1630–1675

1 Roger Clap, *Memoirs of Capt. Roger Clap* (Boston, 1731), p. 4.

2 *Ibid.*, pp. 14, 25.

3 See, for example [Rev. Francis Higginson], *New-Englands Plantation. Or, a Short and True Description of the Commodities and Discommodities of that Countrey* (3d ed., London, 1630), *passim.* "Experience doth manifest," averred Higginson, "that there is hardly a more healthfull place to be found in the World that agreeth better with our English Bodyes."

4 Quoted in Hutchinson, *The History of the Colony and Province of Massachusetts-Bay*, I, 404–405.

5 Melville Egleston, *The Land System of the New England Colonies* (Johns Hopkins University *Studies in History and Political Science*, IV, nos. 11, 12, Baltimore, 1886), p. 30; William Haller, Jr., *The Puritan Frontier: Town-Planting in New England: Colonial Development, 1630–1660* (New York, 1951), p. 94.

6 Francis X. Moloney, *The Fur Trade in New England, 1620–1676* (Cambridge, Mass., 1931), pp. 67–76.

7 John Underhill, *News from America; or, a new and experimentall discoverie of New England* (Charles Orr, ed., *History of the Pequot War*, Cleveland, 1897), p. 81.

8 Nathaniel B. Shurtleff and David Pulsifer, eds., *Records of the Colony of New Plymouth in New England* (Boston, 1855–1861), X, 208.

9 Leo Vincent De Gaetano, "Indian policy in early New England" (New York University, master's thesis, 1948), pp. 12–13; Marshall Harris, *Origin of the Land Tenure System in the United States* (Ames, Iowa, 1953), p. 63.

10 New York Public Library. Bancroft Collection, New England, I, 334–335.

11 Nathaniel B. Shurtleff, ed., *Records of the Governor and Company of the Massachusetts Bay in New England* (Boston, 1853–1854), III, 281.

12 Cotton Mather, *Magnalia Christi Americana* (Hartford, Conn., 1820), I, 523.

13 Examples of pertinent legislation may be found in MCR, I, 112; Max Farrand, ed., *The Laws and Liberties of Massachusetts* (Cambridge, Mass., 1929), pp. 28–29; J. H. Trumbull and C. J. Hoadly, eds., *The Public Records of the Colony of Connecticut* (Hartford, 1850–1890), I, 402; Shurtleff and Pulsifer, *Records of the Colony of New Plymouth*, XI, 41; John Russell Bartlett, ed., *Records of the Colony of Rhode Island and Providence Plantations in New England* (Providence, 1856–1865), I, 236, 403–404; *The Colonial Laws of New York from the Year 1664 to the Revolution* (Albany, 1894–1896), I, 40–42.

14 Connecticut began this practice as early as 1659 with the Golden Hill reservation near Fairfield. See Trumbull and Hoadly, *The Public Records of the Colony of Connecticut*, I, 335–336; Albert E. Van Dusen, *Connecticut* (New York, 1961), p. 75.

15 Connecticut Archives, Hartford. Indians, I, 227. For documentation of this long and painful controversy, see also *Ibid.*, pp. 75–76, 95–96, 100–101, 105–110, 139, 143–145; and Trumbull and Hoadly, *The Public Records of the Colony of Connecticut*, VI, 364, 402; VII, 324–326, 411–412. Such cases seldom were concluded to the full satisfaction of the Indians.

[16] Fred M. Kimmey, "Christianity and Indian Lands," *Ethnohistory*, VII (1960), pp. 44–60.

[17] *New Englands First Fruits* (Sabin's Reprints, Quarto Series, no. 7, New York, 1865), p. 15.

[18] Franklin B. Dexter, ed., *New Haven Town Records, 1649–1684* (New Haven, Conn., 1917–1919), I, 178.

[19] Shurtleff and Pulsifer, *Records of the Colony of New Plymouth*, XI, 143.

[20] *The Colonial Laws of New York from the Year 1664 to the Revolution*, I, 41.

[21] Trumbull and Hoadly, *The Public Records of the Colony of Connecticut*, I, 532–533.

[22] *Ibid.*, I, 353, 576–577.

[23] Shurtleff, *Records of the Governor and Company of the Massachusetts Bay in New England*, III, 322.

[24] Nathaniel Morton, *New Englands Memoriall*, Howard J. Hall, ed. (New York, 1937), p. 111. See also Allyn B. Forbes, ed., *Winthrop Papers* (Boston, 1929–1947), IV, 48–50, 52–53, 60; Shurtleff and Pulsifer, *Records of the Colony of New Plymouth*, I, 96–97.

[25] Trumbull and Hoadly, *The Public Records of the Colony of Connecticut*, I, 13–14.

[26] Bartlett, *Records of the Colony of Rhode Island*, II, 509; *Records of the Court of Assistants of the Colony of the Massachusetts Bay, 1630–1692* (Boston, 1901–1908), I, 21–22; Superior Court, Newport, R.I. General Court of Trials, Record 1, p. 20.

[27] Jeremy Belknap, *The History of New-Hampshire* (Dover, N.H., 1831), pp. 197–198.

[28] Narragansett Club *Publications*, VI (Providence, 1874), pp. 275–276.

[29] Hutchinson, *The History of the Colony and Province of Massachusetts-Bay*, I, 239n., 260, II, 203.

[30] Beverley W. Bond, Jr., *The Quit-Rent System in the American Colonies* (New Haven, Conn., 1919), pp. 439, 456; Harris, *Origin of the Land Tenure System in the United States*, p. 116.

[31] Egleston, *The Land System of the New England Colonies*, pp. 24–25. See also Haller, *The Puritan Frontier*, pp. 33–34.

[32] Bidwell and Falconer, *History of Agriculture in the Northern United States, 1620–1860*, p. 49.

[33] Samuel Eliot Morison, "William Pynchon, the Founder of Springfield," Massachusetts Historical Society *Proceedings*, LXIV (Boston, 1932), p. 80.

[34] Shurtleff, *Records of the Governor and Company of the Massachusetts Bay in New England*, I, 117.

[35] *Ibid.*, IV, Part 1, p. 22.

[36] *Ibid.*, I, 179.

[37] *Ibid.*, III, 45.

[38] Haller, *The Puritan Frontier*, p. 53.

[39] It remains only to point out that new conditions on the frontier by themselves eventually would have forced even a group of pioneers with identical habits to change their practices, whereas the complete absence of new conditions might have made it possible for men of diverse habits to reconcile their differences not by compromise and experiment, but by recourse to majority decision. Thus the frontier experience remains an essential factor in producing these new arrangements.

[40] An informative discussion of the land problems of one town by an observer only a century removed from the town's beginning may be found in the New York Public Library, Hawley Papers, Box 1, p. 28.

[41] Quoted in Morison, "William Pynchon, the Founder of Springfield," p. 88.

[42] The text of the Dover agreement has been published in John S. Jenness, ed., *Transcripts of Original Documents in the English Archives Relating to the Early History of the State of New Hampshire* (New York, 1876), pp. 36–37. See also Hutchinson, *The History of the Colony and Province of Massachusetts-Bay*, I, 93–94.

[43] Farrand, *The Laws and Liberties of Massachusetts*, p. 21; Haller, *The Puritan Frontier*, pp. 36, 44, 52–53.

[44] Victor S. Clark, *History of Manufactures in the United States, 1607–1860* (Washington, 1916), pp. 40–41.

[45] Shurtleff, *Records of the Governor and Company of the Massachusetts Bay in New England*, I, 116; Hutchinson, *The History of the Colony and Province of Massachusetts-Bay*, I, 383.

[46] *Ibid.*, I, 201, IV, Part 1, pp. 101, 288.

[47] Trumbull and Hoadly, *The Public Records of the Colony of Connecticut*, II, 67–68.

[48] Clark, *History of Manufactures in the United States, 1607–1860*, pp. 73–74. For a discussion of the mast trade in New England, see Robert G. Albion, *Forests and Sea Power: The Timber Problem of the Royal Navy, 1652–1862* (Cambridge, Mass., 1926), pp. 206–280.

[49] New York Public Library. Bancroft Collection, New England, II, 274.

[50] Robert Earl Moody, "The Maine Frontier, 1607 to 1763" (Yale University, doctoral dissertation, 1933), chap. 3; Preston, *Gorges of Plymouth Fort*, p. 337; Burrage, *The Beginnings of Colonial Maine, 1602–1658*, pp. 249, 309–310.

[51] James Phinney Baxter, ed., *Documentary History of the State of Maine. Vol. III. Containing The Trelawny Papers* (Portland, Me., 1884), p. 137.

[52] Lois K. Mathews Rosenberry, *Migrations from Connecticut Prior to 1800* (New Haven, Conn., 1934), pp. 2–4; Harris, *Origin of the Land Tenure System in the United States*, pp. 223–224; Van Dusen, *Connecticut*, p. 74; Bond, *The Quit-Rent System in the American Colonies*, pp. 439–440.

[53] O'Callaghan and Fernow, *Documents Relative to the Colonial History of the State of New-York*, III, 67–68.

[54] *The Colonial Laws of New York from the Year 1664 to the Revolution*, I, 44; Richard Nicolls, *The Conditions for New-Planters In the Territories of His Royal Highnes the Duke of York* ([Boston, 1665]). (A broadside, reproduced opposite p. 82 of Flick, *History of the State of New York*, II).

[55] Harris, *Origin of the Land Tenure System in the United States*, pp. 212–213.

Chapter 4: War and Peace, 1675–1689

[1] Herbert L. Osgood, *The American Colonies in the Seventeenth Century* (New York, 1904–1907), I, chap. 13; Morrison Sharp, "Leadership and Democracy in the Early New England System of Defense," *American Historical Review*, L (January 1945), pp. 244–260; Harold L. Peterson, "The Military Equipment of the Plymouth and Bay Colonies, 1620–1690," *New England Quarterly*, XX (June 1947), pp. 197–208; Douglas Edward Leach, "The Military System of Plymouth Colony," *New England Quarterly*, XXIV (September 1951), pp. 342–364.

[2] Starting in 1659 a group of Connecticut and Massachusetts investors, headed by Major Humphrey Atherton, began buying from the Narragansett Indians all the

land lying along the western shore of Narragansett Bay from East Greenwich Bay down to Point Judith. At about this time the Narragansett committed some outrages against white settlers, for which the tribe was heavily fined by the colonial authorities. As security for the fine, the sachems mortgaged the entire Narragansett country, with the consequence that the region soon fell into the waiting hands of the Atherton group, at least nominally. Although the transaction later was rendered void, its implications contributed greatly to Narragansett resentment against the Puritan colonies. There is a more thorough discussion of this case in the author's unpublished doctoral dissertation, "The Causes and Effects of King Philip's War" (Harvard University, 1950), pp. 112–120.

[3] Daniel Gookin, the Puritan supervisor of Indians in Massachusetts, estimated that the Narragansett could muster about a thousand able men. The figure probably is too high. Massachusetts Historical Society *Collections,* 1st ser., I (1792), p. 148.

[4] Thomas Wheeler, *A Thankefull remembrance of Gods mercy to several persons at Quabaug or Brookfield* [Sometimes cited as *A True Narrative of the Lord's Providences . . .*] (Cambridge, Mass., 1676).

[5] For a discussion of the services performed by Indian auxiliaries, see Douglas Edward Leach, *Flintlock and Tomahawk: New England in King Philip's War* (New York, 1958), pp. 152–153.

[6] Hutchinson, *The History of the Colony and Province of Massachusetts-Bay,* I, 378.

[7] The best account of this episode is given by one of the captives, Mary Rowlandson, in her *Narrative of the Captivity of Mrs. Mary Rowlandson* (Cambridge, Mass., 1682). This is available in many editions.

[8] Leach, *Flintlock and Tomahawk,* pp. 187–188.

[9] Douglas Edward Leach, ed., *A Rhode Islander Reports on King Philip's War: The Second William Harris Letter of August, 1676* (Providence, 1963), p. 60.

[10] *A Report of the Record Commissioners, Containing the Roxbury Land and Church Records* (Boston, 1881), p. 195.

[11] Governor Leverett to Count Frontenac, October 24, 1677 (Massachusetts Historical Society, Miscellaneous Papers, III). The most vivid account of the attack on Hatfield is found in the narrative of Quentin Stockwell, one of the prisoners. Stockwell's account was first published in Increase Mather, *An Essay for the Recording of Illustrious Providences* (Boston, 1684), pp. 39–57.

[12] Warwick Records, Book A-2 (Transcript by Marshall Morgan), p. 240.

[13] Trumbull and Hoadly, *The Public Records of the Colony of Connecticut,* II, 328; Massachusetts Archives, Boston. Vol. LXIX, 238.

[14] John Pynchon to Francis Nicholson, August 21, 1688 (Massachusetts Historical Society, Gay Transcripts, State Papers, III, 74–78).

[15] George M. Bodge, *Soldiers in King Philip's War* (3d ed., Boston, 1906), pp. 406–446, is an excellent review of the various land grants made by the colonial governments to the veterans.

[16] Bartlett B. James and J. Franklin Jameson, eds., *Journal of Jasper Danckaerts, 1679–1680* (J. Franklin Jameson, ed., *Original Narratives of Early American History Series,* New York, 1913), p. 96.

[17] John E. Pomfret, "West New Jersey: A Quaker Society, 1675–1775," *William and Mary Quarterly,* VIII (October 1951), p. 494.

[18] William A. Whitehead *et al.,* eds., *Archives of the State of New Jersey* (Newark, N.J., etc., 1880–1906), 1st ser., I, 259.

[19] John E. Pomfret, *The Province of West New Jersey, 1609–1702,* pp. 117–119.

20 The "Concessions and Agreements" are published in Whitehead, *Archives of the State of New Jersey*, 1st ser., I, 241–270.

21 Pomfret, *The Province of West New Jersey, 1609–1702*, pp. 131–132.

22 Edwin B. Bronner, *William Penn's "Holy Experiment": The Founding of Pennsylvania, 1681–1701* (New York, 1962), pp. 64–65.

23 Myers, *Narratives of Early Pennsylvania*, p. 211.

24 Thomas Budd, *Good Order Established in Pennsilvania & New-Jersey in America, Being a true Account of the Country* ([Philadelphia], 1685), p. 8.

25 Paul A. W. Wallace, *Indians in Pennsylvania* (Harrisburg, 1961), pp. 129–130; *Eighteenth Annual Report of the Bureau of American Ethnology, 1896–97*, Part 2 (Washington, 1899), p. 597.

26 Samuel Hazard *et al.*, eds., *Pennsylvania Archives* (Philadelphia and Harrisburg, 1852–1949), 1st ser., I, 47–48.

27 William W. Comfort *et al.*, eds., *Remember William Penn, 1644–1944* ([Harrisburg, Pa.], 1944), pp. 109–110.

28 Indian land transactions in Pennsylvania from 1683 to 1718 are summarized in the *Eighteenth Annual Report of the Bureau of American Ethnology, 1896–97*, Part 2, pp. 594–597.

29 Penn described his township plan in *A further account of the Province of Pennsylvania and its improvements* ([London, 1685]), which has been republished in Myers, *Narratives of Early Pennsylvania*, pp. 259–278. The proprietor claimed that by 1684 his colony contained at least fifty settled townships. See also *Colonial Records of Pennsylvania* (Philadelphia, 1852–1853), I, 39.

30 *Ibid.*, pp. 26–28; Harris, *Origin of the Land Tenure System in the United States*, pp. 238–240.

31 Stella H. Sutherland, *Population Distribution in Colonial America* (New York, 1936), p. 144.

32 Albert B. Faust, *The German Element in the United States* (Boston, 1909), I, 36.

33 For a facsimile copy, see Hazard, *Pennsylvania Archives*, 3d ser., Appendixes 1–10. The map is discussed in Homer Rosenberger, "Early Maps of Pennsylvania," *Pennsylvania History*, (April 1944), pp. 105–106.

34 British Museum. Additional Mss. 5414, Roll 23.

35 Myers, *Narratives of Early Pennsylvania*, p. 278.

36 Budd, *Good Order Established in Pennsilvania & New-Jersey in America*, p. 35.

37 Myers, *Narratives of Early Pennsylvania*, p. 277.

38 This broadside was published in London in 1690. A copy is to be found in the American Philosophical Society, Penn Letters, III, 7.

Chapter 5: The Life of the Pioneer

1 Budd, *Good Order Established in Pennsilvania & New-Jersey in America*, pp. 24–26.

2 These lists are largely derived from *Ibid.*

3 Heath, *A Journal of the Pilgrims at Plymouth*, p. 46.

4 [Sir Ferdinando Gorges], *A briefe Relation of the Discovery and Plantation of New England* (James P. Baxter, *Sir Ferdinando Gorges and His Province of Maine*, Boston, 1890), I, 231; Wood, *New Englands Prospect*, p. 23.

5 *Ibid.*, p. 26.

6 Lechford, *Plaine Dealing*, p. 101; Gottlieb Mittelberger, *Journey to Pennsylvania*, Oscar Handlin and John Clive, eds. (Cambridge, Mass., 1960), p. 61.

7 Wood, *New Englands Prospect,* p. 50.

8 Thomas Church, *Entertaining Passages Relating to Philip's War* . . . (Boston, 1716), p. 8.

9 Wood, *New Englands Prospect,* p. 50; Lechford, *Plaine Dealing,* p. 101.

10 Josselyn, *New-Englands Rarities Discovered,* p. 39.

11 C[harles] W[olley], *A two Years Journal in New-York* (London, 1701), pp. 53–54.

12 Shurtleff, *The Log Cabin Myth,* chap. 1. See also above, pp. 79–80, 212.

13 Morrison, *Early American Architecture,* pp. 9–11. See also Shurtleff, *The Log Cabin Myth,* pp. 20–35.

14 Jameson, *Johnson's Wonder-Working Providence, 1628–1651,* pp. 113–114.

15 Quoted in Waterman, *The Dwellings of Colonial America,* pp. 191–192.

16 Ward, *New Sweden on the Delaware,* p. 140; Bidwell and Falconer, *History of Agriculture in the Northern United States, 1620–1860,* p. 36; Wayland F. Dunaway, *The Scotch-Irish of Colonial Pennsylvania* (Chapel Hill, N.C., 1944), p. 168.

17 Daniel J. Boorstin, *The Americans: The Colonial Experience* (New York, 1958), p. 192.

18 Carl P. Russell, *Guns on the Early Frontiers: A History of Firearms From Colonial Times Through the Years of the Western Fur Trade* (Berkeley, Calif., 1957), p. 44.

19 Wood, *New Englands Prospect,* p. 5.

20 Benson, *Peter Kalm's Travels in North America,* pp. 191–192.

21 Jameson, *Johnson's Wonder-Working Providence, 1628–1651,* p. 114.

22 Morrison, *Early American Architecture,* pp. 20–24, 27–31, 42–43; Waterman, *The Dwellings of Colonial America,* pp. 245–246, 251; John H. Cady, "The Development of the Neck," *Rhode Island History,* II (January 1943), pp. 28–29.

23 Waterman, *The Dwellings of Colonial America,* pp. 118–119; Ward, *New Sweden on the Delaware,* p. 137; James and Jameson, *Journal of Jasper Danckaerts, 1679–1680,* p. 98.

24 Quoted in Morrison, *Early American Architecture,* p. 505.

25 *Ibid.,* pp. 541–542; Waterman, *The Dwellings of Colonial America,* pp. 150, 159.

26 Morrison, *Early American Architecture,* pp. 44–45, 47.

27 Wood, *New Englands Prospect,* p. 19. See also Ward, *New Sweden on the Delaware,* p. 139.

28 A contemporary map of the proposed fortification is reproduced in Burrage, *Early English and French Voyages,* p. 412.

29 Bradford, *Of Plymouth Plantation,* pp. 69, 111.

30 Waterman, *The Dwellings of Colonial America,* pp. 239–243; Morrison, *Early American Architecture,* pp. 76–79.

31 Hutchinson, *The History of the Colony and Province of Massachusetts-Bay,* II, 50n.

32 O'Callaghan and Fernow, *Documents Relative to the Colonial History of the State of New-York,* I, 367.

33 Bidwell and Falconer, *History of Agriculture in the Northern United States, 1620–1860,* pp. 10–12, 101; Robert R. Walcott, "Husbandry in Colonial New England," *New England Quarterly,* IX (June 1936), pp. 229–231.

34 Lyman Carrier, *The Beginnings of Agriculture in America* (New York, 1923), p. 177.

35 *Ibid.,* p. 253.

36 *Ibid.*, p. 151; Bidwell and Falconer, *History of Agriculture in the Northern United States, 1620–1860,* p. 27; Edward Channing, *The Narragansett Planters* (Johns Hopkins University *Studies in History and Political Science,* IV, No. 3, Baltimore, 1886); Walcott, "Husbandry in Colonial New England," p. 240; Edward C. Kirkland, *A History of American Economic Life* (rev. ed., New York, 1951), p. 58.

37 Mittelberger, *Journey to Pennsylvania,* p. 60.

38 Jameson, *Narratives of New Netherland,* p. 169.

39 Wood, *New Englands Prospect,* pp. 24–25, 32.

40 *An Abstract, or Abbreviation Of some Few of the Many (Later and Former) Testimonys from the Inhabitants of New-Jersey, And Other Eminent Persons* (London, 1681), pp. 22–23.

41 Josselyn, *New-Englands Rarities Discovered,* pp. 52–53; Clap, *Memoirs,* p. 25. A frontier saying that persists to the present day is that somebody "doesn't know enough to pound samp" (sometimes corrupted to "sand").

42 Josselyn, *New-Englands Rarities Discovered,* p. 91.

43 Myers, *Narratives of Early Pennsylvania,* p. 265.

44 Bidwell and Falconer, *History of Agriculture in the Northern United States, 1620–1860,* p. 5.

45 *Ibid.*, p. 80; Mittelberger, *Journey to Pennsylvania,* p. 54; Albert L. Olson, *Agricultural Economy and the Population in Eighteenth-Century Connecticut* (New Haven, Conn., 1935), p. 3.

46 Walcott, "Husbandry in Colonial New England," p. 235; Myers, *Narratives of Early Pennsylvania,* p. 253.

47 Clark, *History of Manufactures in the United States, 1607–1860,* p. 165; Kirkland, *A History of American Economic Life,* p. 42.

48 Moody, "The Maine Frontier, 1607 to 1763," pp. 264–265; Clark, *History of Manufactures in the United States, 1607–1860,* pp. 175–176, 187.

49 *Ibid.*, p. 176.

50 Quoted in Bidwell and Falconer, *History of Agriculture in the Northern United States, 1620–1860,* p. 70. See also Benson, *Peter Kalm's Travels in North America,* pp. 97–98. Ellen C. Semple was in error when she asserted that New England long lacked the impulse for westward expansion because its soil was not subject to rapid depletion (*American History and Its Geographic Conditions,* Boston, 1903, p. 43). Thomas Hutchinson wrote that "after three or four years improvement of a piece of ground, they found they had exhausted the goodness of the soil and were obliged to go upon new improvements." (*The History of the Colony and Province of Massachusetts-Bay,* I, 85). There is much additional evidence to support this view.

51 Benson, *Peter Kalm's Travels in North America,* p. 308.

52 Myers, *Narratives of Early Pennsylvania,* p. 319.

53 *The Colonial Laws of New York from the Year 1664 to the Revolution,* II, 228. See also George W. Roach, "Colonial Highways in the Upper Hudson Valley," *New York History,* XL (April 1959), pp. 93–116.

54 James and Jameson, *Journal of Jasper Danckaerts, 1679–1680,* p. 157.

55 Wood, *New Englands Prospect,* p. 48.

56 Seymour Dunbar, *A History of Travel in America* (Indianapolis, 1915), I, 22–23, tells how such canoes were made.

57 *Ibid.*, pp. 38–40.

58 Frederic G. Cassidy, "Language on the American Frontier" (Walker D. Wyman and Clifton B. Kroeber, eds., *The Frontier in Perspective,* Madison, Wis., 1957), p. 195.

Chapter 6: The Early Fur Trade, 1607–1689

[1] Hutchinson, *The History of the Colony and Province of Massachusetts-Bay,* I, 395.

[2] Earl Edward Muntz, *Race Contact: A Study of the Social and Economic Consequences of the Contacts between Civilized and Uncivilized Races* (New York [1927]), pp. 120–121.

[3] H. L. Babcock, "The Beaver as a Factor in the Development of New England," *Americana,* XI (April 1916), pp. 181–195; Donald G. Creighton, *Dominion of the North: A History of Canada* (Boston, 1944), pp. 12–13; Murray G. Lawson, *Fur: A Study in English Mercantilism, 1700–1775* (Toronto, 1943), pp. 2–4; Moloney, *The Fur Trade in New England, 1620–1676,* pp. 14–15.

[4] Wood, *New Englands Prospect,* p. 29.

[5] W[olley], *A two Years Journal in New-York,* pp. 47–48; Harold A. Innis, *The Fur Trade in Canada* (New Haven, 1930), pp. 4, 16.

[6] For examples of fur trading along the coast prior to regular settlement, see John Parker, *Van Meteren's Virginia, 1607–1612* (Minneapolis, 1961), p. 59; Jameson, *Narratives of New Netherland,* pp. 7, 22; Massachusetts Historical Society *Collections,* 3d ser., III (1833), p. 20; Jameson, *Johnson's Wonder-Working Providence, 1628–1651,* pp. 39–40. According to Johnson (*Ibid.,* p. 64), when the Winthrop migration reached Boston in 1630 they found a number of persons already residing in that vicinity engaged in the beaver trade.

[7] Bradford, *Of Plymouth Plantation,* p. 263.

[8] Morton has left us his own interesting views, including aspects of the New England fur trade, in his *New English Canaan or New Canaan,* edited by Charles F. Adams, Jr., as Volume XIV of the Prince Society *Publications* (Boston, 1883). See especially pp. 151–152, 174, 202, 206, 234–240, 256, 282, 295.

[9] A good example is Thomas Purchase, the first settler in the vicinity of the present Brunswick, Maine, at the falls of the Androscoggin River. See Burrage, *The Beginnings of Colonial Maine, 1602–1658,* pp. 241–244.

[10] Richard A. Preston, "The Laconia Company of 1629: An English Attempt to Intercept the Fur Trade," *Canadian Historical Review,* XXXI (June 1950), pp. 125–144; Preston, *Gorges of Plymouth Fort,* pp. 278–280; Arthur H. Buffinton, "New England and the Western Fur Trade, 1629–1675," Colonial Society of Massachusetts *Publications,* XVIII (1917), pp. 164–165.

[11] Preston, "The Laconia Company of 1629," pp. 127–128.

[12] John Winter to Robert Trelawny, June 18, 1634 (Baxter, *Documentary History of the State of Maine. Vol. III*), pp. 27–28.

[13] Shurtleff, *Records of the Governor and Company of the Massachusetts Bay in New England,* I, 394–395; [Francis Higginson], *New-Englands Plantation. Or, a Short and True Description of the Commodities and Discommodities of that Countrey* (3d ed., London, 1630).

[14] Shurtleff, *Records of the Governor and Company of the Massachusetts Bay in New England,* I, 96.

[15] *Ibid.,* I, 179.

[16] *Ibid.,* I, 322–323.

[17] *Ibid.,* II, 225 (Also found in Farrand, *The Laws and Liberties of Massachusetts,* p. 26).

[18] Shurtleff, *Records of the Governor and Company of the Massachusetts Bay in New England,* III, 424; IV, Part 1, pp. 291–292.

[19] Haller, *The Puritan Frontier,* pp. 99–100; Ruth A. McIntyre, *William Pynchon: Merchant and Colonizer* (Springfield, Mass., 1961), pp. 12–15.

20 Trumbull and Hoadly, *The Public Records of the Colony of Connecticut*, I, 20.

21 Moloney, *The Fur Trade in New England, 1620–1676*, pp. 60–61.

22 Jean E. Murray, "The Early Fur Trade in New France and New Netherland," *Canadian Historical Review*, XIX (December 1938), p. 369.

23 Paul A. W. Wallace, "The Iroquois: A Brief Outline of Their History" (Lawrence H. Leder, ed., *The Livingston Indian Records, 1666–1723*, Gettysburg, Pa., 1956), p. 18.

24 Edna Kenton, ed., *The Jesuit Relations and Allied Documents* (New York, 1954), pp. 181–182.

25 Trelease, *Indian Affairs in Colonial New York: The Seventeenth Century*, pp. 114–115.

26 O'Callaghan, *Laws and Ordinances of New Netherland*, pp. 63, 137.

27 *Ibid.*, p. 381. See also *Ibid.*, pp. 378, 383–384, 394, 425–427.

28 *Ibid.*, pp. 426–427.

29 *Ibid.*, pp. 463–464. It was said that some of the Dutch traders employed a special tactic when a dissatisfied Indian was about to break off the dickering and take his peltry elsewhere. Just as the native was on the verge of leaving, he would be invited to enjoy the company of the trader's wife, an inducement supposedly sufficient to complete a faltering transaction. Cadwallader Colden is the authority for this dubious tale. New York Historical Society *Collections*, LI, 259.

30 It has sometimes been argued that the seventeenth-century musket was so clumsy and inefficient that the Indian bow was a preferable weapon. This argument founders on two facts: the English, who certainly could have regained their old proficiency with the bow, made no general attempt to do so; and the Indians soon came to prefer the flintlock gun for hunting and fighting.

31 Preston, *Gorges of Plymouth Fort*, pp. 213, 238, 281.

32 Shurtleff, *Records of the Governor and Company of the Massachusetts Bay in New England*, I, 99–100.

33 *Ibid.*, I, 196, II, 16; O'Callaghan, *Laws and Ordinances of New Netherland*, pp. 18–19, 47; Shurtleff and Pulsifer, *Records of the Colony of New Plymouth*, XI, 33; Trumbull and Hoadly, *The Public Records of the Colony of Connecticut*, I, 79, 529–530.

34 Shurtleff, *Records of the Governor and Company of the Massachusetts Bay in New England*, IV, Part 2, pp. 364–365; Shurtleff and Pulsifer, *Records of the Colony of New Plymouth*, V, 11–12; Trumbull and Hoadly, *The Public Records of the Colony of Connecticut*, II, 119.

35 Hutchinson, *The History of the Colony and Province of Massachusetts-Bay*, I, 394.

36 Budd, *Good Order Established in Pennsilvania & New-Jersey in America*, p. 29.

37 American Philosophical Society. Penn Letters, I, 130. For examples of other colonial legislation against the liquor traffic, see Shurtleff, *Records of the Governor and Company of the Massachusetts Bay*, I, 106, III, 369, 425–426; O'Callaghan, *Laws and Ordinances of New Netherland*, pp. 34, 52, 64, 100, 182–184, 258–261, 310–311, 383–384; Shurtleff and Pulsifer, *Records of the Colony of New Plymouth*, XI, 54; Trumbull and Hoadly, *The Public Records of the Colony of Connecticut*, I, 263; *The Colonial Laws of New York from the Year 1664 to the Revolution*, I, 41. The New England Confederation took cognizance of the problem in 1656. Shurtleff and Pulsifer, *Records of the Colony of New Plymouth*, X, 158.

38 Samuel Lee to Nehemiah Grew, June 25, 1690 (Massachusetts Historical Society, Gay Transcripts, Miscellaneous Papers, I, 85–98).

39 Myers, *Narratives of Early Pennsylvania*, p. 233.

[40] W[olley], *A two Years Journal in New-York,* pp. 28–29.

[41] Bartlett, *Records of the Colony of Rhode Island,* II, 500–503.

[42] O'Callaghan and Fernow, *Documents Relative to the Colonial History of the State of New-York,* III, 462–463.

[43] *Ibid.,* III, 67–68.

[44] The John Miller plan of Albany, which shows the layout of the town in 1695, is included among the illustrations in this volume.

[45] James and Jameson, *Journal of Jasper Danckaerts, 1679–1680,* pp. 216–217.

[46] Arthur H. Buffinton, "The Policy of Albany and English Westward Expansion," *Mississippi Valley Historical Review,* VIII (March 1922), pp. 329–334, 337–338.

[47] Buffinton, "New England and the Western Fur Trade, 1629–1675," pp. 183–188. For an attempt by a Massachusetts company to encroach upon the Dutch-Iroquois fur trade in 1659, see *Ibid.,* pp. 176–181; O'Callaghan and Fernow, *Documents Relative to the Colonial History of the State of New-York,* II, 137; Flick, *History of the State of New York,* II, 53.

[48] O'Callaghan and Fernow, *Documents Relative to the Colonial History of the State of New-York,* III, 262, 400.

[49] Wallace, *Indians in Pennsylvania,* pp. 99–100.

[50] Lawrence H. Leder, *Robert Livingston, 1654–1728, and the Politics of Colonial New York* (Chapel Hill, N.C., 1961), pp. 47–48.

[51] Richard A. Preston and Leopold Lamontagne, eds., *Royal Fort Frontenac* (Toronto, 1958), pp. 22–23, 27, 41, 102–104, 115–116, 155; Buffinton, "The Policy of Albany and English Westward Expansion," pp. 338–340.

[52] Creighton, *Dominion of the North,* p. 91; W. J. Eccles, "Frontenac and the Iroquois, 1672–1682," *Canadian Historical Review,* XXXVI (March 1955), pp. 1–16.

[53] O'Callaghan and Fernow, *Documents Relative to the Colonial History of the State of New-York,* III, 394; Leder, *Robert Livingston, 1654–1728, and the Politics of Colonial New York,* pp. 47–48; Trelease, *Indian Affairs in Colonial New York: The Seventeenth Century,* pp. 276–277.

[54] O'Callaghan and Fernow, *Documents Relative to the Colonial History of the State of New-York,* III, 349. See also *Ibid.,* pp. 341, 347–348, 392–393, 416–418; Buffinton, "The Policy of Albany and English Westward Expansion," pp. 343–344; Paul Chrisler Phillips, *The Fur Trade* (Norman, Okla., 1961), I, 253–254.

[55] *The Colonial Laws of New York from the Year 1664 to the Revolution,* I, 195; Trelease, *Indian Affairs in Colonial New York: The Seventeenth Century,* p. 208; Buffinton, "The Policy of Albany and English Westward Expansion," pp. 334–335.

[56] O'Callaghan and Fernow, *Documents Relative to the Colonial History of the State of New-York,* III, 363, 394, 477.

[57] Leder, *The Livingston Indian Records, 1666–1723,* pp. 106–108, contains documents relating to the Rooseboom expedition to divert the trade of the Western Indians. See also Phillips, *The Fur Trade,* I, 261–262; Creighton, *Dominion of the North,* p. 95.

[58] Colden, *The History of the Five Indian Nations,* pp. 59–60; Trelease, *Indian Affairs in Colonial New York: The Seventeenth Century,* pp. 270–271.

Chapter 7: English–French Imperial Rivalry, 1689–1713

[1] Edward Trelawny to Robert Trelawny, January 10, 1635/36 (Baxter, *Documentary History of the State of Maine. Vol. III*), p. 78.

[2] Douglas E. Leach, "The Question of French Involvement in King Philip's War," Colonial Society of Massachusetts *Publications,* XXXVIII (1959), pp. 414–421.

[3] Hutchinson, *The History of the Colony and Province of Massachusetts-Bay,* I, 335; Cotton Mather, *Decennium Luctuosum* (Charles H. Lincoln, ed., *Narratives of the Indian Wars, 1675–1699* [J. Franklin Jameson, ed., *Original Narratives of Early American History Series,* New York, 1913]), pp. 195–196. The assault seemed especially treacherous because the Pennacook were thought to be well disposed toward Major Richard Waldron, whose garrison house was the special target of their violence.

[4] Colden, *The History of the Five Indian Nations,* p. 102; Edward P. Hamilton, *The French and Indian Wars: The Story of Battles and Forts in the Wilderness* (New York, 1962), pp. 35–36.

[5] Leder, *Robert Livingston, 1654–1728, and the Politics of Colonial New York,* p. 83.

[6] Colden, *The History of the Five Indian Nations,* pp. 98–99.

[7] Massachusetts Historical Society. Gay Transcripts, State Papers, VII, 105–114.

[8] Cuthbert Potter's Journal (Newton D. Mereness, ed., *Travels in the American Colonies, 1690–1783,* New York, 1916), pp. 4–11; Hutchinson, *The History of the Colony and Province of Massachusetts-Bay,* I, Appendix, pp. 459–467; Massachusetts Historical Society. Gay Transcripts, Phips Papers, I, 78–79, 82–86, 103–106, 121–123.

[9] An example of such an offer is found in the Massachusetts Archives, XXX, 435–436. For an extensive listing of scalp bounties, see Ronald Oliver MacFarlane, "Indian relations in New England, 1620–1760: a study of a regulated frontier" (Harvard University, doctoral dissertation, 1933), Appendix B.

[10] *The Acts and Resolves, Public and Private, of the Province of the Massachusetts Bay* (Boston, 1869–1922), I, 194–195.

[11] Lincoln, *Narratives of the Indian Wars,* pp. 263–266; Hutchinson, *The History of the Colony and Province of Massachusetts-Bay,* II, 80–81.

[12] John Gyles, *Memoirs of Odd Adventures, Strange Deliverances, &c.* (Boston, 1736), p. 15. This story is an interesting example of frontier taletelling. One is tempted to doubt that the episode ever happened, at least in the form given by Gyles. Could a group of Indians be so easily duped on ground as familiar to them as to the prisoner? Would any sane captive have risked his life by attempting such a dubious deception? Yet Gyles claimed to speak from first-hand knowledge, and had no apparent reason for fabricating the story. All we can say is that if true, the episode stands out as a pioneer practical joke of the first water; if false, the story may still be admired as an early example of the frontier yarn.

[13] Hutchinson, *The History of the Colony and Province of Massachusetts-Bay,* II, 75.

[14] O'Callaghan and Fernow, *Documents Relative to the Colonial History of the State of New-York,* III, 785.

[15] Leder, *The Livingston Indian Records, 1666–1723,* p. 165. See also Colden, *The History of the Five Indian Nations,* pp. 126–127, 152–153.

[16] Massachusetts Archives, XXX, 439–441, 447–449, 464–471.

[17] British Museum. Lansdowne Mss. 849, ff. 29, 90.

[18] The deed placing the hunting lands of the Iroquois under royal protection is published in O'Callaghan and Fernow, *Documents Relative to the Colonial History of the State of New-York,* IV, 908–911, and also in the *Eighteenth Annual Report of the Bureau of American Ethnology, 1896–97,* Part 2, pp. 552–553. See also Anthony F. C. Wallace, "Origins of Iroquois Neutrality: The Grand Settlement of 1701," *Pennsylvania History,* XXIV (July 1957), pp. 223–235; Trelease, *Indian Affairs in Colonial New York: The Seventeenth Century,* pp. 361–363.

[19] British Museum. Lansdowne Mss. 849, ff. 29, 78. Bellomont's information was based partly upon a tour of the Iroquois country made at his direction by Colonel Wolfgang Römer in 1700. The most tangible result of Römer's exploration is an excellent map of the area, showing his route and the location of various Indian villages. The map is in the British Museum, K. Top. CXXI, 10.

[20] Penhallow, *The History of the Wars of New-England with the Eastern Indians,* p. 27. See also Hamilton, *The French and Indian Wars,* pp. 47–48; Francis Parkman, *A Half-Century of Conflict* (Boston, 1892), I, 40–44.

[21] Arthur H. Buffinton, "The Policy of the Northern Colonies towards the French to the Peace of Utrecht" (Harvard University, doctoral dissertation, 1925), pp. 361–381; Flick, *History of the State of New York,* II, 241.

[22] Massachusetts Archives, CXIII, 350.

[23] John Williams, *The Redeemed Captive Returning to Zion* (Springfield, Mass., 1908), pp. 9–10; Hutchinson, *The History of the Colony and Province of Massachusetts-Bay,* II, 102–104; Hamilton, *The French and Indian Wars,* p. 49. The most vivid account of the attack is to be found in Parkman, *A Half-Century of Conflict,* I, 52–65.

[24] Emma Lewis Coleman, *New England Captives Carried to Canada Between 1677 and 1760 During the French and Indian Wars* (Portland, Me., 1925), II, 44–64. See also Hutchinson, *The History of the Colony and Province of Massachusetts-Bay,* II, 104n.; Colden, *The History of the Five Indian Nations,* pp. 180–181.

[25] Massachusetts Archives, CXIII, 124.

[26] For examples of frontier petitions, see *Ibid.,* 362–363, 365, 419–420, 456.

[27] *Ibid.,* 582.

[28] Hutchinson, *The History of the Colony and Province of Massachusetts-Bay,* II, 121.

[29] Benjamin Church, *The History of the Eastern Expeditions Of 1689, 1690, 1692, 1696, and 1704 Against the Indians and French,* Henry M. Dexter, ed. (Boston, 1867), pp. 99–120; Hamilton, *The French and Indian Wars,* pp. 50–51. See also Hutchinson, *The History of the Colony and Province of Massachusetts-Bay,* II, 107–109; *The Deplorable State of New-England, By Reason of a Covetous and Treacherous Governour and Pusillanimous Counsellors* (Massachusetts Historical Society *Collections,* 5th ser., VI, 1879), pp. 97–131; *A Memorial Of the Present Deplorable State of New-England* (Massachusetts Historical Society *Collections,* 5th ser., VI, 1879), pp. 31–64; *A Modest Enquiry into the Grounds and Occasions of a Late Pamphlet, Intituled, A Memorial of the Present Deplorable State of New-England* (Massachusetts Historical Society *Collections,* 5th ser., VI, 1879), pp. 65–95.

[30] Massachusetts Historical Society. Gay Transcripts, State Papers, X, 19–48; Bruce T. McCully, "Catastrophe in the Wilderness: New Light on the Canada Expedition of 1709," *William and Mary Quarterly,* XI (July 1954), pp. 441–456; Hamilton, *The French and Indian Wars,* pp. 52–53; G. M. Waller, *Samuel Vetch: Colonial Enterpriser* (Chapel Hill, N.C., 1960), chap. 7–8.

[31] Penhallow, *The History of the Wars of New-England with the Eastern Indians,* pp. 63–67; Waller, *Samuel Vetch,* pp. 179–187.

[32] Massachusetts Historical Society. Gay Transcripts, State Papers, X, 81–104, 109–128, 159–179; William T. Morgan, "Queen Anne's Canadian Expedition of 1711," Queen's University *Bulletin,* no. 56 (1928), pp. 18–19.

[33] Massachusetts Historical Society. Gay Transcripts, State Papers, X, 132–142, 187–192; Waller, *Samuel Vetch,* chap. 12; Parkman, *A Half-Century of Conflict,* I, chap. 8.

³⁴ See the maps published in Herman R. Friis, "A Series of Population Maps of the Colonies and the United States, 1625–1790," *Geographical Review*, XXX (July 1940), pp. 463–470.

Chapter 8: The Expanding Frontier, 1713–1743

¹ U.S. Bureau of the Census, *Historical Statistics of the United States, Colonial Times to 1957* (Washington, 1960), p. 756.

² My discussion of the German migration to New York relies heavily upon Walter Allen Knittle, *Early Eighteenth Century Palatine Emigration: A British Government Redemptioner Project to Manufacture Naval Stores* (Philadelphia, 1937). See also Faust, *The German Element in the United States*, I, 74–105.

³ Higgins, *Expansion in New York, with Especial Reference to the Eighteenth Century*, p. 52. The behavior of the Palatines is mentioned with disapproval in a report of the Board of Trade, dated September 8, 1721 (British Museum. Additional Mss. 23615). Some years later the Swedish traveler Peter Kalm attributed the fact that few Germans came to New York after the great migration of 1710 to the unhappy experience of the Palatines in that province. This view has been widely accepted, but Dr. Knittle has suggested that more effective advertising by Pennsylvania was a factor of greater significance. *Early Eighteenth Century Palatine Emigration*, pp. 210–212, 216–218.

⁴ Pownall, *A Topographical Description of the Dominions of the United States of America*, p. 35.

⁵ Higgins, *Expansion in New York, with Especial Reference to the Eighteenth Century*, p. 47.

⁶ Bidwell and Falconer, *History of Agriculture in the Northern United States, 1620–1860*, p. 140.

⁷ Higgins, *Expansion in New York, with Especial Reference to the Eighteenth Century*, pp. 70–72; Henry Jones Ford, *The Scotch-Irish in America* (Princeton, N. J., 1915), pp. 256–257.

⁸ See below, pp. 171–173.

⁹ Ford, *The Scotch-Irish in America*, pp. 226–229; Charles K. Bolton, *Scotch Irish Pioneers in Ulster and America* (Boston, 1910), pp. 154, 177–181; J. P. MacLean, *An Historical Account of the Settlements of Scotch Highlanders in America Prior to the Peace of 1783* (Cleveland, 1900), p. 47.

¹⁰ Bolton, *Scotch Irish Pioneers in Ulster and America*, pp. 239–265; Ford, *The Scotch-Irish in America*, pp. 236–238.

¹¹ Baxter, *Documentary History of the State of Maine*, XXIV, 244–245; Moody, "The Maine Frontier, 1607 to 1763," pp. 361–362; Bolton, *Scotch Irish Pioneers in Ulster and America*, pp. 215–238; William Willis, ed., *Journals of the Rev. Thomas Smith, and the Rev. Samuel Deane, Pastors of the First Church in Portland* (Portland, Me., 1849), p. 87n.

¹² Governor Dummer to Governor Vaudreuil, January 19, 1724/5 (Massachusetts Archives, LII, 106–109. Published in William B. Trask, ed., *Letters of Colonel Thomas Westbrook and Others Relative to Indian Affairs in Maine, 1722–1726* [Boston, 1901], pp. 88–91). See also Hutchinson, *The History of the Colony and Province of Massachusetts-Bay*, II, 198–199; Mary Celeste Leger, *The Catholic Indian Missions in Maine (1611–1820)* (Catholic University of America *Studies in American Church History*, VIII, Washington, 1929), pp. 75–84. An extremely interesting and valuable interpretation of Rale's endeavor, emphasizing the fact that a strong pro-English faction existed among his Indians, is to be found in Fannie H. Eckstorm, "**The**

Attack on Norridgewock: 1724," *New England Quarterly,* VII (September 1934), pp. 541–578.

[13] Massachusetts Archives, LXXII, 147–148. Published in Trask, *Letters of Colonel Thomas Westbrook,* pp. 42–43; Penhallow, *The History of the Wars of New-England with the Eastern Indians,* pp. 89–90; Hutchinson, *The History of the Colony and Province of Massachusetts-Bay,* II, 164–166; Belknap, *The History of New-Hampshire,* p. 198; Henry F. DePuy, comp., *A Bibliography of the English Colonial Treaties with the American Indians, Including a Synopsis of Each Treaty* (New York, 1917), p. 6.

[14] The declaration, dated July 25, 1722, is in Massachusetts Archives, XXXI, 106–108.

[15] The attack on Norridgewock and the killing of Rale has been the subject of much controversy, blown up by religious partisanship. The best available evidence indicates that Rale met his death while actively engaging in combat. Captured documents proved the extent of his involvement in the Indian resistance to English expansion.

[16] Thomas Symmes, *Historical Memoirs of the Late Fight at Piggwacket . . .* (2d ed., Boston, 1725); Penhallow, *The History of the Wars of New-England with the Eastern Indians,* pp. 114–118. When the historian Jeremy Belknap visited the site of Lovewell's defeat fifty-nine years later, the names of the dead could still be seen where they had been carved on trees by the party which came and buried the bodies. Belknap, *The History of New-Hampshire,* p. 212n.

[17] Penhallow, *The History of the Wars of New-England with the Eastern Indians,* pp. 123–127. The agreement subsequently was ratified by groups of Indian leaders in 1726 and 1727. DePuy, *A Bibliography of the English Colonial Treaties with the American Indians,* pp. 11–12.

[18] Willis, *Journals of the Rev. Thomas Smith, and the Rev. Samuel Deane,* p. 48.

[19] Mathews, *The Expansion of New England,* pp. 88–89.

[20] Waterman, *The Dwellings of Colonial America,* pp. 280–281. The site of Fort Dummer is near the present Brattleboro, Vermont.

[21] New Hampshire Historical Society *Collections,* II, 75–77; Walter Hill Crockett, *Vermont, the Green Mountain State* (New York, 1921–1923), I, 165.

[22] Albion, *Forests and Sea Power* pp. 269–273; Moody, "The Maine Frontier, 1607 to 1763," p. 335; Kirkland, *A History of American Economic Life,* p. 43.

[23] Especially helpful for an understanding of the royal policy are Albion, *Forests and Sea Power,* pp. 238–263, and Moody, "The Maine Frontier, 1607 to 1763," pp. 366ff.

[24] Governor Belcher to the Lords of Trade, July 1, 1734 (Massachusetts Historical Society *Collections,* 6th ser., VII, 78–85); John A. Schutz, *William Shirley: King's Governor of Massachusetts* (Chapel Hill, N. C., 1961), pp. 18–19.

[25] Kirkland, *A History of American Economic Life,* p. 43.

[26] Quoted in James G. Leyburn, *The Scotch-Irish: A Social History* (Chapel Hill, N. C., 1962), p. 170. Additional evidence on the volume of the migration is conveniently assembled in *Ibid.,* pp. 179–183.

[27] Solon J. and Elizabeth H. Buck, *The Planting of Civilization in Western Pennsylvania* (Pittsburgh, 1939), p. 9.

[28] Leyburn, *The Scotch-Irish: A Social History,* pp. 190–191.

[29] *Colonial Records of Pennsylvania,* III, 355–356.

[30] Dunaway, *The Scotch-Irish of Colonial Pennsylvania,* p. 61.

[31] Wayland F. Dunaway, *A History of Pennsylvania* (2d ed., New York, 1948), p. 205; Bond, *The Quit-Rent System in the American Colonies,* p. 134.

[32] Historical Society of Pennsylvania. Penn Mss., I, Indian Affairs, 1687–1753, p. 35.

[33] Bidwell and Falconer, *History of Agriculture in the Northern United States, 1620–1860*, pp. 72–73; Joseph Schafer, *The Social History of American Agriculture* (New York, 1936), p. 10.

[34] Historical Society of Pennsylvania. Penn Mss., I, Indian Affairs, 1687–1753, p. 36; Joseph E. Johnson, "A Quaker Imperialist's View of the British Colonies in America: 1732," *Pennsylvania Magazine of History and Biography*, LX (1936), p. 108.

[35] Wallace, "The Iroquois: A Brief Outline of Their History," pp. 23–24; Wallace, *Indians in Pennsylvania*, pp. 104–107.

[36] Paul A. W. Wallace, *Conrad Weiser, 1696–1760: Friend of Colonist and Mohawk* (Philadelphia, 1945), pp. 96–99. For a contrary view, see Julian P. Boyd's introduction to *Indian Treaties Printed by Benjamin Franklin, 1736–1762* (Philadelphia, 1938), p. xxviii.

[37] [Charles Thomson], *An Enquiry into the Causes of the Alienation of the Delaware and Shawanese Indians from the British Interest* (London, 1759), p. 69.

[38] Wallace, *Conrad Weiser*, pp. 42–49; George A. Cribbs, "The Frontier Policy of Pennsylvania," *Western Pennsylvania Historical Magazine*, II (January 1919), p. 12; Wallace, *Indians in Pennsylvania*, pp. 141–143.

[39] [Thomson], *An Enquiry into the Causes of the Alienation of the Delaware and Shawanese Indians from the British Interest*, pp. 42–47; DePuy, *A Bibliography of the English Colonial Treaties with the American Indians*, pp. 17–18; *Indian Treaties Printed by Benjamin Franklin*, pp. 15–39; Wallace, *Conrad Weiser*, pp. 125–132.

Chapter 9: The Fur Trade and English–French Rivalry

[1] British Museum. Additional Mss. 23615.

[2] Colden to Peter Collinson, May 1742 (New York Historical Society *Collections*, LI, 257–263); Colden to Dr. Mitchell, August 17, 1751 (Historical Society of Pennsylvania, Penn Mss., I, Indian Affairs, 1687–1753, p. 79).

[3] *The Colonial Laws of New York from the Year 1664 to the Revolution*, II, 909. See also Peter Wraxall, *An Abridgment of the Indian Affairs . . . of New York, From the Year 1678 to the Year 1751*, Charles H. McIlwain, ed. (*Harvard Historical Studies*, XXI, Cambridge, 1915), pp. 166, 187–188, 195.

[4] Colden to Peter Collinson, May 1742 (New York Historical Society *Collections*, LI, 260).

[5] [Thomson], *An Enquiry into the Causes of the Alienation of the Delaware and Shawanese Indians from the British Interest*, p. 75. For an authoritative, modern appraisal of the problem see Wilbur R. Jacobs, "Unsavory Sidelights on the Colonial Fur Trade," *New York History*, XXXIV (April 1953), pp. 135–148.

[6] *Pennsylvania Archives*, 4th ser., I (1900), p. 854.

[7] Historical Society of Pennsylvania. Penn Mss., I, Indian Affairs, 1687–1753, p. 106. Published in Leonard W. Labaree, *et al.*, eds., *The Papers of Benjamin Franklin* (New Haven, Conn., 1959–   ), V, 107.

[8] Historical Society of Pennsylvania. Penn Mss., I, Indian Affairs, 1687–1753, pp. 98–99. Published in Labaree, *The Papers of Benjamin Franklin*, V, 97. For further evidence of the way in which liquor sometimes was employed by irregular or unlicensed traders to undercut the business of the licensed traders, see *Pennsylvania Archives*, 1st ser., I (1852), p. 261.

9 See above, pp. 94–95.

10 Massachusetts Archives, XXX, 346–347, 445–446, 462. Published in *The Acts and Resolves, Public and Private, of the Province of the Massachusetts Bay*, I (Boston, 1869), 172–173, 384–385. See also Ronald O. MacFarlane, "The Massachusetts Bay Truck-Houses in Diplomacy with the Indians," *New England Quarterly*, XI (March 1938), p. 50.

11 *The Acts and Resolves, Public and Private, of the Province of the Massachusetts Bay*, II (Boston, 1874), pp. 365–366.

12 MacFarlane, "The Massachusetts Bay Truck-Houses in Diplomacy with the Indians," p. 48. In the Massachusetts Archives, XXIX, 283–306, is the record of a conference held with the Eastern Indians in the winter of 1727–1728, which reveals much about the kind of problem that did arise under the Massachusetts system. Two Indians lodged a complaint against Captain Thomas Smith, one of the truckmasters, alleging that he had refused to pay them more than 3s. 9d. per pound for fall beaver that was worth much more. Smith explained, in his own defense, that his practice was to pay 3s. 9d. for both fall and stage beaver, with some skins being worth less than that, and some more. Under this system, he reckoned, things came out about even. But an expert summoned to appraise the pelts in question set their value at nearly twice the amount offered by the truckmaster. Additional testimony tended to cast a further shadow on Smith's integrity or competence, and he subsequently was dismissed from his post. The government promised the Indians appropriate restitution for the losses they had suffered.

13 Hutchinson, *The History of the Colony and Province of Massachusetts-Bay*, II, 241.

14 The long-range effects of the system are ably discussed in MacFarlane, "The Massachusetts Bay Truck-Houses in Diplomacy with the Indians," and in the tenth chapter of the same author's "Indian relations in New England, 1620–1760."

15 See above, p. 117.

16 British Museum. Additional Mss. 32833 (Newcastle Papers, CXLVIII), 402; Wraxall, *An Abridgment of the Indian Affairs . . . of New York*, p. 41.

17 Penhallow, *The History of the Wars of New-England with the Eastern Indians*, p. 41.

18 Phillips, *The Fur Trade*, I, 392–393.

19 Leder, *Robert Livingston, 1654–1728, and the Politics of Colonial New York*, pp. 250–253; Buffinton, "The Policy of Albany and English Westward Expansion," p. 352.

20 Historical Society of Pennsylvania. Penn Mss., I, Indian Affairs, 1687–1753, p. 26; Buck, *The Planting of Civilization in Western Pennsylvania*, p. 47.

21 New York Historical Society *Collections*, L, 131. Iroquois agreement to this proposal is evidence against the theory that the Confederacy built its entire policy on the ambition to play an exclusive middleman role in the fur trade.

22 Leder, *The Livingston Indian Records, 1666–1723*, pp. 233–235; *The Colonial Laws of New York from the Year 1664 to the Revolution*, II, 109–115.

23 Buffinton, "The Policy of Albany and English Westward Expansion," pp. 333–334, 349–350, 358.

24 Albany merchants were not the only English subjects to conduct the fur trade across international boundaries. Some New Englanders, too, made a practice of sending rum to New France in exchange for furs from the West. See Phillips, *The Fur Trade*, I, 391.

25 *The Colonial Laws of New York from the Year 1664 to the Revolution*, II, 8–12, 98–105, 197–198, 248–250. In 1722 England placed furs on the list of

enumerated colonial exports, which meant that Americans were forbidden to ship their furs to foreign markets. This enactment was to a considerable degree aimed against the direct export of furs from New York to Holland. Lawson, *Fur: A Study in English Mercantilism, 1700–1775*, p. 34.

26 Cuyler to Richard Jeneway, October 31, 1724 (American Antiquarian Society, Cornelis Cuyler Letterbook).

27 *Papers Relating to An Act of the Assembly of the Province of New-York, For Encouragement of the Indian Trade, &c.* (New York, 1724), p. 11. Part VI of this volume, entitled "A Memorial concerning the Furr-Trade of New-York," was written by Colden.

28 Michel Bégon to Claude-Thomas Dupuy, October 31, 1725 (Preston and Lamontagne, *Royal Fort Frontenac*, p. 217).

29 *The Colonial Laws of New York from the Year 1664 to the Revolution*, II, 281–294, 350–365.

30 Flick, *History of the State of New York*, II, 178–179, 324. In 1731 John Henry Lydius, a Dutch merchant recently banished from New France, established a trading center at the Great Carrying Place on the upper Hudson, where Fort Edward later was built. This was an excellent location for an enterprising trader interested in exploiting the trade between New York and Canada. Guy Omeron Coolidge, *The French Occupation of the Champlain Valley from 1609 to 1759* (Vermont Historical Society *Proceedings*, New Series, VI [Brattleboro, Vt., 1938]), p. 220. Various letters from the Albany trader Philip Livingston, during the period 1736–1738, provide additional evidence concerning the trade with Canada. New York State Library, Albany. Mss. Misc., V.

31 Clérambault D'Aigrement to Count Pontchartrain, November 14, 1708 (Preston and Lamontagne, *Royal Fort Frontenac*, p. 208).

32 British Museum. Additional Mss. 23615.

33 Leder, *The Livingston Indian Records, 1666–1723*, p. 233; *Papers Relating to An Act of the Assembly of the Province of New-York, For Encouragement of the Indian Trade, &c.*, pp. 11–12.

34 Higgins, *Expansion in New York, with Especial Reference to the Eighteenth Century*, p. 45.

35 *Ibid.*, pp. 45–46; Buffinton, "The Policy of Albany and English Westward Expansion," p. 363.

36 *The Colonial Laws of New York from the Year 1664 to the Revolution*, II, 558.

37 Philip Livingston to Storke and Gainsborough, June 7, 1736 (New York State Library, Albany. Mss. Misc., V).

38 Benjamin Stoddard to William Johnson, July 16, 1749 (*The Papers of Sir William Johnson* [Albany, 1921–1962], I, 236–237).

39 New York State Library, Albany. Johannes R. Bleecker Photostats.

40 Cuyler to Samuel Baker, May 20, 1732 (American Antiquarian Society, Cornelis Cuyler Letterbook).

41 Samuel Baker to Hendrick Ten Eyck, March 26, 1733 (New York State Library, Albany. Harmanus Bleecker Papers).

42 Cuyler to Storke and Gainsborough, November 16, 1734 (American Antiquarian Society. Cornelis Cuyler Letterbook).

43 Johnson to William Baker, [December 24, 1752] (*The Papers of Sir William Johnson*, I, 384).

44 Livingston to Storke and Gainsborough, November 28, 1734, July 16, 1736 (New York State Library, Albany. Mss. Misc., V).

45 Carl Bridenbaugh, ed., *Gentleman's Progress: The Itinerarium of Dr. Alexander*

Hamilton, 1744 (Chapel Hill, N.C., 1948), p. 73; Benson, *Peter Kalm's Travels in North America*, pp. 129, 343.

[46] Edward Shippen's letter of June 19, 1751 (Historical Society of Pennsylvania. Shippen Family Papers, I).

[47] Cuyler to William Darlington, January 20, 1753 (American Antiquarian Society. Cornelis Cuyler Letterbook).

[48] Letter of November 25, 1735 (New York State Library, Albany. Mss. Misc., V).

[49] Louise P. Kellogg, *The French Régime in Wisconsin and the Northwest* (Madison, Wis., 1925), pp. 409–410.

[50] Buck, *The Planting of Civilization in Western Pennsylvania*, p. 3.

[51] *Ibid.*, p. 53; Phillips, *The Fur Trade*, I, 506; Lawrence H. Gipson, *The British Empire Before the American Revolution* (Caldwell, N.J., and New York, 1936–   ), IV, 172, 174–175. For a discussion of King George's War, see above, pp. 192–195.

[52] Gipson, *The British Empire Before the American Revolution*, IV, 177.

[53] Dunaway, *A History of Pennsylvania*, p. 253.

[54] See, for example, Conrad Weiser's Journal in R. G. Thwaites, ed., *Early Western Journals, 1748–1765* (Cleveland, 1904), p. 41.

[55] Phillips, *The Fur Trade*, I, 507. Some of the problems of the frontier traders are revealed in letters addressed to the Philadelphia merchant Edward Shippen (Historical Society of Pennsylvania, Shippen Family Papers, I, 55, 65, 75, 87, 95).

[56] Buck, *The Planting of Civilization in Western Pennsylvania*, pp. 54–55. There are two excellent biographies of Croghan: Albert T. Volwiler, *George Croghan and the Westward Movement, 1741–1782* (Cleveland, 1926), and Nicholas B. Wainwright, *George Croghan: Wilderness Diplomat* (Chapel Hill, N.C., 1959).

[57] Conrad Weiser to Richard Peters, May 8, 1749 (Historical Society of Pennsylvania, Weiser Correspondence, I, 1741–1756, p. 19); W. Neil Franklin, "Pennsylvania-Virginia Rivalry for the Indian Trade of the Ohio Valley," *Mississippi Valley Historical Review*, XX (March 1934), pp. 464–468. The Virginia claim to the forks area rested upon a liberal interpretation of the rather vague geographical boundaries specified in the charter of 1609. It was in 1749 that the aggressive group of investors known as the Ohio Company of Virginia openly began to challenge Pennsylvania's interests on the upper Ohio.

[58] An excellent account of Céloron's mission is given in Gipson, *The British Empire Before the American Revolution*, IV, 191–202. See also Theodore Calvin Pease and Ernestine Jenison, eds., *Illinois on the Eve of the Seven Years' War, 1747–1755* (Illinois State Historical Library *Collections*, XXIX, Springfield, 1940), pp. xxix–xxxi.

[59] Gipson, *The British Empire Before the American Revolution*, IV, 221–224.

[60] Wainwright, *George Croghan: Wilderness Diplomat*, pp. 50–51; Franklin, "Pennsylvania-Virginia Rivalry for the Indian Trade of the Ohio Valley," p. 470.

[61] Phillips, *The Fur Trade*, I, 402–403.

[62] *Pennsylvania Archives*, 1st ser., I, 261, II, 118–119; Labaree, *The Papers of Benjamin Franklin*, V, 96–99; Wainwright, *George Croghan: Wilderness Diplomat*, p. 67.

[63] Labaree, *The Papers of Benjamin Franklin*, V, 110–115.

[64] *Pennsylvania Magazine of History and Biography*, VI, 743; VII, 63, 181–182, 455–459, 463, 759–762; VIII, 19–25, 29, 76–77; Cribbs, "The Frontier Policy of Pennsylvania," p. 30; Theodore Thayer, *Israel Pemberton, King of the Quakers* (Philadelphia, 1943), pp. 158–159.

[65] This solution to an eighteenth-century problem is of no little interest today as an isolated example of state socialism operating in a key industry prior to the American

Revolution. The arrangement was made without large-scale public opposition, for it was seen to be virtually necessary for the general welfare. It is interesting to note that two of the leading advocates of government monopoly in the fur trade, Bowdoin and Franklin, subsequently were patriots of the Revolution and founders of the Republic.

Chapter 10: Land Speculation

[1] See above, pp. 43–49.

[2] Wraxall, *An Abridgment of the Indian Affairs . . . of New York*, p. 30. See also Higgins, *Expansion in New York, with Especial Reference to the Eighteenth Century*, pp. 23–24; Jerome R. Reich, *Leisler's Rebellion: A Study of Democracy in New York, 1664–1720* (Chicago, 1953), pp. 140–141; Trelease, *Indian Affairs in Colonial New York: The Seventeenth Century*, pp. 330–331.

[3] *The Colonial Laws of New York from the Year 1664 to the Revolution*, I, 412–417.

[4] Bond, *The Quit-Rent System in the American Colonies*, pp. 255–258.

[5] Higgins, *Expansion in New York, with Especial Reference to the Eighteenth Century*, pp. 58–59.

[6] *Ibid.*, pp. 27–29.

[7] American Antiquarian Society *Proceedings*, new ser., XIX (1909), pp. 161, 172–173. See also Higgins, *Expansion in New York, with Especial Reference to the Eighteenth Century*, p. 27.

[8] *Ibid.*, pp. 69–70; Flick, *History of the State of New York*, II, 224.

[9] Wraxall, *An Abridgment of the Indian Affairs . . . of New York*, p. 185.

[10] New York State Library, Albany. Mss. Misc., V, *passim*.

[11] Livingston to Samuel Storke, November 22, 1733 (New York State Library, Albany. Mss. Misc., V).

[12] Livingston to Samuel Storke, October 31, 1734 (New York State Library, Albany. Mss. Misc., V). See also Livingston to Storke and Gainsborough, February 24, 1734/5.

[13] Livingston to Samuel Storke, November 13, 1735 (New York State Library, Albany. Mss. Misc., V). See also O'Callaghan and Fernow, *Documents Relative to the Colonial History of the State of New-York*, VI, 67-69.

[14] Livingston to Samuel Storke, December 8, 1735 (New York State Library, Albany. Mss. Misc., V).

[15] Livingston to Storke and Gainsborough, May 3, 1736 (New York State Library, Albany. Mss. Misc., V).

[16] O'Callaghan and Fernow, *Documents Relative to the Colonial History of the State of New-York*, VI, 42, 57–62, 67–69. Two members of the Albany council told of a statement made by Philip Livingston, apparently in the presence of the council, to the effect that until recently he had known nothing of the Livingston-Storke petition to the Crown, and hoped that the petition would not be granted. If Livingston did make that statement, it was a bald-faced lie.

[17] Edith M. Fox, *Land Speculation in the Mohawk Country (Cornell Studies in American History, Literature, and Folklore*, no. 3, Ithaca, N.Y., 1949), pp. ix–x, 1–4. See also the Preface by Curtis P. Nettels.

[18] Wraxall, *An Abridgment of the Indian Affairs . . . of New York*, pp. 179–180n., 246–247.

[19] For examples of antagonism between settlers and absentee proprietors, see Connecticut Archives, Hartford. Towns and Lands, III, 99–100, 108, 201. H. Roger King, "The Settlement of the Upper Connecticut River Valley to 1675" (Vanderbilt

University, doctoral dissertation, 1965), chap. 6, concludes that in the upper Connecticut Valley there were few absentee landlords and little land speculation prior to 1675.

20 Massachusetts Historical Society *Collections,* 6th ser., VI, 481–482.

21 *Ibid.,* p. 194.

22 *Ibid.,* p. 382.

23 Baxter, *Documentary History of the State of Maine,* XXIV, 200–202, 204–217. Subsequently Sir Edmund Andros, Governor of the Dominion of New England, challenged the validity of Wharton's title. Massachusetts Historical Society, Gay Transcripts, State Papers, VI, 106–110.

24 Moody, "The Maine Frontier, 1607 to 1763," pp. 357–359; Baxter, *Documentary History of the State of Maine,* XXIV, 237–244.

25 *Ibid.,* pp. 244–245.

26 Hutchinson, *The History of the Colony and Province of Massachusetts-Bay,* II, 251–252; Mathews, *The Expansion of New England,* pp. 82–84, Matt Bushnell Jones, *Vermont in the Making, 1750–1777* (Cambridge, Mass., 1939), pp. 13–14.

27 See above, p. 61.

28 Clifford K. Shipton, "The New England Frontier," *New England Quarterly,* X (March 1937), p. 32.

29 Trumbull and Hoadly, *The Public Records of the Colony of Connecticut,* VII, 343–344; VIII, 134–137, 169–171.

30 Interested students should consult Charles S. Grant's "Land Speculation and the Settlement of Kent, 1738–1760," *New England Quarterly,* XXVIII (March 1955), pp. 51–71, and *Democracy in the Connecticut Frontier Town of Kent* (New York, 1961).

31 Philip C. Olsson, "The Kennebec Purchase from the Colony of New Plymouth, 1749–1775" (Harvard University, Honors essay, 1962), p. 25. See also Moody, "The Maine Frontier, 1607 to 1763," pp. 427–438; Schutz, *William Shirley: King's Governor of Massachusetts,* p. 179.

32 Massachusetts Archives, XXXII, 343–344, 359, 363–364; Willis, *Journals of the Rev. Thomas Smith, and the Rev. Samuel Deane,* p. 153.

33 Israel Williams to Governor Phips, March 19, 1753 (Massachusetts Archives, XXXII, 336–337); Belknap, *The History of New-Hampshire,* pp. 305–306.

34 O'Callaghan and Fernow, *Documents Relative to the Colonial History of the State of New-York,* V, 180.

35 Baxter, *Documentary History of the State of Maine,* XXIV, 239.

36 Conference between the Governor of New York and the River Indians, May 4, 1745 (New York Historical Society, Horsmanden Papers). See also John W. Lydekker, *The Faithful Mohawks* (New York, 1938), p. 46.

37 Letter of Edward Shippen, November 8, 1752 (Historical Society of Pennsylvania, Shippen Family Papers, I, 143).

Chapter 11: Christianity on the Northern Frontier

1 In this connection it should be noted, however, that in New England, especially, a frontier community might be more rigidly orthodox than its parent community in the East. The reason is that when a community split over some moral or religious issue, it might be the more conservative faction that moved to the frontier in order to preserve its own standards from the influence of a growing worldliness. This tendency is noted in Richard D. Birdsall, *Berkshire County: A Cultural History* (New Haven, Conn., 1959), p. 41. See also Robert A. East, "Puritanism and New Settlement," *New England Quarterly,* XVII (June 1944), pp. 259–263.

[2] O'Callaghan and Fernow, *Documents Relative to the Colonial History of the State of New-York*, III, 101. See also Burrage, *The Beginnings of Colonial Maine, 1602–1658*, pp. 261–263.

[3] Cotton Mather, *The Present State of New-England. Considered in a Discourse On the Necessities and Advantages of a Public Spirit In every Man* (Boston, 1690), p. 32.

[4] W[inslow], *Good Newes from New England*, pp. 38–41.

[5] Benson, *Peter Kalm's Travels in North America*, p. 711.

[6] Trumbull and Hoadly, *The Public Records of the Colony of Connecticut*, I, 78.

[7] *Memoirs of the Rev. David Brainerd; . . . By Rev. Jonathan Edwards, . . . Including his Journal, . . . by Sereno Edwards Dwight* (New Haven, Conn., 1822), p. 193.

[8] David Brainerd, *Mirabilia Dei inter Indicos* (Philadelphia, [1746]), pp. 118–119.

[9] *Memoirs of the Rev. David Brainerd*, p. 376.

[10] Mittelberger, *Journey to Pennsylvania*, pp. 47–48, 80. Charles Thornton Libby, in his preface to the *Province and Court Records of Maine*, II (Portland, Me., 1931), has suggested a reason why in rural New England it became fairly common for engaged couples to have sexual intercourse prior to marriage. Libby's theory is that a young man destined to become a pioneering farmer felt the need for assurance that his intended wife was capable of providing him with children to help with the burdensome work of the farm. Premarital intercourse, then, was a practical testing of fertility, undertaken at the cost of a heavy fine for breaking the law. "Bluntly stated," says Libby, "in order to alter the New England wilderness into a land of homes, it was necessary for the young husbandman to raise his own farm laborers along with his stock; those large court fines were deliberately, and without shame, incurred and paid as a sort of insurance against what was worse than a fire, and almost as unwelcome as death itself" (pp. xliii–xliv). That young couples calculated quite as matter-of-factly as this may be doubted, but the explanation does illustrate how the special demands of frontier living could influence the patterns of human behavior, while the relative freedom from close observation and control made such departures more easily accomplished.

[11] Dunaway, *The Scotch-Irish of Colonial Pennsylvania*, pp. 207–211; Guy S. Klett, *Presbyterians in Colonial Pennsylvania* (Philadelphia, 1937), pp. 190–191; Mittelberger, *Journey to Pennsylvania*, p. 80.

[12] Fredric Klees, *The Pennsylvania Dutch* (New York, 1951), pp. 96–106.

[13] Thomas Chalkley, *A journal or historical account of the life, travels and Christian experiences of . . . Thomas Chalkley* (2d ed., London, 1751), pp. 42–45, throws much light upon the Quaker dilemma.

[14] Samuel Eliot Morison, *Builders of the Bay Colony* (Boston, 1930), pp. 289–290. Joshua Scottow, a Puritan merchant of Boston, was certain that the principal motivation underlying the settlement of New England, under divine guidance, was religious. "That this Design was Super-humane," he wrote, "will be evidenced by the *Primum Mobile*, or grand Wheel thereof. Neither Spanish Gold or Silver, nor *French* or *Dutch* Trade of Peltry did Oil their Wheels; it was the Propagation of Piety and Religion to Posterity; and the secret Macedonean Call, COME OVER AND HELP US, afterward Instamp'd in the Seal of this Colony, the Setting up of Christ's Kingdom among the Heathens, in this Remote End of the Earth, was the main spring of motion. . . ." *A Narrative of the Planting of the Massachusetts Colony Anno 1628* (Boston, 1694), p. 8.

[15] MacFarlane, "Indian relations in New England, 1620–1760," p. 540.

[16] Daniel Gookin, "Historical Collections of the Indians in New England" (Massachusetts Historical Society *Collections,* 1st ser., I [1792]), p. 209.

[17] For a more thorough discussion of these problems, see Douglas Edward Leach, "The Causes and Effects of King Philip's War" (Harvard University, doctoral dissertation, 1950), pp. 70–81.

[18] Jameson, *Narratives of New Netherland,* p. 178.

[19] Brainerd, *Mirabilia Dei inter Indicos,* pp. 56–57.

[20] *Memoirs of the Rev. David Brainerd,* p. 174. See also Massachusetts Historical Society *Collections,* 3d ser., IV, 85; Lydekker, *The Faithful Mohawks,* p. 46.

[21] Morison, *Builders of the Bay Colony,* pp. 291–295. The entire tenth chapter is devoted to Eliot's career.

[22] Shurtleff, *Records of the Governor and Company of the Massachusetts Bay in New England,* III, 246, 294; IV (Part 1), 75–76, 112.

[23] An example of support from Old England is recorded in Massachusetts Archives, XXX, 32, where two Englishmen to whom debts were owed in New England assigned the debts to Eliot for the furtherance of his work among the Indians. For an adverse view of Eliot's endeavors, see *Calendar of State Papers, Colonial Series, America and West Indies, 1661–1668* (London, 1880), p. 346.

[24] O'Callaghan and Fernow, *Documents Relative to the Colonial History of the State of New-York,* III, 394; British Museum. Lansdowne Mss. 849, f. 80; Leder, *Robert Livingston, 1654–1728, and the Politics of Colonial New York,* p. 188. By 1721 the Board of Trade was recommending an expansion of missionary activity in the colonies for the same mundane reason. British Museum. Additional Mss. 23615.

[25] Lydekker, *The Faithful Mohawks,* pp. 53–55. Barclay has the distinction of having aroused the hostility of young William Johnson, freshly arrived on the Mohawk frontier, by leading a move for more effective repression of the liquor traffic. *The Papers of Sir William Johnson,* I, 6–7. In later years Johnson became an influential supporter of Anglican missions.

[26] Klees, *The Pennsylvania Dutch,* pp. 107–109.

[27] Edwin Scott Gaustad, *The Great Awakening in New England* (New York, 1957), pp. 43–44.

[28] Birdsall, *Berkshire County: A Cultural History,* p. 35.

[29] Samuel Hopkins, *Historical memoirs, relating to the Housatunnuk Indians* (Boston, 1753), p. 8.

[30] *Ibid.,* p. 127; *The Acts and Resolves . . . of the Province of the Massachusetts Bay,* II (Boston, 1874), p. 991; Frank G. Speck, "The Wapanachki Delawares and the English; Their Past as Viewed by an Ethnologist," *Pennsylvania Magazine of History and Biography,* LXVII (October 1943), p. 332.

[31] Hopkins, *Historical memoirs, relating to the Housatunnuk Indians,* p. 88.

[32] Brainerd kept a journal that tells us most of what we know about his career. It reveals a sensitive, highly introspective, totally dedicated spirit, steeped in New England Puritanism and vitalized by the challenge of the Great Awakening. For publication data, consult the bibliographical essay.

[33] E. R. A. Seligman, *The Economic Interpretation of History* (2d ed., rev., New York, 1924), pp. 128–129.

Chapter 12: The Overthrow of New France

[1] Richard W. Van Alstyne, *The American Empire: Its Historical Pattern and Evolution* ([London], 1960), pp. 4–5.

[2] John Rutherfurd to Cadwallader Colden, March 2, 1742/3 (New York Historical Society *Collections*, LII, 9).

[3] Connecticut Archives, Hartford. Indians, I, 257–260, 265; Wraxall, *An Abridgment of the Indian Affairs . . . of New York*, pp. 233–235; DePuy, *A Bibliography of the English Colonial Treaties with the American Indians*, p. 22; *Indian Treaties Printed by Benjamin Franklin*, pp. xl–xlii; Wallace, *Conrad Weiser*, pp. 185, 190–195.

[4] Hutchinson, *The History of the Colony and Province of Massachusetts-Bay*, II, 321; Willis, *Journals of the Rev. Thomas Smith, and the Rev. Samuel Deane*, pp. 119–120; Chris Kilby to William Pepperrell, August 10, 1745 (Maine Historical Society. Pepperrell Papers).

[5] Robert Sanders to William Johnson [November 28, 1745] (*The Papers of Sir William Johnson*, I, 43); Governor Shirley to the Duke of Newcastle, December 14, 1745 (Charles H. Lincoln, ed., *Correspondence of William Shirley, Governor of Massachusetts and Military Commander in America, 1731–1760* [New York, 1912], I, 297–298); Flick, *History of the State of New York*, II, 227; Higgins, *Expansion in New York, with Especial Reference to the Eighteenth Century*, 74.

[6] Hutchinson, *The History of the Colony and Province of Massachusetts-Bay*, II, 90n.; Lydekker, *The Faithful Mohawks*, pp. 56–58; Lincoln, *Correspondence of William Shirley*, I, 210. Much additional information about the affair is to be found in the Horsmanden Papers at the New York Historical Society.

[7] Extract from the journal of Conrad Weiser, of a journey among the Six Nations in June 1745 (New York Historical Society. Horsmanden Papers).

[8] DePuy, *A Bibliography of the English Colonial Treaties with the American Indians*, p. 25; New York Historical Society *Collections*, LII, 247–259; *The Papers of Sir William Johnson*, I, 60–61, 72, 95. Conrad Weiser viewed the involvement of the Iroquois with skepticism, noting that when the French captured a Mohawk they treated him well and sent him back to his own people with a gift. Weiser to Richard Peters, September 27, 1746 (Historical Society of Pennsylvania. Weiser Correspondence, I, 1741–1756, p. 13).

[9] Lincoln, *Correspondence of William Shirley*, I, 385.

[10] Buck, *The Planting of Civilization in Western Pennsylvania*, p. 53. See also above, p. 158.

[11] Nicholas B. Wainwright, "George Croghan and the Indian Uprising of 1747," *Pennsylvania History*, XXI (January 1954), pp. 21–31; Wainwright, *George Croghan: Wilderness Diplomat*, pp. 14–15.

[12] See above, p. 175.

[13] Benson, *Peter Kalm's Travels in North America*, pp. 355–359.

[14] Mereness, *Travels in the American Colonies, 1690–1783*, p. 331.

[15] Historical Society of Pennsylvania. Penn Mss., I, Indian Affairs, 1687–1753, pp. 98–99 (Published in Labaree, *The Papers of Benjamin Franklin*, V, 96–99); Dunaway, *The Scotch-Irish of Colonial Pennsylvania*, pp. 69–71.

[16] Elisha Williams to Colonel Israel Williams, July 21, 1749 (Massachusetts Historical Society, Israel Williams Papers, I, 46). See also above, p. 160.

[17] William Johnson to Governor Clinton, September 25, 1750 (*The Papers of Sir William Johnson*, I, 302–304); Historical Society of Pennsylvania. Penn Mss., I, Indian Affairs, 1687–1753, pp. 63–65.

[18] William Johnson to Governor Clinton, May 4, 1750 (*The Papers of Sir William Johnson*, I, 276–279).

[19] A discussion of the role of the Ohio Company in western expansion may be found in W. Stitt Robinson, *The Southern Colonial Frontier, 1607–1763*, to be published in this series.

[20] Historical Society of Pennsylvania. Weiser Correspondence, I, 1741–1756, p. 28.

[21] Historical Society of Pennsylvania. Penn Mss., I, Indian Affairs, 1687–1753, p. 86.

[22] See above, p. 160.

[23] British Museum. Additional Mss. 32735 (Newcastle Papers, L, 129). See also *Ibid.*, f. 119 (Published in Lincoln, *Correspondence of William Shirley*, II, 33–39); J. Wheelwright's letter, April 8, 1754 (Massachusetts Historical Society, Israel Williams Papers, I, 69).

[24] Robert C. Newbold, *The Albany Congress and Plan of Union of 1754* (New York, 1955), pp. 59, 63–65.

[25] Speaking of the Pennsylvania land purchase of 1754, the contemporary observer Charles Thomson said, "In what Manner, and by what Means, this Grant was obtained, is well known to some who attended the Treaty, as well as the Artifices used for near a Week to induce the *Indians* to execute the Deed." *An Enquiry into the Causes of the Alienation of the Delaware and Shawanese Indians from the British Interest*, p. 78. See also Conrad Weiser to Richard Peters, October 12, 1754 (Historical Society of Pennsylvania, Weiser Correspondence, I, 1741–1756, p. 47); Newbold, *The Albany Congress and Plan of Union of 1754*, p. 60; Oscar Zeichner, *Connecticut's Years of Controversy, 1750–1776* (Chapel Hill, N.C., 1949) pp. 30–31; Buck, *The Planting of Civilization in Western Pennsylvania*, p. 78.

[26] Colonel Israel Williams' letter, September 12, 1754 (Massachusetts Historical Society, Israel Williams Papers, I, 80). Published in Lincoln, *Correspondence of William Shirley*, II, 86–89.

[27] Letter of December 17, 1754 (*The Papers of Sir William Johnson*, I, 431).

[28] Samuel Philips Savage to William Pepperrell, July 23, 1755 (Maine Historical Society, Pepperrell Papers, No. 2); Joseph Shippen to Edward Shippen, July 16, 1755 (Historical Society of Pennsylvania, Shippen Family Papers, I, 211); Massachusetts Historical Society. Israel Williams Papers, I, 157.

[29] Peter Williamson, *French and Indian cruelty; exemplified in the life and various vicissitudes of fortune, of Peter Williamson* (3d ed., Glasgow, 1758), p. 51.

[30] Quoted in Wainwright, *George Croghan: Wilderness Diplomat*, p. 98. See also Klett, *Presbyterians in Colonial Pennsylvania*, pp. 246–248.

[31] Thomas Lloyd to Benjamin Franklin, January 31, 1756 (American Philosophical Society, Philadelphia. Benjamin Franklin Papers, I, 41).

[32] American Antiquarian Society. Nathan Fiske Diary.

[33] William Williams' letter, August 30, 1756 (Massachusetts Historical Society, Israel Williams Papers, I, 246).

[34] Thayer, *Israel Pemberton, King of the Quakers*, p. 138.

[35] *Ibid.*, p. 95; Dunaway, *A History of Pennsylvania*, p. 108; William A. Hunter, *Forts on the Pennsylvania Frontier, 1753–1758* (Harrisburg, 1960), pp. 191–193.

[36] Baxter, *Documentary History of the State of Maine*, XXIV, 93–94.

[37] DePuy, *A Bibliography of the English Colonial Treaties with the American Indians*, p. 44; Wainwright, *George Croghan: Wilderness Diplomat*, pp. 145–151; Thayer, *Israel Pemberton, King of the Quakers*, chap. 12; James Thomas Flexner, *Mohawk Baronet: Sir William Johnson of New York* (New York, 1959), p. 196.

[38] Wainwright, *George Croghan: Wilderness Diplomat*, p. 150.

[39] Quoted in Lydekker, *The Faithful Mohawks*, pp. 98–99.

[40] Quoted in Buffinton, "The Policy of the Northern Colonies towards the French to the Peace of Utrecht," p. 11n.

[41] Cornelis Cuyler's letter, November, 1760 (American Antiquarian Society, Cornelis Cuyler Letterbook).

[42] Olsson, "The Kennebec Purchase from the Colony of New Plymouth, 1749–1775," chap. 3.

[43] Belknap, *The History of New-Hampshire*, p. 324. See also Crockett, *Vermont, The Green Mountain State*, I, 180–182; Jones, *Vermont in the Making, 1750–1777*, pp. 42–44.

[44] Rosenberry, *Migrations from Connecticut Prior to 1800*, p. 11.

[45] The New York Historical Society has in its library Lydius' own book of printed land indentures for the town of Hartford on Otter Creek.

[46] Wallace, *Indians in Pennsylvania*, p. 156; Anthony F. C. Wallace, *King of the Delawares: Teedyuscung, 1700–1763* (Philadelphia, 1949), pp. 258–261.

[47] J. E. Wright and Doris S. Corbett, *Pioneer Life in Western Pennsylvania* (Pittsburgh, 1940), pp. 35–36. Charles M. Stotz, in the *Western Pennsylvania Historical Magazine*, XLI (1958), pp. 110–112, gives many pertinent facts about the pioneer settlement at Pittsburgh in the period 1758–1763.

[48] Buck, *The Planting of Civilization in Western Pennsylvania*, p. 98.

[49] O'Callaghan and Fernow, *Documents Relative to the Colonial History of the State of New-York*, VII, 478.

[50] Frederick Jackson Turner, *The Frontier in American History* (New York, 1921), p. 65.

[51] *Ibid.*, p. 18.

[52] *Ibid.*, pp. 3–4.

BIBLIOGRAPHICAL NOTES

Our subject is a large one, and the pertinent literature is correspondingly extensive. Limitation of space requires that only the more important and useful sources be mentioned here.

The public records of the various colonies have been at least partially published, as indicated in Oscar Handlin *et al., Harvard Guide to American History* (Cambridge, Mass., 1954), pp. 127–139. State and private archives from Maine to Pennsylvania hold multitudinous collections of documents, many of which have a bearing on the frontier and its problems. Especially valuable are the collections in Boston, Hartford, New York, Albany, and Philadelphia, which may best be approached through Philip M. Hamer, ed., *A Guide to Archives and Manuscripts in the United States* (New Haven, Conn., 1961). The one indispensable guide to the pioneers' own accounts of their experiences is R. W. G. Vail, *The Voice of the Old Frontier* (New York, 1949).

The advance of the frontier in particular areas may be traced through state and regional histories, of which the following will serve as examples: John Gorham Palfrey, *History of New England* (5 vols., Boston, 1858–1890); William B. Weeden, *Economic and Social History of New England, 1620–1789* (2 vols., Boston and New York, 1890); Jeremy Belknap, *The History of New-Hampshire* (3 vols., Boston, 1791–1792); William Smith, *The History of the Province of New-York, from the First Discovery to the Year 1732* (2d ed., Philadelphia, 1792). An excellent example of more recent scholarship is Alexander C. Flick, ed., *History of the State of New York* (10 vols., New York, 1933–1937), of which the first two volumes are concerned with the period of our study. Among the many books that offer a fairly broad approach to the colonial period, the following are especially recommended: Herbert L. Osgood, *The American Colonies in the Seventeenth Century* (3 vols., New York, 1904–1907) and *The American Colonies in the Eighteenth Century* (4 vols., New York, 1924–1925); Charles M. Andrews, *The Colonial Period of American History* (4 vols., New Haven, Conn., 1934–1938). The most authoritative and useful general text on the westward movement is Ray A. Billington, *Westward Expansion, a History of the American Frontier* (2d ed., New York, 1960), which includes an extensive bibliography.

Stella H. Sutherland's informative *Population Distribution in Colonial America* (New York, 1936) not only provides much useful data but attempts to explain the reasons underlying the patterns of distribution. Herman R. Friis has published "A Series of Population Maps of the Colonies and the United States, 1625–1790," *Geographical Review*, XXX (July 1940), pp. 463–470. These extremely valuable maps show the extent of settlement for the years 1625, 1650, 1675, 1700, 1720, 1740, 1760, 1770, 1780, and 1790. Utilizing this information, Fulmer Mood, in his "Studies in the History of American Settled Areas and Frontier Lines," *Agricultural History*, XXVI (January 1952), pp. 16–34, demonstrates that there were many distinct clusters of settlement, each constituting a frontier of its own. Students interested in the evolution of land systems in the colonies should begin with Marshall Harris, *Origin of the Land Tenure System in the United States* (Ames, Iowa, 1953). The *Eighteenth Annual Report of the Bureau of American Ethnology, 1896–97*, Part 2 (Washington, 1899), pp. 527-964, contains a detailed examination of Indian land cessions and evaluates the Indian land policies of the various English colonies. Henry F. DePuy, comp., *A Bibliography of the English Colonial Treaties with the American Indians, Including a Synopsis of Each Treaty* (New York, 1917) covers the period 1677–1768 but limits itself to treaties that were given separate publication apart from the regular colony records.

Geography of the Northern Colonial Frontier

A number of good atlases are available, but probably by far the most useful for the beginning student of the early westward movement are Charles O. Paullin, *Atlas of the Historical Geography of the United States* (New York, 1932) and James T. Adams, *Atlas of American History* (New York, 1943). Colonial cartography is well demonstrated in Emerson D. Fite and Archibald Freeman, eds., *A Book of Old Maps Delineating American History from the Earliest Days Down to the Close of the Revolutionary War* (Cambridge, Mass., 1926) and Lloyd A. Brown, ed., *Early Maps of the Ohio Valley* (Pittsburgh, 1959). An interesting work on American geography by a well-informed eighteenth-century Englishman is Thomas Pownall, *A Topographical Description of the Dominions of the United States of America*, Lois Mulkearn, ed. (Pittsburgh, 1949). Two excellent studies of physiography are Nevin M. Fenneman, *Physiography of Eastern United States* (New York, 1938) and Wallace W. Atwood, *The Physiographic Provinces of North America* (Boston, 1940), both of which make good use of maps to supplement the text. An especially interesting view of colonial history in terms of geographical and climatic influences is presented in the first part of Ralph H. Brown, *Historical Geography of the United States* (New York, 1948).

Indians of the Northern Colonial Frontier

Virtually all contemporary accounts of the Eastern Woodland Indians are by Europeans or the immediate descendants of Europeans, and are accordingly biased. One of the best early descriptions of the New England Algonkins is found in William Wood, *New Englands Prospect* (Prince Society *Publications*, I, Boston, 1865). Even more perceptive is Roger Williams, *A Key into the Language of America* (Narragansett Club *Publications*, I, Providence, 1866), which presents not only an Algonquian vocabulary but also brief comments on the customs, dress, and diet of the Indians. Thomas Morton, *New English Canaan or New Canaan* (Amsterdam, Holland, 1637) has a long section on the Indians of eastern Massachusetts. One of the richest storehouses of information on Indian life is Reuben G. Thwaites, ed., *The Jesuit Relations and Allied Documents, 1610–1791* (73 vols., Cleveland, 1896-1901), containing the annual reports of Jesuit missionary activity. A convenient one-volume selection from the above has been edited by Edna Kenton (New York, 1954). For the Iroquois tribes of New York, a major source is Cadwallader Colden, *The History of the Five Indian Nations*, first published at New York in 1727 and now available in a modern paperback edition by Cornell University Press. A considerable amount of information on the Indians of Pennsylvania is given in Julius F. Sachse's translation of Daniel Falckner, *Curieuse Nachricht von Pensylvania*, Pennsylvania-German Society *Proceedings and Addresses*, XIV (1903), pp. 45–256.

Among the most recent surveys is Harold E. Driver, *Indians of North America* (Chicago, 1961), an authoritative, detailed work, which demonstrates the cultural approach to Indian studies at its best. Harold E. Fey and D'Arcy McNickle, *Indians and Other Americans* (New York, 1959), also is reliable and useful. The first chapter of William T. Hagan, *American Indians* (Daniel J. Boorstin, ed., *The Chicago History of American Civilization*, Chicago, 1961) contains some material on the Eastern Woodland Indians but is too brief to be of much use in our study. Roy Harvey Pearce, *The Savages of America: A Study of the Indian and the Idea of Civilization* (Baltimore, 1953) is a profound analysis of the evolution of the white man's concept of the Indian. Paul Radin, *The Story of the American Indian* (New York, 1944) includes a good chapter on the Iroquois. Also helpful is Ruth M. Underhill, *Red Man's America: A History of Indians in the United States* (Chicago, 1953). The best recent book on Pennsylvania Indians is Paul A. W. Wallace, *Indians in Pennsylvania* (Harrisburg, 1961), with major emphasis on the Delawares. Charles C. Willoughby, *Antiquities of the New England Indians* (Cambridge, Mass., 1935), while dealing mostly with artifacts, gives a good general description of the tribesmen. Admirable for the general reader are two books by Clark Wissler, *The American Indian: An Introduction to the Anthropology of the New World* (New York, 1938) and *Indians of the United States* (New York, 1940).

There are many special studies of particular aspects of Indian life. Among the more important are M. K. Bennett, "The Food Economy of the New England Indians, 1605–75," *Journal of Political Economy*, LXIII (October 1955), pp. 369–397; Wilbur R. Jacobs, "Wampum, the Protocol of Indian Diplomacy," *William and Mary Quarterly*, 3d ser., VI (October 1949), pp. 596–604; Wendell S. Hadlock, "War Among the Northeastern Woodland Indians," *American Anthropologist*, XLIX (1947), pp. 204–221; Nathaniel Knowles, "The Torture of Captives by the Indians of Eastern North America," American Philosophical Society *Proceedings*, LXXXII (1940), pp. 151–225; and George S. Snyderman, "Behind the Tree of Peace: A Sociological Analysis of Iroquois Warfare," *Pennsylvania Archaeologist*, XVIII (1948), pp. 2–93.

The value of the ethnohistorical approach to Indian studies is explained in Frank G. Speck, "The Wapanachki Delawares and the English; Their Past as Viewed by an Ethnologist," *Pennsylvania Magazine of History and Biography*, LXVII (October 1943), pp. 319–344. That this approach has become of major importance is clearly demonstrated in William N. Fenton, *American Indian and White Relations to 1830: Needs and Opportunities for Study* (Chapel Hill,

N. C., 1957). This stimulating volume contains also an excellent bibliography by L. H. Butterfield, Wilcomb E. Washburn, and William N. Fenton.

Coastal Pioneers, to 1630

The most important source material relating to the Sagadahoc colony, 1607–1608, is in the Massachusetts Historical Society *Proceedings*, XVIII (1880–1881), pp. 94–117; Henry O. Thayer, ed., *The Sagadahoc Colony* (Portland, Me., 1892); and Henry S. Burrage, ed., *Early English and French Voyages . . . 1534–1608* (J. Franklin Jameson, ed., *Original Narratives of Early American History Series*, n.p., 1906), pp. 399–419. For Plymouth Colony, the one absolutely indispensable source is William Bradford, *Of Plimoth Plantation*. There are several editions; the best is edited by Samuel Eliot Morison (New York, 1953). Another important Pilgrim source is Dwight B. Heath, ed., *A Journal of the Pilgrims at Plymouth [Mourt's Relation]* (New York, 1963), which tells much of Indian relations during the first year at Plymouth. A convenient compilation of Pilgrim sources is George F. Willison, ed., *The Pilgrim Reader: The Story of the Pilgrims As Told By Themselves and Their Contemporaries . . .* (Garden City, N. Y., 1953). The subject of Indian relations in early Plymouth is ably handled by David Bushnell in "The Treatment of the Indians in Plymouth Colony," *New England Quarterly*, XXVI (June 1953), pp. 193–218. Thomas W. Perry, "New Plymouth and Old England: A Suggestion," *William and Mary Quarterly*, 3d ser., XVIII (April 1961), pp. 251–265, stresses the persistence of the Pilgrims' loyalty to England and to English ways.

Most of the colonizing activity along the New England coast north of Cape Ann during the early years was sponsored by Sir Ferdinando Gorges and the Council for New England. Three primary sources are of special interest: [Sir Ferdinando Gorges], *A briefe Relation of the Discovery and Plantation of New England* (London, 1622); Sir Ferdinando Gorges, *A Briefe Narration of the Originall Undertakings of the Advancement of Plantations Into the parts of America* (London, 1658); and Christopher Levett, *A Voyage into New England Begun in 1623. and ended in 1624* (London, 1628).

For the Dutch period of New York's history, the two most important sources in the English language are E. B. O'Callaghan, comp., *Laws and Ordinances of New Netherland, 1638–1674* (Albany, 1868) and the first three volumes of E. B. O'Callaghan and Berthold Fernow, eds., *Documents Relative to the Colonial History of the State of New-York* (15 vols., Albany, 1856–1887). Many of the contemporary accounts of the Dutch colony are to be found, in whole or in part, in J. Franklin Jameson, ed., *Narratives of New Netherland, 1609–1664* (J. Franklin Jameson, ed., *Original Narratives of Early American History Series*, New York, 1909). An interesting description of New Netherland in 1643 is included in Father Isaac Jogues, *Narrative of a Captivity among the Mohawk Indians, and a Description of New Netherland in 1642–3*, published in Reuben G. Thwaites, ed., *The Jesuit Relations and Allied Docu-*

ments (73 vols., Cleveland, 1896–1901), XXVIII, pp. 105–115. A modern interpretive survey written in a lively, colorful style is Ellis L. Raesly, *Portrait of New Netherland* (New York, 1945). The standard analysis of the patroonship system is S. G. Nissenson, *The Patroon's Domain* (New York, 1937), which argues that the principal objective of the patroons was to break in upon the Company's monopoly of the fur trade. Clarence W. Rife, "Land Tenure in New Netherland," *Essays in Colonial History Presented to Charles McLean Andrews by his Students* (New Haven, Conn., 1931), pp. 41–73, also deals with the patroonship system. A recent monograph of great value is Allen W. Trelease, *Indian Affairs in Colonial New York: The Seventeenth Century* (Ithaca, N. Y., 1960), of which the first six chapters are concerned with the Dutch period.

A good introduction to the history of New Sweden is Amandus Johnson, *The Swedes on the Delaware, 1638–1664* (Philadelphia, 1915), an abridgment of the same author's *The Swedish Settlements on the Delaware, 1638–1664* (2 vols., Philadelphia, 1911). More recent and sprightly are two books by Christopher Ward, *The Dutch & Swedes on the Delaware, 1609–64* (Philadelphia, 1930) and *New Sweden on the Delaware* (Philadelphia, 1938). The first part of Albert C. Myers, ed., *Narratives of Early Pennsylvania, West New Jersey, and Delaware, 1630–1707* (J. Franklin Jameson, ed., *Original Narratives of Early American History Series*, New York, 1912) contains several important early accounts of New Sweden, including portions of the eighteenth-century description by the Reverend Israel Acrelius.

The Tidal Wave of the English, 1630–1675

Captain John Smith of Jamestown fame, in his *Advertisements for the unexperienced Planters of New-England, or any where* (London, 1631), tells of Plymouth's trials and success, and also describes the beginnings of the Massachusetts Bay Colony. His account has been republished in the Massachusetts Historical Society *Collections*, 3d ser., III (1833), pp. 1–53. One of the best descriptions of conditions in Massachusetts during the first few months after the arrival of the Winthrop migration is found in a letter from Thomas Dudley, deputy-governor of the colony. This letter, together with several other early documents, was published in a volume entitled *Massachusetts or the first Planters of New-England, the End and Manner of their coming thither, and Abode there* (Boston, 1696), usually attributed to Joshua Scottow. Undoubtedly, however, the most valuable personal narrative dealing with the early development of the Bay Colony is the *Journal* of Governor John Winthrop, edited in two volumes by James K. Hosmer (J. Franklin Jameson, ed., *Original Narratives of Early American History Series*, New York, 1908).

The standard work on the first half-century of settlement in Maine, still useful and reliable, is Henry S. Burrage, *The Beginnings of Colonial Maine, 1602–1658* (Portland, Me., 1914). James P. Baxter, *Sir Ferdinando Gorges and His Province of Maine* (3 vols., Boston, 1890) has stood for many years as the major work on the visionary proprietor. It includes most of Gorges' extant writings. Richard A. Preston, *Gorges of Plymouth Fort: A life of Sir Ferdinando Gorges* . . . (Toronto, 1953) is a scholarly reappraisal challenging Baxter's opinion that Gorges sought to impose upon frontier Maine an outmoded and reactionary feudalism. The book contains a table of grants and a map showing various divisions and grants of land from 1606 to 1639.

New England's first serious conflict with the Indians, the Pequot War of 1637, produced several narratives by participants or spectators. The most vivid of these is John Mason, *A Brief History of the Pequot War* (Boston, 1736). Mason and the other narrators were unanimous in their condemnation of the Indians. These accounts have been brought together under one cover in Charles Orr, ed., *History of the Pequot War* (Cleveland, 1897). No thorough, modern treatment of the war is in print. Howard Bradstreet, *The Story of the War with the Pequots, Re-Told* (New Haven, Conn., 1933) is too brief to do justice to the subject. The easy assumption that the Pequot War was caused by the land greed of the English is sharply challenged in Alden T. Vaughan, "Pequots and Puritans: The Causes of the War of 1637," *William and Mary Quarterly,* 3d ser., XXI (April 1964), pp. 256–269.

The process and the implications of Puritan expansionism are examined in a number of works. Especially noteworthy is William Haller, Jr., *The Puritan Frontier: Town-Planting in New England: Colonial Development, 1630–1660* (New York, 1951), which clearly explains the process by which new towns were established. A thorough examination of the same process as it worked in the case of one succession of Massachusetts towns is Sumner C. Powell, *Puritan Village: The Formation of a New England Town* (Middletown, Conn., 1963). Settlement and early community development in another important frontier area prior to 1675 have been analyzed by H. Roger King in "The Settlement of the Upper Connecticut River Valley to 1675" (unpublished doctoral dissertation, Vanderbilt University, 1965). Robert A. East, "Puritanism and New Settlement," *New England Quarterly,* XVII (June 1944), pp. 225–264, shows that religious dissension within a community often was the major cause behind group withdrawal to found a new town and that not infrequently the orthodox rather than the unorthodox were the ones who went to the frontier. Richard S. Dunn has published two articles dealing with the activities of one prominent Puritan expansionist: "John Winthrop, Jr., and the Narragansett Country," *William and Mary Quarterly,* 3d ser., XIII (January 1956), pp. 68–86, and "John Winthrop, Jr., Connecticut Expansionist," *New England Quarterly,* XXIX (March 1956), pp. 3–26. Other articles of special importance to a study of Puritan expansionism are Chester E. Eisinger, "The Puritans' Justification for Taking the Land," *Essex Institute Historical Collections,* LXXXIV (April 1948), pp. 131–143; Wilcomb E. Washburn, "The Moral and Legal Justifications for Dispossessing the Indians," in James M. Smith, ed., *Seventeenth-Century America: Essays in Colonial History* (Chapel Hill, N. C., 1959), pp. 15–32; Alan Heimert, "Puritanism, the Wilderness, and the Frontier," *New England Quarterly,* XXVI (September 1953), pp. 361–382; and George H. Williams, "The Wilderness and Paradise in the History of the Church," *Church History,* XXVIII (March 1959), pp. 3–24.

King Philip's War and Its Aftermath

There are three major contemporary narrative accounts of King Philip's War that are informative and often exciting to read: Thomas Church, *Entertaining Passages Relating to Philip's War* . . . (Boston, 1716); William Hubbard, *A Narrative of the Troubles with the Indians in New-England* . . . (Boston, 1677); and Increase Mather, *A Brief History of the War with the Indians in New-England* (Boston and London, 1676). These are available in more recent editions; the best for Church and Hubbard are those of 1865 edited by Henry M. Dexter and Samuel G. Drake respectively, and for Mather that of 1862 edited by Drake. In addition there is the excellent collection of sources found in Charles H. Lincoln, ed., *Narratives of the Indian Wars, 1675–1699* (J. Franklin Jameson, ed., *Original Narratives of Early American History Series*, New York, 1913). As recently as 1959 a contemporary account of King Philip's War, written by a resident of Rhode Island, was discovered in England. This has been edited by Douglas Edward Leach, and published by the Rhode Island Historical Society under the title *A Rhode Islander Reports on King Philip's War: The Second William Harris Letter of August, 1676* (Providence, 1963). One of the best of the secondary narratives is George W. Ellis and John E. Morris, *King Philip's War* (New York, 1906), which modifies the Puritan view of Philip as a vicious beast. The latest study is Douglas Edward Leach, *Flintlock and Tomahawk: New England in King Philip's War* (New York, 1958).

The Early Quaker Frontier

From early New Jersey and Pennsylvania came a plentiful supply of pamphlet literature, primarily designed to advertise the advantages of this new frontier. Considering the purpose for which these tracts were written, they offer much valuable information on conditions in the settlements and the progress being made or anticipated. A number have been republished in Albert C. Myers, ed., *Narratives of Early Pennsylvania, West New Jersey, and Delaware, 1630–1707* (J. Franklin Jameson, ed., *Original Narratives of Early American History Series*, New York, 1912); others are [William Penn], *A brief account of the Province of Pennsylvania in America* (n.p., 1682?) and Thomas Budd, *Good Order Established in Pennsylvania & New-Jersey in America* . . . ([Philadelphia], 1685).

Especially useful for a study of the Quaker frontier is John E. Pomfret, *The Province of West New Jersey, 1609–1702: A History of the Origins of an American Colony* (Princeton, N. J., 1956). Edwin B. Bronner, *William Penn's "Holy Experiment": The Founding of Pennsylvania, 1681–1701* (New York, 1962) traces the evolution of politics in the Quaker commonwealth. Penn's career is analyzed topically in *Remember William Penn, 1644–1944* ([Harrisburg], 1944), a handbook edited by William W. Comfort and others. The fifth chapter is concerned with Penn's Indian policy. Two well-informed articles relating to early Pennsylvania are John E. Pomfret, "The First Purchasers of Pennsylvania, 1681–1700," *Pennsylvania Magazine of History and*

Biography, LXXX (April 1956), pp. 137–163 and George A. Cribbs, "The Frontier Policy of Pennsylvania," *Western Pennsylvania Historical Magazine,* II (January, April, July, 1919), pp. 5–35, 72–106, 174–198.

The Life of the Pioneer

Two beautifully illustrated volumes giving a vivid impression of pioneer life are Edwin Tunis, *Colonial Living* (Cleveland and New York, 1957), and *Frontier Living* (Cleveland and New York, 1961). These should be in the hands of every young student of early American history. The fifth chapter of E. Douglas Branch, *Westward: The Romance of the American Frontier* (New York, 1930), entitled "Life and Labor in the Backwoods," contains interesting details of pioneer life in the second half of the eighteenth century. An excellent analysis of the ways of the Scotch-Irish pioneers is presented in Chapter 14 of James G. Leyburn, *The Scotch-Irish: A Social History* (Chapel Hill, N.C., 1962). Although dealing mostly with the period after 1763, J. E. Wright and Doris S. Corbett, *Pioneer Life in Western Pennsylvania* (Pittsburgh, 1940) suggests much that is valid for an earlier period and contains some very good drawings of pioneer implements and activities. James T. Adams, ed., *Album of American History* (5 vols., New York, 1944–1960), vol. I, offers many illustrations of the tools, furniture, dress, and dwellings of the frontier folk. Pioneer weapons may be studied in Carl P. Russell, *Guns on the Early Frontiers: A History of Firearms From Colonial Times Through the Years of the Western Fur Trade* (Berkeley, Calif., 1957). Pioneer housing of various kinds is ably discussed in the two leading books on colonial architecture: Hugh Morrison, *Early American Architecture* (New York, 1952) and Thomas T. Waterman, *The Dwellings of Colonial America* (Chapel Hill, N.C., 1950). Of particular importance for a sound understanding of frontier housing is Harold R. Shurtleff, *The Log Cabin Myth: A Study of the Early Dwellings of the English Colonists in North America* (Cambridge, Mass., 1939), which dispels the common notion that all pioneers, the Pilgrims included, lived in log cabins.

Travelers and other occasional observers give us some of the best insights into everyday life on the frontier. Good examples of such accounts are Bartlett B. James and J. Franklin Jameson, eds., *Journal of Jasper Danckaerts, 1679–1680* (J. Franklin Jameson, ed., *Original Narratives of Early American History Series,* New York, 1913); Peter Kalm, *Travels into North America,* Adolph B. Benson, ed. (2 vols., New York, 1937); Carl Bridenbaugh, ed., *Gentleman's Progress: The Itinerarium of Dr. Alexander Hamilton, 1744* (Chapel Hill, N.C., 1948); and Gottlieb Mittelberger, *Journey to Pennsylvania,* Oscar Handlin and John Clive, eds. (Cambridge, Mass., 1960). Other travelers' accounts may be found in Newton D. Mereness, ed., *Travels in the American Colonies, 1690–1783* (New York, 1916). An actual journey made by a pioneering settler in Puritan New England is closely studied in William R. Carlton, "Overland to Connecticut in 1645: A Travel Diary of John Winthrop, Jr.," *New England Quarterly,* XIII (September 1940), pp. 494–510.

Percy W. Bidwell and John I. Falconer, *History of Agriculture in the*

Northern United States, 1620–1860 (Washington, 1925); Lyman Carrier, *The Beginnings of Agriculture in America* (New York, 1923); Albert L. Olson, *Agricultural Economy and the Population in Eighteenth-Century Connecticut* (New Haven, Conn., 1935); S. W. Fletcher, "The Subsistence Farming Period in Pennsylvania Agriculture, 1640–1840," *Pennsylvania History*, XIV (July 1947), pp. 185–195; Frederic K. Miller, "The Farmer at Work in Colonial Pennsylvania," *Pennsylvania History*, III (April 1936), pp. 115–123; and Robert R. Walcott, "Husbandry in Colonial New England," *New England Quarterly*, IX (June 1936), pp. 218–252, are all useful for a study of agricultural methods along the northern frontier. A communication by Warren C. Scoville in *The Southern Economic Journal*, XX (October 1953), pp. 178–181, challenges the prevalent belief that colonial farmers wasted the land. Various aspects of frontier industry, including methods and techniques, are discussed in Victor S. Clark, *History of Manufactures in the United States, 1607–1860* (Washington, 1916).

Students interested in the problem of culture on the frontier should consult Louis B. Wright, *The Cultural Life of the American Colonies, 1607–1763* (Henry S. Commager and Richard B. Morris, eds., *The New American Nation Series*, New York, 1957); and especially the same author's *Culture on the Moving Frontier* (Bloomington, Ind., 1955). The latter volume focuses attention on the conservative influence of those members of frontier society who steadfastly sought to uphold culture during the course of the westward movement. Two essays in Walker D. Wyman and Clifton B. Kroeber, eds., *The Frontier in Perspective* (Madison, Wis., 1957) are especially pertinent. These are Frederic G. Cassidy, "Language on the American Frontier," pp. 185–204; and A. Irving Hallowell, "The Backwash of the Frontier: The Impact of the Indian on American Culture," pp. 229–258.

The Fur Trade

The most important works on the colonial fur trade published prior to 1947 are listed in Stuart Cuthbertson and John C. Ewers, *A Preliminary Bibliography on the American Fur Trade* (St. Louis, 1939) and Joseph P. Donnelly, *A Tentative Bibliography for the Colonial Fur Trade in the American Colonies: 1608–1800* (St. Louis, 1947). Mention of more recent publications may be found in Paul C. Phillips, *The Fur Trade* (2 vols., Norman, Okla., 1961). Also useful as a general study is Francis X. Moloney, *The Fur Trade in New England, 1620–1676* (Cambridge, Mass., 1931). The most complete and authoritative examination of the mercantilist character of the British fur trade is Murray G. Lawson, *Fur: A Study in English Mercantilism, 1700–1775* (Toronto, 1943)—technical, laced with statistics, and extremely useful. Abuses in the conduct of the trade are discussed in Wilbur R. Jacobs, "Unsavory Sidelights on the Colonial Fur Trade," *New York History*, XXXIV (April 1953), pp. 135–148.

A knowledge of the workings of the French fur trade is essential to a full understanding of the English traders and their problems. A thoroughly competent monograph containing many excerpts from documents is Harold

A. Innis, *The Fur Trade in Canada* (New Haven, Conn., 1930). Also helpful for an understanding of the system are William B. Munro, "The Coureurs de Bois," Massachusetts Historical Society *Proceedings,* LVII (1923–1924), pp. 192–205, and Jean E. Murray, "The Early Fur Trade in New France and New Netherland," *Canadian Historical Review,* XIX (December 1938), pp. 365–377. Additional information may be gleaned from Gustave Lanctot, *A History of Canada. Volume One: From its Origins to the Royal Regime, 1663* (Cambridge, Mass., 1963). The role of Count Frontenac as governor of New France during a period crucial for the development of the French fur trade receives its classic interpretation in Francis Parkman, *Count Frontenac and New France under Louis XIV* (Boston, 1877). A less admiring view of the governor, based on more recent scholarship, is presented in W. J. Eccles, "Frontenac and the Iroquois, 1672–1682," *Canadian Historical Review,* XXXVI (March 1955), pp. 1–16.

Two careful studies of the leading merchant in the early days of the upper Connecticut Valley contribute greatly to our understanding of the fur trade in that area. These are Samuel Eliot Morison, "William Pynchon, the Founder of Springfield," Massachusetts Historical Society *Proceedings,* LXIV (1930–1932), pp. 67–107, and Ruth A. McIntyre, *William Pynchon: Merchant and Colonizer* (Springfield, Mass., 1961). New England's interest in the Indian trade of the remote interior is ably discussed in Arthur H. Buffinton, "New England and the Western Fur Trade, 1629–1675," Colonial Society of Massachusetts *Publications,* XVIII (1915–1916), pp. 160–192. The archives and the published records of Massachusetts contain much material on the official truck-house system developed by that colony, but interested students may prefer to begin with an article by Ronald O. MacFarlane, "The Massachusetts Bay Truck-Houses in Diplomacy with the Indians," *New England Quarterly,* XI (March 1938), pp. 48–65.

The Hudson River–Iroquois trade has been intensively studied, and the literature on various aspects of the subject is extensive. Charles H. McIlwain, in his Introduction to Peter Wraxall's *An Abridgment of the Indian Affairs . . . of New York, From the Year 1678 to the Year 1751* (Cambridge, Mass., 1915), maintained that Iroquois policy after 1640 was designed primarily to gain for the Five Nations the role of middleman in the fur trade. George T. Hunt, *The Wars of the Iroquois: A Study in Intertribal Trade Relations* (Madison, Wis., 1940) attributes the Iroquois wars largely to the same economic motive. More recently the McIlwain-Hunt thesis has been sharply challenged by Allen W. Trelease, who argues that Iroquois expansionism is to be explained not so much by a yearning for the middleman role as by a need for better hunting grounds and an urge to despoil other Indians of their peltry. See Trelease's *Indian Affairs in Colonial New York: The Seventeenth Century* (Ithaca, N.Y., 1960) and "The Iroquois and the Western Fur Trade: A Problem in Interpretation," *Mississippi Valley Historical Review,* XLIX (June 1962), pp. 32–51. The policy of the Albany merchants, especially in relation to westward expansion, is reviewed in two important articles. The first, Helen Broshar, "The First Push Westward of the Albany Traders," *Mississippi Valley Historical Review,* VII (December 1920), pp. 228–241, stresses the expansionism of the 1680s.

The second, Arthur H. Buffinton, "The Policy of Albany and English Westward Expansion," *Mississippi Valley Historical Review*, VIII (March 1922), pp. 327–366, emphasizes Albany's more usual reluctance to penetrate the wilderness in pursuit of trade. New York's attempts to suppress the Albany-Montreal trade are illuminated by a number of contemporary sources in addition to the ordinary provincial records. The most important of these include Lawrence H. Leder, ed., *The Livingston Indian Records, 1666–1723* (Gettysburg, Pa., 1956) and Cadwallader Colden, "A Memorial concerning the Furr-Trade of New-York," published as Part VI of *Papers Relating to An Act of the Assembly of the Province of New-York, For Encouragement of the Indian Trade, &c.* (New York, 1724). See also Jean Lunn, "The Illegal Fur Trade out of New France," *Canadian Historical Association Report, 1939* (Toronto, 1939), pp. 61–76; and Lawrence H. Leder, *Robert Livingston, 1654–1728, and the Politics of Colonial New York* (Chapel Hill, N.C., 1961).

The business letters and other papers of Albany men who were active in the fur trade yield much information about the conduct of the business. Mercantile papers of Hendrick Ten Eyck are to be found among the Harmanus Bleecker Papers at the New York State Library. The same repository also has photostats of similar documentary material for Johannes R. Bleecker, and its Manuscripts Miscellaneous, vol. V, contains some of Philip Livington's business correspondence. The American Antiquarian Society owns two letter-books of Cornelis Cuyler, covering the periods 1724–1736 and 1752–1764, excellent for prices of goods, names of ships, and the methods of the business. An insight into corresponding aspects of the Pennsylvania fur trade may be obtained by studying the business papers of Logan and Shippen, as found in the Shippen Family Papers, vol. I, 1701–1755 (Historical Society of Pennsylvania). Two articles dealing with the extension of the fur trade to the upper Ohio Valley are W. Neil Franklin, "Pennsylvania-Virginia Rivalry for the Indian Trade of the Ohio Valley," *Mississippi Valley Historical Review*, XX (March 1934), pp. 463–480, and William A. Hunter, "Traders on the Ohio: 1730," *Western Pennsylvania Historical Magazine*, XXXV (June 1952), pp. 85–92. Pennsylvania's foremost Indian trader has been effectively portrayed in two excellent biographies—Albert T. Volwiler, *George Croghan and the Westward Movement, 1741–1782* (Cleveland, 1926), and Nicholas B. Wainwright, *George Croghan: Wilderness Diplomat* (Chapel Hill, N.C., 1959). Wainwright also has given us an interesting study of the fur traders' problems at mid-century in "An Indian Trade Failure: The Story of the Hockley, Trent and Croghan Company, 1748–1752," *Pennsylvania Magazine of History and Biography*, LXXII (October 1948), pp. 343–375.

English-French Imperial Rivalry, 1689–1713

For sheer narrative excitement, the best place to begin is Francis Parkman, *Count Frontenac and New France under Louis XIV* (Boston, 1877) and *A Half-Century of Conflict* (Boston, 1892). New England's own version of the struggle was effectively presented during the second half of the eighteenth century by Thomas Hutchinson in *The History of the Colony and Province of*

Massachusetts-Bay (Lawrence S. Mayo, ed., 3 vols., Cambridge, Mass., 1936). Less distinguished than Parkman, but still useful, is John Fiske, *New France and New England* (Cambridge, Mass., 1902). John K. Mahon, "Anglo-American Methods of Indian Warfare, 1676–1794," *Mississippi Valley Historical Review*, XLV (September, 1958), pp. 254–275, discusses the evolution of tactics in the colonial wars with the Indians, and concludes that trained units were more effective in forest warfare than were untrained frontiersmen. The continuing problem of defense against the French and Indians is touched upon in John Usher's Report on the Northern Colonies, 1698, which has been edited by Margaret Kinard and published in *William and Mary Quarterly*, 3d ser., VII (January 1950), pp. 95–106. Among the useful works dealing with the activities of the French are Guy O. Coolidge, *The French Occupation of the Champlain Valley from 1609 to 1759* (Vermont Historical Society *Proceedings*, New Series, VI [Brattleboro, Vt., 1938]); and Richard A. Preston and Leopold Lamontagne, eds., *Royal Fort Frontenac* (Toronto, 1958). The latter is distinguished by a helpful introduction and the inclusion of much documentary source material. W. J. Eccles, "Frontenac's Military Policies, 1689–1698: A Reassessment," *Canadian Historical Review*, XXXVII (September 1956), pp. 201–224, is an excellent study of French leadership, tending to correct Parkman's view of Frontenac as a masterful war governor. Especially recommended is a brief, overall commentary on the underlying issues of the wars from 1689 to 1760, Howard H. Peckham, "Speculations on the Colonial Wars," *William and Mary Quarterly*, 3d ser., XVII (October 1960), pp. 463–472.

One subject that became of unusual interest during the colonial wars, producing its own body of literature, was Indian captivity. A good example of a captivity narrative relating to King William's War is John Gyles, *Memoirs of Odd Adventures, Strange Deliverances, &c. In the Captivity of John Gyles, Esq;* (Boston, 1736). The most important captivity narrative of Queen Anne's War is John Williams, *The Redeemed Captive Returning to Zion* (Boston, 1707), which is primarily concerned with the experiences of captives who came into the hands of the French at Montreal and Quebec. Some of the captivity narratives are summarized briefly in R. W. G. Vail, "Certain Indian Captives of New England," Massachusetts Historical Society *Proceedings*, LXVIII (1944–1947), pp. 113–131. The various individual captives have been identified and traced with painstaking devotion in Emma L. Coleman, *New England Captives Carried to Canada Between 1677 and 1760 During the French and Indian Wars* (2 vols., Portland, Me., 1925).

Probably the best contemporary account of New England in King William's War, although colored by obvious bias, is Cotton Mather, *Decennium Luctuosum* (Boston, 1699), which has been republished in Charles H. Lincoln, ed., *Narratives of the Indian Wars, 1675–1699* (J. Franklin Jameson, ed., *Original Narratives of Early American History Series*, New York, 1913), pp. 179–300. Also pertinent is the same author's *The Present State of New-England. Considered in a Discourse On the Necessities and Advantages of a Public Spirit In every Man* (Boston, 1690). Military operations along the coast of northern New England are described by an active participant, Benjamin

Church, in *The History of the Eastern Expeditions Of 1689, 1690, 1692, 1696, and 1704 Against the Indians and French*, Henry M. Dexter, ed. (Boston, 1867). A French and Indian invasion of Mohawk territory during the winter of 1692–1693 is the subject of Adelaide R. Hasse, ed., *A narrative of an attempt made by the French of Canada upon the Mohaques Country* . . . (New York, 1903).

Samuel Penhallow, *The History of the Wars of New-England with the Eastern Indians* (Boston, 1726), covering the period 1703–1725, is a very helpful source for Queen Anne's War. It is perhaps most readily available in the New Hampshire Historical Society *Collections*, I (1824), pp. 14–133. An authoritative biography of a controversial figure who was extremely active in promoting some of the major military expeditions of the war is G. M. Waller, *Samuel Vetch: Colonial Enterpriser* (Chapel Hill, N.C., 1960).

The Expanding Frontier, 1713–1743

Non-English immigrants contributed greatly to the expansion of the northern frontier during the first half of the eighteenth century. Among the more reliable works on the German settlers are Albert B. Faust, *The German Element in the United States* (2 vols., Boston, 1909); Walter A. Knittle, *Early Eighteenth Century Palatine Emigration: A British Government Redemptioner Project to Manufacture Naval Stores* (Philadelphia, 1937); and Fredric Klees, *The Pennsylvania Dutch* (New York, 1951). The activities of the Scots are reviewed in J. P. MacLean, *An Historical Account of the Settlements of Scotch Highlanders in America Prior to the Peace of 1783* (Cleveland, 1900); Charles K. Bolton, *Scotch Irish Pioneers in Ulster and America* (Boston, 1910); Henry J. Ford, *The Scotch-Irish in America* (Princeton, N.J., 1915); Guy S. Klett, *Presbyterians in Colonial Pennsylvania* (Philadelphia, 1937); Wayland F. Dunaway, *The Scotch-Irish of Colonial Pennsylvania* (Chapel Hill, N.C., 1944); Ian C. C. Graham, *Colonists From Scotland: Emigration to North America, 1707–1783* (Ithaca, N.Y., 1956); and Guy S. Klett, "The Presbyterian Church and the Scotch-Irish on the Pennsylvania Frontier," *Pennsylvania History*, XX (April 1941), pp. 165–179.

Other works deal with particular geographical areas during the period of expansion after 1713. Lois K. Mathews, *The Expansion of New England* (Boston, 1909) is strongly Turnerian in flavor. Ruth L. Higgins, *Expansion in New York, with Especial Reference to the Eighteenth Century* (Columbus, Ohio, 1931) is more sharply focused in both time and area. Wayland F. Dunaway, "Pennsylvania as an Early Distributing Center of Population," *Pennsylvania Magazine of History and Biography*, LV (1931), pp. 134–169, traces the movement of population southward and westward after 1730.

There are a number of important sources relating to the outbreak of violence known as Dummer's War, 1722–1725. Conditions in Maine during the period are well described in William B. Trask, ed., *Letters of Colonel Thomas Westbrook and Others Relative to Indian Affairs in Maine, 1722–1726* (Boston, 1901). The details of Lovewell's defeat, as derived from survivors, are excitingly presented in Thomas Symmes, *Historical Memoirs of the Late Fight at Piggwacket.* . . (Boston, 1725). An interesting captivity narrative of Dummer's War is Samuel Bownas, *An Account of the Captivity of Elizabeth Hanson, Now or Late of Kachecky, in New-England* (2d ed., London, 1760). Fannie H. Eckstorm, "The Attack on Norridgewock: 1724," *New England Quarterly*, VII (September 1934), pp. 541–578, is a sound and sober reconsideration of one important episode.

Land Speculation

The subject of land speculation and the westward movement badly needs a scholarly survey such as Paul C. Phillips provided for the American fur trade. Fortunately there are competent works dealing with particular areas and projects, but the needed synthesis has not yet appeared. For Maine we have Robert E. Moody's extraordinarily valuable study, "The Maine Frontier, 1607 to 1763" (unpublished doctoral dissertation, Yale University, 1933), containing detailed analysis of such matters as "The Pejepscot Proprietors," "Thomas Coram and his Proposed Settlements," "The Dunbar Settlements and the Muscongus Company," and "Samuel Waldo and the Early Settlements of the Waldo Patent." Another work of unusual merit, focusing on one speculative company, is Philip C. Olsson, "The Kennebec Purchase from the Colony of New Plymouth, 1749–1775" (unpublished honors essay, Harvard University, 1962). The history of Connecticut's Susquehannah Company has been ably illuminated by Julian P. Boyd in his Introduction to *The Susquehannah Company Papers,* vol. I (Wilkes-Barre, Pa., 1930), and *The Susquehannah Company: Connecticut's Experiment in Expansion* (New Haven, Conn., 1935). A short study which reveals the devious methods by which royal officials in eighteenth-century New York acquired title to large quantities of frontier land is Edith M. Fox, *Land Speculation in the Mohawk Country* (Cornell Studies in American History, Literature, and Folklore, no. 3 [Ithaca, 1949]). Other works dealing with land speculation include Thomas P. Abernethy, *Western Lands and the American Revolution* (New York, 1937); Charles S. Grant, "Land Speculation and the Settlement of Kent, 1738–1760," *New England Quarterly*, XXVIII (March 1955), pp. 51–71, and the same author's *Democracy in the Connecticut Frontier Town of Kent* (New York, 1961); Ruth L. Higgins, *Expansion in New York, with Especial Reference to the Eighteenth Century* (Columbus, Ohio, 1931); and Irving Mark, *Agrarian Conflicts in Colonial New York, 1711–1775* (New York, 1940).

It is probable that our knowledge of the speculators and their methods will be increased in the future primarily by careful study of their private papers and business records. Many collections of such documents are available in archives and historical societies. For example, there is a large volume of General Samuel Waldo papers at the Maine Historical Society, some of which relate to Waldo's dealings in land at Falmouth and elsewhere. Equally important are the various published collections such as James P. Baxter, ed., *Documentary History of the State of Maine*, XXIV (Portland, Me., 1916) which contains some of the records of the Pejepscot Company.

Christianity on the Northern Frontier

The best general introduction to the history of organized religion on the northern frontier is the first eleven chapters of William W. Sweet, *The Story of Religion in America* (2d rev. ed., New York, 1950). The same author provides somewhat more detailed treatment in his *Religion in Colonial America* (New York, 1942). Much useful material in convenient form is to be found in H. Shelton Smith, Robert T. Handy, and Lefferts A. Loetscher, *American Christianity: An Historical Interpretation with Representative Documents*, vol. I, 1607–1820 (New York, 1960).

Missionary activity among the Indians has produced a rich supply of source material, much of it coming from the missionaries themselves in the form of promotional tracts. Despite some bias, these writings constitute our best available sources on the subject. The work of the Reverend John Eliot among the Indians of Massachusetts is described in eleven tracts, of which seven have been republished in the Massachusetts Historical Society *Collections*, 3d ser., IV (Cambridge, Mass., 1834). All eleven are listed and described in R. W. G. Vail, *The Voice of the Old Frontier* (New York, 1949). Similar efforts by the Mayhew family are recorded in Matthew Mayhew, *A Brief Narrative of The Success which the Gospel hath had, among the Indians, of Martha's-Vineyard* (Boston, 1694). A good modern account is Lloyd C. M. Hare, *Thomas Mayhew: Patriarch to the Indians (1593–1682)* (New York, 1932). The work of the Reverend John Sergeant at Stockbridge is described approvingly in Samuel Hopkins, *Historical memoirs, relating to the Housatunnuk Indians* (Boston, 1753). The Reverend David Brainerd reveals a missionary's inner anguish and occasional triumphs in his journal for 1745–1746, published under the title *Mirabilia Dei inter Indicos* (Philadelphia [1746]). Other portions of his journal have been published in *Memoirs of the Rev. David Brainerd . . . By Rev. Jonathan Edwards . . . Including his Journal . . . by Sereno Edwards Dwight* (New Haven, Conn., 1822).

A good overall discussion of the various attempts to Christianize the New England Indians is Frances Godwin James, "Puritan Missionary Endeavors in Early New England" (unpublished master's thesis, Yale University, 1938). William Kellaway, *The New England Company, 1649–1776: Missionary Society to the American Indians* (New York, 1962) traces the history of the English corporation that provided much of the financial support for the work of Eliot, the Mayhews, John Sergeant, and other missionaries. Portions of the same subject are discussed in George P. Winship, "Samuel Sewall and the New England Company," Massachusetts Historical Society *Proceedings*, LXVII (1941–1944), pp. 55–110. The progress of Anglican missions in New York is described in two very useful and perceptive studies—John W. Lydekker, *The Faithful Mohawks* (New York, 1938) and Frank J. Klingberg, *Anglican Humanitarianism in Colonial New York* (Philadelphia, 1940). The former includes excerpts from documents in the archives of the Society for the Propagation of the Gospel in Foreign Parts. Other phases of the missionary endeavor are discussed in Charles E. Corwin, "Efforts of the Dutch-American Colonial Pastors for the Conversion of the Indians," Presbyterian Historical

Society *Journal*, XII (October 1925), pp. 225–246; Frank J. Klingberg, "The Anglican Minority in Colonial Pennsylvania, with Particular Reference to the Indian," *Pennsylvania Magazine of History and Biography*, LXV (July 1941), pp. 276–299; and Kenneth G. Hamilton, "Cultural Contributions of Moravian Missions among the Indians," *Pennsylvania History*, XVIII (January 1951), pp. 1–15.

The two most important and authoritative studies of the Great Awakening in the northern colonies are Edwin S. Gaustad *The Great Awakening in New England* (New York, 1957) and Charles H. Maxson, *The Great Awakening in the Middle Colonies* (Chicago, 1920). Gaustad has demonstrated quite effectively that in New England, at least, the Great Awakening was not primarily a frontier movement.

The Overthrow of New France

The standard narrative accounts such as Francis Parkman, *A Half-Century of Conflict* (Boston, 1892) and *Montcalm and Wolfe* (Boston, 1884) have recently been supplemented by two brief but authoritative summaries embodying the fruits of a half century of research since Parkman's time—Edward P. Hamilton, *The French and Indian Wars: The Story of Battles and Forts in the Wilderness* (New York, 1962) and Howard H. Peckham, *The Colonial Wars, 1689–1762* (Daniel J. Boorstin, ed., *The Chicago History of American Civilization*, Chicago, 1964). International strife on the northern frontier in the mid-eighteenth century receives its most profound analysis in volumes 3–7 of Lawrence H. Gipson's magnificent *The British Empire Before the American Revolution* (Caldwell, N.J., and New York, 1936–1958).

Among the most useful of the many volumes of published sources are Theodore C. Pease, ed., *Anglo-French Boundary Disputes in the West* (Illinois State Historical Library *Collections*, XXVII [Springfield, Ill., 1936]); Theodore C. Pease and Ernestine Jenison, eds., *Illinois on the Eve of the Seven Years' War, 1747–1755* (Illinois State Historical Library *Collections*, XXIX [Springfield, 1940]); Sylvester K. Stevens and Donald H. Kent, eds., *Wilderness Chronicles of Northwestern Pennsylvania* (Harrisburg, Pa., 1941); and appropriate volumes in *The Papers of Sir William Johnson* (13 vols., Albany, 1921–62). Thomas Pownall, *Considerations Towards a General Plan of Measures for the English Provinces* (New York, 1756) is an incisive analysis of the strategic problem of the mid-1750s, and was influential in the shaping of British policy. The character of forest warfare emerges clearly from Howard H. Peckham, ed., *Journals of Major Robert Rogers* (New York, 1961). Thomas Doolittle, *A Short Narrative of Mischief done by the French and Indian Enemy, on the Western Frontiers of the Province of the Massachusetts-Bay* (Boston, 1750) emphasizes the hardships of frontier life during King George's War, and criticizes the war effort of the colonial authorities. Captivity narratives for this war include Nehemiah How, *A Narrative of the Captivity of Nehemiah How . . .* (Boston, 1748) and John Norton, *The Redeemed Captive, Being a Narrative of the taken* [sic] *and carrying into captivity the Reverend Mr. John Norton . . .* (Boston, 1748). Similar accounts for the subsequent decisive war are Robert Eastburn, *A Faithful Narrative of The many Dangers and Sufferings, as well as wonderful and surprizing Deliverances of Robert Eastburn. . . .* (Philadelphia and Boston, 1758); William and Elizabeth Fleming, *A narrative of the Sufferings and surprizing Deliverances of William and Elizabeth Fleming* (Boston, 1756); Howard H. Peckham, "Thomas Gist's Indian Captivity, 1758–1759," *Pennsylvania Magazine of History and Biography,* LXXX (July 1956), pp. 285–311; and Peter Williamson, *French and Indian cruelty; exemplified in the life and various vicissitudes of fortune, of Peter Williamson* (3d ed., Glasgow, 1758).

The early chapters of Clarence W. Alvord, *The Illinois Country, 1673–1818* (Springfield, Ill., 1920) provide a good introduction to international rivalries beyond the Appalachians. A detailed and authoritative account of diplomatic maneuvers and negotiations is to be found in Max Savelle, *The Diplomatic History of the Canadian Boundary, 1749–1763* (New Haven, Conn., 1940). The role of Virginia's aggressive speculators and imperialists is ably analyzed in Kenneth P. Bailey, *The Ohio Company of Virginia and the Westward Movement, 1748–1792* (Glendale, Calif., 1939). Solon J. and Elizabeth H. Buck, *The Planting of Civilization in Western Pennsylvania* (Pittsburgh, 1939) presents the story of one burgeoning frontier in a way that is both scholarly and interesting, with a number of excellent illustrations. Wilbur R. Jacobs, *Diplomacy and Indian Gifts: Anglo-French Rivalry along the Ohio and Northwest Frontiers, 1748–1763* (Stanford, Calif., 1950) emphasizes the importance of gift giving in negotiations with the Indians. Techniques and problems of frontier fortification in the mid-eighteenth century may be studied in William A. Hunter, *Forts on the Pennsylvania Frontier, 1753–1758* (Harrisburg, Pa., 1960), and Alfred P. James and Charles M. Stotz, *Drums in the Forest* (*Western Pennsylvania Historical Magazine,* XLI, pp. 3–56, 59–227 [Pittsburgh, 1958]). The best study of the Albany Congress is Robert C. Newbold, *The Albany Congress and Plan of Union of 1754* (New York, 1955).

The problem of Quaker pacifism and frontier defense in Pennsylvania was of major importance in the 1750s, fostering bitter political strife, as evidenced by two pamphlets attributed to Provost William Smith: *A Brief State of the Province of Pennsylvania, in which The Conduct of their Assemblies for several Years past is impartially examined* (London, 1755) and *A Brief View Of the Conduct of Pennsylvania, For the Year 1755* (London, 1756). More sympathetic toward the Quakers is Peter Williamson, *Some Considerations on The present State of Affairs* (York, Eng., 1758). Ralph L. Ketcham, "Conscience, War, and Politics in Pennsylvania, 1755–1757," *William and Mary Quarterly,* 3d ser., XX (July 1963), pp. 416–439, is a close analysis of this factional strife. Also useful in considering the problem are Theodore Thayer, "The Friendly Association," *Pennsylvania Magazine of History and Biography,* LXVII (October 1943), pp. 356–376; Theodore Thayer, *Israel Pemberton, King of the Quakers* (Philadelphia, 1943); and Anthony F. C. Wallace, *King of the Delawares: Teedyuscung, 1700–1763* (Philadelphia, 1949).

The international negotiations, 1759–1763, which determined the future of the northern frontier, are carefully examined in Zenab E. Rashed, *The Peace of Paris, 1763* (Liverpool, 1951).

INDEX

Abnaki Indians: attack Wells, Me., in Queen Anne's War, 118; in Dummer's War, 131–132; influenced by the French, 109. *See also* Eastern Indians
Acadia (Nova Scotia), 123–124, 205
Adirondack Mountains, 6
Agriculture, 5, 18, 19, 22, 30, 32–33, 41, 46–48, 62–63, 70, 74, 77, 78, 80, 82–83, 86–87, 129, 171, 215, 234
Albany, N.Y., 111, 114, 118, 121, 123–124, 127, 128, 150–155, 165, 169, 170, 192, 193, 194, 199, 200, 232
Albany Congress, 198–199, 203, 237
Alexander, James, 113
Algonquian Indians: and the Iroquois, 60, 97, 105. *See also* under tribal names
Allegheny Mountains, 6, 161. *See also* Appalachian Mountains
Allegheny River, 141, 156, 158–160
Amish, 138
Andros, Gov. Edmund, 104, 110, 233
Androscoggin River, 131, 133, 172–173, 221
Appalachian Mountains, 5–6, 92–93, 140, 191–192, 196, 198, 206–208. *See also* Allegheny Mountains
Architecture, 26–27, 75–77, 78–81, 212
Atherton, Humphrey, and land speculation, 216–217

Barentz, Pieter, 21
Belcher, Jonathan, quoted on land tenancy, 172
Bellomont, Gov. Lord: 117, 165–167, 255; quoted on the condition of New York's forts, 118
Bethlehem, Pa., settled by Moravians, 138, 182–183, 187
Beverwyck. *See* Albany
Bleecker, Johannes, fur merchant, 154
Board of Trade, 144–145, 152–153, 235
Boston, Mass., 32, 36, 83, 111, 124, 131, 133, 134, 172, 221
Bowdoin, James, 160–161, 232

Braddock, Gen. Edward, 200, 206
Bradford, William, quoted on the aid given by Squanto, 18
Brainerd, Rev. David: missionary among the Indians, 189–190, 235; preaches to frontiersmen, 181–182; quoted on religious conditions on the frontier, 181–182
Bridger, John, surveyor of the woods, 134
Broad Arrow Policy, 134–135
Brookfield, Mass.: attacked in King Philip's War, 56–57; petition from, during Queen Anne's War, 122–123
Brunswick, Me.: settled by the Pejepscot Company, 131–132, 173; settled by Thomas Purchase, 221
Budd, Thomas, quoted on pioneering in Pennsylvania, 71
Burnet, Gov. William, 129, 150–153
Burnetsfield, N.Y., 131; settled by Palatines, 129

Canada. *See* New France
Cape Ann, 20, 31–32
Cargill, James, and scalp hunting, 202–203
Casco Bay. *See* Forts
Cattle frontier, 83
Caughnawaga Indians, 105–106; and the Albany-Montreal fur trade, 151, 154
Cayuga Indians, 11, 197
Céloron de Blainville, P. J., 160, 196–197
Champlain Valley, 5, 111, 118, 124; as a route for the fur trade, 151-153, 198
Charles River, 32, 186
Chelmsford, Mass., 35
Cherry Valley, N.Y., settled, 129, 131
Church, Benjamin, leads expedition against Acadia, 123
Clarke, George, and land speculation in New York, 170
Clinton, Gov. George, in King George's War, 193